Praise for *The White Blackbird*

"Moore offers no easy answers. . . . It is a virtue of this autobiograph-
ical biography that it succeeds in evoking the unfathomable nature of
a personality."   —*New York Review of Books*

"Thanks to her granddaughter's sensitive reconstruction of her life,
Margarett Sargent's memorable personality and extraordinary sensibility have been given a second chance of surviving oblivion."
                           —*Wall Street Journal*

"Moving, penetrating, and true; it evokes the destiny of women like
Zelda Fitzgerald. Well written, well researched, and insightful."
                           —Françoise Gilot

"Honor Moore has painted a vivid picture of an era. Most fabulous
of all is the picture of that tormented woman wandering through life
searching for truth and beauty that she could see and feel but couldn't
get her arms around."   —Ben Bradlee

"Moore translates Sargent's paintings into rich word-portraits . . .
her writing is delicious. She describes a culture in which establishing
connection with the pleasurably erotic pulse of creativity requires
exactly the same risk as jumping off a high cliff."
                           —*Women's Review of Books*

"Never has the life of a woman artist been rendered with such exquisite
detail, with such excitement, insight, and compassion. Anyone who
cares about triumph—and the psychic cost—of making art must read
this book."   —Louise DeSalvo

ALSO BY HONOR MOORE

Memoir

The Bishop's Daughter

Poems

Red Shoes

Darling

Memoir

Play

Mourning Pictures

Edited by Honor Moore

Poems from the Women's Movement

The Stray Dog Cabaret: A Book of Russian Poems

Amy Lowell: Selected Poems

The New Women's Theatre: Ten Plays by
Contemporary American Women

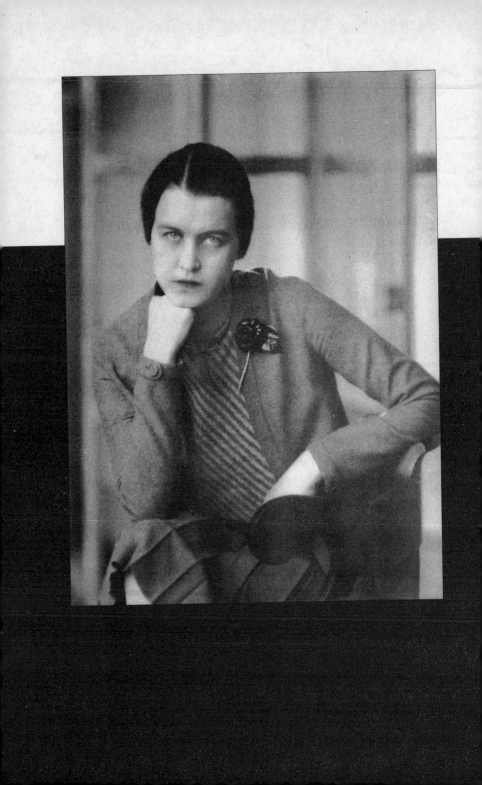

Honor Moore

THE WHITE BLACKBIRD

A life of the painter

Margarett Sargent

by her

granddaughter

W. W. NORTON & COMPANY
New York • London

Page 379 constitutes an extension of this copyright page.

Frontispiece: Margarett Sargent in Paris, 1928.
(Photograph by Berenice Abbott)

For information about permission to reproduce selections from this book, write to
Permissions, W. W. Norton & Company, Inc., 500 Fifth Avenue, New York, NY 10110

For information about special discounts for bulk purchases, please contact
W. W. Norton Special Sales at specialsales@wwnorton.com or 800-233-4830

Manufacturing by Courier Westford
Book design by Francesca Belanger
Production manager: Devon Zahn

Library of Congress Cataloging-in-Publication Data

Moore, Honor, 1945–
The white blackbird: A life of the painter Margarett Sargent
by her granddaughter / Honor Moore.
p. cm.
Originally published: New York : Viking, 1996.
Includes bibliographical references and index.
ISBN 978-0-393-33611-5 (pbk.)
1. Sargent, Margarett, 1892–1978. 2. Painters—United States—Biography. I. Title
ND237.S313M66 2009
759.13—dc22
[B]
2009005666

W. W. Norton & Company, Inc., 500 Fifth Avenue, New York, N.Y. 10110
www.wwnorton.com

W. W. Norton & Company Ltd., Castle House, 75/76 Wells Street, London W1T 3QT

1 2 3 4 5 6 7 8 9 0

For Margarett Vernon

Contents

viii

Isolation is delicious, especially in a crowd

213

A section of photographs follows page 148.

Color plates of paintings by Margarett Sargent may be viewed at
www.margarettsargent.com.

If you bring forth what is within you, what you bring forth will save you. If you do not bring forth what is within you, what you do not bring forth will destroy you.

—The Gnostic Gospel of Thomas

i

Sundays of course were different—
I wore plumes . . .

(1892–1908)

Margarett and her father
at Wareham, c. 1903

"YOU WILL HAVE A BOSOM like your grandmother's," my mother says. I am eleven, standing with her near the brass-fixtured highboy on the second-floor landing of our house in Indianapolis. My mother is black-haired, olive-skinned, and lean. My brother teases me for being too pale, too round—"white and gooshy, white and gooshy"—and I reassure myself: I am like my grandmother Margarett. She had black hair and very white skin. Like mine. She was not called pale. She was an artist, and she was called wonderfully fair.

"I was flat-chested until I had children," my mother says, pulling my first bra from the underwear drawer. "I envy you your bosom." At thirteen, alone in the mirrored dressing room, I cup new breasts with small, wide hands: a "bosom" like my grandmother's. The bosom grows. And the buttocks. "What's that behind you?" my mother jokes as we walk together down the street. Fat. Fat as Margarett's face in that photograph she sent from Brittany in 1953. It was the only picture of her in our house. A fat face. Too fat for the Breton headdress. Too sad to look at for long. I finger the red felt jacket from Saint-Malo. It lasts. Grandma sent it from France! She taught me to draw. To want to write letters in strange-colored inks on unusual paper.

It could have been any day in the years before the truce my mother and I reached when I left home. It happened a lot in the years my figure was becoming like my grandmother's. Standing in the twenties-vintage maroon bathroom so the other children won't hear, my mother and I scream at each other for "reasons" having to do with hair— "Sweetie, keep it away from your face!" And she pushes it from my face. And I yank her hand away. Silence, then, "There, that's lovely," the side of my face revealed when the hair goes behind the ear. "Bitch," under my breath. My room is messy. A slap across my face—punctuation to the fights with my mother. One long fight. She is cool. I am not. Margarett was not.

Margarett is dead now, and so is my mother. I am left with the reports of war correspondents. "All the time," my brother says. "She screamed at you. Screamed." And my sister: "Once I asked Mom, Why are you so mean to Honor?" "What did she say?" "Nothing." And my father: "My psychiatrist told me to stay out of it: mothers and daughters . . ." Twenty years later, my brother: "She was fighting something back in you. Definitely. Tamping it down. It was her mother in you. She saw Margarett growing in you."

My mother at the telephone when telephones were black: "Grandma's in the hospital again." "What's wrong with her?" "Mentally ill." My mother stands there touching her head. "It means her mind is sick." Her brain? The feeling inside my own head. Nothing in my mother's voice tells me her fear. Fifteen years later, I hold a white telephone as my mother tells me she herself is going into a sanitarium: depression. Margarett's sad face. Oh, yes, her brain. Her mind. Oh, yes, I understand—that kernel of pain in my own head. A feeling starts to hurt and you have no words for it.

I help my mother set the table for a dinner party. From the high cupboard we lift white china cupids holding luscious fake grapes, gifts from Margarett, to decorate the long dining table, Margarett's wedding present. "You know the story of this table," my mother says as we place the silver and the red goblets. "She promised it as a wedding present, then she had more shock treatments, and when we went to claim it, she wouldn't give it to us! The shock treatments made her forget even our wedding!" My mother talks in a perfectly normal voice. "Finally we got it, but the whole thing was *just* awful."

"I don't want you to have to cope with her," my mother said when I told her I wanted to go to Radcliffe. Cambridge was less than an

hour from where Margarett lived. Of course I wanted to go nowhere
but Radcliffe. When the time came, Margarett was in a sanitarium.
At Radcliffe, I was a midwestern immigrant even though all the men
in my mother's family had gone to Harvard for generations, even
though Radcliffe had been founded by my mother's paternal great-
great-grandmother. I cry from fear the night before my first exam. I
am too ashamed to speak the secret wish: I want to write. I skate a surface, the dark water of possible creativity well below, frozen from me.
Unspoken, even unthought, is the fear: If it thaws and I plunge through,
if I write, will I go mad? "You look so much like Margarett," all the
Boston relatives say.

Crazy Margarett, the woman always described as having been startlingly beautiful, to my child's eye bestially fat, stuffed into high heels,
still attempting chic. Crazy. Scent of her perfume cut with heavy nausea smell. Image of my mother on the phone, news again of Margarett
drunk, manic, sent for a few weeks to this or that sanitarium. I do not
want to be crazy, and yet I want something this grandmother has.
Everything she does, she does with taste so original its sensuality is palpable: letters written in brown ink on butcher's paper; a green satin
purse with cream satin lining, a Christmas present for the granddaughter she barely knows; her sensitive responses when I send her an
example of my own art: "Your poster is safely on my wall. When I
watch it, it really moves. I admire very much the distribution of letter-
ing you were obliged to do—I would be helpless with the problem. As
I wired you, I love it. . . ."

"That week at Grandma's wrecked my life," I say. My father laughs.
"We were all so worried, but you had a great time." Wrecked my life?
What mystery, what example, what illusion would have formed the
yearning of my imagination had I not, at the age of five, visited that
grandmother in that house?

Her house. An old saltbox my grandfather bought while he was
still at Harvard, built in 1630, lived in first by the king's tax collector
for the Massachusetts Bay Colony, then during the Revolution by

General Burgoyne. Margarett and Shaw restored it and, after their marriage, added onto the house so that, to a small girl's eye, it seemed a castle. Its entrance hall, first built as Margarett's sculpture studio, became, with later additions, a mammoth living room. Off one corner, an octagonal tower walled with mirrors Margarett left outdoors one winter to weather to an appropriate cloudiness. A pool walled with trimmed arborvitae, its entrance hidden so the hedge seems a maze. Apple trees like candelabra, espaliered against the dark clapboard.

In her Spanish bedroom, Margarett directs as a photographer positions me. I ride a tiny antique rocking horse. Flash. On the wall above the mantel hangs a De Chirico: two stallions, creamy manes lifted by desert wind, creamy tails streaming to the sand. I sit pasting paper, intent; nearby, Margarett, pen in hand, sketch pad on her knee. Or Margarett sits near my bed, sketching as I fall asleep. When I wake, she's gone. I remember Jack, her green macaw, screaming "Margarett!!!" over and over. And the darkened bedroom. "Shhh. Quiet," the cook says. "Your grandmother was up late." I remember shafts of sun coming through skylights breaking the gloom of the living room. The quiet emptiness. But I don't remember what she sketched. I don't think I ever saw the drawing.

Margarett stopped painting in her early forties, and one day I had the nerve to ask her why. "It got too intense," she said, at eighty-two having survived five strokes, divorce, years in and out of sanitariums. "For twenty years, I worked," she answered, gravelly rasp rendered nearly incomprehensible by partial paralysis. "And then I turned to horticulture." This was the first and only time in my relationship with Margarett, a friendship that began and grew in the last seven years of her life, long after she had become bedridden, that we spoke of her art, the closest we came to speaking of her manic-depression, the "madness" I interpret as the inevitable result of conflict between art and female obligation in upper-class, old-family Boston.

I do not see a painting of hers until I have my first apartment: "I want one you painted." My letter to her says something about lots of blank white walls. I am tentative because I have seen only one drawing of hers, never a painting; tentative because I know she stopped painting and don't know how many of her paintings there are, if any. *The Blue Girl*, its arrival announced weeks before by a note scrawled in pink on hot-turquoise stationery, comes crated. I unwind gleaming screws, one by one, lift the lid, whiff of fresh wood, peel back the cardboard.

"It has a wonderful Spanish frame," she'd written. Yes, and dazed black eyes staring as if interrupted. A stranger. A huge black hat's shadows smudge her white forehead; lips set, red, disturbed. Color: Light blue collars a pale neck, behind writhe thick green vines, exploding ultramarine blooms. Brown hair to the shoulder, she sits, volcanic, holds the graceful white arm of an orange chair with both hands, as if to hold herself to the canvas. I am twenty-one. This is my first adult intimacy with a woman who has given up.

"Who is she?" I ask Margarett later. Her voice is already muffled by the first paralytic stroke. "A model." Of despair. Hands roughly articulated. After the first stroke, Margarett's hands shake too much to draw. The Blue Girl's hands, painted in 1929, splay like fans, prophetic. "Who did that frightening painting?" a visitor asks. "My crazy grandmother." I laugh, knowing that at night when I sit down at my blue typewriter I won't be able to dismiss her piercing disturbance as I type, fingers splaying across the keyboard, drumming to tame that countenance, the steady acidic gaze that follows me everywhere in the room, watching, communicating some warning I cannot yet hear.

I am sitting with Margarett's oldest daughter, my aunt Margie, near her pool, minutes from the house I visited at the age of five. Margarett has been dead two years. My mother's spell has worked. Margarett won't fit into the poem I keep trying to write, and every time I contemplate her, I am frightened. While she was still alive, I'd sit by her bed, chest tight, unable to ask what I wanted to know. "Tell me about your life, Grandma. Tell me how you became an artist." Unasked were other questions: "What must I do not to 'go mad' as you have? What must I do to live fully both as an artist and a woman?" In Margarett's absence, I ask questions of the daughter who was close to her, of whom she made so many drawings and paintings.

"She was not a very cozy mother," Margie says. "We'd visit her studio. We wouldn't stay long. She'd be intent on her work." And so it was true, Margarett was a working artist. "She never stopped drawing. She stopped exhibiting. I think she hated herself for not continuing." Margie, it seems, will tell me anything I want to know. She gives me names of people to talk to, assures me Margarett's brother Dan will be happy to see me. "But you better hurry up," she says. "He's nearly ninety, and so many of those left are dying." When I leave, she gives me a big portfolio, full of photographs and drawings. "The story starts in Wellesley," she says. "Hurry up."

§

IN THE PORTFOLIO, I find a photograph taken in Wellesley in 1952: Grown-ups lean against Corinthian columns or sit on chairs set on the front steps of an immense white house. Children sit and sprawl on the grass—babies, not-yet-teenage girls with braids and quizzical faces, little boys wearing ties, bigger boys wearing striped tee shirts, adults in fine pale linens. You can't miss Margarett. Near the center she sits, sixty years old, wearing the only dark dress in the photograph. On her head is an elegant black hat.

This was how Margarett chose to appear among her mother's family. Though she was a Sargent by name, she grew up in the domain of her maternal grandfather, Horatio Hollis Hunnewell, the son of a country doctor, who made a fortune in railroads, built the big house in the photograph, and transformed its surroundings, a "pitch pine forest with a barren soil," to an earthly paradise. As a child, Margarett visited him in the conservatory, where he sat in a wicker wheelchair among his orchids and palms. His mouth in old age had a vague expression, which, if a grandchild wound his mechanical nightingale enough to make it sing, wreathed to a smile.

When Margarett turned to horticulture, she was returning to Wellesley, where, in her childhood, the fruits of Hollis's cultivation were at their prime. He hybridized scores of rhododendron, cultivated fruits and tropical plants in a dozen greenhouses, and proudly collected conifers for a pinetum that would include specimens from every continent. His tour de force was his Italian Garden, the first topiary display in North America. "No Vanderbilt, with all his great wealth, can possess one of these for the next fifty years," he wrote in his diary in 1899, "for it could not be grown in less time."

Judgment of topiary took into account not only the harmonious effects of the shapes of trees—a green cone by the side of a darker green pyramid, a tall pine clipped to look like an Olympian game of horseshoes—but also the effect of clipping on the texture of foliage. It was no small feat to adapt European pruning to trees that would survive in New England, and Hollis achieved it. After fifty years, two hundred sculpted trees occupied three sloping acres at the shore of Lake Waban in Wellesley. Seventy granite steps, edged by century aloes in granite urns, descended from a columned pavilion, past stone goddesses, to the water.

Margarett's brother Dan took my curiosity about his sister seriously and invited me to Wellesley for the annual Independence Day softball game the Hunnewells hold every year on the lawn of the big white house. He and Margarett were not yet born in 1889, when their aunt Isabella instituted the festivities as a way for Hollis, widowed by then, to gather his children and grandchildren. This was to be the first time I visited the Hunnewell estate. Wellesley, as the white house is called, had been designed by Arthur Gilman, architect of the Arlington Street Church in Boston. Nearby, each on a landscaped property, loom the Victorian "cottages" Hollis built, one each for his children, an extra for guests. The big house was named in honor of his wife Isabella's family, who had originally owned the land; later, grateful for his gifts of a library, a town hall, and a park, the town of West Needham changed its name to Wellesley.

At the lawn's edge, young Hunnewells stir strawberry-and-ginger-ale punch in a massive blue-and-white Chinese porcelain footbath. A breeze moves the tops of a huge tentlike stand of weeping beech, a giant catalpa, old maples, an ancient white oak—prized lawn trees whose circumference Hollis recorded in his diary every time his son John visited from France to measure them. In 1889, the year of the first softball game, he wrote that the white oak, the one tree he had not planted, had grown half an inch a year, which made it "fully 200 years old at this time. . . . I hope that in due time it will reach the good old age of one thousand years, and that some of our descendants will be on hand to admire it."

The game is set to begin at ten-thirty. The umpire takes her seat, clipboard in hand, in the old fringe-topped buggy Hollis drove in his old age. Nonplayers (octogenarians or pregnant cousins) watch from under the trees, perched on outdoor furniture. A loud toot announces the large red jeep hurtling across the lawn, crammed with children, miniature American flags flying. This generation's Arnold leaps from the front seat and strides onto the lawn with a megaphone. "Okay," he shouts. "Everyone whose name I call, get out on the field!" He begins the list. "Hollis! Walter! Frank! Jenny! Isabella!" As he calls, players of all ages run to take their positions, as they had in response to the same names on ninety prior occasions.

Afterward, at the punch bowl, I am introduced as Cousin Margarett's granddaughter, a writer. Immediately a clamor of voices begin a story: Margarett at the softball game at age sixty-eight. If you're over sixty, you can have a younger surrogate run your bases, but Margarett hit a long ball that sent children scurrying to Washington Street, abruptly lifted her long black skirt to reveal a red taffeta petticoat, whose flounces rustled as she ran one, two, three bases—a home run.

"Why are you writing about her?" a cousin asked.

"I'm interested in her career."

"Her career?"

"She was a painter."

Lifting black to expose red among white-clad cousins, Margarett was painting, painting a banner that signaled not only her own otherness but that of her long silenced grandmother. Like Margarett the painter, Isabella Hunnewell goes virtually unmentioned on the great scroll of Hunnewells, and yet her family's money and land were the foundation of her husband's extraordinary triumph. It was Isabella's uncle Samuel Welles who gave impoverished Horatio Hollis, his twelve-year-old cousin by marriage, the great opportunity of his life, a job at the Welles banking house in Paris; and it was Isabella's parents who took her and her young husband in after the great crash of 1837 drove them back from Europe, penniless, with two small children. After writing home that she felt old as Methuselah after giving birth to her two eldest children, Isabella had seven more, affording Hollis's dynasty the dimension of which he was so proud.

Though she was timid, with a fidelity to home and family that amounted to passion, Isabella traveled at sixteen with her sister to stay for a year in Paris with her uncle Samuel and his elegant wife. As she sat one day in her uncle's banking office, copying out his correspondence, she noticed Hollis. The two were soon betrothed, but Hollis had no intention of leaving Paris. When Isabella, in protest, resisted setting a wedding date, a favorite aunt was dispatched from Massachusetts to reassure her, and the young couple were promptly married.

Twenty-nine years later, Hollis, by now made extremely wealthy by real estate and railroad investments, took his wife and his three youngest children, including Margarett's mother, Jenny, on a grand tour of the Continent. For the winter, the children were left in school in Paris. In her diary, Isabella recorded roadside piracy, a blizzard that overturned their coach in the Alps, and the pomp of the Pope's Sunday appearance. In Venice, after a few lines about alighting from a gondola, the pages go blank. "It was in Europe," her youngest son, Henry, wrote, "that my poor mother had a nervous breakdown from which she never fully recovered." Jenny remembered that after Europe, her mother's eyes no longer met hers. At thirteen, she was effectively motherless.

For Isabella, after the trip to Europe, the tonic effect of a week in Charleston or a trip to take the waters at Saratoga was never more than fleeting. If she was not away in a sanitarium, she sat in a wheelchair in her spacious, sunny room at Wellesley, dressed in black and weeping, obsessed by a certainty her husband would run out of money. Except at her death, in 1888, when he noted "the beloved wife has found rest at last," Hollis never hinted in his diary of his wife's illness, hardly mentioned her at all.

Jenny grew up suppressing terror at any sort of separation, avoiding adventure, and fearing for her sanity as the Hunnewell enclave moved between the summer palace on Lake Waban and a winter one Hollis built in 1862 on a Beacon Street lot he bought at auction as an alphabet of streets (Arlington, Berkeley, Clarendon) displaced the brackish Back Bay to accommodate Boston's new industrial rich. The household ran so smoothly, Jenny had no opportunity to express her lack of ease, and so she was considered shy and retiring, in contrast to her older sister, Isabella, who had her father's unconflicted assertion and strength.

When Jenny was eighteen, she made her debut at a ball her father gave in the ballroom of his Beacon Street mansion. She had grown into tall, black-haired good looks and was given to forgetting her nervousness in laughter. When she was twenty-four, her older sister was married at Wellesley, and a year later Jenny gave a "german"—a hundred and sixty friends danced the waltz and turned the intricate figures of the cotillion. The winter she was twenty-nine, she gave two dancing parties for her friends—most of whom were married—and for her sister and older brothers—all of whom were married. She had resigned herself to living the spinster life her mother's sisters had. It was 1880, fifteen years after the truce at Appomattox, and there were seventy-five thousand marriageable women in Boston. Late that winter, Frank Sargent headed east from Wyoming.

§

"THE HUNNEWELLS AREN'T AS ARISTOCRATIC as the Sargents," Margarett declared one day when she was fifteen and out on a walk with Dan and a Hunnewell uncle. She assigned aristocracy to the qualities of her father's family, distancing herself from the Hunnewells. As an adult, she prided herself on her weeping Sargentia, the hemlock shrub first discovered by her cousin Henry Winthrop Sargent, and when she became an artist, she proudly declared her individual ambition by announcing that she was a "dissident" and hated the painting of her fourth cousin John Singer Sargent. As a child, she hung on her father's stories of Sargents—mesmerists, tubercular poets, famous generals, and clipper ship captains—far more interesting than the Hunnewells she saw every day, whose courtesy restrained her as an arborist would a conifer in her grandfather's Italian Garden.

Margarett's first American Sargent ancestor, William, came to Massachusetts from Bristol, England, and in 1678 was granted two acres on Eastern Point in Gloucester. Margarett's generation was the seventh of his descendants born in America. His son Epes fathered fifteen children by two wives, and it is for him that the Sargent genealogy, published in 1923, was named. Of his five surviving sons, two fought for the crown during the Revolution and three for the colonies; during the siege of Boston, one Sargent brother retreated with the British on a ship for Nova Scotia, while another led a victorious regiment into the city.

It is from two of Epes's sons that Margarett and the painter John Singer Sargent descend. Singer Sargent's great-great-grandfather Winthrop was a patriot merchant instrumental in founding the Universalist Church in America. His brother, Margarett's great-great-grandfather Daniel, made a fortune in the "triangle trade," fishing cod, shipping it to Gloucester for salting, then to the Caribbean as cheap food for the plantation slaves who loaded cargoes of sugar bound for Boston's distilleries.

Daniel Sargent had six sons. Two were merchants like their father, one was a Temperance writer, and the youngest, Henry, was a history painter, a friend of Gilbert Stuart and creator of the monumental *Landing of the Pilgrims* that hangs in the museum at Plymouth. The two remaining sons are described by their descendants either as n'er-do-wells or as poets, and one of them was Margarett's great-grandfather, John Turner Sargent. I found no poems, just his brother's assurance he had "the finest head and chest I'd ever beheld for a man" and the tale of his courtship of the beautiful Christiana Keadie Swan, the spirited heiress to a Salem shipping fortune, who defied her mother to marry him, and was disinherited as a consequence. When John Sargent died young and her mother refused her any assistance, Kitty Swan rolled up her sleeves, took in laundry, and put three sons through Harvard.

After excelling at the study of law, her middle son, Margarett's grandfather Henry Jackson Sargent, was invited to become secretary to the great senator Daniel Webster. He turned Webster down and, when he inherited a fortune from his grandmother, abruptly abandoned law for the writing of poetry: "Lawyers must lie; I am a gentleman and can't." The Sargent genealogy offers the excuse of "poor health" for Harry's choices, but years later, a nephew, bemoaning his own compulsion to drink, blamed his uncle's genes.

Harry Sargent had a handsome head of black hair, pale skin, and bright eyes, and affected a Byronic appearance. He sang a sweet tenor in the evening when his family gathered at the fire, but when he drank, he turned cruel. He commandeered his sons to carry his guns when he hunted plover on the Boston Common, and his wife was forced to plead that he allow their three daughters to marry—he considered them an insurance policy to be redeemed for their dowries at his whim. At a dinner his brother gave for the abolitionist Theodore Parker and the runaway slaves he'd brought to Boston to promote his cause, Harry angrily refused to escort a black woman to the table, struck his brother, and left the party. The two never spoke again.

When her father died, in 1920, Margarett, then twenty-eight and living in New York, returned to Boston. In his will, Frank Sargent had distributed cherished family objects among his five children. Because Margarett was an artist, he left her Washington Allston's portrait of Kitty Swan Sargent. Because Dan was a poet, he inherited the desk at which drunken Harry Sargent wrote his poems. The desk had been in the library as long as Dan could remember, and there was no key. One afternoon while Jenny Sargent was out, Margarett hired a locksmith, opened its drawers, and began to read what she found. When Dan arrived for supper, his mother was in an uncharacteristic rage: "Margarett has done the most dishonorable thing!"

Jenny burned the contents of the desk, and Margarett never told Dan what she found there, but Dan, at ninety-one, remained convinced the unlocked drawer contained letters written to the ladies his womanizing grandfather addressed in the poems he published in *Feathers from a Moulting Muse*, his only book of verse:

> Thou art lost to me for ever!
> We must part, whate'er the pain.
> A blight hath touched my passion-flower:
> It may not bloom again. . . .

By the time Margarett's father, Frank Sargent, was ten years old, Harry had squandered his inheritance, and his oldest son had gone to sea to support the family. In 1862, that son, also called Harry, took command of a ship called the *Phantom* and became the youngest clipper captain in history. In 1863, he died, lost in the China Sea, and Harry pulled fifteen-year-old Frank out of Boston Latin School and sent him to work. He got a job as a lamplighter and never spoke a word against his father. He'd never cared about books, he said, and by working he could help his mother.

But Frank soon realized he'd never make enough money quickly enough in Boston. His sisters married well, but when he courted Grace Revere, grandniece of Paul, she rejected him for someone richer. The clipper trade was dead and had killed his brother, and now that Frank was old enough to enlist, the war was over. Friends of his had moved west to make fortunes now that livestock was shipped by railroad from the great range to Chicago. The burly physique that suited him to amateur boxing would serve him well on the frontier, and so, in 1870, Frank Sargent packed up and headed for Wyoming.

He and a Boston friend bought a ranch in Laramie and raised sheep, then steer, on the open range. In a photograph Margarett always kept on the piano, Frank wore a ten-gallon hat and black-and-white ponyskin chaps. He won road races and met Buffalo Bill and, though he wouldn't admit he liked her, took General Custer's daughter, Belle, for buggy rides. One summer evening, Belle broke their musing silence: "It would be so wonderful if we could just drive on and on and on." Frank told the story as a marital cautionary tale: "I stopped the horses and turned around the wagon." His friend Harry Balch could never go home, because he had married a Wyoming woman, but Frank still had Boston ambitions. He would remain out west as long as it took him to return to Beacon Street rich enough to marry well and recover the family honor. He stayed ten years.

Frank Sargent did not make a fortune in Wyoming, but the brawn he acquired wrestling steer set him clearly apart from the men with whom Jenny Hunnewell was familiar, men who wrestled with figures in the banks on Devonshire Street. At thirty-two, Frank was thickset and looked shorter than his five feet ten inches. He had a bull neck, auburn hair that fell in damp weather into waves, and twinkling vivid blue eyes. Perhaps Jenny was encouraged by mutual Sargent relations to invite their cowboy cousin to her parties the winter of 1880; perhaps the two noticed each other on Beacon Street on the blocks between his mother's house at number 73 and her father's at 130; or perhaps they danced together at someone else's cotillion. Whatever the case, there were grounds for intimacy when Jenny crossed the Common and pushed through the bustle of Tremont Street one spring morning in 1881.

Jenny, blushing, told the story not as a narrative but in exclamations and bursts of delighted laughter. As a footman opened the door of H. H. Tuttle's, Boston's most fashionable cobbler, whom should she see, trying on a pair of shoes, but Frank Sargent! There survives no description of shoes purchased, but Frank Sargent and Jenny Hunnewell emerged from Tuttle's secretly betrothed. On May 26, Hollis noted in his diary "great news from Jenny," and on June 3, that "the gentleman from Wyoming arrived yesterday."

Frank Sargent's days of penury were behind him, but he was determined not to live the kind of wasteful life his father had. He drank only milk, and every cent Jenny or her father gave him, he left in trust to his children. "I am a practical man," he'd repeat, as if reminding himself, under his breath. Soon after the marriage, he took a position at S. M. Weld Company, a cotton brokerage, and was soon as rich as his wife, prosperous enough to feel secure in the brick town house Jenny's brother Henry, an architect, built for them at the corner of Hereford Street on the modest, shady side of Commonwealth Avenue.

At first, the memory of her mother's illness dissolved in the pleasure of her extraordinary domestic happiness. Jenny had never expected to marry, and she adored Frank Sargent. But by 1886, she was thirty-five, with three children under four, and the complexity of her household had begun to fray her composure. The Sargents moved four times a year—a hundred trunks, seven servants, two nursemaids, carriages, dogs, horses—and the details of each migration were Jenny's exhausting responsibility: Wellesley to Boston at Thanksgiving, Boston to Wellesley after Easter, Wellesley to the seashore in Wareham on July 4, Wareham to Wellesley at the beginning of September. "Our family lived very simply," Dan said, "but in three houses."

When Jenny became pregnant for the sixth time, late in 1891, she hoped for a second daughter and an easy birth. Alice, born six years before, had died at two of scarlet fever, and Jenny kept her photograph always, chubby baby face in a silver frame, on her desk. None of the children's births had been physically difficult, but the vulnerability that gave her a capacity for frequent laughter also made Jenny frightened of pain. After Dan's birth, during the summer of 1890, her depression had been debilitating and extreme, had unhinged her.

On Wednesday afternoon, August 31, at South Station in Boston, Frank Sargent boarded, as he had every weekday all summer, the 2:30 for Tempest Knob, the station on Buzzards Bay near Wareham where the "Three on Three" club train let off its passengers. Dr. Swift, who had delivered Margarett's brother Dan almost exactly two years before, accompanied Frank on the special train, called the "dude train" not after its well-heeled passengers but because its conductor was a dandy.

Perhaps Frank and the doctor chatted as the train sped toward the Cape, or perhaps they read the *Transcript*, that day dominated by news of pretrial hearings in Fall River in the case of Lizzie Borden, a young

woman accused of taking an ax to her father and stepmother one heat-
wave afternoon just three weeks before. Professor Wood, a chemist
from Harvard, had testified that laboratory examination of the mur-
dered Bordens' stomachs evidenced no trace of poison and that the
hair and blood on the ax were not human. Perhaps Frank, who loved a
good story, read first about the Bordens, or perhaps he noticed first, at
the bottom of the front page, an advertisement that presumed to fore-
tell a Boston daughter's life:

> When Baby was sick, we gave her Castoria
> When she was a child, she cried for Castoria
> When she became a miss, she clung to Castoria
> When she had children, she gave them Castoria.

Hammond, the Sargents' coachman, drove the buggy to meet the
train, which arrived on time at 3:13. Jenny Sargent was in labor, and
Mary Carey, who had also attended Dan's birth, sat by her bedside.
Mary Montgomery, the cook, and her two kitchen maids worked
more quietly than usual in the large kitchen, heat from the huge black
coal stove sucking up the afternoon breeze. Ocean-reflected light played
on the dark-green paneling in the parlor, on the crisscross exposed
beams in the dining room, and on the buffalo head, a Wyoming tro-
phy of Frank's, that hung in the front hall. Jane, the Sargents' oldest
child, and the children's nurse were playing with Harry and Dan,
three and two, on the beach below, and young Frank, eight years old,
was fiddling with the dinghy.

Dr. Swift delivered Frank and Jenny's sixth child during the early
evening. The infant girl was immediately named Margarett Williams
Sargent for her paternal grandmother, who was eighty-three and ail-
ing. The next morning, from his office in Boston, Frank dispatched a
message to his father-in-law in Wellesley, who wrote in his diary,
"Jenny Sargent confined of a fine girl, nine and half pounds."

No break in the flow of Horatio Hollis Hunnewell's handwriting
indicates he considered this birth less ordinary than the progress of a
rhododendron from one spring to the next. Margarett was his twenty-

ninth grandchild and the second to be called by that name, though the other Margarett was not distinguished by two *t*'s. The two *t*'s, which seemed, as Margarett grew up, to encourage her emphatic and exuberant individuality, were the legacy of English ancestors who felt no need to conform to what was ordinary but who certainly did not intend that a name's spelling confer any untoward uniqueness.

§

ONE JUNE AFTERNOON when Margarett was four, Mary Sutherland, called "Nanna," dressed her in a light cotton dress, brown everyday stockings, and tie-up shoes. She parted Margarett's black hair down the middle, splitting her widow's peak, and tied the top back with white ribbon, leaving the rest soft around her ears. When Frank (called Papa, pronounced "Puppa") got back to Wellesley from his office in Boston, the family gathered on the veranda and arranged themselves for a photographer. The portrait gives the impression, not of a young family exhibiting a concerted rush of solidarity, but of a constellation of individuals, each caught in a moment of settled, if not entirely comfortable, contemplation.

Jenny (Mama, pronounced "Mumma") sits in a chair to the left, a bemused smile on her broad face. She wears a dark print dress with a black lace collar; her large hands rest on her lap. She is six months pregnant, but her figure looks merely matronly. There were no maternity clothes, and pregnancies were never mentioned.

In the center chair is Jane, the oldest, now fourteen. She's dressed in a light print guimpe with full leghorn sleeves. Her delicate, dark-blond prettiness contrasts with her mother's dark hair and olive skin. Her right elbow rests on the right arm of her chair, and her right hand cradles her small, inward-looking face. Her features are her father's.

Harry, named for his father's clipper ship brother, straddles a high stool between his mother and older sister, his right arm lolling across Jenny's knee. He still wears a sailor suit, the cowlick at his hairline gives his forelock a life of its own. He gazes at us full on with a half-smile and wide-open eyes. Dan, a year younger, fixes us with steady six-year-old seriousness, standing as straight as the soldier uncle for whom he was named. His blond curls, still long, feather out below his ears, and his evenly trimmed bangs are undisturbed by cowlicks. No one else looks at the camera.

Frank, the eldest son, is twelve, old enough to wear a jacket and tie. He stands behind his mother and sister, arms at his sides, dark hair slicked back. He has his mother's eyes and nose and smiles his mother's smile. He looks down, perhaps at Jane; or perhaps at Margarett, with an older brother's proprietary sweetness.

Papa and Margarett form the right flank of the photograph. Frank's bald forehead seems inordinately vast because he looks down at the child who sits at his feet. Like her father, Margarett has an expansive brow. Like him she folds her hands in her lap, like him sits with legs firmly apart, her lace-yoked frock as slightly askew as the rumpled vest buttoned over his portly belly. It seems that his tender, concentrated gaze is all that keeps the unhappy, precociously disdainful, full-cheeked face of his "dear little Chump" from breaking into tears.

No more concrete diagnosis of Margarett's early physical contrariness survives than that she was "sickly." With her black hair and demanding temperament, she was not the daughter Jenny had hoped for. Alice's replacement, a little girl named Ruth, arrived in 1896, and four-year-old Margarett protested vehemently with mind, body, and spirit. In Dan's memory, she was "always crying, all the time."

Even if her relations with her mother had been easier, Margarett would not have run to her. The Sargent children, in the care of their nanny, saw their parents only fleetingly. As time went by, Margarett's protests became increasingly physical. She was sick so often that the Sargents eventually heeded Nanna's complaints and hired a trained nurse to care for their difficult daughter. With Miss Whiteside, Margarett formed a kind of satellite realm, isolated from the hurly-burly of her brothers and from her baby sister. When her eyes, which were as startlingly blue as her father's, weren't shot red with tears, she was vomiting, and Miss Whiteside was cleaning up after her. As she lay pallid and green, swaddled in a steamer chair in the Wareham sun,

Ruth toddled about, blond curls flowing to her shoulders. Jenny was enthralled. Ruth was the "pet of us all," "never cried," had "the most smiling face," "always seemed to be happy."

John Eldridge, the boatman at Wareham, took a look at Margarett one day and announced to Miss Whiteside that he could already see the flies gathering on her. Frank consulted specialists, but in spite of treatment after treatment, Margarett "did nothing but wail, day and night." When she was six or seven, she was finally diagnosed as anemic and prescribed beef juice. If Miss Whiteside wasn't looking, Margarett tossed it out or gave it to her cousin Gertrude Hunnewell, who always eagerly drank it. By the time a Viennese child specialist named Dr. Farr arrived in Boston to treat an Armour meat heiress, Frank was desperate enough to hire a foreign physician. "Dat is de stomach," Margarett mimicked as Dr. Farr poked at her. "Doze are de looongs."

Whatever her organic symptoms, Margarett's ailment had the feel of rage and grief. Jenny was comforted by Jane and delighted by Ruth, but Margarett was a different kind of daughter. With her, Jenny was apt to feel uncomprehending, as powerless to comfort as she had been with her depressed and agitated mother. In a photograph taken at Wareham, her two younger daughters stand with their backs to the ocean. Margarett, taller and almost gawky, has her hand on Ruth's shoulder. Ruth smiles right at the camera; Margarett looks down.

By the time she was eight, Margarett had recovered, and Miss Whiteside had left the household. His sister had become, in Dan's words, "a cheerful little girl who happily raised tumbler pigeons in the barn at Wellesley." Now that she was healthy, protest against her mother took a new form. Jane was demure and Ruth was adorable, so Margarett became a wild tomboy. Whenever she could, she played with her brothers and rose to their challenges. When they insisted she always be "it" in hide-and-seek, she did so. When her older brother Frank dared her to dive from the nursery sofa like the white angels on its red chintz, she did it and, landing on her head, didn't cry at all.

Her brothers marveled as she became a family contender. At the Sargent dinner table, the currency was wit—and Margarett became the wittiest in a family of quick and charming tongues. When the boys teased her about her asymmetrical ears, she'd think up a retort that turned asymmetry to her advantage. When Harry, who tormented her about her looks, reported his fighting weight at the breakfast table, Margarett replied, "Was that before or after I manicured you?"

At Wellesley, Margarett enlisted her cousins Gertrude and Mary. She urged them up the circular stair of the tent Hollis built each June to shelter his blossoming rhododendrons; the three giggled down on his stuffy horticultural guests and zinged spitballs at Dan and their cousin Arnold Hunnewell, who played tag below. She coaxed them to take off their clothes, dive with her into the oat bin in the barn, and pretend to wash themselves with the dusty grain. Gertrude and Mary were content to watch their family sows cavort, but Margarett jumped into the pen, played with the piglets, and emerged proud and muddy. Her cousins considered the worst possible punishment a day without Margarett Sargent.

The three—Hunnewells dressed identically, Margarett a disheveled third with a strand of black hair in her mouth—were looked after by Nanna and the Hunnewells' nurse, Marmie. They were given lessons by a succession of governesses, who came out on the train to supplement what they were taught during the winter at Miss Fiske's kindergarten in Boston. One of the governesses, who happened to have a cold sore on her lip, so annoyed Margarett that she threw a ruler at her. When Gertrude asked if she regretted it, Margarett replied, to her astonishment, "Only that I missed."

At the turn of the century, Wellesley was at its peak. French parterre gardens adorned the front lawn, and palm trees that wintered in the conservatory were planted outdoors for the summer. Greenhouses produced orchids and bananas, bushels of peaches, nectarines, and grapes, and the pinetum seemed a forest primeval when the three little girls gazed up at its murmuring hemlocks. From the shore, they would wave at their playboy cousin Hollis who'd shout salutations from the gondola he'd brought back from Venice, as the gondolier Rossetti, also imported from Venice, navigated.

On Sunday, the Sargents went to the Unitarian church down the road in South Natick, where Mr. Daniels, the fiery minister, preached emulation of the world's three greatest men: the abolitionist senator Charles Sumner, the abolitionist agitator Wendell Phillips, and Jesus Christ. In a drawing she later made of herself as a child, Margarett, all dressed up, stands outdoors watching Tiger, her Boston terrier, relieve himself against a brilliant green bush hot with pink blooms. She has her back to us and wears a big feathered hat. "Sundays of course were different," she scrawled in red across the bottom. "I wore plumes."

In the spring of 1901, Frank Sargent went to Europe for the first time. He considered the Continent a world of undifferentiated wickedness and danger but declared he was now rich enough to afford to be cheated. Jenny, who hadn't returned to Europe since her mother's breakdown, refused to accompany him, so he took Jane, who had recently made her debut. Young Frank was at Groton, preparing for Harvard. Jane had passed the entrance exam for Radcliffe but had decided not to go; college would have been an unusual choice even for a serious young woman who voraciously read Channing's sermons, Emerson's essays, and William James. When they returned from Europe, Jane embarked upon the rituals of post-debutante life—gentlemen callers, house parties, and a club for young ladies called the Sewing Circle.

The four youngest—Harry was now thirteen, Dan eleven, Margarett nine, and Ruth five—still gathered, like Longfellow's offspring, "Between the dark and the daylight, / When the light is beginning to lower" for that "pause in the day's occupations, / That is known as the Children's Hour." Since they ate early and Nanna saw to all their needs, the hour when the servants had supper was the only scheduled time the younger children saw their parents. At five o'clock, Frank finished reading the *Transcript*, and Jenny put aside her needlework.

The summer parlor was a modest-size room hung with hunting prints, overstuffed and comfortable rather than stylish, dark rather than airy. Frank and Jenny had tea, and after the children chattered out news of the day, Ruth might sit on the floor, building cities with colored blocks, and Harry play a boisterous game of checkers with

Mama. Dan watched Ruth, and Margarett climbed onto Papa's lap.
When the checkers were finished and the blocks built, all four clustered
around Frank: Would he please tell them a story about Wyoming?

His stories always had a point. If he told how his brother Harry
escaped Chinese pirates in two rowboats and saved the *Phantom*'s gold,
it was to remind them of their uncle's courage. If he related how his
brother Uncle Dan won swimming races in a river in Virginia with everyone in his company, then took up the challenge of the commander of
the Confederate regiment camped on the opposite bank, it was to say
something about the ironies of the Civil War. But Margarett always
wanted a story about the West. They all wanted a story of the West.

"How many Indians did you kill?"

"Not a one."

"How many cowboys did you shoot it out with?"

"Not a one, but I did hang one."

"Tell us, oh tell us!"

And Frank would tell of being recruited for a posse, of a cattle
thief who'd worked for him whom all the ranchers knew, and how
such thieves were the ruin of ranchers. "We rode and rode and caught
up with him," Frank said, "then tried and convicted him and hung
him from a tree." But, he added, "I felt just a little seasick watching his
face as the noose tightened around his neck!"

Some days Frank didn't give in to their lust for true-to-life adventure. Instead, he simply burst into song—he had studied voice before
going to Wyoming—"Daisy, Daisy, give me your answer true," or, a
favorite of his father's, "I dreamt I dwelt in marble halls." Once in a
while, instead of singing or telling a story, he offered the specialty he
reserved for Margarett, a recitation from memory, with stunning dramatic flair, of Longfellow's "The Wreck of the Hesperus."

A ship's captain takes his daughter to sea on a stormy night, bundling
her "warm in his seaman's coat / Against the stinging blast." A fog bell
sounds in the distance. The daughter is frightened. She thinks she
hears "the sound of guns," but he pulls her closer, as Frank does Margarett, on his lap. Finally the ship hurtles like a matchbook from wave

to wave, and the father lashes his daughter to the mast to keep her safe. Margarett puts her arms around Papa's neck as the sea captain succumbs to "whistling sleet and snow," leaving his daughter alone to pray to "Christ, who stilled the wave / On the Lake of Galilee."

When morning comes, a fisherman walking the beach at Norman's Woe, a short distance from where Margarett would spend her adult life, stops

> . . . aghast,
> To see the form of a maiden fair,
>   Lashed close to a drifting mast.
>
> The salt-sea was frozen on her breast,
>   The salt tears in her eyes;
> And he saw her hair, like the brown sea weed,
>   On the billows fall and rise.

In a photograph of Margarett and her father at Wareham taken the summer she was nine, she stands close to him on a dock. Both look past the camera into the distance. Frank sits on a railing, white trousers, shirt and tie, straw hat, eyes squinted against the sun. Margarett's white eyelet collar billows from her shoulders, her small straw hat is held on by elastic under her chin. Her blue eyes are eerily pale, her face pretty and concentrated. She and Frank look like conspirators. This Margarett is safe in her father's protection. The Weld boys down the road would have been surprised to hear she needed any protection at all. They named their rabbits Thunder, Chained Lightning, and Margarett Sargent.

§

In Wareham, the Sargents imagined themselves the Swiss Family Robinson. Their elephant of a house was subordinate to no white mansion, and no Commonwealth Avenue calling cards urged return visits. Margarett fished to her heart's content and worshiped her brother Frank, who wore his necktie as a belt. Papa sang at dinner, "Do you remember Alice, Ben Bolt?" Unlike Wellesley or Boston, where the children ate separately, here everyone ate together at the large rectangular table, watched over by the mounted head of a Wyoming elk, all talking and arguing in good-humored loud voices.

Young Frank could not rest: Would he win a pennant at the yacht club next week? Would Papa consent, in a few years' time, to his marrying the quiet young woman in the pink dress? The girl's father had bad manners, Papa said. "And yet," Frank declaimed, "it is written in the stars that we are to marry." Harry and Dan, so inseparable a cousin called them "Harridan," hung on their brother's every miraculous word. He proclaimed his dreams, pacing the bluff, waving his arms. When Margarett learned her first words of French, her handsome older brother became her beloved François.

Papa was known to get so angry at Frank he would send him from the table, but his anger always passed like a summer storm, and it was his imperturbable temperament that kept the family on an even keel. Jenny rarely lost her temper, but she worried, and her worry hung on like a heat inversion, intensifying when her emotions were stormy, receding when they were calm.

Once, young Frank was late for dinner. He was seventeen, old enough to cross the bay by himself. Jenny fretted, wrung her hands. He could have drowned rowing back from the yacht club. He could have tripped and fallen walking back through the woods from Widow's Cove. Unspoken was her real anxiety, his burgeoning sexuality. She insisted that everyone put on a wrap and set out in a search party. Papa carried a lantern, lighting the way down the long, narrow dirt road that led away from the house through a scrub pine forest. He didn't say a word, nor did the children, but Jenny wailed, "O God, bring him back. Dear God, please bring back my son!"

After they had walked half a mile, Jenny turned abruptly back. Papa and the children followed. The house glimmered through the trees, blazed against the black salt grass, the royal-blue evening sky. There in the living room sat Frank, calmly reading the *Boston Herald* by the light of a kerosene lamp. "Where have you been?" he asked, standing up. "I arrived late for supper, having got stuck in the flats with my boat. I expected to find you all here." Papa made sure Jenny never learned the truth, which Frank admitted some time later: he had spent the afternoon in Onset with a prostitute.

The summer Margarett was nine ended with the shooting of President McKinley, on September 6, 1901, in Buffalo. By September 11, the Sargents were back in Wellesley and the President was dead. "The assassination," Hollis wrote in his diary, "by a vile anarchist, of our President McKinley, is causing profound grief and consternation throughout the whole country, and eighty seven millions of our people are mourning their great loss."

One afternoon at the children's hour, soon after the Sargents returned to Wellesley, Mama and Harry were playing checkers, Papa was telling Margarett and Dan a story, and Ruth was sitting in an easy chair, diddling with a small American flag. All at once she lay back, closed her eyes, and held the flag to her chest. Soon she had everyone's mystified attention. "What are you doing?" they asked. No answer. They repeated the question, but she held her position, the serious expression on her face. "What on earth are you doing, Ruth?" Her mother's emphasis provoked a reply. "I'm the little dead President," she said with a smile. "Oh, Ruth," Jenny gasped, her horror bringing everyone's amusement up short. "You must never make fun of the dead!"

On New Year's Day, 1902, Margarett began a diary: "January 1. 9 degrees. Pleasant. Skating with Harry and Dan." She recorded a visit to Aunt Isabella's "parrit," an expedition to Miss Knight's to get a new dress trimmed with a blue bow: "It is very pretty." On Monday, January 6, she noted that she'd taken her broken skate to school to be fixed and that Ruth had "skarlet fever." Tuesday it snowed all day, and on Wednesday, with Hope Thacher and Lily Sears, she built houses of snow. The following Monday, she stayed home: "they have got to have the school fumigated cause so many people in our school have got the skarlet fever."

By February, Margarett was back at school, and Ruth had recovered enough to go outside. Late Friday morning, February 7, Nanna took Ruth up to Boylston Street to see the new streetcars. A coal wagon was backed up to a cellar hatch, its loading ramp obstructing the sidewalk. As Nanna took Ruth by the hand out into the street, the horse hitched to the coal cart shook its head. The rattle of his harness frightened Ruth, who let go of Nanna's hand and ran across the tracks past an outward-bound streetcar onto the inward-bound track. A streetcar was coming down a grade, and the motorman's vision was blocked by the car passing in the other direction. When he saw Ruth, he struggled to brake but succeeded only in preventing the car's wheels from passing over her body, which the fender had already struck twice, killing her.

According to the *Boston Herald* report, "the nurse's shrieks had attracted the attention of people for a block each way, and a crowd gathered in a twinkling. A multitude of brawny shoulders carefully raised the forward end of the car sufficiently to release the body, and it was conveyed to station 16, nearby." Frank arrived at the station and "had no word of blame for the nurse." He scarcely spoke to anyone.

Margarett had gone from school to the skating rink. Frank, home from Groton, had a game with Ruth planned for the afternoon but was out when Dan and Harry got home. Delia, the second parlormaid, met them at the door with the news, and because Jenny was at her father's bedside in Wellesley, Hammond took them up to the New Riding School on Hemenway Street for the afternoon. "Was that your sister who was killed?" the riding master asked Dan.

The funeral was in the living room at 40 Hereford Street, pictures and mirrors draped in black. As Mr. Foote began the prayers, Gertrude Hunnewell saw Frank's hand disappear into the fur muff Jenny wore on a chain around her neck. They stood that way, discreetly consoling each other for this break in their family, their five surviving children clustered around them, until the service was over. That night, Margarett wrote in her diary, "Ruth is dead. Imagen how I feel. She was run over by a car. It is ofly lonsome without her. If she was only liveing, how good I would be to her."

After she confided Ruth's death to her diary, Margarett did not write for a whole month. She told no one until she was in her eighties that when she misbehaved, Nanna scolded her by saying, "To think dear little Ruth was killed and you were left alive!" To have reported this would have required her to approach a mother caught up in a fever of grief. Eighty years after Ruth's death, the walls at Wareham were thick with enlarged photographs of the little girl with blond curls, mere remnants of stacks stored in the attic after Jenny Sargent died.

No one spoke of Ruth after the funeral, and no one questioned Margarett about her feelings, all too clear in her diary entry: "If she was only liveing . . ." Well, Ruth was not alive, and so it was too late to be good to her. Margarett was now almost ten, and she began to put her considerable energy to the business of gaining her mother's attention. In response, Jenny often enlisted Harry and Dan to keep their sister occupied, a task to which they did not take kindly. They were particularly irritated when Mama insisted one day that Margarett accompany them to Mr. Foster's Saturday morning dancing class. She was still too young to join. Her looks would do them no credit—she was pale and always chewed that wisp of black hair—and aside from the fact that it was embarrassing on principle to have your younger sister and her nurse in tow, you never knew what Margarett would do.

The Tuileries stood on the shady side of Commonwealth Avenue and had, Dan wrote later, "a granite facade that befitted a building named after the royal palace in Paris." The ballroom was to the left, and, in 1902, its chandeliers threw glistening blurs on a flawless parquet floor. Dan and Harry barely introduced Margarett to their friends, wary of seeming too responsible for her but not wishing to seem unchivalrous. Dancing was the pretext for Mr. Foster's class, its actual purpose the passing on of etiquette.

Margarett waited as Nanna gave her wrap to the attendant, and then she entered the ballroom. When she saw the older girls curtsy to the two hostesses, she imitated them and then carefully took a seat on one of the painted gold chairs that stood in a row in front of a baroquely paneled, voluptuously rendered scene from the siege of the Tuileries in Paris on August 10, 1792.

Mr. Foster, a tall, lean man with a pointed red beard and white kid gloves, rose and called the march that always began the class. Margarett was behaving, and Dan was relieved enough to be able to notice how garishly the slaughter of the Swiss Guards was composed, when Mr. Foster, in the French accent he affected to camouflage his Cape Cod lineage, called the cotillion. Since Mademoiselle Sargent was the guest, she would lead off.

Margarett felt the thrust of Mr. Foster's begloved wooden hand as he escorted her to the gold chair at the center of the room. She eagerly took the mirror and the lace handkerchief he handed to her, and listened to his instructions. In some cotillions, gentlemen were required to jump hurdles to greet ladies who offered lit tapers or biscuits. In this one, a gentleman came up behind until the lady saw his face in her mirror. If she did not wish to dance with him, she dismissed his attentions by brushing her lace handkerchief across the mirror's surface.

Dressed in white, Margarett crossed her spindly legs, smoothed by Sunday-best stockings. She sat gazing into the mirror. The music began, and the boy whose name Mr. Foster called came up from behind. Margarett brushed his face from the mirror, and Mr. Foster called another name. Whom would she choose to escort her in the two-step? She dismissed the second boy, and a third. It was not proper to pass over more than two, but the music swelled, and Margarett dismissed one boy after another.

Dan and Harry looked at each other. There was just one boy left to be called. Mr. Foster maintained his composure: If acceptable manners were a paddock, Mademoiselle Marguerite had not yet jumped the fence. Would she choose Carl Searle? Dan and Harry could barely look. Margarett turned, smiled at her young man, and rose from the chair. As the pair two-stepped awkwardly around the hall, Dan gazed again at the slaughter of the Swiss Guards, wondering why on earth his sister had chosen a partner whose family was new to Boston and newly rich. When she heard the story, Aunt Mamy Hunnewell, Gertrude and Mary's mother, told her daughters their cousin would surely come to a bad end.

If the Sargents were concerned about Margarett, they did nothing about it; they had a more pressing problem. Harry had become a bully who slugged his playmates; once, he hit Wanda, the Polish nurse who taught the boys German, and broke her finger. At fourteen, he could not tell right from left and had difficulty reading, so he was also considered "slow." His anger wasn't helped by the fact that Dan was a natural student, who, though a year younger, skipped a grade and surpassed Harry in his own class. Frank and Jenny determined to send the two boys to different boarding schools, but Dan wept until they broke their resolve. "A terrible mistake," Aunt Mamy whispered to her daughters. The two were not separated until Dan was kept back at Groton so Harry could enter Harvard first.

It was Dan whom Margarett missed most when he left home. The spring before he went off to Groton, they'd had measles together. "We have a maid named Kelleher / I would not say that she has curly hair," was only one of the rhymes they composed as they lay sick. They also lampooned their brother Frank's girl chasing and made a poem of Hammond at Wareham whistling to summon the crow with one white feather from the forest to his shoulder. During the days in the darkened room, they forged an alliance, which grew stronger as they grew up and she became an artist and he a poet. They were the family vaudeville team, contriving skits for family gatherings in which they ruthlessly mimicked this or that aunt, uncle, or cousin; rendered Hunnewell life from the point of view of the Wellesley gatekeeper, who taxidermized songbirds and enshrined them in glass globes; or, years later, acted out the sinking of the *Titanic*.

The theater fed their imaginations. Frank Sargent was a man apt to slip alone from his office to see Houdini, and he loved to take his children to Buffalo Bill's Wild West Show or to Keith's, the most reputable vaudeville house in Boston. "They say Buster Brown is a dwarf but I can't believe it," Margarett wrote when she was fourteen. "There were 491 children that went on the stage to get Buster Brown's photo. We did not go but as the curtain went down, Buster Brown threw us half a dozen." The act that drew her attention was Primrose's Min-

strels, led by Lew Dockstader, a big, lumbering man who performed in
outsize clothes and huge shoes, combining clowning with blackface. "I
laughed my insides out," Margarett wrote. "Awfully good take-offs on
'Deary' and 'Waltz Me Around Again Willie.' Bully show."

On the stage at Keith's, the Irish, Italians, Jews, and blacks, mute
or careful when Margarett encountered them as servants or saw them
at a distance, became, with the actors' magic, outspoken, brash, and
funny. In the dark of the theater, audiences roared with laughter at behavior that in the light of day would have prompted them to purse
their lips with disapproval. In her 1907 diary, Margarett wrote that she
and Lily Sears had "fooled with a nigger." The word her grandfather
employed in his diary was "coon," and one of Lew Dockstader's hit
songs was called "Coon Coon." The minstrel show imported to the
quiet boulevards of the Back Bay a diluted form of the racist terror
then building in the South. Ironically, vaudeville, which imprisoned
its performers in slapstick distortion, was Margarett's first introduction
to people different from herself. The performers she saw onstage seemed
free and spirited, their behavior and difference an escape from the life
against which she was forming a habit of rebellion.

To render the appearance of that life—animal, flower, beautiful
household object—was considered a female skill like embroidery, and,
like her cousins and friends, Margarett was sent to drawing class. At
first, she drew things as she was taught, but soon she began to see how
drawing could alter the world she found so dull: "Drew lion which I
made look like a dachshund!" At Keith's, she had learned that things
were not always what they seemed, and now, in her drawing, she
performed similar feats of transformation. Directed to sketch the gar-
goyles on the Gothic facade of a house across the street on Commonwealth Avenue, she told the instructor she would prefer to draw a glass
of water, half empty. When he refused, Margarett left the class for
good. Drawing had become part of her, but drawing on her own
terms. Now she added quick caricatures and portraits to her entertain-
ments at Hunnewell parties.

Margarett went to these drawing classes with E. and O. Ames,

who appear often among the names that swarm her diaries. These were
the daughters and sons of those her cousin Gertrude called "all the best
people," the covey of companions to whose lives Margarett's life would
be compared for the next seventy-five years. E. and O. and their cousin
Helen Hooper preceded Margarett at the dressmaker's, and Gertrude
and Mary and she went to the same sewing class. Margarett took fancy
dancing with Libby Silsbee and Hope Thacher—"I danced like a cook
on a tightrope"—and ice-skating with Lily and Phyllis Sears—"Loads
of lessons. Hang it."

Like Gertrude and Mary at Wellesley, her Boston friends were
willing lieutenants in mischief. E. Ames became Margarett's best friend.
They were "intimate," E. said, using the word to describe the confi-
dentiality of friendships in which certain rules of decorum are suspended. They were inseparable, Dan said, constantly spending the
night at each other's houses. "Margarett always made us do things," E.
said. "She made us have a play at the Arlington Street Church." Everyone remembers that the play was called *Edith and the Burglars*; no one
remembers the plot. Margarett wrote it, talked all her friends into doing it, and talked Paul Revere Frothingham into letting them perform
it in his pristine sanctuary for a packed Back Bay audience.

When she was twelve, Margarett entered Miss Winsor's School,
located in buildings on Newbury and Marlborough Streets, within
walking distance of the Sargents' house on Hereford. Jane and the
boys had commuted each day to Boston for school, but Margarett did
her fall and spring work in Wellesley, supervised by tutors she shared
with Gertrude and Mary. Mary Pickard Winsor was an austere and
gifted teacher, who believed that a student's behavior was as important
as her academic performance. Gertrude Hunnewell joked that the only
girls who met Miss Winsor were those who excelled and those who
misbehaved. She herself hardly knew the headmistress, but Margarett,
in time, came to know her very well.

Miss Winsor's School did not capture Margarett's imagination.
She performed only when she was interested, and at least one teacher
complained that she had no "power of concentration." In science and

math, she arduously progressed; cooking class was "fun"; and in French and German, she applied herself. She became a crack speller and an "appreciative and thoughtful" reader, and when the history teacher assigned a county map, she drew it with enthusiasm. She was judged "most unsteady" in preparing her daily theme, but she wrote with relish in the diary her teachers never saw: "Bully Great Danes and vile lap dogs, peachy setters . . . Delicious drooly English bulls . . ."

"Boys go back to Groton. It'll be rotten without them," Margarett wrote in January 1907. She was fourteen and the only child left at home. Riding was her salvation. She rode her pony, Logo, indoors at the New Riding Club, and Mr. Speare, the riding master, led trail rides in the Fenway. Girls rode sidesaddle, and Mrs. Ames, concerned her children would become "one-sided," had a saddle made with its pommel on the right and special habits tailored so that E. and O. could alternate, riding right one day, left the next.

Margarett rode sidesaddle only when it was impossible to do otherwise. "Rode astride," she exulted, "but I'll get Hail Columbia. . . . We went like greased lightning. Jumped over stone walls, hurdles and brooks." At the club, her riding soon drew the admiration of the older girls. "Am smashed on Alice Thorndike," Margarett wrote. And later, "Am smashed on Eleo and A. Thorndike." To be "smashed" was to have a crush. Eleanora Sears had greeted Margarett once at Wareham with a patronizing "Hello, Freckletop." Now Alice had asked her to ride Jack Rabbit, her pony, in the club horse show! Margarett jumped her own Logo "splendidly," and then rode Jack Rabbit to first place. Victory brought "the dearest pin" from Alice and a surge of invitations to ride other ponies in the next show. Even the riding master was impressed; "Mr. Speare wanted me to ride Miss Wheelwright's horse." But "Ma and Pa say jumping two horses is enough. Damn it!"

"I am always looking for Margarett to make a start in her lessons," Miss Winsor wrote on her 1907 report card. "A change in behavior must come first, and it is my firm belief that that is coming at once." She was wrong. Margarett had her own priorities. She considered her pony an "angelic angel," but called her teacher "a pig." A week after the 1907 report card, the school boiler burst and school was dismissed. Margarett let out a whoop of pleasure, and the headmistress sternly tapped her on the shoulder. "Miss Mary P. Winsor has got a prison," Margarett snarled in her diary later that winter.

The Sargents did nothing about their daughter's discontent. Jenny thought she could scold it away, and Frank was bemused, believing that in time Margarett would naturally follow Jane into the rites of womanhood. But the two sisters were very different. Jane had never been known for fights with teachers or desires to ride too many horses. Late in 1906, at twenty-four, she became engaged to David Cheever, Harvard '97, a young surgeon and an instructor at the Harvard Medical School. They would marry in June. On February 7, 1907, Margarett wrote in her diary, "Jane has asked me to be bridesmaid. I am thrilled!"

The day of the wedding, Hammond, in borrowed high boots and a top hat, drove Jane and Papa to the Unitarian church in the Sargents' only closed carriage, and Paul Revere Frothingham led the couple through their vows. After a reception for six hundred in a tent near the Sargents' house in Wellesley, the newlyweds left for a honeymoon on Cedar Island in Vermont. "It was quite an undertaking," Jenny wrote a friend, "but I am delighted that Jane is settled for life." Margarett, almost fifteen, had a different ambition: "When 30," she scrawled on the back binding of her diary, days after the wedding, "am going to have a horse and millions of animals. Am going to be a nice cantankerous old maid."

She kept no diary in 1908. The only record of her fourth year at Miss Winsor's are her grades, which plummet at midterm. No warning preceded Miss Winsor's final "blow up," which came to Hereford Street by letter and survived in Dan's memory: "I'm afraid we can't take back your daughter Margarett. She's a born leader, but unfortunately she always leads people in the wrong direction."

ii

*If only we hadn't sent her
to Europe!*

(1908–1913)

Margarett, her debutante year

MISS PORTER'S SCHOOL in Farmington, Connecticut, still inhabits its extraordinary original buildings, porticoed Federal mansion houses which line a street that was, when Margarett arrived in 1908, a dirt road as apt to be marked with the hoofprints of a yoke of oxen as with the tracks of a carriage. Built of brick in 1830 as the Union Hotel, "Main" was the first building purchased by Sarah Porter, and it was on its steps that Elizabeth Hale Keep, Miss Porter's successor, always stood the first day of school to greet the young women asked to present themselves "during the day or the evening." In a photograph taken in 1909 of "The School," all one hundred thirty subjects wear white dresses, and all but Margarett look at the camera.

Margarett's sister, Jane, had suggested she go to Miss Porter's. Margarett's friend Frances Saltonstall had just finished, and Dorothy Draper, another Bostonian, was in her last year there. Jenny had misgivings—no other Hunnewell daughter had gone away to school, and she remembered palpably her lonely year at school in Paris—but Jane had a clear sense of her younger sister's intelligence and believed Margarett's enthusiasm might be engaged at a good school away from home.

Sarah Porter was the intellectually voracious eldest daughter of Noah Porter, who was for sixty years the pastor of the First Church of Farmington. She became the first female student at Farmington Academy and at sixteen its first female instructor, later teaching at schools for girls in Springfield, Buffalo, and Philadelphia. When she was twenty-eight, she came home to teach a few young women in an old stone store. A dozen years later, she was teaching more than fifty girls and attracting pupils from as far away as California.

Every afternoon, whatever the weather, Miss Porter took her students on a walk in the countryside or had them driven in a carriage up Talcott Mountain for a picnic, while she led on horseback. At fifty, she learned Greek, and at sixty-five undertook Hebrew. The depth of her knowledge of philosophy brought visits from scholars, and luminaries like Mark Twain often lectured at the school. For most of her career, Miss Porter taught all the academic subjects—Latin, French, German, chemistry, natural philosophy, and rhetoric. She had a physical constitution "hardly less remarkable than Gladstone's," *Century Magazine* reported, and "astonishing reports grew up as to the little sleep she required."

When Margarett came to Farmington, Sarah Porter had been dead eight years, but her portrait still hung in Main. The girls made secret fun of the gaunt New England likeness, which revealed little of the founder's expansive character and nothing of her belief that the essence of teaching lay not in "the fixed organization of matters educational" but in "the contact of mental and spiritual life in the teacher with the answering love and spiritual life in the pupil."

In a photograph in Margarett's scrapbook, Elizabeth Keep rises majestically from a sea of pompadoured girls in white dresses, a figurehead. Her contribution to the school was organizational; Mrs. Keep didn't teach. She was as Edwardian as Sarah Porter was Puritan, as full-bodied as Miss Porter was gaunt. Her expression is one of satisfaction rather than hunger, and she wears, pinned meticulously to beautifully coiffed nearly white hair, an enormous black hat. Miss Porter inspired her students with after-dinner readings from the classics of English fiction and poetry; Mrs. Keep entertained with chapters of popular novels. When she "sailed imposingly" into a room, Clover Todd, class of 1912, was reminded "of the Winged Victory of Samothrace." To sixteen-year-old Margarett, Mrs. Keep was, as Miss Winsor had been, an authority with whom to negotiate.

Margarett's initial "Homesick if I stopped to think" was subsumed quickly by a routine that, unlike life in Boston, burst from her diary's tiny pages. She was awake at 6:45, then downstairs for breakfast, prayers, and hymns; classes began at 8:40. At first, Margarett was insecure in her studies. She reacted to low grades or criticism with fury and to the possibility of a test with high anxiety: "If we have an algebra exam, I meet the ghost." A mark of 64 for a "hang old Spenser exam" enraged her, and when she and a classmate were caught misbehaving in French she threw a tantrum.

But Jane's prediction proved accurate. The title page of Margarett's psychology text listed vices of defect to the left, vices of excess to the right, and virtues down the center. In time, she attained, if not virtue, a modicum of equanimity. She did well enough in French to be advanced her second year—"I was petrified. There are girls who have been in Mademoiselle Pierrard's classes for ages." She found Bible "most exciting" and ethics, though "ghastly" on Aristotle, "so interesting," but it was where algebra, psychology, and Miss McDonald converged that her heart and mind awakened to intellectual curiosity.

Jessie Claire McDonald, whose fiancé, it was rumored, had died tragically, was tall, brunette, and slender, and, by the time Margarett came to Miss Porter's, the constant companion of Miss Duclos, the English instructor. Her charisma and warmth made her the object of many a student crush, and Margarett was no exception; Miss McDonald entered her diary on a least thirty occasions. "Went to call on Miss McDonald. We talked of the big trees in California. She is the most fascinating hostess." "She is so interesting on the earthquake, Italy & The Republic, etc." "Went to call on Miss McDonald. Heavenly and melancholy."

In turn, Miss McDonald took an interest in Margarett. She was the first to encourage her intellectually, keeping her after class to tell her when she'd improved and chastising her when her work fell off: "Got slightly stung by Macy Doo who told me that I could compete with the finest mathematicians in the school, but that I had left my heart in Groton or some such thing." Miss McDonald was more sympathetic than Jenny, who, when Margarett wrote "a discouraged letter," replied by "telling me to stop complaining."

"Macy Doo's" concern and attention soothed Margarett's insecurity, provincial shyness in the face of girls from New York and Chicago, who seemed unassailably worldly bedecked in their sophisticated clothing, their pompadours combed higher than anyone dared in Boston. "I have absolutely the clearest memory of Margarett coming down the stair in Main," said Marjorie Davenport, a New York girl who wore a velvet hat even on her afternoon walk. "She didn't have very pretty clothes. She dressed the way Boston girls did in those days—rather unattractively—and her hair was braided and turned up and nothing very attractive about it."

Margarett soon came to be admired for her independence and sought after for her wit. She cut required evening prayer meetings when she didn't feel like going, something her classmate Fanny Perkins never had the courage to do. "She was very sarcastic, like a knife," Fanny said, "and she made quite a few enemies." She remembered Margarett carefree, entertaining the Farmington railroad car to Boston with Harry Lauder songs, singing his "Whistle, daughter, whistle" as she jigged down the aisle, her classmates overcome with laughter. Fanny did not recall that her nervy classmate had headaches that sent her to bed with hot-water bottles.

"Woke up with a rancid headache. Got excused from Church," Margarett wrote one Sunday. In February, she announced her first period—"I am no longer an Amazon!"—but noted no accompanying pain. She could get a headache after sketch class or after indulging herself with cake or candy. There were mornings she woke feeling "rottenly" and recovered quickly, but her "old family tricks," the harrowing headache and nausea of her childhood, could devastate her for two days. Margarett had violent reactions—"Dead with loneliness," she wrote when her roommate had a visitor—and headaches often accompanied them. She got a headache when she was thwarted, as when Edith Parkman couldn't be her partner at gym, or when she asserted herself, as when she told Eleanor Hubbard she didn't want to room with her. The more she made her desires known to herself, the more brutal, it seemed, the attacks became. One morning, sufficiently sick to leave a class in Main, she climbed the stairs to Miss McDonald's room. "I had my nerve with me enough to sleep on her bed."

"Don't Crush," read a headline Margarett cut from an ad to paste on her diary's marbled endpapers. "Sorry you were not in," reads Kaa Thompson's calling card affixed to one inside cover; Marian Turner's sew-on clothes tag flutters from the other. These are relics of the all-girls social life at Miss Porter's, which matched, in excitement and intrigue, regulated, infrequent congress with the young men who visited on the train from New Haven.

Girls were allowed to attend, by invitation, the Yale Prom or the Yale-Harvard game and to have gentlemen callers on Saturday afternoons, but weekend walks on Farmington Avenue, where Yale men were said to lurk uninvited, were forbidden. That one of her classmates had callers and flirted with local Irish boys made Margarett uneasy. "I may be a New Englander," she wrote indignantly, "but I prefer the dump and Boston any time to the behavior of New York. Grace Allen kicked her legs and behaved altogether like a chorus girl on a spree." The only admiration of the opposite sex in Margarett's diary involves a Mr. Samuel Archer King of London and Bryn Mawr College, who visited Miss Porter's to teach declamatory reading and voice placement: "Great shock—he is young and good looking."

"It was all the style to have crushes," Fanny Perkins said. "New Girls" had crushes on "Old Girls," and one's crush was often one's "date" for all the school events of the weekend. A crush was exclusive, and everyone knew its status. "What a strain," Margarett wrote after an afternoon with Eleanor Hubbard. "I am so sick of being told I am in a peeve with E. Hubbard!"

During the week, one invited a girl one admired for an afternoon of sledding, riding, or tennis, depending on the season. If you walked, you did so arm in arm. "PM with 'little Daven,'" Margarett wrote of an afternoon with Marjorie Davenport. "The first date I've had with her and lets hope not the last." In the spring, girls walked to Diamond Glen or through Hill-Stead to Hooker's Woods, in the fall to a cider mill at the edge of the Farmington River, where they drank cider they hoped would be hard. More than once a hot-water bottle filled with cider burst in the back of a closet, for a chambermaid to find. Afternoons ended at the Gundy, the school teahouse, a short walk up the hill.

Like everyone else, Margarett had a date for Saturday evenings, who accompanied her to dinner, to the weekly theatrical entertainment, to dancing in the gym afterward. "Delaware and I sported up for a waltz, our first standing date." Mrs. Keep's secretary taught popular dances in the gymnasium Monday mornings, and on several Wednesdays each term Miss Ethel Bury-Palliser of London arrived on her circuit of girls' schools to teach deportment and carriage. "Did it with E. Orr," Margarett wrote. "I got so mad trying to do the scarf dance."

The girls attended each other like suitors. Tottie Evarts, two years younger, surprised Margarett one day by polishing her shoes "like an angel," and another admirer left this poem:

> The one was tired
> And her head ached
> For she'd had an awful day
> That was the reason when the other laughed
> She shouted "Keep out of the way!"
>
> The other was tactless
> And noisy too
> And feeling by far too gay
> Therefore her conscience smote her
> When you shouted "keep out of the way!"
>
> "The other" leaves
> These violets here
> Hoping when you see them
> You won't say (as you did to me
> the other day) "Keep out of the way!!"

But Margarett wasn't interested in the girls who pursued her. Marian Turner also sat at the table Miss Duclos supervised at supper, and it was she whom Margarett began to court: "I am glad to get to know M. Turner. I think she's sweet but too clever," she wrote after visiting her room one night. Marian was an Old Girl from Saint Louis. She was small and dark-haired, and dressed modestly. Fanny Perkins described her as "not bad looking," but to Margarett she was "so attractive." It was not a comfortable friendship. They argued about Miss McDonald and about the advisability of a girl becoming engaged before she left Miss Porter's—"I think it's childish," Margarett sniffed.

A week after their argument, Margarett wrote Marian a poem (it has not survived) and delivered it with a bunch of violets, a gesture she'd previously reserved for Miss McDonald. After Easter vacation, they had a walk, but Margarett was soon insecure: "I am afraid she is not sincere, and I like her so much." Marjorie Davenport told her reassuringly "that she thought people always would want to show me their finer side and that I was the kind of girl to bring it out!" But on the heels of a rumor that Marian was engaged came the news she was leaving before the end of term. "It is worse than I expected," Margarett wrote the day Marian left. To distract herself she went shopping in Hartford with Elinor McLane: "I bought a hat like a loon and had to borrow and borrow."

"Little Clara," or "C.C. Lemons the star of French III," looks from the likeness in Margarett's diary to be rather plain, but it's "a quick sketch," she wrote, "so I don't do her justice." Opposite is the haughty profile of a stylish young woman wearing a hat trimmed with grapes. Margarett used ink to emphasize grapes, collar, and earrings—"Girls you would not have for your friends," she captioned it. "Sleep gentle sleep," she wrote one night, then dashed off with pen and ink Cupid nesting in a cloud.

Miss Porter's was famous for its art department. Its art history course had the benefit of "all the best means of illustration: electric

lantern, lantern slides, photographs and plaster casts." Because drawing and painting were always taught by professionals, the art curriculum was unusual, but it was not progressive. In 1856, women students
at the Philadelphia Academy had won the right to sketch from a cast of
Apollo Belvedere provided he wore a "close-fitting but inconspicuous
fig leaf." By 1868, they were allowed to draw a live female nude, but
when male nude models were permitted ten years later, Philadelphia
was scandalized. At Miss Porter's in 1909, students sketched plaster
torsos and each other, fully clothed.

Margarett's portraits were mediums for scrutiny and admiration.
At Tuesday sketch class, she filled a book with her schoolmate models
and, in her diary, catalogued her impressions: Eleanor Hubbard in a
big black hat was "stunning," Rebekah Mills was "not very interesting for me as she was in costume," and Mary Plum "wonderful to
sketch—I managed to get something quite a little like her." When she
was interviewed years later, Margarett brought out the sketchbook she
kept at Miss Porter's as an example of her early work. The reporter
described the drawings as "Ingres-like," done in "a carefully delineated
style with the shadows well blacked in."

The years Margarett was at Farmington, Theodate Pope, a Miss
Porter's graduate and one of the first American women to become a
licensed architect, was putting finishing touches on Hill-Stead, the
grand country house she had designed for her parents on one hundred
fifty acres adjacent to the school. Girls from Miss Porter's wandered
through "Miss Pope's place" as if it were part of the campus. In the
house hung a small but exquisite collection of Impressionist paintings
assembled by Theodate's iron-baron father on his travels abroad, among
them two Monet haystacks, a Degas nude bather, and a Mary Cassatt
mother and child.

Cassatt was actually a friend of Theodate's, and it was at Miss
Porter's Margarett learned that a young woman from Philadelphia had
made her way in Paris as a serious painter. Cassatt visited the Popes in
Farmington on her last trip to America. The artist was in her sixties, it
was the autumn of 1908, and Margarett was in her first term at Miss

Porter's. There is no evidence of a meeting or of the artist's visiting the
school, but three years later, when her father gave her a thousand dollars for her nineteenth birthday, Margarett went to New York and
bought a Cassatt, the pastel that now hangs in the Philadelphia
Museum of Art—a young woman dressed in yellow in a balcony at the
opera, face half hidden by an open fan. Cassatt became a talisman for
Margarett's own artistic aspirations; later, she would collect three of
her aquatints and a bronze head of the artist by Degas.

That Margarett mentioned in her diary neither Mary Cassatt nor
Rosamond Lombard Smith, who exhibited paintings as Rosamond
Smith Bouve and whom the 1908 Miss Porter's circular listed as an
instructor in drawing and painting, was not a sign of her indif-
ference to art. Her drawing had become as organic to her as the jot-
tings in her diary, and her classmates at Farmington were the first
models to lend themselves to her most expressive subject—what is revealed when a woman sits alone for a woman artist. Long after Margarett stopped painting, she would continue to draw, capturing with
the quick movement of a line what she saw and the particular intensity
with which she saw it.

At first when Margarett got back to Wellesley in May, she was relieved. There were "no bells," and she could present herself for formal
calls now that boarding school had made her a "lady." But Miss Porter's
had changed her in ways her ascent to a new plateau of female obligation did not acknowledge. She now had dreams of a life beyond
Wellesley and domesticity, and she knew she dreaded the summer at
Wareham. Dan was traveling in Europe, Frank and Harry were also
away, and she did not look forward to Gertrude and Mary's annual
visit. She wrote madly to Farmington friends, to Fanny Perkins: "Please
come see me. I am so bored!"

Between furious games of tennis, books rescued her. By the end
of August she had read at least twenty. She read *Up from Slavery* and
made herself "disagreeable to the rest of the family" by describing
Booker T. Washington's ideas about the people to whom they routinely

referred, in the slang of the time, as "coons." She read F. Marion Crawford's *Marcella* and announced she had "serious thoughts of being a socialist." She read Thackeray's *The Virginians* and George Meredith's great novel declaring the intellectual equality of women with men, *Diana of the Crossways*. Jenny had brought her set of George Eliot to Wareham, and Margarett soon finished *The Mill on the Floss*. "I have started it so many times, but this is the first time I have persisted. Mad about G. Eliot. Teary book."

Back at Miss Porter's in September, Margarett became the school's most sought after leading man. In *Nephew or Uncle*, she played a prospective bridegroom, and in *Trying It On* sat grimacing, frock coat brushing the floor, as she banged away on the piano. When a classmate left the cast of Thackeray's *The Rose and the Ring*, Margarett was drafted as Hedzoff, captain of the guard. The play was rehearsed six weeks, programs were printed, scenery was wallpapered, costumes were dug from the school's trunks of flounced gowns, powdered wigs, waistcoats, and britches. Tuesday before the opening, "getting nervous," Margarett took a walk, ate maple sugar at the Gundy, wore no rubbers, got soaked, woke feeling "rottenly," and landed in the infirmary. On Sunday, her nose ran "like thin ink," but by Tuesday she was ransacking Main for dress rehearsal—"nothing to keep moustache on with." In a photograph as a swain, her assumed virility is utterly convincing as, wig in place, she casts a lustful eye at Polly Foster, the ingenue. "She was the best actress they ever had," Fanny said. "They begged her to stay a third year."

Margarett had other ideas. Her roommate, Elinor McLane, was going to finishing school in Florence. Margarett had read George Eliot's *Romola*, set there, and had studied Italian painting in art history. A year abroad would postpone her debut, the thought of which she found "just repulsive." She begged Mama and Papa to allow her to go, and at last, Frank and Jane prevailed over Jenny's fear of sending a daughter off to Europe. When the Florentine School denied her application, Margarett borrowed money and sent a telegram—"Please reconsider our marvellous daughter"—and signed it Mr. and Mrs. Francis W. Sargent.

§

MARGARETT STANDS ON THE DECK of the SS *Princess Irene* next to Catharine Bond, "my attractive blond Baltimore friend," one of the flurry of new acquaintances who will be her schoolmates in Florence. It is October 1910, and she is eighteen. Louise Delano of New York holds aside her camera to pose on the ship's bridge with Captain von Letten Peterssen, whose navy-blue uniform is brass-buttoned over a generous belly. Margarett snaps Miss Sheldon, chaperone of the Florentine School, and two schoolmates lounging on deck chairs. Catharine closes what she's reading and looks at the camera. A few popular novels balance on the ledge behind them: *The Motor Maid*, *Arsène Lupin*, *All in the Same Boat*.

Later, without Miss Sheldon, three girls, including Margarett, "the new member of The Florentine School," posed on the same chairs, books nowhere in sight, "all busy being silly." Margarett looks matronly, uncannily like her mother in a dark tweed suit that seems too big, her forehead obscured by an outsize, awkward hat. She stalked everyone with her camera: the captain, who postured in several uniforms; a uniformed gentleman she called "an intruder"; the doctor, terribly severe in his uniform.

There was no sign of her traveling companion from Miss Porter's, Elinor McLane. According to Fanny Perkins, news of their "irreperable" falling-out crackled along the Farmington grapevine as soon as protestations from Tuscany could reach New England. In a deck snapshot, Frances Breese grins impishly at the camera and Margarett smiles, eyes lowered, arm tight around the waist of her new friend.

The Florentine School, run by an American, Miss Nixon, mainly for American girls, was one of three finishing schools in Florence in 1910. In Margarett's year, thirteen girls inhabited the towered ivy-clad villa Miss Nixon leased on the Via Barbacane, a narrow street that led up steeply from the square in San Gervasio, a village near San Domenico in the hills below Fiesole, about thirty minutes from the center of the city.

When Miss Nixon's students took the tram down the hill for pastries, a teacher went along. Miss Nixon feared the young men who loitered on Via Tornabuoni near Doney's—titled young Florentines without a cent, who, in search of an American wife, routinely questioned the concierges of the Excelsior and the Grand Hotel about the lineages of young American female guests: if she wasn't rich, they weren't interested. As an antidote, Miss Nixon invited American, English, and Italian young men of whom she approved for thés dansants. On at least one occasion, Margarett escaped the headmistress to rendezvous in a park, not with an Italian princeling but with Mr. Ringling, whose circus was touring Italy. "You never knew how Margarett met people," Dan remarked. At home, she entertained her brothers with the episode, boasting she had not been caught and mercilessly mimicking Miss Nixon saying "the most banal things."

Haze obscured the heights above Florence in the morning, so the girls piled into the school's touring car to sightsee in the afternoons. Margarett snapped the famous view of Florence from Piazza Michelangelo, the Duomo rising in the distance, cedars in silhouette between her camera and the city. When the girls gathered in the square at Fiesole, she snapped seven of them, "all in suits and hats." They toured Fiesole's Romanesque cathedral, saw its schools of Giotto Madonna and saints. When they walked out back to scrutinize the Teatro Romana, they found it occupied by a Franciscan monastery and therefore, as the Baedeker put it, "not accessible to ladies."

Miss Nixon's intention was that a young girl's year at the Florentine School familiarize her with the great sights of Italy. Before Christmas, she took her students to Levante on the Riviera to escape the cold, then south to Rome and Pompeii, and, in May, to Venice. At Portofino, they climbed Monte di Portofino with its views of both Rivieras, and in Genoa, Margarett, Frances Breese, and Catharine Bond linked arms for a photo, "The Three Musketeers." Margarett's love of what she saw showed in her photographs: in Rome, the looming walls of the Colosseum; in Pompeii, the Casa dei Vettii's frescoed cupids sacrificing to Fortuna.

Though her studies in Florence consisted, Margarett said later, largely of "just looking," "just looking" had, for her, a transforming intensity. The elegance and care with which she preserved her lecture notes rather than her crowded snapshots testified that she was vulnerable to Florence. Matched brass florets mark the corners of the three leather volumes that contain them, and delicate brass chains fasten their bindings. Each front cover is stamped with a gold "MWS," each spine with a subject: Florentine History, Italian Literature, Italian Art. Inside, in black ink, Margarett recorded what she learned. Nothing of the rapscallion Farmington girl jarred her scholarly seriousness. Though Miss Nixon was strict and the situation new, caution was not what kept Margarett's penmanship precise: the enchanted city was weaving its spell.

In the margin of Margarett's history notebook, alongside a note that "Visconti becomes sole lord of Milan by the murder of his uncle," a teacher inserted, "92% Corrected to Feb. 1, 1911." Margarett sustained a high standard of achievement throughout the year, but she couldn't resist making her notebook personal. Instead of copying coats of arms, she drew and painted freehand. One of her black Urbino eagles has fallen from its shield; her blue Visconti serpent—a tiny nude shrieking from its mouth—gazes, gluttonous, from a bright-yellow ground.

E. Ames remarked that her friend came home from Florence "sporting Italian." In a scrapbook photo of the room Margarett shared with Louise Delano in Venice, a sign tacked to the organdy canopy of a rumpled bed announced, "Si prequo di non sputore," a misspelled attempt at "Please don't spit." Next to it, emphatic arrows pointing left, was another sign: "Rittrato," it said, for "Ritirata," which means WC. Whatever Margarett's mistakes, her interest in Italian was earnest and enthusiastic; when assigned the transcription of an Italian poem from each literary epoch, she chose works that expressed her own temperament: "If I were fire, I'd burn the world away; / If I were wind, I'd turn my storms thereon."

Soon after her arrival in October, Margarett left school to visit

Edward Boit, whose sister had married her uncle Arthur Hunnewell and whose daughters were the subjects of his friend John Sargent's great group portrait. She had never visited the home of an artist, and Edward Darley Boit was a working painter who had studied in Rome and Paris and exhibited at the Paris Salon of 1876. His villa crowned the summit of a hill in Pegli, in the hills above the Italian Riviera. Margarett had grown up with the topiary of Wellesley's Italian Garden, flower beds that waxed and waned with the harsh New England seasons, but she was still unused to the effortless profusion of a garden in Italy, the timeless presence of barns and granaries built and rebuilt with the same ancient stone.

Florrie, the Boit daughter who at fourteen slouched against a huge vase in the Sargent painting, led her visitor through the gardens. In the rose garden, Margarett posed, not smiling at the camera but contemplating a fountain, captivated, it seems, not only by the beauty of what she looked at but by the idea of herself in such a place. "Al cor gentil ripara sempre amore," read one of the poems in her literature notebook. "Within the gentle heart," translated Rossetti from Guincelli, "Love shelters him / As birds within the green shade of the grove."

At a fancy-dress tea soon after their arrival, the girls dressed as characters from the paintings they were studying. Frances Breese was Botticelli's Primavera, Emily Von Armin, a darkly hooded Angelico monk, and M. MacLaren so precisely Piero della Francesca's *Portrait of a Lady* that she seemed sprung from the Uffizi. Margarett walked demurely across the lawn, the startling embodiment of a portrait by Ambrogio de Predis that Bernard Berenson called simply *Profile of a Lady.* Wearing a dress that revealed her slender figure, her hair coiled in Renaissance fashion, Margarett showed signs of leaving behind the "ugly duckling" to whom her Boston friend Kay Saltonstall had bid farewell and becoming the "lovely swan" whom she would welcome home.

Margarett was assigned John Addington Symonds's *Fine Arts,* Walter Pater's *Essays on the Renaissance,* and Bernard Berenson's *Florentine Painters* to read, but it is Berenson's approach that glimmers through her notes like an original through overpainting. She recorded that Signorelli's works had "gigantic robustness" and were "replete with primeval energy," Berenson having praised his "gigantic robustness and suggestions of primeval energy." Margarett wrote of Raphael as "the greatest master of Composition in the sense of grouping and arrangement"; Berenson, "the greatest master of Composition—whether considered as arrangement or as space."

By 1911, Bernard Berenson had lived in Florence for more than ten years, and renovations of I Tatti, his villa at Settignano, were close to completion. His "four gospels," the famous essays that constitute *Italian Painters of the Renaissance*, had long since established the authority that his breathlessly awaited "lists" enhanced every few years. A new Berenson inventory of known Italian Renaissance paintings with changed or refined attributions caused wild price swings in the art markets of Paris, New York, and London, and significant activity among the students at Miss Nixon's school, which lay just two miles northwest of I Tatti.

His influence was evident when Margarett chose which Alinari postcards she would paste into her art notebook. From the Sistine Chapel's *Incidents in the Life of Moses* she scratched "della Francesca" and inserted "Baldovinetti." In 1898, Berenson had published an article in which he reattributed a della Francesca Madonna just sold to the Louvre to the rarer Baldovinetti. On her postcard of the Uffizi Annunciation, Margarett crossed out "Da Vinci" and wrote "Verrochio"—"Berenson gives it to him."

Whether her allusions to Berenson originated with Margarett herself or with the unidentified art instructor at the Florentine School, it is his insistence a great painting "rouse the tactile sense" that explains the impact of "just looking" on her untrained but sensitive eye. It was a sculptor, not a painter, who particularly attracted her: "She came home," Dan said, "crazy about Donatello." "However tastes may differ about the positive merits of his several works," Margarett wrote in her art notebook, "there is no doubt that his principles—sincerity, truth to nature and technical accuracy—were of immense value to his age." To the left, she glued a postcard of the sculptor's bronze David, which in

1910 stood where it does now, in the large, daylit upstairs gallery of the Bargello.

Imagine it! A curious seventeen-year-old from Boston who has never seen a naked man, perhaps no bare flesh other than her own, encounters Donatello's boy hero, his foot resting on the severed head of Goliath. There he is, near her age, freestanding, genitals exposed, pure sensuality of bronze and gleaming flesh, of flank and buttocks, louche hand on hip. And the details!—hair cascading down a wide back, slim nude hips, brimmed hat, its tassel suspended, the sword held languidly, the stone easy in his hand, the feather of Goliath's helmet slithering up his taut inner leg.

Margarett was, I suspect, not shocked—was, rather, drawn in by the slippery, fluid surface, the sculptor's choice to render David's triumph as a victory of youth over age, of erotic ebullience over stentorian torpor. She saw Donatello's twin pulpits at San Lorenzo, his fulsome Judith lifting an ax to Holofernes, and his haunted, aging Magdalene. "Margarett came home," Dan repeated, "crazy about Donatello, and she started to talk about becoming a sculptor." Why not? Once moved by sculpture, she had a glimmer of its purpose. With his hands, an artist half a millennium away had given shape to something she felt, to thoughts, as she wrote in her notebook, "too deep for formulation."

I remember the look on Margarett's face when I visited her after my own first trip to Florence. "Donatello!" she said, taking a long time with each syllable. Let us say that in his work, she saw for the first time, in concrete and material form, an alternative to the sensibility into which she had been born. "Donatello," she repeated at eighty, with a nostalgic and conspiratorial smile.

§

THE EFFECTS on Margarett's character of the year abroad registered as a shock on the unsuspecting family seismograph at home. On her way back to Boston, she traveled in Switzerland with two friends from school. It was June 1911, the end of a year of mourning for Edward VII, and Margarett arrived in London in time to stand with thousands cheering the coronation procession of George V. Just weeks before, in Boston, Jane Sargent Cheever had given birth to a third son, and it was Jenny Sargent's hope that Margarett would return to Boston prepared to become a flourishing matron like her sister. But the Florentine School had not polished away her rough edges. It was as if she herself were a souvenir brought home to herald the passing of the Edwardian Age, news that otherwise might not have reached the Back Bay for a year or two. "I don't understand my daughter Margarett at all," Jenny exclaimed to E. Ames, throwing up her hands.

Immediately on her return, Margarett had the walls of her room at 40 Hereford Street stripped of flowered wallpaper and painted the color of cement. After her birthday, at the end of August, she went to New York City and bought the Mary Cassatt; when she got home, she removed her bedroom curtains and replaced "those dreadful hunting pictures" with her beautiful pastel. "It was very outré," her old friend E. Ames said of the new decor. Gertrude Hunnewell, who had cautioned the departing Margarett not to expect to become a successful deb, expressed concern that her cousin, now "a sophisticated beauty," might burn the hair she waved—onduléed—like the French. "What am I saving it for?" Margarett retorted. The Miss Porter's grapevine reported "spectacular" news: Margarett Sargent had returned from Italy wearing *extraordinary* clothes.

Margarett had gone to Florence to complete the self-creation Miss Porter's had begun. Her success was acknowledged by those closest to her. "It was after Florence," Gertrude said, "that Margarett began to be different from other people." E. Ames was proud the friend who'd gone to Florence a Hunnewell had returned "a person in her own right," but Margarett's difference tore at her mother's fragile temperament. Always, in subsequent years, when her daughter did something she considered un-Bostonian, Jenny Sargent expressed her agony in one resonant, hopeless sentence: "If only we hadn't sent her to Europe!"

"Look!" Ellen Curtis said to Marian Valliant as the two girls eyed guests at a wedding at the Arlington Street Church. "There's Margarett Sargent!" Marian had heard talk of Margarett, and here she was, "a vision" on the usher's arm, walking down the aisle. Marian didn't remember who the bride was, but she remembered what Margarett wore: "I promised myself then and there that when I could buy my own clothes, I would have a tartan velveteen just like Margarett Sargent."

Margarett did not record her interest in art in the diary she began early in 1912. She noted an occasional Italian lesson, the writing of an Italian poem, but Florence soon receded in the gathering momentum of her debutante year. Cries of wonder at her beauty and sophistication had not healed the wounds years of plainness had inflicted; she now applied herself to a sustained performance—she would play not the swain she'd perfected at Farmington but the damsel who attracted his admiration.

For support, she turned to E. Ames, who had come out the year before and whose clothes—"perfection"—Marian Valliant also admired. Margarett visited E. at the Ames house on the North Shore, charted E.'s winter bronchitis in her diary, lunched with E., dined with E. before the theater, and "adjourned to E.'s" in Boston so often that Fran and Kay Saltonstall teased her. "The Salts are so funny about my going there all the time as if I never used to." It seemed to Dan that the friendship thrived because Margarett did all the talking and E. did none. "Rather ashamed at the way I let my tongue run away with me," Margarett wrote once, but of another conversation she exclaimed, "E. and I had such a gasbag talk and the more I see of her the more wonderful I think she is the way she sizes up people."

It was with E. that Margarett assessed the enterprise of coming out into the world of courtship and marriage. On one "delicious drive," they ended up at The Country Club in Brookline, where they'd sledded as children. "We were comparing wives to suits. Serviceable colors, etc. E. is a pretty color but might not wear well—and you couldn't wear every hat with her." Margarett found herself more complicated: "I am made of rough cloth—and dirt does stick to it so."

Margarett was aware of her difference as she looked ahead to what was called "the season." In mid-September, she was one of ten debutantes invited to join and choose the membership of the 1911 Sewing Circle. The original Sewing Circles had evolved from the Sanitary Commissions formed in Boston during the Civil War, when young women gathered to roll bandages. Two years before Margarett's coming-out season, a group of debutantes, Margarett's riding friend Alice Thorndike among them, transformed what had become society lunch clubs into "a philanthropic employment bureau" for young women, like the Junior League founded in New York in 1901.

Like their New York counterparts, Alice and her friends chafed against the example of Lady Bountiful, "with her promiscuous giving," and trained themselves for the city's settlement houses, schools, and hospitals. By 1911, they had put four hundred young women to work. Margarett's year in Italy and discovery of art had already given her a taste of the independence others looked for in helping others, but membership in the Sewing Circle, her mother told her, was an honor she could not refuse. As the year progressed, Margarett would note the Sewing Circle in her diary with mounting annoyance, but she did not decline when her sister debutantes elected her president, which made her, in the opinion of one society writer, "the most preeminently popular girl of the season."

Throughout the fall of 1911, Margarett gained prominence as a member of "the rising generation," filling cups and offering sugar or lemon at a succession of occasions that would often, but not always, culminate in informal dancing. In the third week of December, cards went out for her ball, to be held on Friday, January 12. To whom were the invitations sent? "Just everybody, I guess," Gertrude Hunnewell said. A daughter's debut could clear one's social slate for a year.

Jane's party had been given at home, but now Frank was more prosperous; Margarett's would be given in the ballroom of the Somerset Hotel, which could accommodate scores more guests. The Somerset was smaller than the newer Copley Plaza, older than the Ritz, and more equipped for chauffeured cars than the Vendôme, whose ballroom Marian Valliant said was "hopelessly dowdy." But neither the choice of place nor the invitation list was up to Margarett. Jenny did it all: preparations for a party of hundreds, the hiring of forty-eight butlers and maids, two doormen, two carriage men, a valet, two extra checkroom men, and a band of fifty to play until dawn. She arranged the menu for the breakfast to be served after midnight, and chose favors for the cotillion—long beaded chains and sleigh bells on red and green ribbon for gentlemen to offer ladies, boutonnieres and boxes of cigarettes for the ladies to offer in return.

On January 12, the front page of the *Herald* predicted a cloudy day with snow and featured an account of a hearing during which Andrew Carnegie, seventy-seven years old, "frequently pounded the table with his hand" and denounced the banking system of the United States as a "threat to civilization." That afternoon, a *Boston Traveler* headline, "Miss Sargeant to Make Debut at Ball Tonight," drew attention to an item that proclaimed Margarett's party "the fashionable event of the day scheduled on society's calendar," and "one of the most important affairs of the season." Next to it appeared a three-column photograph of a lady in white lace—the late Stanford White's paramour and his jailed murderer's wife, Evelyn Nesbit Thaw, "fighting to have her husband freed."

That morning, Margarett wrote in her diary, "The day of my ball at last. Taking it easy all day—trying to be beautiful." If her aim since her return from Florence had been to create herself as a beauty, the ball was her vernissage. During the afternoon, her hair was piled high on her head and crowned with a filigreed tiara by Miss Murphy, the hairdresser. In the early evening, she put on a gown of white satin and chiffon, and at about seven, her brothers escorted her to her sister Jane's house on Marlborough Street, where a dinner was given in her honor.

Soon after nine, Frank and Dan, distinguished as head ushers by the color of their boutonnieres, assembled their corps of twenty at the Somerset. The gold-and-white ballroom was festooned with flowers from Wellesley; a basket of pink roses hung from each chandelier, and masses of pink blooms framed every window and door. After greeting Margarett, who stood between her parents, one was escorted toward the ballroom.

If a guest was female and alone, the usher took her to the "dump" (slang for "sitting-out room"), where, Gertrude said, "you sat hoping someone would come along and talk to you." A "great belle" might arrive at a ball with too many partners for the dance card she found placed in the dressing room. A younger girl might find her roster filled when an older brother returned the card he'd taken from her at the entrance. "Young ladies should be very careful not to forget their dancing engagements, and should never refuse one gentleman and then dance with another," cautioned Florence Hall, Julia Ward Howe's daughter, in a book of etiquette published the year before Margarett came out.

The *Transcript*'s reporting that evening culminated in a catalogue of its female guests, distinguished by hues, stuffs, and trim of gown. A hundred fifty descriptions burst from thirteen kaleidoscopic paragraphs that took up thirty-five column inches of Sunday's paper. E. Ames's dark hair was set off by a gown of "peach colored satin under flounces of white lace." Young ladies should wear white or light colors, Mrs. Hall advised, but color might deepen as age advanced. Margarett's sister, Jane, twenty-nine years old and the mother of three sons, wore rose velvet, and Jenny Sargent wore "a beautiful gown of royal purple velvet," its bodice embroidered with "purple beads shading to rhinestones."

As Berger's orchestra from New York played, scores of young men in formal black and white led partners through whirling rainbow figures of schottische, german, and waltz. When, at the height of the evening, Margarett led the cotillion with Philip Sears, "one of the veterans in that capacity," the guests saw a young woman with fair skin, black hair, and wide light-blue eyes. Her five-foot-ten-inch height was enhanced by coiffure and slippers, and the beaded embroidery of her white gown shimmered in the glitter of electric chandeliers. One reporter, as if writing about horseflesh, described her as "a tall, slender girl with the distinction which marks her mother."

"She was a wonderful dancer," Dan said, using the word "lithe" to describe how she moved. The confidence with which she wielded her charm stunned him. He had not expected Margarett to become glamorous. "There was a whole row of boys lined up for her!" he exclaimed at ninety. Shaw McKean, a Harvard man from Philadelphia, fell in love with her on the spot, as did Hamilton Fish, Harvard 1910, all-American football hero and captain of the Harvard team. "She was good-looking. She had a lovely figure. She was charming, intelligent, and vivacious. All the attributes and a good family background. She was," he asserted, "the most unusual woman I met up there." Years later, when her eleven-year-old daughter asked about her coming-out ball, Margarett declared, "I looked marvelous!"

"Margarett?" her cousin Beebo Bradlee said. "Why, she was as pretty as a red wagon."

§

MARGARETT'S FRIENDS who had come out the year she was in Florence were becoming engaged, and after her ball, her life became a press of well-chaperoned opportunities for courtship: dances, house parties, theater evenings, football weekends. "I adored the Beals dance. I certainly deserved to after the dinner seat I had between F. Motley and Junius Morgan!!!" Activities of the marriage market were everyone's business. The announcement of Lily Sears's and Bayard Warren's engagement provoked Miss Ruth Gaston to express what Margarett considered "the extraordinary point of view" that it would be risky if Lily married Bayard because of her mother. Mrs. Sears, believing her husband was unfaithful, had thrown herself from a window.

"Mein Gott, how dreary," Margarett wrote in June at the prospect of trimming a hat for Margaret Richardson's marriage to Hall Roosevelt, but a month later, when Lily Sears visited Wareham, Margarett listened, riveted, to the details of her engagement, and two weeks after that, when her brother Frank clinched her suspicion that Kay, the youngest "Salt," had become engaged to Philip Weld, the son of Papa's business partner, Margarett couldn't stop talking about it: "I suppose the engaged bug is in my bonnet." But no one—not "Beau" Gardner, Bey Meyer, or Francis Gray; not Fat Cutler, who had actually proposed—emerged as a candidate for Margarett's undivided attention until Dan's "very best friend" sent her a "wild telegram" the summer of 1912.

Margarett first met Eddie Morgan when Dan was at Groton. He visited Wareham in 1909, the summer after her first year at Farmington and his freshman year at Harvard, and Dan encouraged a romance. Margarett found Eddie attractive and "refined looking" that summer but made no other mention of him. In an undergraduate photograph, his darkly handsome face has an air of earnest innocence. But he had "dash," his son said, and, Dan said, was "gallant." Like Margarett, he had very dark hair, and like her father, he sang beautifully. Like his own father, Eddie was tall, six feet one. When he turned up at Hereford Street late the winter of 1912, Margarett noticed his temperament: at dinner he let it be known he was "very sore at E. Ames for turning him down at the Strong's dance."

Eddie was from New York but, in spite of what society reporters wrote later, was only distantly related to J. P. Morgan. His family lived on Long Island and in Newport in two grand houses, "Wheatly" at Old Westbury and "Beacon Rock" at Newport—both designed by Charles McKim. "But the Morgans had no swank," Eddie's son said; "no butlers or anything. They were interested in the sailing."

Eddie's "rich, racy, pithy English," the tossed-off ease with which he quoted long passages from Milton and Shakespeare, the brilliance that brought him surprise top marks on Groton's Harvard entrance exam, made him popular. At Harvard, like all of Margarett's brothers and like Teddy Roosevelt, another New Yorker, he was asked to join the Porcellian, the oldest and most quintessentially Bostonian of the college's clubs, and when he was initiated into the Hasty Pudding, he deftly met the requirements: to climb a telephone pole, smoke a cigarette, and give a speech on woman suffrage. He majored in Egyptology, then a rage, not out of interest but because it was, in Cambridge parlance, a "gut"—an easy major. Eddie's real passion was rowing—he studied only enough to stay on the crew.

Margarett had a gift for flirtation, but she was not prepared for the consequences of real sexual feeling, nor was there anyone, even a friend, in whom, if she'd had the language, she could deeply confide. What she and Eddie felt for each other had no place in the life they had been directed to lead, no destination aside from marriage. They carried on the substance of their romance clandestinely, by letter and in secret meetings, and presented a carefree front to their families.

When Eddie Morgan began to pursue her the summer after her debut, Margarett was just back from a trip to Bermuda with Frances Breese. On the Fourth of July, she found herself at the Ameses' on the North Shore, yearning for an expected letter from Eddie and beside herself that it had not arrived. Nothing helped—not a letter from John Parker on Monday or a card from Styve Chanler on Wednesday, not expressions of interest from Walter Paine, "the only boy who doesn't repulse me in a bathing suit," or watching polo at the Myopia Hunt Club: "I can't say without profanity what I thought of it." Finally, on Saturday afternoon, between the "retouching" of her hair and a dinner party, the letter arrived. Wednesday, back at Wareham, there was a "wild telegram," and Margarett wrote in her diary, "Can I call him a beau?"

She could tell her mother nothing. Jenny Sargent watched warily. Even though he was Dan's best friend, Eddie Morgan, a New Yorker, was not who she had in mind for her younger daughter, and Margarett, at nineteen, was too young to become engaged—Jane had courted decorously at twenty-four. "Jane back soothing Mama," Margarett wrote at Wareham in July. She found the example of her older sister "furiously irritating." Jenny tried to make peace. "If you two don't become friends," she once declared, "I'll walk down to Wellesley barefoot." But Margarett's experience with Eddie separated her from both her sister and her mother. She considered herself an adult, and presumptions of authority, coming as they did in the absence of real sympathy, galled her. "Jane infuriated me about looks and dress," she wrote on July 17, and four days later, "Jane and I played tennis together. Jane irritated me beyond words making me wait on her."

At the end of the summer, days before her twentieth birthday, Margarett addressed the subject more fully: "I realize really absolutely now, in spite of any effort—which I realize I am incapable of making—that I could never in this wide world be truly intimate with Jane—or even begin to be. She doesn't interest me—and I don't care what anyone says—she is not truly, truly sympathetic."

Her brother Frank, on the other hand, was her idol and counselor. At twenty-eight, he was still unmarried. His passion, aside from women, was steeplechasing, where skill required wild daring. Riding a horse through a risky, daredevil course showed off his most compelling qualities—startling good looks, athletic ease, and charm. His unpredictability dazzled the young and unnerved those who'd lived longer. "He was a *great* beau of mine," Kay, the youngest "Salt," boasted in her eighties, "but he was very agitated." His charisma and brilliance at Parkinson and Burr prompted an elderly and scholarly client to exclaim, "Young man, don't throw away your life being a stockbroker."

As Margarett began to fall in love, she sought him out, and he gave her what advice she got on matters of the heart. As the romance proceeded, she became restless. She was late to meals, "sassed the family til they shut up." She read her love letters alone in the woods. Even in her diary she didn't express her anxiety directly. "I lack that spirit of dash and 'en bon point' that characterized my style formerly. Sighed quite a lot." She wrote Italian poetry—"not in my best vein"—and meandered through the newspaper. "Happened to see an interesting 'want ad': reads Western oil magnate wants good looking, clever stenographer. Must have lots of self confidence.' That last rather implies 'Cheek.' Cheek of course would not apply to me."

"Margarett got engaged to Eddie to escape her mother," Dan said in his eighties. "It was my first kiss," was how Margarett excused her first engagement when her daughters asked about it as children. On a Monday late in July, she set off for a visit to the Pollards in Manchester. Eddie had spent the weekend at Wareham, and they took the train with her brother Frank, Margarett "in a white heat" that Eddie didn't sit next to her. At South Station, Eddie picked up his car. Margarett said good-bye to Frank, skipped appointments with the dentist and the hairdresser, and embarked with Eddie on a secret drive, "mostly thro' slums"—parts of the city where they would not be recognized. An angular star, code for the momentous first kiss, was the extent of her candor about the rest of the afternoon. "Conversation in the Common watching a frog pond," she wrote mysteriously. "Boy with an umbrella and the consequences."

When Eddie dropped her in Manchester after the two-hour drive north, Margarett found her hosts "distinctly at their worst." Eddie was all she could think of. The next day, a letter arrived special delivery, and she dreamed about the kiss: "Talked last night in my sleep about EDM. Crazy to get to bed so as to think." Back at Wareham, Margarett kept her secret as if it were the trump in a family game of whist. "Can't make up my mind whether to discuss a certain matter with Frank or not. I certainly have the easiest family to fool."

On Friday, Eddie came again for the weekend, and that night everyone went out dancing in the honky-tonk town of Mattapoisett, chaperoned by Frank and a crew of his friends. When they got home, thinking Papa and Jenny were asleep, Margarett and Eddie drove alone out into the bracken, "until Papa's irate voice sounds like a melodrama and we had to come in." Eddie left early the next morning, after the two took a mosquitoey walk through the woods, and later that day Margarett let her brother Frank in on her secret, that she hoped to become engaged. "He was sweet and all I knew he'd be, but encourages the idea of both seeing other people." The next Saturday night in Mattapoisett, Margarett took his advice: "I adored dancing with Gom Goodale, Mr. Wolcott, Mr. Parker & Mr. Richardson."

As the romance proceeded, Eddie's darkness revealed itself. Beneath his charm, he was moody, mercurial, and oversensitive. He was as insecure as Margarett but more vulnerable to her than she was to him. "If only you could have seen the letter I wrote you about an hour ago! You always thought of me as emotionless. Well thank heavens I waited an hour, read it and tore it up," he wrote Margarett during a lovers' quarrel. "I had a lonely, gloomy fit. I felt that I more or less lost ground with you, wore the welcome off the mat, showed my 'shallow, stupid' side once too often." He began to drink too much. After the incident in the bracken, he stayed away a day. When he returned after lunch on Sunday, he was pale, wan, and hung over. Out on a drive in the afternoon, he vomited. "Disastrous turn of events in short automobile trip," Margarett wrote, "managed not to have hysterics."

Margarett apparently excused him. On Monday, August 5, two weeks to the day after the first kiss, on a bench at the Arnold Arboretum, Eddie proposed, and she accepted. They had taken another secret drive: "Don't you think we should kiss?"

Two lions guarded the entrance to The Orchard, the Breeses' estate in Southampton, built by Stanford White in 1906 and completed just before his murder. Doric columns soared two stories across its facade, a spectacularly vast garden stretched out behind. Margarett photographed the house in the distance at the end of a long paved walk bordered with Roman heads on tall pedestals, cedars, flowering trees, abundantly planted perennials. At the center of a courtyard close to the house splashed Janet Scudder's sculpture *Frog Fountain*. It was a week after her secret agreement with Eddie, and Margarett was visiting her Florence schoolmate Frances Breese. The "Salts" had not let her hear the end of her going to Long Island: "I hate to have people talk as if I had been to the Hindoo Isles."

James Lawrence Breese made his money as a stockbroker, but he also worked as a semiprofessional photographer, specializing in erotic studies of young girls he sponsored, supported, and brought to his studio for late-night parties, a pleasure he'd shared with his late friend Stanford White. In the late nineties, at the climax of a stag dinner he gave, a gigantic "Jack Horner Pie" was wheeled into the dining room. A naked girl burst through the crust, and the guest of honor reeled her in on a ribbon leash. Breese noticed Margarett immediately and on the first day of her visit made his move, "patting me all over." "Disgusting," she wrote in her diary, and the next day, "Mr. Breese tired of me."

Enthusiastically squired to polo matches, luncheons, swims, and tennis matches, Margarett did not miss Eddie. Even in solitude, contemplating "the Club piazzas all deserted," she did not miss him. She was quickly caught up in the Southampton social whirl. At a dance Saturday evening, Chalmers Wood and Bill Tilden, the tennis player, were her suitors. At the Breeses' thé dansant Sunday afternoon, Frances's married older brother Sydney praised her dancing; in the evening, Oliver Harriman came for supper and was smitten. Monday at Steeplechase Park, a young man familiar enough to be called "Bob" became "quite 'devoné'—and we had quite a clutch in the scenic railways."

But Eddie yearned after Margarett. A telegram reached her on the train on her way home, and he met her at Barnstable. They took a drive and missed the last train to Wareham. Margarett was terrified. There was no telephone at Wareham. Her parents would discover that Eddie met her every time she took a train, that she had kissed him in his car: "Got myself all porked up & upset." She telephoned the Herricks, who lived down the road in Wareham, and Eddie left for Newport. She took the train to Wellesley, in nervousness dropping her money on the platform. She couldn't talk, even to Uncle Frank Hunnewell or Cousin Walter. She cried and sobbed herself to sleep, poured herself into a long letter to Eddie. The next morning, she boarded the 8:26 to Barnstable and changed for Wareham. "Papa apparently hasn't slept, otherwise not half the furor I expected." The attention of the household was elsewhere. The Herricks' daughter, Katharine, had run over and killed a child in New Bedford: "Horrible."

For her twentieth birthday, on August 31, Eddie gave Margarett a puppy, named Pilgrim for the automobile in which he'd driven her to the Arnold Arboretum the afternoon he proposed. Pilgrim came with a leash, a red collar, a comb, and a supply of dog biscuits. Eddie also presented Margarett with an oar pin: he rowed seven on the Harvard varsity crew.

When she heard about the engagement, Jenny protested violently. Aside from the fact that Margarett was too young, Eddie's temperament frightened her, and she had a Boston prejudice against his New York origins. New Yorkers drank too much, entertained too lavishly, and were ostentatious and wasteful with money. Another year or two at home, followed by marriage to a prudent Bostonian, was what she had in mind for her younger daughter. Another year or two at home was exactly what Margarett did not want. Jenny did not prevail, but in deference to her feelings, Margarett and Eddie agreed to a year's engagement and a postponed announcement.

In spite of their betrothal's supposed secrecy, Margarett and Eddie became a "famously beautiful couple." In 1912, the rhythm of Irving Berlin's "Everybody's Doin' It Now" began a dance craze that so departed from the decorous waltzes of hotel thés dansants that a New York grand jury was moved to investigate. Margarett learned the turkey trot from her brother Frank and passed it on to Eddie. Afternoons at Wellesley, they cranked the Victrola and gyrated to ragtime. Margarett was "*so very* attractive," said Eddie's younger sister, Kassie, fourteen at the time. "She wore a very modern bathing suit."

But betrothal began to wear on Margarett. Seven decades later, Dan's voice was earnest with horror when he told me that while she was engaged to Eddie Morgan, his sister "saw other men." "It was Shaw McKean who was the culprit," Kassie Morgan said. Dan confirmed that Margarett walked around the lake at Wellesley with Shaw McKean while she was still engaged to Eddie. Uncle Frank Hunnewell accosted her with a young man after dark on the lake path: "What are you doing here?" Eddie's son reported that Bertie Goelet was the villain. "No," snapped Kassie, "Shaw McKean," and explained that it was all much worse than it might have been, since Eddie and Margarett had been engaged "a *full year*."

Margarett did not mention other suitors in her 1912 diary, but on every page from September 24 until her last entry, written on October 17, she crossed Eddie's initials resolutely out. "I guess I want the impossible," Eddie wrote that winter "to catch a fine fish with a baitless hook."

"I didn't know you two didn't get along," Dan said to Eddie when he heard the news of the breakup. He had come home from France in May to prepare for the wedding, had given up a job in Bordeaux to be his best friend's best man. He angrily confronted Margarett. She had spent time with the Morgans in Old Westbury, she told him. Newly married Morgans lived in "The Lodge," attached to the big house. What would she do while Eddie was at the stables with the Morgans' one hundred horses? While he exercised hunters? Trained ponies for polo? And then there was Mrs. Morgan.

" 'Margarett dear,' " she mimicked, " 'this is little Katherine, who will be your new sister-in-law.' "

"I don't want a sister-in-law," she shouted at Dan, "and I can't bear little Katherine!"

What Margarett did not tell Dan was that Eddie drank too much, that he had promised over and over again that he would stop, and that he had gone back on his promise once too often.

Margarett broke it off at Newport. She and Eddie were at a big dance, perhaps at Beacon Rock, possibly at another house whose ballroom overlooked the sea. They left the heat of dancing and went outdoors, and as they stood, pressed against a balustrade, Margarett said, "Eddie, I can't marry you." It wasn't that she didn't love him, she said. "I want to marry you, but I can't."

"Why not?" Eddie said, quite stunned.

"I'm terribly sorry."

"Margarett, why not?"

She didn't answer immediately. Then, "I'm going to Italy to sculpt."

To those around her, the announced reason for Margarett's extraordinary step seemed so mysterious it hardly registered: "I'm going to Italy to sculpt." Reasons she gave that were more understandable, that Eddie drank too much, that she couldn't bear the cloying domesticity she might expect as a member of the Morgan household, that Eddie had "no small talk"—did not, even if true, warrant such radical action in the minds of her friends and family, particularly after a year of betrothal, the setting of dates, the arrival of early wedding presents.

"Eddie took to drink over his jealousy about Margarett!" Dan exclaimed. Jane felt Margarett had treated Eddie "very badly." Jenny was "mortally wounded" that her daughter had done such a thing. "You didn't *break* it!" she exclaimed. It was as if her daughter had gotten a divorce. Frank was more merciful. "Don't be so hard on Peggy," he said. Mrs. Morgan was "shocked and furious." "She was his only girl," Kassie said, "and she dropped him." The fault, in Dan's eyes, was Margarett's, but the tragedy was equally his. The broken engagement had—"of course," he nearly shouted decades later—broken his closest friendship. "Margarett had 'immortal longings,'" he explained, intending the deepest parallel to Cleopatra: "She wanted more than you could get. Nothing banal was good enough for her."

Margarett had been, she always said, in love with Eddie, but the desire to sculpt had turned her away. "Oh clay," she said. "How I loved clay!" With portents of war rumbling in Europe, the Sargents would not hear of her sculpting in Italy. Instead, Jenny asked Frank's business partner, General Weld, to take her daughter away from sculpture and away from Eddie, out of the country to Mount Talbot, the castle he leased in Ireland in County Roscommon. A fancy-dress ball after Margarett returned to Boston in December was the former lovers' first encounter since her precipitous action. There was barely a breath, as the revelers, who included Eddie, waited. Margarett made her entrance dressed as Joan of Arc, in a full suit of armor.

When her daughters were little, but old enough to remember, Margarett took them upstairs to the cedar closet at Hereford Street. She opened a cavernous cupboard and showed them wedding presents never returned from the first-kiss engagement. They were wrapped in coal-black tissue paper that rustled when she touched it. There were china bowls and a silver tray for calling cards. "She didn't explain the calling cards," her daughter Jenny wrote. "She made a point of never telling us of such conventions."

iii

a rose the world
has dreamed . . .

(1913–1918)

Margarett, October 1915
(photographed in New York
by Arnold Genthe)

"IT WILL BE REMEMBERED," *Town Topics* observed, "that one of the prettiest and most dashing girls of the exclusive Boston set broke an engagement just at the end of her debutante year with a Harvard man who boasts one of the most prominent names in the world of finance as well as of society. It caused a great deal of talk at the time because it was said that a classmate was the cause of the trouble and rumor points to a young man who is at work in the mines." It was not reported that Margarett's break with Eddie had required courage and that in spite of her apparent arrogance, she had suffered. Gertrude Hunnewell had a clear memory of her once triumphant cousin, "the poor thing," coming to visit. She was "covered with boils" and had brought along a suitcase of trousseau linens monogrammed in Paris, which she attempted to rescue with needle and thread, doctoring the Morgan *M* with a cramped *ck*.

The young man implicated was, of course, Quincy Adams Shaw McKean. The mines were the Calumet & Hecla copper mines, near Lake Superior, where Shaw McKean worked as a gentleman laborer from autumn 1914 through the summer of 1915, gaining, he wrote, "experience underground and in mill and smelter." The Calumet & Hecla Mining Company was a family enterprise, and Shaw was a member of the family. In 1866, his mother's uncle, Alexander Agassiz, son of Louis Agassiz, the Swiss-born naturalist famous for *Recherches sur les poissons*, the basis of modern knowledge of fish, and *Études sur les glaciers*, traveled to Michigan to inspect an undeveloped mine his brother-in-law Quincy Adams Shaw had purchased the year before.

He returned to Boston with a proposal to purchase land to the south of the mine, even richer in copper.

His ambition was to support his own zoological research and to endow his father's dream, a Harvard Museum of Comparative Zoology, without spending his life as his father had, dunning Lawrences and Thayers. His sister Pauline presented him with an unexpected opportunity when she married Quincy Adams Shaw, the son of a wealthy merchant and real estate entrepreneur whose family had made a fortune in the China trade and who, after graduation from Harvard in 1845, had explored the Oregon territory with his cousin and classmate, the historian Francis Parkman. After his trip west, Quincy lived in Paris, where he began to collect art; the schoolroom where Shaw's mother, Marian, learned to read was hung with twenty-one pastels by Jean-François Millet, meant to illustrate the sacredness of peasant labor. Throughout the house, which stood on a bluff overlooking Jamaica Pond, resided twenty-five Millet oils, paintings by French nineteenth-century artists, Dutch old masters, and works by artists of the Italian Renaissance, including Donatello.

Because he was born rich, Quincy Shaw's interest in the Michigan mines was at first more casual then Alexander Agassiz's. It was Alex who convinced "a party of Boston men," chiefly friends and family, to join in purchasing the land that became the dazzlingly profitable Hecla mine, and Alex, with his degree in mining engineering, who persuaded the investors that retooling the old shafts would increase productivity. What began for many, including Horatio Hollis Hunnewell, as a gesture of support for two young men became a bonanza. Calumet & Hecla renovated more than one tired Boston shipping fortune and made a younger generation rich.

Shaw McKean was the son of Quincy Shaw's daughter Marian and Henry P. McKean, a Philadelphia gentleman farmer. Though he wintered in Philadelphia, he went to Harvard and summered on the North Shore, which made him, to Jenny's mind, an ideal suitor for Margarett. Dan disagreed. He had roomed with Shaw for two years at Harvard, and they had not become friends. Dan was a serious student who had contempt for the sporting life, and Shaw escaped Cambridge whenever he could to play polo. "He was too well dressed, too shiny," Dan said. "I couldn't understand his emotions." At her debut, Margarett had turned Shaw aside, but she remained struck by his dark-haired, blue-eyed looks and his shy, diffident manner. When she returned from Ireland, he was in his first year at Harvard Law School, and for some months they saw one another.

In March 1914, at the Arlington Hotel in Santa Barbara, a letter from Shaw reached Margarett, thanking her for "postals." "The Grand Canyon looks too marvelous—I have never seen such an extraordinary view in my life," he wrote. Margarett and Louise Delano, a Florence classmate, were on a tour of the West. "I'm trying to become an out-door girl," Margarett wrote her brother Harry from Pasadena. "Tomorrow I ride astride." She, Louise, and Miss White, their chaperone, sailed to Santa Catalina, cheered "cowboy races" at the country club, and surfed Sandylands Beach.

"I hear they have the only dirt polo field—which is made with dirt & oil—in the world at Pasadena," Shaw wrote. "If I didn't know I'd go to the devil doing it & if I had the money necessary, I should like to play polo all year round. California—Long Island—Narragansett etc. with three months off in the fall so as not to get stale at it." At Monterey, Margarett photographed a tree in the shape of an ostrich, and at Yosemite, Billy Wilson, their Indian guide.

From Santa Barbara, Margarett wrote to Eddie Morgan. She got no answer and wrote again. "It was my accident that prevented my answering sooner," he protested. Playing his father's polo ponies, he had taken a fall and broken his collarbone. Margarett wanted him to return the photograph of herself she'd given his mother. He replied that it might be some time before the family returned to Newport, but that when they did, his mother would either destroy the photograph or return it. She also asked about the future. "At the time I got your letter," he wrote, "I was amusing myself by drinking a good deal and half heartedly looking unsuccessfully for a girl I might fall superficially in love with, merely as a pastime." He added that since the accident, he had cut out all "rum," with the exception of beer, for good. Margarett's final question concerned Pilgrim. "He long since fulfilled his sphere of usefulness so far as I am concerned," wrote Eddie, newly the owner of a pack of beagles. "When you marry, would it not be kinder to all four of us—you, the man, Pil and myself—to send the little fellow (Pil, I mean, not the man) in the most merciful possible way to his happy hunting ground."

Eddie doubtless assumed that "the man" was his former roommate Shaw McKean, who himself would soon learn it was through no weakness in his rival that Margarett's hand remained her own.

Before her trip, Margarett had written Shaw, "I know you love me. I hope you will like me just as much and more—for I don't think it is just for the satisfaction of your attention—or your attraction—but knowing you is a real enjoyment to me. And above all don't forget me." Shaw quoted these declarations back to her in "a page of serious stuff" he sent her to Santa Barbara:

> You have told me you liked to feel I cared for you & would hate to have to cease. . . . This all sounds pretty much as if you did not put me on entirely the same plane as your friends & that you expected something more than mere friendship would come of it. Then you turn around and berate me soundly for presuming to take you to task— You say that you don't want me to call you dearest and when you come home you don't expect to keep so much in touch with me— Well, can't you see that the two attitudes can't go together?

It was on the train east that Margarett saw the cowboy again. A hulking rancher she'd met in Wyoming had resolved to marry her, and was pursuing her. She liked him, she said later. Had talked to him, that was all. The day she reached Boston, he knocked on the door at Hereford Street and asked for Mr. Sargent. "I'd like a shot of whiskey, straight," he said, and, when he got it, knocked it back. "I'm going to marry your daughter." Frank, who had known many Wyoming ranchers, did not hesitate. "No," he said. The cowboy was shown to the door.

Margarett did not need her father's help in turning Shaw McKean away. She had declared in no uncertain terms that he had no claim on her. She intended to pursue sculpture, and no matter what sort of art collection his family had or how fascinated he seemed with her chosen career, she would not marry him.

§

IF MARGARETT'S DECLARATION that she was "going to Italy to sculpt" had been made fifty years earlier, her parents might have sent her to Rome, where the sculptor William Wetmore Story, a Bostonian and a friend of Henry James, presided, from elegant apartments in the Palazzo Barberini, over the American expatriate colony. Story might have taken Margarett as a student, but she would also have been drawn to the group of American women sculptors, then in their twenties and thirties, who thrived in Rome at midcentury. Story nervously called them "the emancipated females," and Henry James, famously, "that strange sisterhood who at one time settled upon the seven hills in a white Marmorean flock."

Quintessential among them was Harriet Hosmer, like Margarett an energetic, unmanageable, and ambitious young woman, who prevailed over childhood sickliness to become a willful tomboy. Her school declared her incorrigible, and Harriet was sent to Miss Sedgwick's in Lenox, Massachusetts, where she met Fanny Kemble, the British actress and feminist, who encouraged her to turn a talent for modeling animals into a career in sculpture. When Harriet was twenty-two, the celebrated actress Charlotte Cushman admired her sculpture and invited her to Rome. Four years later, in 1856, Harriet sold her *Puck* to the Prince of Wales; thirty marble copies were made, and the profits were said to have amounted to thirty thousand dollars. Within ten years, she had a palatial studio, a staff of male stonecutters, and as many commissions for British gardens and American great men as she could manage.

"Hatty takes a high hand here with Rome," William Story sniffed, "and would have the Romans know that a Yankee girl can do anything

she pleases, walk alone, ride her horse alone, and laugh at their rules."
She cut her hair short and wore a velvet beret, a man's cravat, and
baggy Zouave trousers. She had not declined an offer of marriage to
achieve her independence, but she waged an "eternal feud with the
consolidating knot," aware she'd stepped from the beaten path: "I
honor all those who step boldly forward," she wrote, "and, in spite of
ridicule and criticism, pave a broader way for the women of the next
generation."

When Hosmer's most audacious artistic descendant, Janet Scudder, decided she wanted to sculpt, American women in search of training were at the mercy of master sculptors reluctant to hire them. One
man changed their destiny. When asked to take charge of all the sculpture for the 1893 World Columbian Exposition in Chicago, Lorado
Taft asked if he could recruit the young sculptors working in his studio, several of whom were women. Certainly, came the answer, "white
rabbits if they could help you out."

The six self-named "white rabbits," all with Taft's support, altered
the course of American sculpture. At the height of her career, Scudder,
offered the commission for a memorial to Longfellow, suggested a
sculpture garden rather than a statue. When the committee insisted on
a statue, she refused the job: "I won't add to this obsession of male
egotism that is ruining every city in the United States with rows of
hideous statues of men—men—men—each one uglier than the other—
standing, sitting, riding horseback—every one of them pompously
convinced that he is decorating the landscape!" Later, in 1907, Gertrude Vanderbilt Whitney, herself a sculptor, encouraged the National
Sculpture Society to promote garden sculpture. Women like Scudder,
Malvina Hoffman, Harriet Frishmuth, and Whitney herself leaped at
the opportunity to sculpt "pagan" figures like Pan and Diana, in which
sensuality and charm replaced funereal pomposity.

By 1913, when Margarett declared her ambition, Scudder was a
successful sculptor juggling commissions, and articles about female
sculptors crowded the pages of the new illustrated periodicals. "If we
men do not look out, we may be pushed from our stools by women,"

an unidentified male sculptor told *Scribner's* in 1910. Edith Deacon, briefly a girlfriend of Margarett's brother Frank, was pictured in the *Boston American* when her grandmother offered her $100,000 to lure her back to the marriage market from "the study of melancholy art in the studio of a sculptor," and in 1915, when the Boston artist Marion Boyd Allen painted a portrait of Anna Vaughn Hyatt modeling the maquette for her Joan of Arc—the saint in full armor, sword raised, astride a powerful steed—the painting won the popular prize at the Newport Art Association.

The summer of 1915, Margarett returned to Southampton to visit Frances Breese and looked with new eyes at the fountain that adorned the court at The Orchard. The frolicsome marble child kicking water into the mouths of frogs was one of the most famous garden sculptures by an American woman. Margarett photographed it twice and pasted both photographs into her scrapbook. "Janet Scudder," she wrote, "Frog Fountain."

"I have found something that I think might interest you." It was ten o'clock at night, and the man's voice on my telephone was not familiar. "Just last week at auction, I picked up a sculpture by Margarett Sargent." In the 1960s, Margarett's studio had burned to the ground, and many of her sculptures were destroyed. I had seen only a few—works in the family and fragments that, for one reason or another, escaped the fire.

"Yes, I'm interested."

A week later, I met the collector at a warehouse in Boston. The work was cast in bronze and stood fifteen inches high. A young woman stands in front of a wall. She is caught, seems to pull away from the wall as if unable to escape, as if her hands are tied behind her. She wears a flared dress to her ankle and looks to be from the past, a character from a novel, perhaps. The work has no title, but at the base is inscribed "M. Sargent" and a date, 1916.

In the fall of 1914, for the first time in her life, Margarett had become "occupied," as she put it. She was sculpting, she wrote later, with "passionate application," inspired by a sculptor her own age, a young woman named Bessie Paeff. Bessie was Jewish and had come from Russia with her family when she was less than a year old—"their crowded little flat down in the North End simply dripped melody," wrote a reporter, "and one or another of the six children of the dreamy Russian intellectual was always hurrying off to the Conservatory, clutching a violin case or a roll of piano music."

Margarett, Dan was sure, read at least one of the accounts of Bessie's triumphs published between 1913 and 1915 in the *Globe* and the *Transcript*, and in periodicals as far away as New York and Washington. Bessie drew pictures with more passion than she devoted to the violin, and her parents sent her to the Boston Normal Art School. One of her teachers showed her work to the sculptors Bela Pratt and Cyrus Dallin, who saw to it she got a scholarship to the prestigious Museum School. There she won more prizes than any student in the school's history, while earning a living making change in the Park Street subway, a lump of wet clay always at her side.

When Bessie Paeff came to lunch at Wellesley in the fall of 1915, she had just been praised in the press for "the figure of a little crouching boy, intently watching a bird that has alighted on the tips of his outstretched fingers," which was later placed at the Arlington Street entrance of the Boston Common. The war had kept her from studying in Paris with Rodin, but she would soon realize "one of the ambitions of her life"—to sculpt the great Jane Addams in Chicago. At lunch, she announced her intention to change her name to Bashka Paevi. Margarett protested. It was pretentious, she insisted, and drew allied opinions from her brothers, finally convincing "Bashka" to keep "Paeff," at least.

The two had a partnership: Bashka instructed Margarett in sculpture, and Margarett encouraged friends to give her teacher commissions. Shaw ordered a sculpture of his champion fox terrier, and Bayard Warren a portrait of his champion Sealyham. Margarett was enthralled by this woman of her own age, with black hair and flashing eyes, who dressed with bohemian glamour and moved with such assurance

among the Jewish art-collecting elite of Boston, families like the
Koshlands and the Kirsteins, whom Margarett herself would not have
known, even though their houses on Commonwealth Avenue were as
grand as anyone else's. Under Bashka's tutelage, Margarett was soon
earning her own commissions.

Late in 1915, Frank and Jenny ordered a group portrait of their
Cheever grandsons. The little boys were escorted one at a time to Margarett's studio in Copley Hall by their nurse. "It was strange to be six,"
Sargent Cheever said, "and to tell your friends that you had to go pose
for your aunt." He remembers the smell of wet clay, and Margarett,
with whom he had always laughed, as having been quite serious. He
remembers her discussing with Miss Paeff whether he should be
clothed or bare-shouldered—in the end only the youngest, Zeke,
didn't wear a shirt—and that Bashka encouraged and advised as Margarett modeled. Unlike the children captured in mischief or glee by
Scudder or Paeff, Margarett's nephews lower their eyes. The forms are
clear, but in the youth and shyness of the portraits, I see the youth of
Margarett's talent. Cast in bronze, the sculpture's surfaces were smooth,
as well-behaved as her nephews.

When Margarett got Dan to sit for her, in late 1915, he had just published his first book of poems and was about to join the American
Field Service Ambulance Corps in France. His decision to volunteer
was as much the consequence of rebellion against his parents as of
courage—he'd fallen in love, and Jenny had forbidden marriage. Trips
to France and study of its literature had opened him to real emotion
about the war, and like Margarett, he was uneasy in the life to which
he had been born. In poems, he expressed his discomfort: "My freedom is a torture cell," he wrote, "My peace the rack of thought." In
another, he imagined himself a priest on the battlefields of his adopted
country, "But tonight my fingers have a stain / The blood of men, the
touch of the dead."

Margarett intended that her portrait honor Dan's new sense of
self, that the bust be more than a commemorative likeness. As he sat in

her studio, no shirt on his strong young chest, she worked until his familiar face gave way to an expression that embodied her belief in his poetry and her support for his courageous choice. "She did my normal face from memory," Dan exclaimed; he had been hit in the jaw with a hockey stick, and his lip had swelled. When a Boston paper ran a photograph of the portrait, its readers saw a young man, his proud face turned fearlessly toward the dangers ahead. The reporter characterized the sculpture as "a keepsake should anything happen to him while in Europe," but there was nothing sentimental in Margarett's forthright view of her brother's heroic aspiration. It was a portrait of hers as well.

There was good reason for worry about Dan's safety; German submarines had sunk the *Lusitania* a year before, and the Kaiser would not make a commitment to spare passenger vessels. Dan sailed for France on March 16, 1916, and cabled Wellesley before embarking at Southampton to cross the Channel on "a frail swift passenger steamer" called the *Sussex*. Because the number of Channel crossings each week had been reduced, nearly five hundred passengers crowded aboard that afternoon.

At 3:05, Edwin H. Huxley of New York, on deck for a stroll, glanced at his watch. A moment later, Samuel Bemis of Harvard, also on deck, saw the wake of a torpedo moving briskly toward the steamer. Dan, in the dining room for lunch, was thrown to the deck when the ship halted "as if it had struck a rock." He rose to his feet in time to see the people at the next table disappear beneath the waves. "The Sussex had been cut in two at the bridge," Huxley told the *New York Times*, "as cleanly as though it had been done with a knife."

The rear half of the ship remained afloat, electric lights eerily ablaze, as passengers crying for help clung to bits of furniture. Men on board pulled the wounded and the mangled bodies of the dead from beneath collapsed debris. President Wilson announced he would not sever diplomatic ties with Germany until there was proof the *Sussex* had been hit by a torpedo. When the *New York Times* interviewed Frank Sargent on Saturday evening, he said he "had not received any word regarding the safety of his son." Margarett waited for word at Wellesley with everyone else.

Dan was rescued by a French trawler at almost midnight and, when he disembarked in Boulogne at dawn Saturday, took a train for Paris. "It was broad daylight when I arrived at Paris, at the Gare du Nord. I bought a newspaper there and read that all the passengers on the *Sussex* had been drowned and that among them was an American, Daniel Sargent—a bit of news that was reported to my parents in Boston, six hours later." It was hours before the Sargents received his one-word telegram, "Safe," or heard the reports that there had been no American casualties.

§

UNTIL DAN'S CLOSE CALLS, Margarett's life had not been much affected by the war, but gradually, in the months following, the American reality began to change. During the summer of 1915, General Leonard Wood opened the first Plattsburgh camp to train civilian volunteers, and in December, Wilson asked Congress for a standing army of 142,000 and a reserve of 400,000 men. In another year, he would announce the United States ready to fight for a just cause, but now, in spite of relentless German victories and virtual German control of the Eastern front, he steered a course of neutrality, and Americans went about their ordinary business.

In early October, Margarett traveled to Southampton, Long Island, for the double weddings of Frances Breese and her brother. A train was hired to transport guests from New York, and automobiles greeted them at the station and ferried them to Saint Andrew's, a "quaint little wooden structure," which stood on the dunes close to the sea. Robert Breese and his new bride processed from the church, followed by the full choir of Grace Church, New York, singing Mendelssohn's wedding music, and the guests were conveyed to The Orchard, where, in the music room, Frances married Lawrence McKeever Miller, Harvard 1911, of Tuxedo Park.

The portieres were pulled closed in the vast high-ceilinged room, and candles provided the only illumination. Margarett, the lone attendant, wore a mist of pale-blue chiffon over mauve and a shepherdess hat, and preceded Frances down the aisle carrying a basket of blue asters suspended from a shepherd's crook. *Town Topics* reported that next to the bride, "Miss Margaret [*sic*] Sargent, the Boston bridesmaid, commanded the most attention and admiration."

One of Margarett's admirers that afternoon was the famous photographer Arnold Genthe. Three days after the wedding, she had a sitting in his New York studio. It was characteristic of Genthe, when a young woman caught his eye, to ask to photograph her. A girl on a New York street reminded him of the Venus de Milo, and the *Sunday World* gave his photograph a full page, headed "Finding a Venus on Broadway." A discouraged singer arrived at his door, and her face reminded him of Rossetti's *Beata Beatrix*; days later, his portrait was published as "The Girl with the Rossetti Mouth."

Margarett could not have been unaware of Genthe's stature as a photographer. He had attracted a prestigious clientele for unique portraits in which his subjects' likenesses seem to emerge unbidden from an ethereal chiaroscuro. A month before Margarett sat for him, Genthe photographed the artist Florine Stettheimer and her sister Ettie. Two weeks afterward, he photographed Pavlova in a leap—the only record of the dancer in motion—and two weeks after that, Theda Bara. He photographed Edna St. Vincent Millay and Dorothy Parker, Sinclair Lewis and William Butler Yeats, President Taft and Alice B. Toklas. He made famous photographs of Isadora Duncan, with whom he had an affair, and misty studies of her young dancers, which were published in *Vanity Fair.*

Dorothea Lange, who worked as his assistant, called Genthe "an unconscionable old goat, in that he seduced everyone who came into the place," but admitted, too, that he was a great photographer of women, "because he really loved them." In his skylit top-floor studio at 1 West 46th Street, he cut a breathtakingly romantic figure. He was six feet two, kept fit by riding daily in Central Park, and always wore jodhpurs to work. Margarett had never met a man like this among her Harvard beaux, even among her racy Southampton admirers. "A real roué," Lange said.

Margarett had been instructed to dress simply, but Genthe asked her to pose in one of his Japanese kimonos, and then, stomping around in his riding boots, muttering to himself in German, he posed her, adjusted the light, and peered through his lens. The young woman he saw was neither a giggling schoolgirl, a serene debutante, nor a smiling fiancée. Her hair was loosely pulled back, widow's peak distinct; her dark eyebrows perfectly shaped above large, haunted eyes. Her mouth was full, and a half-moon of light accentuated the lustrous curve of her lower lip. She faced the camera with a look that was intense, sexual, almost savage.

"Thanks for your letter, dear Margarett," Jenny wrote not long after the sitting, "it told me quite a lot of things I wanted to know." A mother would have been incautious not to worry about this daughter, and Margarett knew it. In the pose she had printed for her family, her face is half hidden in shadow, the curve of her cheek quiet and lyrical, her hair smooth, and her gaze indirect.

§

WHEN MARGARETT BEGAN her career as a sculptor, Boston was a city of artists. In 1903, a New York critic had excoriated the Athens of America as "merely a metropolis of a locality, a provincial capital," but a Boston critic refuted him, citing his city's "army of professional artists—six hundred painters, three hundred fifty architects, more than a hundred engravers, almost as many picture dealers." The educated rich of the Back Bay bought paintings for their walls and commissioned sculpture for their city's "Emerald Necklace" of Olmsted parks. Collectors mixed with gentlemen artists at the St. Botolph and Boston art clubs, and a group of painters known as the Boston School perfected an elegant aesthetic, which they passed on at the Museum of Fine Arts School of Painting and Drawing. Two of them, Edmund Tarbell and Frank Benson, were also members of "the Ten," a group of artists who led an Impressionist secession from the Society of American Artists in 1889 and whose work dominated the mainstream of American art as the century turned.

In 1891, Tarbell had painted *In the Orchard*, a group of young men and women gathered outdoors on a summer afternoon. Using high color shot through with light, he emulated the Renoir of *The Boating Party*. Like other Boston artists, Tarbell had come under the influence of the Impressionists while studying in Paris, but his work changed. In 1892, Isabella Gardner purchased Vermeer's *The Concert*, in 1897 exhibited it in Boston, and in 1907 hung it in her house museum, Fenway Court. Subsequently, in the paintings of the Boston School, *plein air* and loose brush acquiesced to indoors and tight brushwork, to paintings *of* light rather than *with* light, and Vermeer and Velázquez replaced Monet and Renoir as aesthetic models.

The spring of 1914, which Margarett had spent out West, confirmed Boston's art conservatism. After triumphs in New York and Chicago, the notorious Armory Show opened at Copley Hall; because of limited space, no paintings or sculptures by American artists or pre-Modernist work by Europeans blunted its avant-garde edge. "Exhibition of Post-Impressionists at Copley Hall like Dream of Psychopathy," read the *Herald*'s headline the day after the opening; "Art Branded with the Mark of Cocaine." The turbulent shapes and surfaces of Modernism had been welcomed in New York and Chicago, but Boston wanted no revolution, and most of its artists joined the ridicule with which reviewers greeted the exhibition. Philip Leslie Hale, one of the few Boston painters in the New York show, dismissed Marcel Duchamp's *Nude Descending a Staircase* with a limerick:

> . . . a lady, quite bare,
> Descended the stair,
> Now wouldn't that rattle your slats?

By the time the Armory Show reached Boston, the verve of Impressionism had entirely left the work of what *American Art News* called "the near-Vermeer Boston School," and its signature painting was an exquisitely painted luminous interior in which the quiet presence of a beautifully dressed woman competed for the eye with porcelain brought home by an ancestor in the China trade, a richly decorative screen, or the play of light through an open window. In Tarbell's *The Breakfast Room*, painted in 1903, a woman sits at a table, gown off one shoulder, a bowl of grapes in front of her. In the background, a maid, visible through an open door to the pantry, reaches toward a cupboard.

Margarett had an aversion to the Boston School. By breaking her engagement, she had left behind the life its painters depicted, and she knew that the women they painted as contemplative dreamers were often nothing of the kind. Tarbell's *Mrs. C.* was actually Blanche Ames, a cousin of E.'s and an illustrator, botanist, and suffragist; and Elizabeth Okie Paxton, whom her husband, William, painted dressed for a ball, was a painter in her own right. When Margarett began to make sculpture in Boston in 1914, she joined a considerable population of women artists.

The Museum School had declared its mission the transformation of "a boor of rather superior natural tastes and refinement into the well-educated and cultivated gentleman that an artist needs to be," but in fact it trained more women than men, and many of its female graduates worked in Boston as professional artists. Lillian Westcott Hale was more gifted and sought after as a portraitist than her husband, Philip; Lila Cabot Perry worked at Giverny with Monet for ten summers beginning in 1889; and Gertrude Fiske rebuked her mentors by painting women in other than domestic circumstances, women who seemed to contemplate their own individual destinies, among them Margarett herself. "John Doe," writing for *American Art News* in 1915, was sure "the march of Art Amazons" exhibiting at the St. Botolph Club that winter was "quite a shock to the 'old fogy members' who think the proper place for 'Woman' is 'The Home' (especially if it can be on Beacon Street)."

Every winter, a simple pamphlet was circulated in the art quarters of Boston, announcing the Woodbury Summer School of Drawing and

Painting, set in the ravishing landscape—seashore, pine forest, undulating farmland—of Ogunquit, Maine. E. Ames and her family spent part of each summer in Biddeford Pool, not far from Ogunquit, and during the foggy summer of 1915, Margarett and E. took a few classes with Charles Woodbury, the admired and respected Boston painter who ran the school. The next summer, Margarett returned to Ogunquit by herself, rented a studio, and enrolled for the full session of instruction in "painting & drawing from nature in oil, watercolor & pencil."

By 1916, artists had painted in Ogunquit for two decades, and the tiny fishing village perched on a bluff overlooking the ocean had become what a 1920 tourist brochure called "a highclass resort." The Ontio Hotel had a "hop" on Friday nights, and the Sparhawk, where a dance was held each Saturday, was the largest of the half-dozen hotels that rose like baroque castles along the shore. When Margarett came to Ogunquit, three summer art schools flourished, and the town was a magnet for painters and sculptors, a place where the conflict brought to a pitch by the Armory Show was reenacted each summer in earnest miniature.

Through the small fishing settlement at Perkins Cove ran a trickle called the Josiah River. On the west side, in and out of his large shingled studio, Woodbury presided over his students, most of whom were women. One mean-spirited Boston painter called them "fanatically adoring disciples," and an Ogunquit literary man dubbed them "virginal wayfarers," after the Marginal Way, the path that edged the bluff high above the Atlantic. In fact, Woodbury was genuinely supportive of women artists, perhaps because his wife, who had died in 1913, had been a painter.

In his friend John Singer Sargent's 1921 portrait, Woodbury is a handsome, delicately featured man with silver hair, a trim beard, and evidence of charm and humor about the eyes. Like Tarbell, he had studied at the Académie Julian in Paris, but he was almost exclusively a marine painter, whose fierce, raw approach to his subject belied his slight build and gentle nature. Though his painting retained the Impressionist spontaneity abandoned by the Boston School, he represented, in the binary system of Ogunquit, the traditional and academic.

In 1911, on the other side of Perkins Cove, Hamilton Easter Field, a painter and art critic from Brooklyn, had established another school of art. Field was ten years younger than Woodbury, tall and dark-haired, Byronic in appearance, bohemian by temperament, and said to be homosexual. Educated at Harvard and at the Columbia School of Architecture, he went in the late 1890s to Paris, where he stayed for several years, studying painting at the Accademia Collarossi. Paris exposed him to the beginnings of Cubism, and he returned to America ready to put his inheritance to the service of Modernism. He supported individual artists financially, and before long Perkins Cove lured them north. Field ran his school with the sculptor Robert Laurent and settled his students in converted shacks, cheek by jowl with artists who would become great American Modernists—Marsden Hartley, Gaston Lachaise, and Stuart Davis among them.

While Woodbury encouraged painting outdoors from nature, Field hired models, who posed nude in fishing shacks or, to the delight of the fishermen, on rocks at the far end of the cove. Woodbury's young women worked to render nature "as it seemed," and Field's young men, influenced by Europe, distorted the coastline to suit their avant-garde ardor. Parents like Margarett's trusted Woodbury to protect their daughters, but Field, citing Monet's peasant sabots at Giverny, exhorted his students to mix with the fishermen at Perkins Cove. Once, on a dare, a European countess, posing nude for Field's class, grabbed a kimono, ran across the footbridge, and flung herself naked on the steps of Woodbury's studio, but there is no record of a virginal wayfarer crossing the bridge in the other direction.

Realistically, though, the bridge was passable and the distance between Woodbury's studio and Field's shacks a mere hundred yards. Some of Field's students regularly attended Woodbury's classes, and the Ogunquit beach welcomed artists of both persuasions. It is altogether possible that the Boston girl who met Mr. Ringling in Florence managed to meet some of the artists who worked with Field. The summers Margarett was in Ogunquit, Walt Kuhn, George Bellows, and Robert Henri were in residence, and the summer of 1916, she took her meals at Eva Perkins's boardinghouse, where many artists, including the young Josephine Nivison and her future husband, Edward Hopper, ate desserts piled high with whipped cream.

§

"GOOD-LOOKIN'," was how Phyllis Ramsdell Eaton, aged eighty, described Margarett as she was in 1915. "Tall, slender. She wore very nice clothes." Phyllis was a child then, and her mother cleaned the shingled studio Margarett rented behind the Riverside Inn. Each cottage had a kerosene stove, a hot-water heater run on kerosene, an icebox that held one block of ice, and a small bed, and each day Lizzie Ramsdell tidied up, dusted, swept, and did the laundry. At the end of the summer, Margarett was so grateful she gave Mrs. Ramsdell a gold bangle.

On weekends, the rich whose grand houses lined the sea north from York gave parties, but during the week, there were cultural activities. Thursday evenings, Hamilton Field sponsored the Thurnscoe Forum, meetings held "for the open discussion of art, music, literature and kindred subjects," where questions addressed ranged from "Which is better fitted to express the emotions of our modern world, music or painting?" to "Has William Dean Howells contributed to American Literature anything which will be valued a century hence?" At the Village Studio, there were musicales and lectures by Nathan Dole or the humorist John Kendrick Bangs, owner of the newspaper in neighboring York, whom a local reporter called "the generator of more hearty, healthful, purely good-humored laughs than any other half-dozen men of our country today."

Margarett had brought Pilgrim to Ogunquit, and in no time at all, she met Libby Burgess, a giggly, chubby fellow art student who lived with a whippet named Covey in another Riverside studio. Class was held in the morning, so if Margarett and Libby weren't painting, they could play tennis at the Sparhawk, take tea at the Whistling Oyster, or shop in town for what a guidebook called "rich and expensive importation of all kinds."

If they took their dogs to walk on Pine Hill, they were apt to encounter Gertrude Fiske and Boy, her Boston bull terrier, whose bronze portrait Bashka Paeff had exhibited in Boston that spring. Like Amy Cabot and Charlotte Butler, two painters who lived together across from the Ramsdells, Gertrude was one of the "Pine Hill Girls," former virginal wayfarers who, after many summers painting with Woodbury, bought houses on the hill where the trolley ran above town, forming a community around the Woodbury School. It must have heartened Margarett to work among women who had committed themselves to art over marriage, and who welcomed and supported younger women.

Margarett was one of between seventy and a hundred students at the Woodbury School that summer. They came from New York, from Boston as she did, and from as far away as Chicago, Saint Louis, and the West. Woodbury always wore a starched collar and a necktie under a gray smock, and an old battered hat. As he lectured, he chain-smoked, the gold rims of his spectacles glinting in the sun, and his class, young women in large hats, shading themselves with umbrellas, and a few young men in shirtsleeves, leaned against the fish shacks, straining to hear every word.

Woodbury's first lecture of the season concerned the impact of the new movements in art. "The divergence of opinion is so great," he said, "as to make it possible for a picture to be held up by one person as an absolute masterpiece, and by another an unforgivable atrocity." In just a few years, Margarett would be a convert to Modernism, excoriating as "a dreadful picture" *El Jaleo*, John Singer Sargent's audacious panorama of a flamenco dancer, a jewel of Isabella Gardner's collection. Woodbury cautioned his students against such extremism, warning that the "futurists" would "throw away all tradition and manufacture something new." He advocated a quiet middle course: "It would not seem likely we should need to sweep away everything that has been done before . . . we still must use it."

To make the first assignment, Woodbury placed several paintings of the same tree on an easel to demonstrate how land, sky, and sea— in the manner of Monet's haystacks—changed color as light moved through the day. "I will say then that a picture is a sensation of emotion expressed in terms of nature," he said, and directed his students to make nine sketches of a single scene under varying conditions. Each sketch was not to take more than half an hour, and when looked at together, the series should demonstrate continuous change, however slight.

On Saturday mornings, each student placed her series on racks set up by the cove, and Woodbury inspected the work, criticizing gently in order to encourage improvement. Each subsequent assignment built on the previous week. "You will always find color interesting," he told them. "Light and form may not be, but color is." Woodbury repeatedly emphasized that his words should not take the place of experience with paint. "I am not trying to teach you to paint," he said. "I am trying to teach you to think pictures, with the hope that some day you may paint them." Whatever Woodbury taught, Margarett could see in his tempestuous and rather startling oceanscapes what happened when an artist worked directly from feeling, feeling that without the discipline of art might have proved overwhelming. His was an example she would put to use when she began to paint ten years later.

At the end of the summer, Margarett sent home her boxes of canvases, brushes, and paints, and though Woodbury advised his students to keep their summer's work for reference, no specimens document what she produced in his classes. What survived from that summer were four works by Charles Woodbury: a woodcut of porpoises, an etching of two men in a boat, and two portraits of Margarett. One was called *Portrait of Miss Sargent.* The other, a lithograph—*Artist (Miss Sargent) Painting on a Bluff*—shows her at a windswept distance, a virginal wayfarer poised at an easel high above the sea, somewhere along the Marginal Way.

❦

IN OGUNQUIT during the summer of 1916, Margarett began to leave behind the Boston of Shaw McKean. Grace Allen, whom she had known slightly at Miss Porter's, had married George Peabody of New York in 1911. Now the mother of two small sons, she was a divorcée who wrote on stationery engraved "Mrs. Grace Allen Peabody" and the mistress of a large house on the ocean in York Harbor, just south of Ogunquit. There she entertained her contemporaries, young people drawn to Maine not only by its beauty but by the atmosphere of bohemian excitement around its art colonies.

Margarett had never liked Grace, of whom Archibald MacLeish wrote that summer, "Lily, red wool lily, / Flaunting fairy lily." It was precisely Grace's "flaunting" that had provoked Margarett's disapproval when they met at Farmington and Grace "kicked her legs, and behaved altogether like a chorus girl on a spree." Now Margarett was attracted by Grace's experience with men and by the interest in ancient Greece she held to with such passion that her friends called her "Helen of Troy." Grace looked like a goddess—dark-blond hair tumbling down her back in curls, skin that turned tawny in the sun, and a classically beautiful face.

At a party at Grace's late that August, Margarett met Frank Bangs, an English teacher at St. Paul's School in New Hampshire. He was immediately "fascinated." Margarett was curious. Unlike many of the young men she was used to, who talked about sports, cards, or dogs, Frank was literary. Not only did he read books, he talked about them. He had wit and was born to using it—his father was the humorist John Kendrick Bangs. He called Margarett "Sargent" and insisted she call him "Bangs." He saw her as an artist and understood what she meant when she told him she was resting her eyes by doing watercolor that summer rather than sculpture.

After a small party Margarett gave at her studio, it was Bangs she invited to stay behind. She shortened Shaw McKean's planned weekend visit to a few hours Sunday afternoon. Frank hardly left her side the rest of her stay in Ogunquit. When Margarett left, he was in love, and his letters, literary and self-conscious, followed her home. "Why should you distrust the bronze strength I send you?" he wrote, and she responded, "O my brazen prophet . . ."

Bangs was not the only person in love when Margarett left Maine. On her way back home from Ogunquit, she spent the night at Grace's in York, and there had a reunion with another friend from Miss Porter's. Marjorie Davenport had not seen Margarett since her dowdy Farmington days and was stunned at the transformation. "She was marvelously dressed, and she had fifteen million bags. Why I thought she was the most exciting thing I had ever known!"

Margarett was also pleased. She planned to rent a house the next summer in Ogunquit, and Marjorie was a companion of whom her parents would approve. Marjorie also had domestic talents. She made her own beautiful clothes, and she could cook. Margarett extended the invitation, and Marjorie accepted. "This glorious person wanted to spend a summer with me!" When Margarett left York Harbor in her parents' chauffeured car, wearing a yellow linen dress, Marjorie yearned after her. "You don't know when your life takes a sudden direction," she said, "and mine took one which went on for many years when Margarett spent that night at Grace's."

Margarett also had plans to see Grace again, and soon after she returned to Wellesley, Grace wrote: "I can't see a Green Sea-Bus without longing to set sail on one with you. The too few hours we spent together remain very vivid—" Margarett had invited her to Boston, but Grace hoped Margarett would return to Maine "for a few days of sand-dunes and hours in which to tell you how deeply I feel your friendship which I can only hope to deserve in the future." Margarett was interested in Grace's knowledge of the classics. She planned a sculpture of the goddess Diana, and she had asked Grace to do some research. Grace relished the opportunity to respond: "I send you a few lines on the Keen-Sighted, Untouched, Fair-tressed Artemis—Diana Huntress of Men and Stags," she wrote. "Curious you should turn to the Goddess so very like yourself in many ways. . . . This divine creature surpassed all in strength—beauty of courage and activity—I think she loved women because she gave them gentle and painless deaths."

Margarett accepted Grace's invitation and during her visit photographed her hostess as Diana and in the results seemed to return her hostess's erotic admiration. Her eyes took in Grace's statuesque beauty, her long limbs, studied her profile and cheekbones. Grace, contemplative, rested on a rock, and Margarett photographed her in profile, legs bare to the hip, the sea beyond. Grace stood in her garden, Greek-style chiton flowing, and Margarett photographed her fingering the late-summer hollyhock, which towered above her considerable well-proportioned height. They talked of their mutual friend Bangs and of his friend Archie MacLeish, who had flattered Grace with the "flaunting lily" poem when he visited Bangs in July.

When Bangs visited Margarett at Wellesley in October, he was eager to have her meet his poet friend. Ever since their years together at Yale, where they shared their passion for poetry, he had delighted in startling Archie with introductions to extraordinary women. Now Bangs looked forward to his friend's reaction to "what he deemed a marvel," as he put it in his diary. Margarett played the part with gusto when she and Bangs had lunch with MacLeish and his new wife, Ada, at the Hotel Touraine in Boston. Archie was suitably impressed.

But when he and Ada met Margarett alone, MacLeish was a bit put off: "One doesn't tell a lady he admires that her personality is a brazen trumpet about Jericho—be Jericho a city walled or not." Later, they met without Ada, and afterward Margarett wrote Bangs with wild enthusiasm. She was enchanted by the beauty that came into Archie's face when he read and the expressiveness with which he moved his hands. He'd read aloud poems by others, but she was thrilled when he read her something of his own. "She is all you claim for her," Archie wrote Bangs, enclosing a poem to Margarett, which, he said, "I dare not show her for fear of annihilation."

When "The 'Chantress" later appeared in MacLeish's first book, he removed one of Margarett's two *t*'s, but when Bangs sent it along to Margarett, in November 1916, her name had two *t*'s and its subject was evident and undisguised:

> Lo, the Lady Margarett
> Spreadeth beauty for a net,
> Springeth souls thereby
> Springeth souls to light her clay.

Margarett was delighted, and when Archie sought her out to read the poem to her, she watched and listened, never letting on she had already seen it: "Cunningly her fingers fret / Witcheries in clay," he intoned. "Her dark hair is springes set, / Her two hands a spell. / Whom she tangleth, him they bind," and so on. Margarett wrote Bangs that Archie "never would have known I knew aught of it," but she was lying. After MacLeish, with excruciating self-consciousness, read her the poem, Margarett told him she had previously read it. He was devastated. His proud reading voice shattered into stammers of embarrassment. Margarett wrote Bangs, "Did he fear our dual laughter?"

In spite of Archie's reaction that day, Margarett became, to Bangs's satisfaction, "a considerable stimulus to MacLeish's poetic faculties." In early spring, when he imagined Helen for "Our Lady of Troy," a dramatic poem inspired by Faust, it was Margarett he conjured naked on the hearth, her limbs that shone "like silver in the light."

> Lo! I am she ye seek in every maid
> Ye love and leave again. I am desire
> Of woman that no man may slake in women.
> This thing am I,—a rose the world has dreamed.

Bangs was astonished at the success of his introduction. In May, he received a sonnet after MacLeish encountered Margarett at a wedding:

> . . . she sat, self-mimicking,
> The center of her inward-looking world,
> And costumed her, and tuned her mood, and curled
> The cap-plumes of her soul, and strummed a string.
> Her words were swift as swallows in a gale—
> Darted and flashed and poised, and then in flight
> Essayed the sun, and then vanished quite
> In some perplexing eddy . . .

"Sargent, that Archibald should be casting such lines your way is beyond my comprehension," Bangs wrote jealously, while denying knowledge of any "personal relations" between his friend and his beloved. "I could shriek but instead in half an hour I shall pull an oar in the rowing tank." For MacLeish, Margarett remained safely a muse, but Bangs lacked the shields of poetry and wedlock. He was in love and wished actually to do what his friend, he assumed, only imagined, "To wind her tresses this way 'bout the thumb, / or twist the heavy thunder of her hair. . . ."

Archie didn't trust Margarett's intentions toward Bangs, and he feared for his friend. He was not alone. Bangs took Margarett to dinner with his former Yale instructor, Lawrence Mason, and Margarett folded a dinner napkin on her head like a wimple and impersonated a nun. It was a trick that always made her family roar with laughter. Mason, who taught English literature, was reminded of all "the great Nun-passages in Milton" and wrote Bangs that Margarett's performance had been "one of the great triumphs of the American stage."

But he found her terrifying, comparing her to the audacious heroine of George Meredith's *Modern Love*. "She does indeed bear out all your preposterous praise," he wrote, "BUT is there anything sacred to her? Has she a soul? The transfiguring life-force that so wonderfully streams through her is like so much meaningless electricity unless there be a higher sanction." Bangs himself found Margarett "always extraordinarily simple and direct." He did not tell Mason that on June 25, 1917, at midnight, he had proposed marriage, and that she declined: "Maybe after the war."

The draft was passed on May 18, 1917, and in late July, MacLeish and Bangs enlisted in the Yale Mobile Hospital Unit in New Haven and sailed on the SS *Baltic* for France. One night, they leaned over the rail, peering out into the utter darkness of the submarine zone. Later, in his cabin, Archie wrote a poem with, he wrote Bangs, thoughts of Margarett and his wife:

> Like moon-dark, like brown water you escape
> O laughing mouth, O sweet uplighted lips.
> Within the peering brain old ghosts take shape
> You flame and wither as the white foam slips
> Back from the broken wave. . . .

iv

The White Blackbird

(1917–1919)

Margarett at Borgland, 1918

"WAR HAS BEGUN," was the *Transcript*'s laconic lead headline on Friday evening, April 6, 1917. The young men of Margarett's circle acted quickly. Eddie Morgan, who had already passed competitive civilian exams and earned a commission of second lieutenant, sailed immediately for France. E. Ames's brothers, Oliver and Dickie, enlisted, and before she saw them off, Marian McKean sent her sons, Shaw and Harry, to John Singer Sargent's studio at the Copley Plaza to sit in uniform for charcoal portraits. Harry Sargent passed officer training at Plattsburgh and sailed for France at the end of August, and Dan, who had been fighting in North Africa for the French, returned to Paris to receive a commission of second lieutenant in the American infantry.

Only Margarett's oldest brother, Frank, remained at home. In 1914, at thirty years old, he'd finally married. Margery Lee was the dark-haired granddaughter of an equerry to the king of Italy; the daughter of George Lee, a Bostonian yachtsman, steeplechaser, and painter; and widely considered "the most beautiful girl in Boston." But marriage did not calm Frank's temperament; once, after Sunday lunch at the Cheevers', the newlyweds bolted the table and retired for an hour to a guest room upstairs.

Frank had married for love, but he timed the wedding to avoid the draft. Only as the country turned toward war and he read Dan's account of heroism at Verdun was he inspired to fight. At the end of his officer training stint at Harvard the summer of 1918, he stood expectantly as the names of those commissioned were announced and, when his was not among them, fell to the ground in a dead faint. The training officer found him "over-intense," Dan later said; his barrage of questions, his brilliant and unbridled talk, had seemed evidence of "nervousness." The army offered a commission in the quartermaster corps, but Frank proudly refused and gamely enlisted as a private. It was good this way, he told himself; he'd be a better officer, having suffered the "hard knocks" of rising through the ranks.

But his failure was a bitter comedown. His career at Harvard and in sports, his marriage to Margery, his precocious achievement in business, all paled beside the military stature of his younger brothers. His sister Jane advised him to conceal that he'd been denied a commission, and he assured her he'd be discreet. "I've never lost *faith* in myself," he wrote her in a determinedly upbeat letter. But he must have felt he failed his father; although Papa would not have reproached him directly, he was no longer the family's golden hero. "I hate to think of them going to the front," Papa wrote to Margarett about Harry and Dan, "but if they had turned out slackers I should have been a very unhappy man."

As families disguised their anxiety in the bright trappings of patriotism, the rituals of betrothal and marriage were displaced by the ministrations of leavetaking, letters from the front, photographs of young men in uniform, newspaper casualty lists. In the face of the real danger to the boys in combat, everything at home seemed temporary. To those left behind, the dislocations of war extended a freedom that would not have been allowed in peaceful times. For Margarett, this suspension of social and domestic life was an opportunity.

Her sculpture career was already flourishing. In October 1916, a form postcard had arrived at her studio from the Art Institute of Chicago: "Dear Sir," it addressed Margarett, "I have the pleasure of informing you that the following works have been accepted for exhibition." The sculpture jury, all sculptors of national reputation, had chosen *The Cheever Boys* and *Outdoors: A Sketch* (now lost) for the institute's annual in November.

The Twenty-ninth Annual Exhibition of American Oil Painting and Sculpture of the Art Institute of Chicago was the first public display of Margarett's work. Since it opened the museum's new wing and was joined by a sculpture show organized by the National Sculpture Society, hailed as "the most comprehensive and remarkable ever shown in America," it was not a mere annual. Margarett's pieces stood among seven hundred by two hundred of the most prominent contemporary American sculptors, more than sixty of them women. "It's all there," commented the *Chicago Herald*, "busts, animals, Indians, Greeks, Egyptians, cowboys and lovers."

In the months before America entered the war, Margarett was absorbed in her work. She stayed long hours in her studio, making portraits and "statuettes" on commission to earn her own money. She advertised herself among her family and family friends. Portraits of animals and children sold easily, so she made a lot of them. She worked in the traditional way, constructing an armature, sculpting in clay, refining a plaster, then having the piece cast at a foundry. Each season, she had her pieces photographed and submitted them to annuals. In March 1917, at the age of twenty-five, she exhibited the bust of Dan and a work called *Bronze* at the 92nd Annual Exhibition of the National Academy of Design in New York.

It was the mother of her childhood friends the "Salts" who recommended Margarett's next teacher, Gutzon Borglum, later the sculptor of Mount Rushmore. Mrs. Saltonstall's friend Joseph Lindon Smith, a Boston muralist and painter, had been impressed with Borglum's instruction of his son, and arranged an introduction. Margarett had learned all she could from Bashka Paeff, and the idea of leaving Boston was exciting. Borglum was a hardworking artist with two studios, in New York and in Connecticut. Margarett would work at the country studio, where he undertook his largest pieces, commissions for public sculptures all over the country.

Gutzon Borglum was an ambitious man, to his own mind a visionary. It was hard to miss him in the newspapers. Recently it had been reported that the Daughters of the Confederacy had commissioned him to carve a Civil War memorial into the bare face of Stone Mountain near Atlanta. The Daughters had in mind an equestrian relief of General Lee, but Borglum offered a grander proposal: Lee on horseback, leading a full regiment across the virgin granite expanse.

He did nothing uncontentiously. He joined the Association of American Painters and Sculptors because he shared their rage at the strictures of the National Academy of Design, but when their plans for the Armory Show expanded to include works from the European avant-garde and it became clear that Modernism's "personal note distinctly sounded" had prevailed, he withdrew his work, resigned as chair of the sculpture committee, and raucously took his case to the press: "we wish Mr. Borglum walked to the battlefield upon ankles not quite so thick," remarked the *New York Globe*.

It had taken the force of pure ambition for John de la Mothe Gutzon Borglum to emerge from the Mormon household where he was born on the Idaho frontier in 1867, the first son of the second of his father's sister wives. At twenty he went to San Francisco, and at twenty-two married his painting teacher, Lisa Putnam, who was forty and a working artist. A painting of a stagecoach drawn by six horses hurtling down a Sierra chasm attracted his first patron, Jessie Benton Frémont, the brilliant wife of the explorer John Charles Frémont. When Lisa, eager to civilize her young husband, planned a trip to Europe, Mrs. Frémont provided letters of introduction.

In London, Gutzon painted portraits of patrons his wife cultivated with lavish entertaining—at one party, a young Isadora Duncan, scattering rose petals, danced "out into the garden." But his frontier ambition soon chafed at the civilized British life Lisa encouraged, and he turned from painting to sculpture and exhibited at the Paris Salon. When his younger brother Solon triumphed as a sculptor of the great American West at the 1900 Paris Exposition, Gutzon walked out on Lisa and sailed alone for America. On shipboard, he met Mary Montgomery, twenty-four years old, who had just earned a doctorate in Sanskrit from the University of Berlin. Eventually she became his second wife.

Brazen with self-righteousness, Gutzon Borglum assaulted the civilized gates of the New York art world. When Augustus Saint-Gaudens threw his entry out of competition for an equestrian sculpture of General Grant, Borglum took revenge in a tirade published in Gustave Stickley's *The Craftsman*. He would liberate his work from "the top-notch of mediocrity" to which this vaunted artist, in his opinion a mere "workman," had brought American sculpture. It was Saint-Gaudens's influence, with its smooth and careful surfaces, that Bashka Paeff had passed on to Margarett. Borglum, who had met Rodin in Paris, believed expression of America's "unsatisfied hunger" required sculpture with a raw, gestural surface. Given ten million dollars, he would dynamite all the public memorials in the United States and set about erecting his own Washington monument, his own Lincoln memorial. Then he would endow a real art school: "There is no such institution in America."

It was to Borgland, Borglum's estate and studio at Turn of River, Connecticut, rather than to Ogunquit, that Margarett invited Marjorie Davenport for the summer of 1917. Six years earlier, joining "the search for country homes by city men," Borglum had purchased land to create an "estate" near his brother Solon's home in the Wire Mills district, near Stamford. Margarett was his only pupil that summer. Gutzon had taught at the Art Students League in New York, but he preferred informal arrangements, usually with young women from prominent families. In lieu of tuition, Margarett bought him a gold cigarette case which she charged at Cartier: "My name is Margarett Sargent, and I come from Turn of River," she told the clerk by way of identification.

At Borgland, Margarett found a paradise—wild orchids, a lake stocked with trout, a canoe from which her host fished with a barbless fly: "Oh no," he explained, "I do not catch them. I only play with them." Nor was one permitted to pick the wildflowers. Borgland was that "most sacred recess in the life of human beings," a haven for the hungry creative soul. Gutzon and Mary and their two children lived in a renovated farmhouse, but his studio was a distance away, on the other side of the river, so he could ride his horse to work. Built of pink granite mined from its site by Italian stonecutters who camped there, the vaulted studio was heated with ten-foot logs cut from Borgland's forests, which burned in a looming Gothic fireplace of Gutzon's design. Outside, the Rippowam River ran so swiftly its roar penetrated the granite walls.

Margarett brought Pilgrim to Borgland, and eventually she kept birds—a parrot and a crow. Relieved of the suits and dresses required in Boston, she wore long loose skirts, pullovers, a scarf around her shoulders. She and Marjorie shared a small outbuilding near the studio. Marjorie took charge of the household, as Margarett had hoped she would. She did the mending and, when they didn't eat with the Borglums, the cooking. On summer days, they swam in a pool gouged from the river, with Mr. Borglum, as they called him, and his children.

In the studio, Margarett measured contours— "Through the neck 7 one degree—under ears, chin to eyebrow 10 one degree," she noted on a drawing. Each day she pulled muslin tarpaulins from sculptures and sprayed them with water to keep them wet and workable. She worked sections of Borglum's pieces under his direction, and she worked in the office. In exchange, he gave her suggestions and criticized her sculpture. For *The Spirit of Aviation*, a memorial to the first American flier killed in the war, Gutzon had hired a model with flat feet, so Margarett posed for the feet. "You can see it," she would say later, "if you go to the University of Virginia."

At first, Margarett was in thrall to Borglum's charisma and the "vision" to which he held with religious zeal. His masculinity had the roughness of the West, his courtliness the veneer of Europe. He had technique and discipline, and he insisted she measure up. In the beginning, Margarett thrived. It didn't occur to her that his assignments condescended to the skill she'd already achieved; he was the master. She didn't mind that he was volatile, that his criticism was pompous and his praise patronizing. When he ranted about his debts, she talked her father into buying his sculpture. When he told her to make sculptures of animals, she did. Borglum, in turn, found his apprentice talented and attractive. "He was crazy about her," Marjorie said. "He thought she was glamorous." As time went on, Margarett would see Borglum in a harsher light. "Those three years were a horror," she said, "but I didn't know it at the time."

In fair weather, Margarett worked on her own pieces outside the studio, its enormous door propped open with a chunk of granite. Behind her, in Borglum's workroom, huge animal figures stood in the half-dark. In a photograph of Margarett working, a sculpture of Pilgrim sits looking down as if at his reflection, and Margarett, Pilgrim himself jumping up on her, models his head and front legs. His rear haunches are still an undefined mass of clay, and she works his right shoulder with no instrument but her long fingers, his other side with a scraping tool.

Margarett made three sculptures of Pilgrim, sculpted the Borglum children, forced Marjorie to pose for hours: "She seemed to think I was Oriental-looking," remarked Marjorie. And she sculpted her birds. Two parrots were accepted for the 1918 Pennsylvania Academy Annual. Margarett and Marjorie had expected to leave Connecticut at the end of the summer of 1917, but instead they stayed on. In the winter, they moved, as the Borglums did, to New York, where Margarett continued her apprenticeship in Gutzon's city studio. Early in the spring, she and Marjorie moved back to Borgland, where things had changed dramatically.

A granite worker had won Mary Borglum to the cause of Czechoslovak unification, and Gutzon, with typical grandiosity, donated a hundred fifty acres at Borgland as a training camp. In Europe, thousands of young Czechs and Slovaks had risked execution by deserting the Austro-Hungarian Army for the Allies; their recent heroism at the pivotal battle for Vladivostok had inspired support for their cause. In America, Czech and Slovak immigrants clamored to join up, and soon young men poured into Borgland from Pittsburgh steel mills, Detroit factories, and Omaha farms. They cleared a parade ground through the woods, converted an outbuilding to a hospital, built log barracks, which they whitewashed and painted with bright folk patterns. Each week, a hundred volunteers passed through the camp, and by late August two regiments had sailed for France.

Gutzon was devoted to the Czechoslovak cause, but he was infuriated by the wild behavior of its young recruits. Where was their discipline? How would the cause be won if its soldiers could not fight? He wrote letters of protest to Tomáš Masaryk, who came to Borgland and exhorted his followers from a platform festooned with stars and stripes, but the camp got no calmer. Spanish flu raged, and killed four volunteers. Marjorie contracted it, and the Sargents called Margarett home for a vaccination. Futilely, Gutzon wrote begging Masaryk to finance provisions, and the Borglums fed the volunteers with their own money. Margarett and Marjorie loved the carousing and singing they heard at night, the sergeant's commands echoing through the forest during the day. Very soon Margarett had young men in uniform sitting for portraits and amorous officers competing for her attention.

Word of the camp attracted notice in New York and, at the height of the summer, brought to Turn of River an artist who would profoundly change Margarett's life. George Luks was Borglum's contemporary, an icon in American art, and a celebrity. He was the most flamboyant of "the Eight," the group of artists whose 1908 show had rebuked with "new art realism" what Luks called "the pink and white painters," the American Impressionists led by Edmund Tarbell and the New Yorker William Merritt Chase. Luks had as much fame and as much energy as Gutzon, but he also had charm and a sense of humor, qualities Borglum utterly lacked. He dressed Mary Borglum in Moravian costume to paint her, persuaded an officer to sit for a painting he titled *Czechoslovak Chieftain*, and, after listening to officers tell stories from the Russian front, painted *Czechoslovak Army Entering Vladivostok*. Margarett asked him to sit for her and began to model his head.

At fifty-one, George Luks was a robust, compactly built man of five feet six, with twinkly blue eyes and fading blond hair. Like Margarett's father, he was an amateur boxer, but with what she later called "the dangerous habit of insulting people in bars." Like Frank Sargent, he might burst into song—he sang while he painted—and could enthrall with a story. Margarett adored him, and he was struck by her insurgent spirit. As he watched her, he set about encouraging that quality in her sculpture. Go ahead, he told her, get your *self* into the texture of that surface. She should throw away her sculptor's tools and attack the clay with "any odd kitchen implement." He arrived in time, Margarett said, "to protect me from the grandiloquence of Borglum's work." Luks was to become her close friend, her mentor, and her most important influence.

One Sunday at the end of the summer, the Borglums arranged a pageant to benefit the camp. The volunteers built thatched huts, and citizens of Stamford, dressed as Bohemian villagers, arrived to inhabit them. Guests came from New York, including Louisine Havemeyer, the collector, suffragist, and intimate friend of Mary Cassatt. Gutzon, Margarett, and Luks dressed as peasant artists and wandered the "village" peddling cartoons and drawings "that would not," a newspaper said, "be termed pro-Teuton." In a dramatic sketch she wrote, Margarett portrayed "in a thrilling manner" a Frenchwoman "robbed by the Huns of all that was dear to her." Suddenly gunfire broke out. "Occupying Germans" had just managed to handcuff the artists, when soldiers, dressed in the horizon blue of independent Czechoslovakia, galloped down the hill, shouting that peace had been declared.

The camp celebrated with folk dancing and singing, Mrs. Havemeyer presented an American flag, and the artists auctioned off drawings and posters and raised fifteen hundred dollars. One of Margarett's sales was to Mrs. Havemeyer.

§

WHEN MARGARETT and Marjorie moved to New York for the winter of 1917, they lived together in an apartment on Forty-ninth Street near Madison Avenue. Their housekeeper, Jane Barnato, brought her monkey along to work, or her two parrots. Marjorie earned money by sewing, and Margarett went out to work at Borglum's studio on Thirty-eighth Street, where live models might include a buffalo, a Per-

sian dancer, or an Indian brave. Margarett and Marjorie had transferred their life together to New York, but the city soon threatened
their contentment.

Though Marjorie was Margarett's verbal and intellectual match,
she did not have Margarett's ambition. Nor did she have a career.
Margarett, with a talent for seduction Marjorie did not share, had always overshadowed her with men, and Marjorie watched her exploits
with a complicated mixture of delight, awe, envy, and horror. "I tell
you," Marjorie said, "she was so popular and men were so crazy about
her that one would make an appointment to meet her at the train,
then another one drive in the taxi with her to the apartment, then
she'd be having dinner with somebody else."

Marjorie was eighty-eight when she said this, dark-gray hair to her
shoulders, dressed for tea in a long red dress.

"Do you remember their names?"

"Yes, but they married. I don't know whether their families . . ."

"It was a long time ago."

"Well, there was a Harriman," she said, but she would not tell me
his first name.

For Margarett, the city was a new arena, and any constraint an echo
of her mother's infuriating worry. The limits of convention were hers to
scorn. Kay Saltonstall and her husband, Philip Weld, were now living
in New York. Margarett took a beau to their apartment for dinner and
scandalized her old friends by visibly holding his hand. Kay may have
been a great belle when they were coming out in Boston, but Margarett, in her fashion, was the belle now. Hamilton Fish, determined to
marry her, wrote daily letters: meet me on that corner, at that restaurant. Shaw wrote from France, accommodating his dreams of wedded
bliss to her "independent—free life." Margarett did not respond.

Marjorie viewed her friend's admirers as hopeless victims, no match
for their predator. After a while, she also had compassion for them
and, though she disapproved of Margarett's behavior, took smug pleasure in the fact that it was she with whom Margarett had chosen to
live. In turn, Margarett, with intermittent warmth and extravagance,

included Marjorie in her success. The "miserable man" took them to Delmonico's. Everyone ordered a full dinner, and then Margarett, pretending the man had said something wrong, berated him, stood up, and announced that she and Marjorie were leaving.

"We hadn't had a bite to eat!" Marjorie said. "They must have brought the dinner and he must have paid for it."

When Marjorie criticized what she'd done, Margarett shut her up, full force, with the sarcasm she'd honed for years on her mother.

Marjorie was also jealous. She and Margarett shared a bed, and though nothing documents what they did there, Marjorie, at the end of her life, raged against Margarett with the fury of a thwarted lover. At its best, their friendship had the pleasures of a conspiracy, the two of them poised against a world with expectations of women neither intended to fulfill. At its worst, their relationship was unequal and exploitative. Margarett was the artist, Marjorie the admirer. Marjorie did the housework, Margarett paid the bills. Margarett got angry, Marjorie cowered. Anything might trip the spring: Marjorie sewing, Marjorie not sewing; Marjorie leaping with terror in the night as mice ran across their pillows. But Marjorie considered her years with Margarett "great days," days she would remember forever. Going home for Christmas with her widowed mother was, by contrast, "retiring to a quiet life."

In Margarett's last bedroom, a painting hung so that she could see it from the bed to which she was, by then, confined. It was her portrait as a young woman, which George Luks painted from memory in early 1919. If I turn from my desk now as I work, I can see the young woman, sitting in profile. Her pale hands are folded, disappearing into the black of her lap. She wears a dark hat, its swath of auburn feather trailing down her back. Her dark dress has a creamy collar and cuffs, daubed with salmon trim. Luks invented the clothes, he said, to make her look timeless.

Because of her black hair, her very light complexion, and the contradictions in her character, Luks called Margarett "The White Blackbird," and that is what he called the painting. The young woman's decorous pose contrasts with the low, open neck of her gown. The re-

straint of her expression belies the worldly rush of her life in New York
and her racy reputation. In the warm whites of cheeks and chin, the
dark of eyes steadily forward, mouth gently closed, Luks caught uncer-
tainty and sadness, a vulnerability Margarett rarely revealed. Against
the old-master darkness of the rest of the surface, the pale flesh of her
neck and décolletage takes on the luminous shape of a white bird in
moonlit flight.

At nearly twenty-four, Margarett knew the power of her looks.
Frank Bangs wrote lyrically of "unusually light-blue eyes, a countenance pale as marble, and amazingly thick dark hair." She dressed to
emphasize her height, her long neck, and her voluptuous figure, but
childhood plainness had taught her that beauty was currency, and just
as ephemeral. "My memories," wrote Archibald MacLeish of Margarett, "are of vividness—almost a glitter it was sometimes—and movement." She held her own in conversation, with what friends called "the
Sargent gift for brilliant language." Out from under the sheen of elegant manners came the wit she'd honed to disarm her brothers into a
collapse of laughter. If repartee didn't shock or charm, she performed.
Once, at a party, to Gertrude Hunnewell's astonishment, she "accidentally on purpose popped out of a black velvet evening dress."

"Hundreds" of passionate letters Margarett received during this
period were destroyed by her children. Many of her correspondents
were friends or classmates of her brothers, Harvard boys on their way
to managing inherited money or family property. Others she had met
at parties in Newport or Long Island—New York boys of whom her
mother disapproved simply because they were not from Boston. All of
them were attracted by her beauty, enthralled by her talk, and drawn
in by her seductiveness. "I know, Margarett darling, that I cannot do
without you, & the only thing that has enabled me to leave you is the
thought & hope of your being with me before so very long," wrote
Oliver Harriman, en route to Mexico, from the Metropolitan Club in
Washington. "I had a long dream about you the other night which was
very encouraging if true," wrote "Freddy" from the University Club in

Portland, Oregon, begging her to write "a little more often." One unsigned letter set forth an island tryst:

> . . . just as the canoe touched the beach you ran down to meet me leaving the turtle soup to burn or boil over to its heart's content, and I am ashamed to say that you didn't have any clothes on at all . . . a big moon came up over the water and threw shafts of light among the trees. We very slowly awoke . . . our lips moved and our mouths met in a long kiss and our bodies stirred and came closer together and your hand stole down from my shoulder and touched an old friend and wakened him. . . .

Margarett's anonymous correspondent was not impertinent; he was responding to the sexuality that infused her speech, dress, and movement. What he could not have known, because she would not have told him, was what suffering intense feeling had always brought her. The cost of breaking her engagement had taught her to seek seduction without obligation, physical passion without loss of virginity, love without the consequence of marriage. Her desire for independence set her apart not only from the lives of most of her friends but from their understanding. It was this solitude that George Luks caught in his portrait, but it was not what most people saw. Betty Parsons met Margarett in 1919: "She had such magnetism, Margarett. Such physical magnetism plus that fantastic, witty brain. The combination was just devastating. You could see them being knocked down, right and left."

In the fall of 1919, Margarett and Marjorie moved to New York for good and settled into an apartment at 10 West 58th Street, across from the Plaza Hotel. Margarett continued to work for Borglum— "mentally I feel I have not lingered and my hands are better prepared," she wrote him. She was soon getting portrait commissions, charging for them, she quipped, "no more than a man would pay for a car." She also had the income from a trust, and she furnished the flat with enthusiasm, worrying her father with the amount of money she spent. Always, Dan said, she complained she was hard up. "She wouldn't buy potatoes, but she'd buy a wonderful rug." Margarett took a room with north light as a studio, and their pet rabbit had the run of it—"his . . . you know," Marjorie said, "got mixed with the clay." Downstairs, in a dark, sculpture-filled duplex, lived the Ziegfeld star Fanny Brice, with her husband, just back from prison, the tall, handsome gangster, of Norwegian descent, Jules Arnstein (called Nicky for the nickel-plated wheels of his motorcycle).

Margarett may have seen Brice perform in Boston in 1911 at the height of the rage for ragtime, singing "Ephraham Played Upon the Piano" in the *Ziegfeld Follies*. Now Fanny was at the peak of her career, headlining in Ziegfeld's *Nine O'Clock Review* and *Midnight Frolic,* cabaret shows that played in nightclub luxury on the roof of the New Amsterdam Theatre on Forty-second Street. At the Roof, Margarett saw Ziegfeld's best acts up close. Backed by thirty-six chorus girls, the black comedian Bert Williams sang, and Bird ("Bird on a Wire") Millman swung on his trapeze. Affecting a Yiddish accent, Fanny vamped "I'm Bad," slouching in tight black silk across the stage in an angular spoof of Theda Bara. Later in the show, dressed as an Apache squaw who unaccountably sang Yiddish, she hooted out a new number called "I'm an Indian."

After her shows, Fanny gave parties. For the first time in Margarett's life, a party was not an occasion to greet her parents' friends and relatives or a ritual assembly of boys in tails and girls in gowns. Even Grace Peabody's Maine gatherings paled beside the heady crowd at Fanny's, where at least one of Nicky's near-underworld cronies noticed a tall sculptress from Boston with blue eyes and elegant clothes. Ziegfeld girls and Broadway impresarios pressed up against Whitneys and Astors, and just across the room, where Margarett could easily meet them, mingled the people who made her laugh so hard when she saw them on the stage—Eddie Cantor, W. C. Fields, who had just made his first silent movie, and Bert Williams. Margarett learned at Fanny's that entertaining might be an occasion for invention, and when she married and had her own household, she planned parties that surprised, even enlightened, with their mix of guests.

Margarett and Fanny encountered each other at a time and in an atmosphere where both their differences and their resemblances brought them together. Each had fled a childhood that predicted a destiny she would work hard to reject; each might have chosen the other's life to make up the deficits in her own. Margarett envied the romance of Fanny's nomadic youth in the saloons her mother ran in Brooklyn and Newark, the freedom of a girlhood on city streets, the blaze of theatrical triumph. Fanny envied Margarett's education, the luxurious security of her Boston girlhood, her beauty and her glamour. As interested in art as Margarett was in theater, she drew and painted a little herself. She knew she was funny, but she had no sense that she was attractive; later, she would bob her nose to play down the appearance she believed kept her from serious acting roles. She had a long, lanky figure, beautiful skin, dark hair, lively green eyes, looks that lit up with extraordinary vitality and warmth. Like Margarett, she was mercurial, an extrovert who was terribly shy, a courteous woman who shocked with her candor.

Margarett was twenty-six and Fanny twenty-seven when they met, so theirs was the friendship of young women. Margarett and Marjorie went eagerly to Milgrim's, a dress shop in which Fanny had invested, and Fanny slept on their sofa when she lost her keys and came upstairs to talk the nights and days Nicky Arnstein disappeared. Margarett and Marjorie were intrigued that Nicky was an actual gambler, and they thought him devastating. He gave Margarett one of his mono-grammed silk shirts to use as a smock. As far as Fanny was concerned, Nicky could do no wrong; when he was arrested for fraud in 1916, she sold her jewels to pay his lawyers. "He was elegant—very swell," Marjorie said. "How he must have hated prison."

&

In Margarett's studio, a damp cloth drapes a head to keep the clay damp. Under the towel, her sculpture of a woman's head is erect, the profile definite. The trace of fingers has given the eyes vitality without detail of iris, pupil, or sclera. Under another cloth, the portrait head of an old man: For wrinkles, Margarett has delicately creased the clay near his eyes, and the eyes, rough suggestions, directly fix one's gaze. She's kept the clay very wet, so the hair near his ear is not heavy or inert but lifted and light. She is no longer smoothing surfaces until texture disappears.

Margarett takes a fistful of clay and presses it to an armature made of wire and wood. The soldier sits on a chair. In the structure of the armature is the beginning of her idea of what he looks like. Perhaps, as she works, they make conversation. This is the first of a number of sittings or the only sitting. It goes on for hours or until she has something of his shape. A plain but handsome face. How will she communicate the light color of his hair? She shoves the clay to resemble his face, moves the head—as if holding a living face in her hands—to position it on the neck.

Soon it doesn't matter if he is sitting there or has gone. Something had taken hold. Margarett has looked at heads on necks, and she has looked at soldiers. She has loved her brothers and her brothers' friends, and she has watched them in uniform. As the clay softens in her hands, the experience of looking becomes knowledge of the soldier's form. Now she pulls that knowledge through the clay, which, as long as it stays soft, has the pliancy of flesh. She works outside thought, or thought enters the motion of her hands. The soldier will look the way she believes he looks, and as her fingers move, a face will emerge, a face that does not change. The work is long, but the clay returns her effort. When she has finished, she has no idea how tired she is.

Later, the soldier stands, his portrait beside him on a sculpture stand. Margarett photographs the sculpture in profile and the soldier in profile just behind it: a double image. The portrait's hair has texture; the soldier's is smooth, as if slicked down to pass an inspection. The portrait's mouth seems resigned, the soldier's mouth weak. The curve of his ear is smooth; she's modeled it rough. The roughness will catch the light when the portrait is cast in bronze, and the light will catch the eye.

On September 26, Margarett delivered a sculpture to the Roman Bronze Works, a foundry in Long Island City. The woman's head was small enough to hold in her hand; with it, she sacrificed precision for emotion, restraint for abandon. Thick locks of hair snake and entangle, seeming to take mysterious shape—a figure, almost, a bacchante in motion. The woman's head is thrown back, her neck long and bare. Her eyes are closed, her mouth is partly open, breaking the surface of a stormy face. This head is too intimate to be a portrait. Margarett called her Hagar, for Abraham's concubine.

Margarett's hand loosened under the influence of George Luks, and it showed in a portrait of him she finished in late 1918. As with Hagar, she expressed her personal sense of a moment—a surge of feeling for a man she loved as she loved her father. Life-size, Luks rises from a swirl of clay—an impression of shirt, balding head, slightly smiling face. He had been still, it seemed, for barely a moment, but his character came across with more expression than the soldier's, more clarity than Hagar's. In the spring of 1919, after the Pennsylvania Academy accepted the head for its annual, Margarett heard from her father: "I am glad you have been successful with Mr. Luks's head, and although I have never seen him I should like to see photographs of it."

Luks was pleased as well. "Get *Town and Country*," he scrawled, and jammed the note into a small envelope; "the March 10th issue has something in it that may interest you." He had helped a photograph of the portrait make its way into the magazine. "Miss Sargent still has been unusually deft-fingered in catching the flexibility of Luks's Old Master mouth and unquenchable enthusiasm," read the accompanying review, Margarett's first critical praise. To the reviewer, Luks's friend Frederick James Gregg of the *New York Herald*, the head suggested "a cross between a bookmaker and a trainer of successful prizefighters." It might have been "carried further," but it was certainly, he wrote, "a refutation of the theory that nobody ought to pay attention to the work of a woman sculptor."

Luks drew Margarett into his New York world of painters and hard drinkers. She was mesmerized. He did not condescend, and he made her laugh with a combination of melodramatic humor and language so obscene even his most progressive friends censored it when they wrote about him. No Boston painter would have attempted to settle an aesthetic difference like Luks did when he punched Edmund Tarbell in the jaw. His excess of vitality mirrored and encouraged Margarett's own. "The eye was made to see; the hand to paint; the nose to smell good food, the earth after rain and the pushcarts of the East Side," he proclaimed.

When asked about her training, Margarett said, "I had the good fortune to become the lone and solitary pupil of George Luks." In the winter of 1917, she'd entered the women's modeling class at the Art Students League, taught by Robert Aitken, famous at the time for memorials to President McKinley. She quickly left, finding, as Luks had, that formal study tried her patience. Luks claimed he learned to paint looking at works by those he considered great—Rembrandt, Hals, Velázquez—and he taught by a combination of anecdote and exhortation: "Don't tell me. Show me!" he would shout.

Margarett asked him to teach her to draw. She wanted the accuracy and speed he'd perfected during years as an artist reporter for the *Philadelphia Press*, the depth he managed in fast portraits of a Czech volunteer or an ordinary woman, the humor distilled from drawing *The Yellow Kid*, America's first comic strip. Margarett was a voracious student. She saw that Luks drew everywhere he went. She watched him sketch her birds at Borgland, marveled as he disappeared into a vortex of speeding pencil to emerge with a double portrait, "Gutzon Borglum critiquing Miss Sargent's sculpture." She saw how he derived a watercolor from a drawing, an oil from a watercolor. His approach freed her from the careful lyricism of Bashka Paeff and Borglum's ponderous formality. She worked harder than she ever had.

During the day, Margarett carried a sketchbook, and it became a diary of drawings. At night, she hired a model, whom she drew again and again. She drew in charcoal and she drew in pencil and, in the manner of Rodin's late erotic drawings, applied a watercolor wash when she finished. A careful line of charcoal edged the figure who lay, legs erotically akimbo, on her stomach, hands concealed beneath her pelvis. Once, as Margarett drew, the doorbell rang, and a tall, rangy man burst in and began to make love to the woman posing on the floor; he was a sculptor, the model his girlfriend. Margarett continued to draw, adding to the nude the faint image of her lover bent over her. "I know I should have been shocked," she said, "but I wasn't."

If Margarett had any remaining allegiance to the gentility of Boston, Luks decimated it. His brutal way of sizing people up satisfied the temperament beneath her manners. "To hell with your hats!" he snorted. He rewarded her hard work with late-night excursions to Chez Mouquin, a favorite haunt of artists, under the Sixth Avenue el at Twenty-eighth Street. They climbed canopied stairs from the side-walk to eat and drink with the writers and painters who were Luks's friends. Red-upholstered banquettes lined the mirrored walls of gaslit dining rooms, where straightforward food described in ersatz French was served with plenty of booze until two A.M. Soon Margarett was at work malleting into shape a bust of Chaffard, Mouquin's famous headwaiter, and Luks was at her shoulder, insisting, she wrote later, on "spontaneity and freedom of attack."

"Art!—my slats. . . . I can paint with a shoe string dipped in pitch and lard," Luks would shout, drinking and sketching wildly on napkins, tablecloths, menus. His emotion, John Sloan observed, drove "the paint before it to the end his heart desired," but, as Margarett learned, when Luks drank, his rapturous facility abandoned him, and he could work a painting until he destroyed it. He had started to drink as a boy, and now, at intervals, he landed at the Northern Dispensary on Waverly Place, where his brother, its director, saw to it he abstained until he was ready to go back to the world. Eventually a drunken brawl landed him in jail, and Margarett introduced him to a young lawyer, Harrison Tweed, a Harvard classmate of her brother Frank, and one of her beaux. Often Margarett found herself in Harrison's company, escorting a barely coherent Luks home to his wife or downtown to his brother.

Margarett began to experiment with watercolor. She showed Luks a series of washes of women in draped garments. "Very good, in fact the best," he wrote in bold pencil across one of them. He took her to see Maurice Prendergast, whom he considered a master of watercolor. Prendergast was tall and lean, still handsome, but going deaf. He was fifty-nine when Margarett met him, but to her he seemed a thousand years old. He was a bachelor given to quoting Kipling's "If a man would be successful in his art, art, art / He must keep the girls away from his heart, heart, heart . . ." But he also encouraged women artists. When he pulled out portfolios and sketchbooks from his early years in Boston and Paris, Margarett saw color that seemed to flow unguided into the most delicate and lifelike images. She left his Washington Square studio with three studies of single female figures done in Paris, gifts from the artist.

Luks also took Margarett to see Alfred Maurer, one of the first Americans of his generation to paint in Paris. By 1905, under the influence of Matisse, hot color and exaggerated form burst his Whistlerian boundaries, and his paintings hung among the Fauves at the Salon d'Automne. In 1909, Alfred Stieglitz summoned him to New York for a triumphant exhibition at "291." Maurer returned to Paris, but in 1914 the war wrenched him home. When Margarett met him, he was struggling to paint in a small room in the Hell's Kitchen apartment of his father, a once prosperous Currier and Ives illustrator who held his son's work in cool contempt.

Looking at Maurer's paintings, Margarett saw a style that matched the spirit of Luks's blunt brush sensuality, but she also saw the influence of Paris, which Luks had summarily rejected when the Armory Show turned American dealers toward Europe. Luks, who valued the integrity of work no matter what its school, urged Margarett to buy Maurer. She purchased a watercolor and two oils—one a regally luscious still life—and talked to everyone about the wonderful painter she'd found so despondent in his tiny studio. Weeks later, she got a letter. Maurer thanked her for "having bought more pictures and having influenced more people to buy him in a month than he sold in years." When she began to paint, Margarett would harken in her own portraits to paintings like his 1907 *Woman with Hat*, the planes of her face daubed yellow and red. By then, Maurer would be in his last depression, which ended, after his father's death at one hundred, in suicide by hanging. He was sixty-five.

George Luks was singularly qualified to introduce Margarett to the world of progressive art. During his years in New York, he had been at the center of the great changes that culminated in the Armory Show in 1913. He regaled her with stories that instilled a belief in the importance of what was new. He told her about the Eight, the group of painters of which he and Prendergast were part, which broke the grip of the National Academy of Design and opened American art to subjects outside the world in which Margarett had grown up, the world portrayed by painters of the Boston School and by John Singer Sargent. She learned how, in the wake of the Eight's legendary exhibition and the movement of artists it inspired, the Armory Show had irrevocably altered the circumstances and sensibilities of American art.

In 1907, fresh to New York, Luks had submitted his *Man with Dyed Moustachios* to the annual of the National Academy of Design. Kenyon Cox, juror and critic, took one look and knocked it from its easel, shouting "To hell with it!" Luks's friend the painter Robert Henri took immediate action, resigning from the Academy and seeing to it that the offending painting was exhibited at the Macbeth Gallery on lower Fifth Avenue. Then he approached William Macbeth with the idea of a nonjuried exhibition of painters whose independent ways of seeing and painting had kept them out of the Academy.

Henri, Luks, and three artists who had worked with them in Philadelphia—John Sloan, Everett Shinn, and William Glackens—invited three other anti-academic painters—Arthur B. Davies, Ernest Lawson, and Prendergast—to join them. Each was stylistically distinct. "We've come together because we're so unlike," they told the press, with a snicker at the boilerplate Impressionists. In the months that followed, as John Sloan photographed works for the catalogue and Gertrude Käsebier posed each artist for a publicity shot, the New York critics chose sides. Heavy snow on February 3, 1908, did not deter three hundred people an hour from filing through two small rooms to view the sixty-three paintings, six of them by George Luks. "Vulgarity smites one in the face at this exhibition," *Town Topics* sneered, but hostile reviews were drowned out by the cheers of critics who welcomed Luks's city people, Sloan's back streets, and Davies's symbolist landscapes.

The Eight's exhibition broke the power of the Academy and inspired the movement that culminated on February 17, 1913, when the International Exhibition of Modern Art opened at the 69th Regiment Armory on Lexington Avenue. The Armory Show included many insurgent American artists, but it was the work of the European avant-garde, brought before a large American public for the first time, that changed the course of American art. Until then, Alfred Stieglitz had been the only New York dealer to take notice of what had happened in Paris since the Impressionists. In 1908, he'd shown the late watercolors of Rodin and works by Matisse, both for the first time in America, and in 1911, he'd mounted Picasso's first American one-man exhibition. In 1912, as Margarett led the march at her debutante ball, he showed Marsden Hartley, and during the weeks her bronze of Dan was exhibited at the National Academy of Design, visitors to "291" saw works by the Italian futurist Gino Severini and Georgia O'Keeffe's first one-woman show. By 1917, when Margarett arrived in New York, Stieglitz's contribution had been subsumed in the breaking open wrought by the Armory Show, and European Modernists and their American followers were no longer hard to find.

"He was a mean old bastard," Betty Parsons said of Stieglitz. When she'd asked the price of a John Marin watercolor, he said six thousand dollars when in fact he'd priced it at under three hundred. "He thought I was some kind of socialite, and he didn't like me," she said. In 1919, Margarett made the acquaintance of this "socialite," a young woman from New York and Newport who had been in love with modern art since her governess took her to the Armory Show as a beribboned thirteen-year-old.

When Margarett encountered her, Betty was Betty Pierson, nineteen, and studying sculpture in New York. The Armory Show had instilled in her a passionate and insistent ambition to be an artist, and after a standoff with her stockbroker father, she was allowed to work with Solon Borglum, Gutzon's brother, who had her sketch bones until she was "blue in the face"—not what she had imagined doing when she looked at Bourdelle and Brancusi at the 69th Regiment Armory. Betty was an exquisitely beautiful young woman, small and blond, with startling, very blue eyes. Her figure was boyish, and she was not afraid to swagger. She had a wry sense of humor and a penchant to explore what was on her mind by talking passionately.

Margarett had heard of Betty Pierson; Betty had been seeing Eddie Morgan's brother, Archer, until she broke it off for Schuyler Parsons, whom she chose because he made her laugh. And Betty had heard of Margarett Sargent. She remembered later that Margarett introduced herself at a formal party, approached her across the dance floor. Margarett was a head taller than she and wore, that night, a low-necked gown and white kid gloves nearly to her shoulders. Betty remembered Margarett's black hair and her pale, beautiful skin. "We began to talk," she said. And they didn't stop. Margarett talked about the artists she knew, about Luks, and, Betty remembered, Hartley, Marin, and Arthur Dove, all Stieglitz painters.

The next morning, Margarett sent a bouquet of violets and lily of the valley, "with quite a note." Betty was shocked that a woman would send her flowers, and fell, she admitted, a little in love. Though Betty was eight years younger, Margarett recognized in her someone who was as strong as she; that, more than anything, attracted her. They talked, gossiped, argued, agreed, disagreed. Soon Betty was at Fifty-eighth Street, sitting for Margarett and staying on for supper with Marjorie. "Always the art," Betty said, "but it was an emotional thing too. Margarett used to madden me, madden me, but I always had the utmost admiration for her." They became lifelong friends.

Despite the war, there was a great deal of art activity in New York during the fall of 1918. Margarett had been asked to show her bust of Dan in November as part of "Carry On," an exhibition at the Gorham

Galleries to benefit the war effort. Also among the thirty-five sculptors invited were Bashka Paeff, Daniel Chester French, and Solon Borglum, whose massive war sculpture, riderless horses and men with rifles raised, was to be the show's centerpiece.

In April, Margarett had got a letter from Dan in which he wrote that his French landlady "passes a visit here only in order to be sure that a speck of dirt has not fallen in the kitchen, and that the tongue of the great clock is always swinging to and fro." He wrote his sister only cheerful news, so the letter in which he described his narrow escape at Cantigny during the Americans' first independent offensive went to his brother Frank. The splinter of a shell had ripped into his haversack, pierced his canteen, and halted just short of his ribs at the metal case of his Gillette, "on which it made a memorable dent."

Now that Americans were fighting in earnest, news of casualties was in the air. Margarett passed on a rumor that MacLeish had been killed, which he corrected in a crisp letter to Bangs. Frank's Harvard roommate was killed, as was Margarett's onetime beau Oliver Ames, E. and O.'s brother. Mothers of sons who didn't fight were secretly relieved, but men kept from combat wrote letters tinged with shame. In August, Shaw McKean wrote Margarett from France. He was making the best of "a whale of a job" in the Classification Camp, supervising the suiting up and equipping of replacement troops. Margarett did not respond.

After six months at the front, Dan was assigned to Fort Sill, Oklahoma, as an instructor. Margarett pestered the War Department until they divulged his day of return from Europe, then met him at the pier and brought him, joyously, to Fifty-eighth Street, to see Marjorie and to meet Fanny. She worried about Harry, still in France, who in mid-October had been transferred from supply to combat. "You needn't worry however," Harry wrote their parents, "because you know how many have gone to the front and never got even wounded. Of course my only worry is whether I can make good."

News of Austria's surrender came on November 3, and all the next week New York headlines bannered certain armistice, as Harry's division fought in Pershing's "sensational advance" in the Meuse-Argonne. On November 5, the *Times* ran a report that the retreating Germans had been "told to apply to Foch." On Sunday the Kaiser abdicated, and on November 11, at five A.M., Paris time, peace was signed in French Marshal Foch's private railway car. In New York, Margarett and Marjorie, roused by the tooting of horns and the wailing of sirens, watched from their window as a sailor leaped into the fountain in front of the Plaza Hotel.

"After this armistice I feel like writing everybody," Harry wrote to Margarett from France. Dan, who would soon receive a Croix de Guerre from the French, complained from Fort Sill of a victory parade of artillery regiments and "several thousand students" that filed through the streets of Lawton, Oklahoma: "If only I were in France or in some city where the feeling about the end of the war were not so local, so unpardonably down east." Margarett traveled to Boston for Thanksgiving at Wellesley, and Dan turned up in person. Frank was discharged soon after. On a morning in May, Margarett and Dan were at the pier in New York to meet Harry, finally back from France.

Now that her brothers had come home, Margarett made frequent visits to Boston. She particularly wanted to spend time with Frank, whose state of mind all through the war had worried her. Margarett was not alone. Letters exchanged among the family assessed the degree of his depression. In the summer of 1918, when Dan was home on leave, Frank had seemed happier than at any time since he failed to win his commission, but after the armistice, his swings of mood intensified. He was either overactive and too talkative or sluggish and silent—"so nearly," Margarett wrote years later, "without life." Finally he committed himself to a sanitarium, and after several months was sent home with a male companion. In June 1919, when he visited her in New York, Margarett found him near his old self.

On June 18, two days after he returned home to Dover from New York, Frank was considered well enough to ride out alone. Hours later, the horse came back without a rider, its flanks bloodied. A search party fanned the countryside. On the second evening, David Cheever and his friend Jack Parkinson found the body. Dan always said Frank cut his own throat, Jack that he hanged himself. "I always understood he did both," said David Cheever's grandson. On seeing him, Jack, with some hope, said, "We must cut him down." But David, a surgeon, knew better: "It's a task for the coroner."

Margarett took the train to Boston, where the family, reeling with shock, did not discuss the details of the death. After relating the bare facts of the suicide decades later, Dan looked away, shuddering to keep his composure. All Margarett could think of was how well Frank had seemed in New York—he was her adored oldest brother, her valued adviser, and, when he was himself, her most delightful companion. "She worshiped him, and it haunted her," Margarett's oldest daughter, Margie, said. Margarett returned to New York after the funeral. "I remember she looked so wonderful," Marjorie Davenport said. "She wore mourning with a little widow's turban. Oh, she looked great."

V

I guess I will
marry you

(1919–1926)

Margarett with her family, 1924

Jenny Sargent and Marjorie Davenport were alone in a room upstairs at 40 Hereford Street. Jenny was pacing, opening and closing bureau drawers. "Oh, Marjorie, in life we have lots of experiences, don't we?" she said. It was just weeks after Frank's suicide, and Marjorie and Margarett were visiting Boston. "Yes, I think so," said Marjorie. "I knew I was queer," Jenny continued, using the word to mean something irreparably flawed. She talked about Ruth's death, opened another drawer, took something out, turned to Marjorie. "Well, I never should have married."

But she did not conceive of unmarried life as a solution. Her fear for her daughter, twenty-six and single, was palpable: another child under the spell of her inherited, fatal queerness. She herself had not married until she was thirty, but she'd had no suitor until Frank Sargent. Margarett was glutted with suitors but insisted on her art—something to be tolerated in a girl, but not, Jenny believed, in a woman. Jenny chided and argued; Margarett countered with indignant rage. "Why, you serpent! How dare you!" Or seduction: a perfect scarf from New York, accompanied by a tender note, "Can I do any shopping for you, Mama?"

In July, Margarett left home again. With Marjorie, she rented a tiny cottage at the edge of a dairy farm in Dorset, Vermont. She spent the summer doing watercolors. A local resident, Carleton Howe, home from the war, delivered milk and butter and admired the two young city women, who had such unusual taste. In September, Margarett and Marjorie returned to New York.

• • •

On a Monday in October 1919, in Margarett's studio, a model stands naked. She reaches forward with her left arm, lifts her left foot like a shore bird, holds it at ankle height, balancing. Then she crouches, and Margarett draws her from behind. She sits on the floor, folds her legs beneath her, face forward, one arm high—hand cropped by the paper's edge. She is a large woman, hair knotted at the base of her neck, a narrow ribbon strung around her head like a Greek fillet. Her figure is womanly, but as Margarett draws her, the force of her sensuality is androgynous. Margarett's line is spare, no longer bound to the figure or excused by drapery.

The following day, the model sits as if on a bench or chair, but Margarett leaves out everything but the woman in seated position— elbows resting on her parted knees—quick lines digging at her edges. In another sketch, the model sits, arms folded across her belly, legs crossed like a man's. In another, hands between her knees, she begins to pull open her thighs. Finally she leans to one side, presses a palm to the floor, and with her other hand guides her left thigh, leading her torso into an upward twist. In a sketch Margarett makes the last day of the series, the model stands face forward, hands covering her sex.

At twenty-seven, Margarett was drawing with the line she would use all her life, seeing with an eye that permitted a young woman raised Bostonian to draw a naked woman and her lover writhing on the floor, sketching with a line so economical a woman's eyeless face required just five lines. Because it was 1919, six years after the Armory Show, these drawings are distinguished not only by what they include. "Look!" Betty Parsons said, seeing them for the first time. "Look what she leaves out."

In New York in 1919, Margarett and Betty saw exhibition after exhibition, talked, Betty said, "always about art." Modern art crowded the galleries: in January, Marsden Hartley's pastels of New Mexico; in March, Man Ray and Marguerite Zorach; in May, "Modernists"— Max Weber and John Marin. Margarett cultivated her eye, and Luks continued to mark up her watercolors: "You will notice what I mean in my suggestions on the others, in that the washes are not so cottony in this one."

Margarett had left behind her family, but not her grief. "One simply did not speak of suicide," her daughter Margie said. Asked about his father decades later, Francis Sargent, five when Frank killed himself, said, "I know it will seem strange to you. I really know very little about my father. I was so young when he committed suicide, and my mother *never* spoke to me about him!" Margarett spoke only to those closest to her. "It always came up," Betty said, "sooner or later."

In the night quiet of her studio, the silent pulse of an artist's concentration, the whisper and scratch of a pencil, the grace of a carefully rendered hand, a forceful body, hands folded over sex. The woman who draws is not the clown who coiffed herself with table linen to imitate a vaudeville nun, the beauty who spurned one admirer for another. In the transforming quiet of the night, what infuses her line expresses a deeper self. She draws a face for which a line at the brow suffices for eyes, then a face with no eyes at all. She does not wish to see anything outside this room.

The model's eyes look forward, range to some middle distance, then are lowered. Or they lead the body's movement upward: fear, hesitation; desire awakened; modesty; a reach beyond grief, past what Margarett has lived and known, into imagination.

§

IN MAY, Papa had been ill, unable to come to New York to welcome Harry back from the war. But he'd recovered, the bull-necked loving father who always teased, coddled, and encouraged Margarett, doted on her charm, smoothed the wakes of her Hereford Street departures. They adored each other. In a small scrapbook, she pasted a photo from a magazine—a young woman with black hair, wearing a filmy nightgown, lolls in bed, looking joyously out a morning window. "When did you have this photo taken?" Papa joked hastily across the bottom.

Frank did not entirely understand Margarett, but he trusted her, and he saw in her New York adventures a mirror of his own out west. His attention and trust gave her jocular ease with men and what acceptance she had of her own forceful character. As Jane was Jenny's daughter, Margarett was Frank's. It was he who allowed and encouraged the path of her ambition. He did not know art, but he listened when she talked about what she was doing. His gifts as a storyteller gave him an instinct for what was expressive, and he knew how to look for it in what she did. When Jenny pressed to get Margarett home to marry, Frank turned a bemused ear until his wife abdicated her worry to his overarching confidence in their talented daughter.

On January 16, 1920, Margarett and Marjorie, each with a beau, spent the eve of prohibition with George Luks and his wife. Like much of the city, Luks was in mourning. At one restaurant that night, guests were directed to wear black, tables were draped in black, and black bottles overflowed a casket. At another, each diner took home a miniature coffin. "Instead of passing from us in violent paroxysms," the *New York Times* reported the morning of January 17, "the demon rum lay down to a painless, peaceful, though lamented by some, death."

Early the next morning, there was a call from Hereford Street. Margarett immediately caught a train to Boston.

Even in retirement, Frank Sargent kept to his routine, but one morning in October 1919, after going to Boston on his usual train, he'd telephoned Jenny: "Please come pick me up." His illness progressed quickly. He was bedridden in Wellesley until the family moved to Boston in November. Soon he could not climb the stairs without help. Eventually he could not leave his bed, even for an occasional meal. In late December, Jane Cheever brought his first granddaughter, two week old, to visit. He died on January 17, 1920, and an obituary in the *Transcript*, the paper he read every evening, marked the event with economy: "Francis Williams Sargent died today at his home at 40 Hereford Street, following a severe illness which had been prolonged through two months. He was in his seventy-second year."

Margarett, disoriented by grief, moved back home to be with her mother. At first, Jenny could not speak. When she began to speak again, her boisterous laughter was gone. Her mother Isabella's legacy of depression had always threatened her happiness; now it overcame her, and the strength and stability fostered by thirty-nine years of companionship fell to pieces. More than once when she had grandsons to dinner, she excused herself midsentence and hurried out to the vestibule off the living room. There she wept and fought to compose herself before returning to the parlor with a small, pinched smile.

Margarett thought she would live at home indefinitely. Her father's death had shaken her feeling of safety and moved her to new tenderness for her mother. But Jenny's vulnerability soon gave way to clinging desperation: "To have the children happy is the only bright spot I have before me," she wrote. Over her mother's protests, Margarett returned to New York. She was not the only child who fled. When Dan began to court Louise Coolidge, one of three daughters of J. Templeman Coolidge, a Beacon Street collector and painter, Jenny immediately made it clear this young woman was not an appropriate choice for her now most promising son.

Louise had been frail since the death of her mother, when she was eleven, and her father's remarriage when she was sixteen occasioned the first of three internments in Swiss sanitariums. A marriage of Hunnewell "queerness" to the Coolidge version, manifested most notably in the mental instability of Louise's late uncle Francis Parkman, historian of the West, filled Jenny with dread. Joined by Mr. Coolidge, who agreed his daughter was not marriage material, Jenny emerged from the gauze of bereavement to forbid the union.

To Dan, Louise's delicate blond looks were irresistible. Her jaggedly frail temperament mirrored his own disorientation, her breakdowns his return in nightly dreams to the moans of the dying at Verdun. Louise had briefly nursed wounded soldiers in Paris, and her Catholicism affirmed Dan's own new faith. Priests on the battlefield, the beatific faces of French soldiers as they passed to death, had inspired him to turn from a "naturalistic view of life" and become a Catholic. To his parents, the departure of their heroic son to the hocuspocus faith of their Irish servants had been appalling. Now, supported by his belief and steadied by his distinction as a soldier, Dan brooked a new torrent of family disapproval. His mother had succeeded the first time she obstructed him in love; he would resist her now.

As it turned out, Jenny's anxiety was prophetic. In late winter, Louise collapsed. Dan faltered, but his indecision dissolved by April: their gentle love and Christian faith would return her to sanity. "I cannot wait any longer to send you a line of welcome into the family," Jenny wrote Louise, bowing to the inevitable on black-bordered stationery. In late spring, Louise sailed for Europe. They would marry in August in the sanitarium chapel in Lausanne. Dan booked a first-class stateroom, but when Louise pressed for an earlier date, he left his position as a Harvard tutor. "Sails Steerage for Wedding," read the Boston headline.

Margarett had made some effort to overcome an initial dislike of Louise, but Louise considered her a threat, and it soon became clear that Dan would always accommodate his wife, even if it meant pulling away from his sister. That abandonment of their intimacy and his plans for a year's honeymoon abroad turned Margarett's already ruptured family landscape utterly stark. As the unmarried daughter, she was now expected to return to Boston and take charge of her mother's household. She had no defender against this requirement, just Mama and Jane amplifying an inner, dutiful voice Papa would have freed her to ignore.

What lay before her was the darkened sitting room at 40 Hereford Street, heavy furniture, dreary pea-green upholstery ("shit green," her daughter Margie would call it), fading brocade walls. Or Wellesley: the Hunnewells, from whom her New York life had estranged her, more heavy furniture, hunting prints, her sister Jane ("the compleat Bostonian," E. Ames said) across the street. Margarett had no intention of living with her mother. "I simply couldn't bear the thought of it," she said more than once. "That is why I married."

There was an obvious candidate. Shaw McKean was Bostonian, rich. He was seeing "a girl" in Philadelphia, to whom it was rumored he intended to propose, but he had pursued Margarett for nine years.

She loved his looks, and when he stood up to her, she found him very attractive. He had always lived among paintings and he appreciated them—his final letter from France had rapturously described his officers club, appropriated from an artist, its walls "simply a mass of paintings—a great number of Early Italian. . . . I wish you could see the house & everything just as it is."

Married to him, Margarett could continue her career—he had said, always, that he wanted her to. She could marry in good faith. Shaw would be a wonderful father. They would grow to love each other as devoutly as her parents had done. And, as she put it to Betty Parsons, he was a fine stud. One day during the late winter or early spring of 1920, Margarett picked up the telephone. Shaw was courting in Philadelphia. He was unnerved by what he heard but utterly thrilled. "It's Margarett," she said. "I guess I will marry you." Seven years earlier, she had retreated from marriage to protect her career; now she would marry to defend her independence.

It's not clear when she left New York. She was still there in February when Fanny Brice telephoned: Would Margarett take her daughter, six months old, out into Central Park? Fanny did not want the child at home when the police arrived to question her. Nicky Arnstein, "known internationally as a criminal," the paper said, "having been arrested in Paris, London and Monte Carlo at various times in the last ten years," had now conspired to steal five million dollars in securities from brokerage houses and banks. Margarett walked the baby in a perambulator until she saw the police leave the building hours later. The next day's *Times* headline read: "500 Banks Watch for Arnstein Loot; Quiz Fannie Brice." A month later, Nicky's photograph on "wanted" posters hung in every U.S. post office. By the time he slipped into Fanny's limousine to turn himself in, Margarett had arrived in Boston to meet her betrothed face-to-face.

Shaw's mother awaited her. Unlike Margarett's parents, Marian Haughton had a taste for elegance. She wore beautiful clothes and cherished the paintings, French silver, and import china that had passed down to her through generations. She financially supported the Boston Symphony, would count among her friends its most famous music director, Serge Koussevitzky, and religiously attended its Friday afternoon concerts, all her life purchasing an extra seat for her coat.

Marian's love of style was in part a reaction to her mother, Pauline Agassiz Shaw, who had rescued herself from the depression she suffered as a young wife by committing herself, with her husband's blessing and fortune, to an extraordinary life of service. In 1877, she opened her first kindergarten for poor children, and eventually she supported thirty-one of them. Her day nurseries evolved into the first Boston settlement houses, and in 1897 she became a major contributor to woman suffrage, a position that did not meet with unanimous sympathy in her Boston circles. As a girl, Marian was embarrassed by her mother's philanthropy, but later in her life, when Emma Eames and Myra Hess, refugee musicians from Europe, needed financial help, she quietly provided it.

At twenty-three, Marian married Henry Pratt McKean and moved with him to his gentleman's farm outside Philadelphia. "Harry" was a direct descendant of Thomas McKean, governor of Pennsylvania and a signer of the Declaration of Independence, but his pedigree did not keep the Episcopalians of Philadelphia from ostracizing his Unitarian wife. Marian found no solace in her marriage. Harry was alcoholic; on their wedding night, drunk, he locked the door and chased her, terrified and ignorant of sex, around the bedroom. When her sons were ten and twelve, Marian moved back to Boston and put them in boarding school; when they were safely at Harvard, she took the audacious step of divorce. The experience set her apart—"She was as hard as nails," her grandson Shaw said—and estranged her sons from their father. Eventually Marian married Malcolm Graeme Haughton, a genial, red-haired beau from her school days. She could do what she wanted; in 1913, her income was a million dollars a year.

After his discharge, in December 1918, Shaw McKean had returned to Boston. He'd seen no "action," had spent his months in France as captain of a headquarters troop. In late 1919, his friend George Putnam, at Harvard Business School while Shaw was an undergraduate, asked him to join Richardson, Hill, a brokerage in Boston, "who were at the time," Shaw later wrote, "active in industrial financing." The thousand-dollar monthly salary, extravagant for a beginning partner, made Marian nervous. She suspected that Shaw's interest as an heir to McKean founding shares in the Insurance Company of North America and to Calumet & Hecla copper were a greater factor in his hiring than his potential as a broker. If she warned him, Shaw did not heed her. He began work in December 1919.

Weekends he spent north of Boston in the dark clapboard saltbox he'd purchased with his old friend Bayard Warren and his law school classmate, the songwriter Cole Porter. Eventually he bought them out, moved his registered fox terriers from Marian's estate, and named the place Prides Hill Kennels. When the war threatened to interrupt his polo, he took his ponies along to Fort Devens, Massachusetts. Now he was laying out a polo field next to the house. His social life enlisted those of his generation who weekended and summered, often at their parents' grand houses, in the cluster of seashore towns that by 1909, when President Taft leased a summer White House in Beverly, had become Boston's Gold Coast.

Early in the century, the new industrial rich arrived from New York, bought land, and laid out grand estates, displacing old Boston families. "Goodness!" Katharine Peabody Loring said when Henry Clay Frick offered to buy her house and land. "What on earth would I do with a million dollars?" Frick built a mansion on the ocean in Prides Crossing, behind a hundred-thousand-dollar fence. Frank Sargent had chosen Wareham because the North Shore's opulence offended him, but Marian's family had vacationed there for generations. Even when she lived in Philadelphia, she'd moved her sons to Prides Crossing each June.

When Shaw took Margarett to Prides Hill Kennels, she saw an unusually large old saltbox, fitted up for a bachelor. In the library were foxhunting trophies and silver cups his dogs had won, and throughout the house were paintings he'd inherited from his grandparents' legendary collection—two Corots, a Delacroix, a Rembrandt, an exquisite, tiny Géricault. "The most I can say of him is that he was a good dancer," was how Dan Sargent characterized the Harvard roommate he considered in no way worthy of his sister. Margarett chose Shaw, Dan always believed, in a rage at Jenny, who was predictably relieved her untamed daughter finally became engaged.

Marian Haughton did not share Jenny Sargent's happiness at the match. Ever since Margarett passed over her son for Eddie Morgan in her debutante year, she had hoped Shaw's obsession would run its course. When his trips to Philadelphia indicated that at long last it had, she was delighted. The charms that ignited Shaw left her cold. Margarett Sargent had broken a year-long engagement, and nothing she had done since had retrieved her reputation. Marian had lived with Graeme Haughton before she married him and had sympathy for resistance to certain aspects of Boston propriety, but she objected to what she considered Margarett's brazen disregard for the feelings of other people, particularly those of her son. Finally, and discreetly, she feared Frank Sargent's suicide was evidence his sister's behavior was not bad form merely, but bad blood.

To Shaw, Margarett offered a direct and spirited approach to life. When lived through her, everything had a heady, almost dangerous edge—and she made him laugh. He defended Margarett to his mother, his argument rooted in an intuition he could not put into words. He insisted she was not wanton or mean-spirited, but he had not grasped that the behavior Marian found cruel was an expression of Margarett's genuine desire to protect the freedom she found in art. He argued that in marriage, what he believed to be her confusion would be quieted. Whatever his love and respect for his mother, he would not, in his decision to marry, bow to her wishes.

Shaw's arguments did not calm Marian's fears, but his obvious happiness subdued her protests, and when Margarett arrived at Prides Crossing for Independence Day, she offered an embrace and turned a cool, pale cheek to her future daughter-in-law's kiss. At the close of a fortnight's visit, the engagement of Miss Margarett Williams Sargent and Quincy Adams Shaw McKean was announced on the front page of the *Transcript*. They were married at Kings Chapel two weeks later, on Saturday morning, July 31, 1920.

Kings Chapel, built in 1749, stood on Beacon Hill, blocks from the Bulfinch capitol, with its glinting, gilded dome. Its painted white interior—Corinthian columns rising, enclosed pews with red damask upholstery—was cool on the summer morning, and the sun shone bright through arched, clear-glazed windows. Because of Frank's suicide and Papa's death, the wedding was simple and quiet. That and its haste led to *Town Topics*' catty assessment, "the biggest kind of a surprise." Margarett wore a light-gray traveling suit and a demure gray hat with short lace veil. She carried wild roses. The wedding party was so small she greeted everyone before the ceremony.

Margarett might have chosen Dan to take their father's place at her side, but he was honeymooning in Italy, so her brother Harry gave her in marriage. Shaw slipped a plain gold band onto the finger where she already wore an engagement ring, three large diamonds set simply in gold. Because the Sargents were in mourning, there was no wedding lunch. Margarett and Shaw received embraces and congratulations on the steps outside, then embarked in Marian's touring car, stocked for the day's journey with a picnic and champagne.

That day in New York, Marjorie Davenport had received a telegram: "Leaving for Kings Chapel . . ." Margarett had not told her of the engagement. Marjorie herself would never marry—not because there were no offers, but because she espoused free love. When she quoted Margarett's telegram decades later, remembered feeling drove her voice. If the surprise marriage was not an end to their friendship, it was the end of a domestic arrangement, a shared bed; a farewell, too blithe for Marjorie's feelings, to three years of association that had formed the center of her daily life. Marjorie had known Margarett nearly as long as Shaw had pursued her, and she knew that at the very least, her love for him did not match the quality of his for her.

After the service, sometime past noon, the chauffeur maneuvered the car through the narrow streets of Beacon Hill north to New Hampshire, deep into farming country. As the newlyweds settled into the four-hour trip, the excitement of triumph over family disapproval receded. Suddenly Shaw turned to Margarett. "You think that you married me for my money," he said lightly. "Well, I don't have any; I'm going to live on yours; you'll have to live on your looks."

What Margarett did not know was that the day before the wedding, Calumet & Hecla had plummeted to a six-year low. Nor did she know that Richardson, Hill had entered shaky times and that George Putnam expected Shaw to bail it out. Calumet & Hecla's highs had sustained Marian's vast wealth throughout his memory. This new low reduced her holdings, at least temporarily, but it obliterated Shaw's. "Not all his money was lost," his daughter Margie said, "but a good deal of it." Was the news of financial reversal enough to explain his uncharacteristic outburst? Or did his triumph, so actual now, sitting in his mother's car, fail to calm the anxiety that had lifted for an instant when he heard her voice on the telephone in Philadelphia?

Margarett was unnerved. Once, during their engagement, Shaw had told a riddle as they danced. "What's the definition of dancing?" The coarseness of his answer had scared her—"a naval engagement without a loss of seamen"—but she had never known him to be cruel. She sat quietly as they continued toward their destination, a shingled cottage with a white porch at the edge of a secluded lake. Shaw broke the silence: "Don't expect me to spend much time with you. I shall be fishing. I hope you've brought your paints."

Toward afternoon, he rapped on the dividing window and asked the chauffeur to stop. He carried the picnic hamper as they walked out of sunlight into the cool, dark forest, still dressed in wedding clothes. He placed the hamper on the ground, spread a cloth. Or the chauffeur, walking ahead, carried the hamper, spread the cloth, returned to the car. Alone, the newlyweds sat on the ground, and over her protests, Shaw made love to his wife, a virgin at her marriage. For Shaw, the outdoor encounter was a first exercise of conjugal right, Margarett's resistance anachronistic, even coy. For her, it was something else. She hardly knew what she felt as she rose, brushed forest debris from her wedding suit, smoothed wrinkles, composed herself in order to face the chauffeur. More than once, when she spoke of the incident, she used the word "rape."

Over a woman drawn with sketchy lines, loose hair pulled up, downward-looking face half hidden by a cloak, Margarett applied watercolor wash—a faint red to the hair and, to the drapes of the cloak, pale yellow and then pale blue. She dated the watercolor November 23, 1920. Just a year before, alone with a model in her New York studio, she had drawn a woman naked, moving through a room, self-possessed and self-assured, sensuality infused with calm power. Her direct, single line had been simple but also curious and willing. A face achieved with five lines hid nothing. What was economy there had become lassitude—lines for eyes uncommitted, a mouth in shadow. Margarett wrapped the woman in a shroud and hid her hands. This watercolor is the only surviving work from the months after she married.

After spending their first summer at Prides, Margarett and Shaw moved to the Agassiz Hotel on Commonwealth Avenue, not far from Jenny, at the corner of Hereford Street, or Marian, across from the Ritz. Margarett leased a studio at 30 St. Botolph Street in the South End, a street where Frank Benson, Philip Hale, and Edmund Tarbell had all painted at one time or another. There, recovering from the rupture of her father's death and adjusting to marriage, she resumed her work. She continued to sign herself "Margarett Sargent," though in what society pages called "private life" she was now Mrs. Quincy Adams Shaw McKean.

"They were spellbinding walking into a room," was a frequent description of the new couple. He was slightly taller than she, his dark hair pomaded to the curve of his handsome head, and he had his mother's long nose and dark-blue eyes. The tall woman on his arm was given to wearing black or white to set off the strong contrasts in her own coloring—hair nearly black against very pale skin and dark-lashed pale eyes. Their physical allure was set to music in the unusual grace of their dancing and set off by the care and elegance with which they dressed.

Margarett's sensibility, refined by her years in New York, gave her a sophistication that seemed exotic in Boston, and she had what were always described as *beautiful* manners. "Drop dead attractive, I mean it," said C.Z. Guest, born and brought up as Cizzie Cochrane in Boston in the twenties.

One of Margarett's new friends was C.Z.'s mother, Vivian Cochrane, whose husband, Alexander, older by twenty years, had plucked her, young and blond, from the cast of a Broadway musical. When they were all in their cups after dinner at Prides, Vivian might perch on the grand piano, strike a pose, and sing a song from her chorus girl past. She had something of the toughness that attracted Margarett in Fanny Brice; with this Boston outsider, Margarett had more in common than with her girlhood friends. She and Vivian laughed at the same jokes and ridiculed the same conventions. Margarett christened Vivian "VV," and Vivian returned the compliment with "Big Marge." When they met, Vivian had just had her first daughter. By April, Margarett was pregnant.

Pregnancy did not keep her from working—in the studio, or on the grounds at Prides Hill. When Margarett arrived as a bride, the house stood in a fallow field, electrical poles askew, no trees except for a large old elm out front. Her grandfather Hunnewell's gardens at Wellesley began as a cow pasture; this was no worse. Mr. Coughlin came with his horses to plow up the witchgrass, and Margarett's imagination was stirred, as much as by clay or a blank sheet of drawing paper. She went to Wellesley to look again at her grandfather's gardens, her eyes hungry for inspiration. She visited her cousin Charles Sprague Sargent at the Arnold Arboretum and took home a shrub, *Tsuga canadensis "Sargenti,"* a weeping hemlock named for their cousin Henry Winthrop Sargent, who had first collected it.

At Prides, Margarett planted the hemlock as if the act were sacred, as if digging it in assured her landscape a place in the Sargent and Hunnewell horticultural pantheon. The feel of earth relieved her like the feel of clay. She began to get up early to work outdoors, made friends of the men who helped her in the garden, always sharing with

them what she was learning about particular trees and shrubs. When
Betty Parsons came for the weekend, she enlisted her to plant tulips.
She got Shaw to dig holes for new trees and wait as she determined the
most aesthetic placement. In the next fifty years, Margarett planted
almost as many trees at Prides as Grandpa Hollis had in seventy-five
at Wellesley. Her gardens would rival his in ambition, and horticulture would become for her, as it had for him, a source of exhilaration.
Soon a wide and sumptuous perennial border curved out into the new
lawn, clematis framed the doorway, and a riot of zinnias edged the
front walk.

     In the spring, the foundation was laid for an addition to the house.
A studio for Margarett, its beamed ceiling broken by skylights, would
soar to two stories. A loggia, eight French doors opening onto a garden, would connect the addition to the old saltbox, and upstairs there
were to be two new bedrooms. The architect, Joe Leland, his Harvard
sensibility burnished at the Sorbonne and by years in Paris, was inspired by the fervor of Margarett's imagination; in the next ten years,
he would spin from the seventeenth-century saltbox an unlikely American version of a Florentine villa. He considered Margarett a collaborator. "She thinks like a man," he said. He considered the house at
Prides the crown of his career.

§

BY THE TIME Fanny Brice and the *Follies* arrived in Boston at the end
of September 1921, Margarett and Shaw had moved to Marian's
house to avoid the construction at Prides and await the baby. The new
show was Fanny's triumph—"She has the fattest lines and the skinniest
legs in the troupe," the *Variety* critic wrote. "It is," he continued, "by
far the most conspicuous work this veteran funner has ever offered."
She played a lanky George Carpentier boxing tiny Ray Dooley as Jack
Dempsey, and Ethel Barrymore as La Dame aux Camellias to W. C.
Fields's John Barrymore and Ray Hitchcock's Lionel. At the end of the
evening, alone on a bridge across a painted Seine, she brought down
the house singing, full voice and as herself, a new number adapted

from a French *diseuse* tearjerker. In the wake of months of headlines about Nicky's incarceration, "My Man" was a sensation.

On Halloween night, Marian's immense shingled house, empty for the evening, burned to the ground. On November 1, Shaw turned thirty, and on November 2, Margarett gave birth to her first child, a daughter, Margarett Sargent McKean, at the Phillips House, a smaller hospital attached to Massachusetts General. There Margarett slept on her own linens and had her meals sent in; her infant was watched over by Miss Barron, her private baby nurse. When she returned to the Agassiz Hotel with the infant Margie, a pair of tiny red shoes awaited them, a gift from Fanny, gone with the *Follies* on to Philadelphia.

Miss Barron, nicknamed "Ba," changed the diapers, and Margarett attended Margie with sketchbook and pad, pencil and watercolor: dash of pencil for an eye, looped scribble for a mouth. She had fallen in love—with the sensual pleasures of taking care of a baby, with the creative rush of forming a child's sensibility. When Ba brought Margie to the studio, Margarett wrote pages of poems on 30 St. Botolph Street stationery, which she illustrated with sketch after sketch of her namesake's round-faced prettiness:

> You're such a happy baby
> I'd like to be one too,
> It's easier to be big like me,
> Than to be good like you.

At home, she took the baby into her bed and read to her—"*Romeo and Juliet* by the time I was two," Margie said later. Margie's earliest memory was not her nanny's ministrations but the fragrance of her mother's bedclothes and the deep sound of Margarett's voice reading Shakespeare. It became a matter of passionate principle to Margarett that her daughter not learn merely by rote, as she had at Miss Winsor's. She determined to bring her children early to the excitement of learning awakened in her at Miss Porter's.

Shaw was, as Margarett had predicted, a loving and enthusiastic father, and in the transforming aura of Margie's birth, Margarett became, briefly, a devoted wife and a doting daughter-in-law. Unaccountably, everything fell together. She celebrated Marian in baby poems:

> Grandma's fingers are just ten
> But they seem a hundred, when
> She plays game for Baby!
> Churches, tables even chairs
> Grandma makes while baby stares . . .

In the late summer of 1922, the addition to Prides was completed and Margarett moved her clay bins and sculpture stands into the new studio. By September, she was pregnant again, and in November, George Luks telephoned. He arrived on the train, freshly divorced, just out of a sanitarium after a bout with alcohol. Neither the divorce nor the binge was a surprise to Margarett. Emma Luks had initiated the divorce; the settlement—dozens of his best paintings—sent Luks out on a ten-day drunk. When he got to Prides, he was physically broken and penniless, with no paintings to sell.

Margarett was shocked at how frail he looked, and immediately began to buoy him up. "How *could* that awful woman harass and torment you so!" Because she was pregnant and working at Prides, she insisted he take her St. Botolph Street studio. By the time she moved to Boston at Christmas, Luks had fallen in love: "I have lived in Paris and all those other places, but there is nothing like Boston!" The city, he said, preserved what New York had "wiped out with the onrush of events." He painted Commonwealth Avenue, governesses and children in the snow. He painted Kings Chapel as a looming monolith in a crush of narrow streets, a rebuke to the Boston painters who haloed landmarks in Impressionist fuzz. As the warm weather came, he painted swan boats in the Public Garden, prostitutes on Malcolm Street on a languid summer night.

Through Luks's eyes and in his headlong drawings, Margarett saw a living city sheared of Back Bay claustrophobia: Copley Square darted at with pencil, sailors lounging with girls in the Common, naked bathers at the L Street pier. She could watch Shaw's polo as Luks's pencil caught it—players, mallets, horses at full gallop—the dense rhythm of the game rather than niceties between chukkas, the preen and gloat of competitors.

Shaw appreciated the grit of Luks's painting. He guffawed at his nonstop jokes, and continued to welcome him as his visit extended through the spring into the summer. Luks spiced Margarett's dinner parties with his irreverence—he joked with the men, flattered the women, and cut loose occasionally to a barroom. Dan found him "a bruiser" but was enthralled when he illustrated the margins of his book-length poem about Noah's ark.

Soon after his arrival, Luks was elected an honorary member of the Boston Art Club. Edmund Tarbell told a story for years of Luks turning up at a club dinner with a black eye and a torn shirt. "Sorry I'm late," Luks announced. "I couldn't find my collar button." The club men were less tolerant of his painting. In midwinter, John T. Spaulding, a Boston collector, lent Luks's vertiginous *Wrestlers* to the club for exhibition. The huge painting depicted two men, bodies straining in a visceral grip threateningly close to the viewer. "The works wreaks [*sic*] not with perspiration, as I might more politely say," sputtered the *Transcript*, "but with common sweat."

Margarett and Luks were aware that the conservatism the Eight had vanquished in New York lived on in Boston. Just that February, Tarbell's first show in four years had drawn twelve thousand viewers in two weeks. Harley Perkins, a 1909 graduate of the Museum School, combated the thrall of the Boston School with John Marin–influenced abstraction; since the Armory Show, he and other younger artists had fought an uphill battle to bring progressive art to Boston. When Margarett announced a Luks exhibition at Prides, Perkins trumpeted her effort in the *Transcript*, of which he was junior art critic. He also noted that Mrs. McKean, the sculptor Margarett Sargent, evidenced "in her artistic efforts a sympathetic understanding of the full free manner which characterizes the work of the painter."

For five afternoons, Ameses, Cochranes, Searses, and others to whom Margarett sent printed cards, clustered by the light of Joe Leland's north-facing skylights to see George Luks's Boston: a lone vendor shouting up to a resident on Mount Vernon Street, the riotous bustle of a Saturday night market in the immigrant North End, roustabouts striking a circus before dawn. Margarett had hoped for a Boston run on George Luks, but only John Spaulding made a purchase. She vowed that when the time came, she would show her work not in the backwater of Boston but in New York.

On March 12, 1923, Margarett gave birth to a second child, my mother—a black-haired, bright-eyed daughter whom she named Jenny. When Jenny Sargent, still wearing black, came to her namesake's christening, Margarett posed the baby for a photo on her lap in a long white dress. Jenny's evident pleasure, as she tipped a parasol to protect the infant from the sun, was momentary. Mourning her husband and son had become a chronic and debilitating depression akin to what had institutionalized her mother. Since her husband's death, she had abdicated leadership of the family to Dan and to Jane's husband, David Cheever. The departures of her children into their own lives, no matter how physically close their residences, left her full of dread. She had never recovered her laugh. Now she was almost always soft-spoken, given to whispering a quick "much obliged" in response to any kindness. Even her daily visits to Jane failed to stem her melancholy. Finally her children sent her to Dr. Edgerly's in Concord, a sanitarium that offered basket weaving, quiet, and not much else.

Left with nothing to battle in her mother, Margarett ministered to Jenny with an ebullience that infuriated the Cheevers. She'd arrive at Wellesley, little girls in tow, with abundant and luxurious gifts—a piece of jewelry, a dress her sister Jane would never have chosen. After a few hours, she'd depart, leaving behind ideas for brightening the parlor, or opinions on the employment of chauffeurs, suggestions for the resentful David Cheevers to carry out.

In 1921, after a Christmas of profligate bonuses, Richardson, Hill again fell on hard times, and Shaw shored it up with half a million dollars of his McKean inheritance. When the company failed completely two years later, Shaw did not declare bankruptcy. Instead, he paid back the investors he could from what remained of the inheritance and borrowed the balance from the Boston bank of which he was a third-generation client. The debt was not cleared until he inherited half of Marian's fortune more than thirty years later.

Shaw spoke of his bad luck only to those who had to know: his mother and his brother. He had a gentleman's inclination to spare his wife worldly troubles and concerns, and Margarett a lady's corresponding lack of interest in finance. She knew only that Shaw's contributions to the household now came entirely from his mother. Throughout their marriage, Marian provided an ample monthly allowance, capitalized additions to the house, and was consulted on all family matters, even those that did not involve money. If the monthly disbursement ran low, Margarett, drawing on the trust her father had left, wrote Shaw a check. Later, when she inherited money from her mother, Shaw's secretary, John Spanbauer, would drive up from Boston with checks for payment of household bills, typed and ready for her signature.

Shaw never recovered from the failure of Richardson, Hill. All his life he resented George Putnam, whom he watched rise from the ashes of disaster and move on as if there were no such thing as adversity. Shaw had been brought up in untold luxury and was used to having his own money. The fact that his finances were now controlled by his mother, and therefore limited, irritated him. When asked what he did, he replied that he "engaged in what might be termed private banking . . . placing going businesses either with investment banks or with businesses that wished to expand."

He took on several enterprises, but their exact nature was always obscure and there were no evident profits. In spite of his social charm, he could be tactless and insensitive in business unless a partnership had the feel of sporting companionship. His most conspicuous reversal was the collapse of an effort to capitalize a chain of restaurants for Howard Johnson, a loss he always described as a swindle at his expense. He had, his daughter Jenny wrote, "a Boston arrogance, just missing eccentric-

1. Margarett, aged four, with her family. *L. to r.*, Jenny (Mama) pregnant with Ruth, Harry, Young Frank, Jane, Dan, Frank (Papa), and Margarett.

2. Two hired men hoist the family's catch the summer before Margarett's sister Ruth was killed. *Front, l. to r.*, Margarett, Ruth, and Dan. *Rear,*   Mama and Papa.

3. Margarett became the most sought-after leading man at Miss Porter's School.

4. RIGHT: Margarett as a Renaissance portrait by Abrogio de Predis, at finishing school in Italy.

6. Against the wishes of her mother, Margarett became engaged to Eddie Morgan, *c. L.*, Margarett's brother Harry; *r.*, Styve Chanler.

5. Q.A.S. "Shaw" McKean began his eight-year courtship of Margarett at her debut ball in 1912. This 1917 portrait is by John Singer Sargent.

7. RIGHT: Margarett's adored older brother, Frank, just before he killed himself in 1919.

8. Margarett worked for Gutzon Borglum, the sculptor of Mount Rushmore, at his studio estate in Connecticut. Here, she sculpts her dog, Pilgrim.

9. George Luks's 1919 portrait of Margarett, *The White Blackbird*.

10. Ziegfeld's star comic Fanny Brice and her gangster husband, Jules "Nicky" Arnstein. Margarett became Fanny's confidante.

11. For this portrait of her mentor, George Luks, Margarett earned her first serious praise from the New York critics. *(Bronze, 1918, ht.: 38.1 cm. Gift of Frederic C. Bartlett, 1928. 707. Photograph © 1994, The Art Institute of Chicago. All rights reserved.)*

12. LEFT: Margarett's roommate and frequent subject, Marjorie Davenport.

13. ABOVE: Betty Parsons, artist and renowned dealer. Their meeting sparked a lifelong friendship.

14. Margarett's Boston studio became her retreat. After twin sons were born in 1924, she was the mother of four children under three. The plaster reliefs were exhibited at her first New York show in 1926.

15. Prides, spun from a seventeenth-century saltbox, was designed by Joseph Leland.

16. Margarett's four children, *(l. to r.)* Shaw, Jr., Margie, Jenny, and Harry shoveling snow in front of the McKeans' Boston townhouse.

17. Margarett and Shaw at the Myopia Hunt Club, after their return from the year spent in Europe to repair their marriage. "She took to affairs," said Margarett's friend Mrs. Henry Cabot Lodge, "as easily as to brushing her teeth."

18. The catalogue of Margarett's last New York show, in 1931, illustrated with a portrait of her friend Harpo Marx. Soon after, she stopped painting.

MARGARETT SARGENT

C. W. KRAUSHAAR ART GALLERIES
680 FIFTH AVENUE, NEW YORK

JANUARY 3rd to 17th
1931

EZRA STOLLER © ESTO

19. The great hall at Prides, built to be Margarett's studio, became a gallery where she displayed her treasures—by Gauguin, Calder, Degas, Lachaise, and others.

20. Margarett and *(r.)* her close friend Vivian Pickman, a New York chorus girl turned Boston socialite. They fell out in the 1940s over Margarett's drinking.

Margarett often sketched her lovers.

21. The French art dealer Roland Balay

22. The sportswoman and "notorious lesbian" Isabel Pell

23. LEFT: Shaw's cousin by marriage, Florence Shaw, with her Pekingese dogs

24. The writer Jane Bowles, half Margarett's age when they became involved in 1944

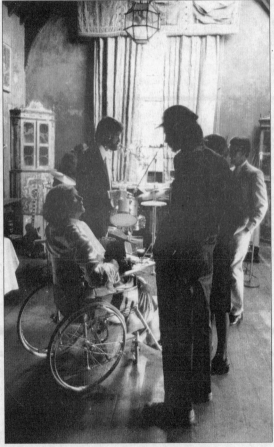

25. ABOVE: The family at Shaw's forty-fifth birthday party. Margarett turned the great hall into a stable, and brought a donkey and a horse through the entrance originally built to accommodate outsized sculpture.

26. After the years of breakdown and loss, Margarett began a new life, entertaining artists, old friends, lovers, and family. At eighty, she gave a final party at Prides.

ity, which convinced him bad times were bad dreams—most of the time." His son Shaw put it more bluntly: "He was a born loser."

Spanbauer got the telephone call at Shaw's office in Boston, someone from Prides summoning Shaw home to see to Mrs. McKean. Or Margarett, weeping, called Dan, and Dan called Shaw at his office. Dan would say only that "sometimes Margarett behaved very badly." Spanbauer put it more directly: "At times she drank a little bit." Shaw would leave the office immediately, take the train to Prides "to quiet things down." If Margarett had drunk too much at lunch, he would put her to bed. If she was lying down, he sat at her bedside and talked to her.

Naked of confidence and will, she seemed again to be the isolated child with a mysterious illness, blanketed in a deck chair on the seaside porch at Wareham. Nothing Shaw said or did could comfort the old despair, which tugged like an undertow: brothers fleeing her red-faced crying, hands over their ears; headaches at Farmington; the mornings, her debutante year, she awoke "feeling deathly" and stayed in bed. Marjorie Davenport remembered sharp rebukes and black moods, but "of course, in the early days, she didn't drink." Dan became familiar with this particular distress. It started, he said, "only after her marriage to Shaw McKean."

As time went on, Margarett learned to navigate her circumstances. Though her parents' devotion was her ideal, it was not possible for her to surrender without conditions, as her mother had, to marriage and motherhood. Nor was she the sort of woman who could calmly accept the imperfection of her situation and adjudge her marriage "an arrangement." Instead, the relationship became a battleground. Margarett tried to change Shaw, and he tried to change her. His desires were simpler than hers. He loved his children, his dogs, his gardens, his sporting life. He expected Margarett's artistic nature to enhance his domestic arrangement, and it did; but he assumed what she did in her studio would remain there, and it did not. In the moment Margarett decided to become Shaw's wife, she believed she could satisfy him and that, in exchange, he would conform to her specifications. As it turned out, neither was able or willing to change, and neither could forgive the other. Shaw was in the wrong marriage, but Margarett was in the wrong life.

Margarett was also a creature of her historical moment. On the crest of suffrage, the 1920s had promised new opportunity for women, but in fact, Margarett was as reined in as her mother had been as a young matron. Even her older sister, Jane, a woman without Margarett's talent or temperament, felt thwarted by the administration of an upper-class Boston household, the complexity of which—servants, multiple houses, and entertaining—required a great deal and returned little. One did not, after all, engage in domestic tasks that might offer actual satisfaction—the handling of food, the small attentions to the needs of one's children.

Nothing has survived in Margarett's words from these years—no diary, no letter to Luks, no testimony from Betty Parsons, who had moved to Paris to sculpt after divorcing her husband. Instead, there is a self-portrait called *Distance*. Margarett has drawn her expression as fearful. She wears a smock. She clasps two large brushes, right hand over left, to her breast. The pastoral surroundings indicate that she intended she be seen as contemplative, but how her hands hold the brush, the angle of her head turning to the right, the degree to which her eyes strain right, as if what is behind her could come into view, contradict the serenity in the drape of the smock, the ease of her line, the Vermont hillside stretching out behind her.

In early spring of 1924, Margarett supervised the planting of an arborvitae hedge to enclose the new swimming pool at Prides. At one end, she placed her sculpture of Pilgrim, so he could gaze into the water at his reflection. In January, she had become pregnant, and in the spring learned she was going to have twins. By early summer, she could no longer walk unassisted. A new phase of work on the house was completed—the octagonal tower, with its mirrored interior, and a new master bedroom. In August, Margarett hired horses and a flatbed wagon and moved Marian's music room, the only outbuilding to survive the fire, to a wooded hill at Prides. Her studio had evolved into a living room; with two small daughters and the two babies on the way, it would be utterly impossible to work in the house.

In mid-September, Margarett went to the hospital and, on Sunday, September 22, with some difficulty, gave birth to two boys, Quincy Adams Shaw McKean, Jr., and Henry Pratt McKean II, named for Shaw's brother. Now thirty-two, she had four children under three years old. "May God bless the wonderful mother, the twins & the distinguished father," Luks wrote. Margarett was exhilarated. The twins proved her talent for motherhood to be as protean as her other gifts. "I don't remember what time you were born," she said to her daughter Jenny years later; "I remember only when I had two sons."

The household was already staffed by cook, kitchen maid, waitress, parlormaid, upstairs maid, lady's maid, valet, kennelman, laundress, chauffeur, gardener, and two stable hands. Now it became a circus of doubles: double nurses, double pram, double bassinet. To look after Margie and Jenny, Margarett hired a governess, an eighteen-year-old girl from Manchester named Catherine Neary, whom Margie christened "Senny." In early summer, Margarett posed the twins' baby nurses, photographing them, each with an infant on her left hip, each with a little girl at her side holding a brother's tiny foot.

That winter, Margarett returned to the studio. The chaos of her household had changed her work. Her new sculptures were of women, but not of living models like the 1919 drawings for which a woman's physical motion had provided suspense and surprise. Nor were they documents of volubility and exchange, like the head of Luks. Working in plaster and in two dimensions, Margarett began to make reliefs, studies of the female figure that were mysterious and quiet. Until now, she had used sculpture as a way into character and passion; now, with large figures that represented no one in particular, she explored silence and contemplation.

As the plaster set in a freestanding wood frame six feet high, Margarett textured its surface to hold the wet plaster she would add later and model into relief. As that plaster thickened from the consistency of milk to the feel of heavy cream, and then to a paste almost as dense as clay, she raced its loss of malleability, feeling on her hands the heat it gave off as it hardened. Across the surface she modeled drapery—a rhythmic roil of plaster—and the rising contours of face and hand. Next, she incised the surface—long sweeping lines for drapery, short lines for eyebrow or mouth, an edged-in pattern for the roughness of hair. Finally, at the suggestion of Luks, who, she told a reporter, "claimed the Greeks had employed it," she tinged the panel with color to achieve an effect "faintly reminiscent of Pompeiian frescoes and Egyptian tomb decorations."

A seated woman takes up the entire surface of *The Wheel*, spokes opening behind her. Fifteen nudes move through a mythic forest scribed onto a second panel. When the third relief—three standing figures, Graces or Fates, classically draped, each facing a different direction—is viewed from a distance, the women become one form, a huge amaryllis-like flower, opening. "To a remarkable degree," Harley Perkins wrote after he saw the panels at the studio on St. Botolph Street, "they seem to express the quite natural and unaffected unfolding of their creator's thought." By the end of the winter, Margarett was ready to show.

❧

THE SEASON of Margarett's first New York exhibition was marked by two events. In December 1925, Alfred Stieglitz opened his first gallery since he closed "291" in 1918. The Intimate's first exhibition was of John Marin, followed by Arthur Dove in January and, in February, Georgia O'Keeffe—large flower paintings and one cityscape. But Stieglitz's American modernists were no longer isolated in their innovation; other New York galleries that winter exhibited Chagall, Archipenko, and Fujita.

The second event was a memorial exhibition of the collection of John Quinn, the explosive red-haired lawyer of Irish descent who had represented the organizers of the Armory Show and defended James Joyce's *Ulysses* against obscenity charges in 1921. "Art World Amazed at Contents of Quinn Memorial," read a front-page *Art News* headline on January 2, 1926. Below it reclined Henri Rousseau's *The Sleeping Gypsy,* and an alphabetical inventory—Braque, Cassatt, Cézanne, Picasso, Prendergast, et cetera—enumerated works offered in the first sale to test the market for the Post-Impressionists. After a year of sales in New York and Paris, the proceeds totaled a stunning, for the time, $700,000. The "artistic anarchists" of whom Kenyon Cox warned after the Armory Show were now worth real money.

American museums and a new generation of American collectors scurried to catch up. The 1920s were the years in which "Modern Art" would make it way into the American mainstream, displacing forever the sensibilities that had nurtured Margarett as a young artist. The gallery where she chose to exhibit, and with which she had a six-year association, embraced Luks and his contemporaries, while looking abroad to the School of Paris, the painters who would be her later influence.

Margarett had met John Kraushaar through Luks when she lived in New York, but she must have approached him herself when she wanted a show, because by 1925, Luks was exhibiting elsewhere. Kraushaar was Luks's contemporary—they had met as young men playing scrub baseball on Long Island—and nine days after the Armory Show closed, he'd opened Luks's first one-man show. The Kraushaar Galleries, founded in 1885 by John's older brother, Charles, made its reputation showing nineteenth-century paintings by French and Dutch artists, but when John joined the business, he began to acquire French modernists—Matisse, Rouault, eventually Modigliani and an occasional Picasso. By the time Margarett came to New York in 1918, he also showed Sloan, Glackens, and Prendergast, all members of the Eight. After Charles died, in 1918, John took over the gallery, by then one of the three or four most important in the city. He continued to exhibit French paintings and, from time to time, showed American modernists like Marsden Hartley and Gaston Lachaise. The year of Margarett's first show, he began his season with John Sloan and ended it with a group that included Constantin Guys, Maurice Vlaminck, and Aristide Maillol.

Margarett's first one-person exhibition opened on March 1, 1926. It was advertised in seven newspapers, and five hundred announcements, illustrated with *The Wheel*, were mailed. The catalogue listed twelve watercolors and four sculptures. *Town Topics* hadn't had so much to say about Margarett Sargent since her broken engagement: "the fascinating Mrs. Q. A. Shaw McKean, known to the artistic world at Margaret [*sic*] Sargent, is showing her things this week at the Kraushaar Galleries in New York. . . . While Margaret has her art, Shaw has his dogs which he loves almost as much as she loves her creations."

The watercolors, the three large plaster reliefs, and the bronze head of the Mouquin headwaiter, Chaffard, were installed in one of the gallery's two rooms. Among the watercolors were the self-portrait *Distance* and a portrait of George Luks, which *Art News* praised for its economy: "hardly more than a soft brown hat." The panels were priced at $1,000, the head at $500, and the watercolors between $50 and $200. Two watercolors sold, *Distance* and *Birches*—a woman in a purple jacket standing in a grove of the white trees. To Antoinette Kraushaar, in her early twenties and working as her father's stenographer, Margarett seemed terribly glamorous: "She had a *lot* of admirers." But she didn't remember talking to her: "She couldn't have been, probably, less interested in me."

The critics greeted Margarett warmly. Several remarked on the likenesses of Luks and Chaffard, whom they knew from Chez Mouquin. Henry McBride found "an innovation" in the surfaces of her plaster panels, *Art News* praised her "amazing talent for leaving out of her delicate watercolors all that is not strictly essential," and the *Herald Tribune* spoke of "the glamor of a new and ingratiating talent." Helen Appleton Read, the only woman critic to review the show, wrote a long piece in the *Brooklyn Eagle*. She saw in "the movement of the body suggested by a great sweeping curve, the head by a simple egg shape," that Margarett had "observed the beauties of abstract sculpture with profit to herself." She praised her freedom in the face of Modernism, "a tyrant," she said, "to which scarcely a talent has not paid homage."

Read was the only critic to refer to the fact that Margarett was a woman. She had struggled with the issue of femininity in a review of Georgia O'Keeffe's flower paintings in 1924 and, in writing about Margarett's watercolors, raised it again, drawing the vague conclusion that the artist's gender was evident and, as with Berthe Morisot, Marie Laurencin, and Mary Cassatt, "a full half of her distinction." But it was the quality of her line, Read concluded, that was Margarett Sargent's "most striking characteristic, her outstanding contribution as an artist."

Margarett had achieved what she envisioned for herself when she turned aside Eddie Morgan, and neither the death of her father, marriage, nor the quick arrival of four children had obstructed her way. Now, at thirty-three, her first show mounted by one of the most prominent dealers in New York and welcomed by the critics, she was not only an exhibiting sculptor but "that rare apparition," an enraptured critic wrote, "a stranger coming here wholly unheralded and yet with an astonishing number of things to say for herself."

vi

It was a time of hope,
that was the thing

(1927–1930)

Margarett at Prides, c. 1928

HER LINE RUSHES as if attracted to each object in the room: the dark wood bed frame, its tall, ornamental headboard; a small American bedside table—on it, telephone, tumbler, pocket watch; a child's chair at bedside; pictures on the wall; a woman's shoes askew on the floor; the bed itself, linens rumpled, a hat hurled on mussed pillows—all sketched with charcoal. Then, as if composing a variation, she lays in pastel: white-green striates walls, buff paper shows through where light doesn't reach; sky-blue diamonds on the seat of the chair, black telephone rendered blue, white-green to model one pillow, heavy cream etching curves of another, bright white for the creases of sheets, all leading the eye to two garments—one rose, the other robin's-egg blue—slung on a bedpost toward the lower right of the drawing. Below, on the slightly tilted floor, the shoes—black with rose insides.

If you enter the room, you see something else: an artist at work, tray of pastels set out beside her, paper on a small easel. This was the bedroom Margarett shared with Shaw, but his bed is not in the picture. In this room, its walls lined with silk, there were two Venetian beds, one unlike the other; Margarett has left out her husband's. What you see is a woman's sleeping room, sunlight falling across the voluptuous shapes of an unmade bed, sheet, pillow, beautifully made nightclothes.

"There were five, six, or seven remotely happy years," Margie said of her parents' marriage. "It was a terribly abnormal, strained, difficult, tenuous relationship," said young Shaw. And Harry, his twin: "I never knew any happiness between them, ever."

In 1927, when Margarett reencountered Eddie Morgan, Margie was six, Jenny four, and the twins three. As they got older, they became aware that their parents led separate lives, that Margarett had many affairs, and that Shaw, in spite of an abiding fascination with his wife, had, as young Shaw put it, "his share of girlfriends." Eventually they learned that Margarett was once engaged to someone named Eddie Morgan, but never that she saw him again, except to arrange for his two sons to come to Prides and play—"they could run very fast," Jenny remembered, "and had mysteriously dark eyes."

"It went on for quite a while," said Eddie Morgan's son. Years. "There were even rumors that Shaw McKean went down to Philadelphia to dig them out of some hotel." Eddie had become a partner in the Wall Street brokerage Richard Whitney and Company, which traded for big banks and big clients, notably J. P. Morgan and Company. In 1927, he was thirty-seven years old: black hair slicked back, handsome face symmetrical enough to carry off a part down the center of his widow's peak. He'd handily paid off the eighty thousand Mike Vanderbilt lent him to buy a seat on the New York Stock Exchange and had made a quick fortune in steel stocks. Now he ran what his son called "the Old Westbury rat race—social life and alcohol."

In just a few years, the sheen of luck would be off Eddie Morgan's life. His wife would die in 1934, just months after Eddie, knowing she was terminally ill, announced to her his plans to leave her for her best friend. In 1938, Richard Whitney, whose efforts to stem the fall at the stock exchange late Black Thursday had earned him its presidency five years in succession, would defraud his clients of more than a million dollars to shore up the applejack distillery in which he had a controlling interest. Eddie, innocent of knowledge or complicity, would read the news on the front page of the *New York Times*; Whitney would go to Sing Sing, his wife and daughters to work. Bankrupt and socially disgraced, Eddie would move his new wife, her two children, and his to a Maryland farm purchased for him by a group of friends, Dan Sargent among them.

But in 1927, Lybba Morgan was alive and beautiful, Richard

Whitney trading in a booming market, and Eddie eager to pursue the woman who had broken his youthful heart. "The old man told the story more than once," said Eddie Morgan, tall and dark like his father. Margarett would come to New York and check into a hotel. She would telephone, and he'd be summoned from the floor of the stock exchange. " 'Eddie, I'm here,' she'd say in that deep voice, and he'd leave the floor and go shack up with her." Young Eddie was a bit embarrassed to report the detail his father most often boasted of: Margarett would arrive in New York, check into a hotel, telephone, and Eddie would rush from the floor of the New York Stock Exchange "with an erection."

Margarett was, as Betty Parsons put it, "a highly sexed woman." "She took to affairs," her old friend Emily Lodge said, "as easily as to brushing her teeth." War and the reality of her marriage had sundered all obligation to her parents' expectations. The difficulty of the twins' birth had prompted her obstetrician to prescribe an abortion when she got pregnant in 1927 and, soon after, in spite of her desire for more children, a hysterectomy, which, she said, "made me careless with men." Fifteen years after the broken engagement, her attraction to Eddie was muddled neither by youth nor by the threat of matrimony. They resumed their relationship, young Eddie said, "in a red-hot sexy affair."

Aside from Betty, who was in Paris, Marjorie was the only person in whom Margarett confided. "I've been seeing something of Eddie Morgan," was how she phrased it, with a particular grin, relishing her friend's familiar horror and delight. In 1927, Marjorie was thirty-six, Margarett thirty-five. Differences that had seemed slight when they were in their early twenties now bore social weight. Margarett paid Marjorie's rent in Vermont until an uncle left her enough money to buy a house, enough to go to Paris. Margarett traveled whenever she pleased, and she was married. "Margarett could have had anything, you know," Betty Parsons said, "and Marjorie was Little Miss Muffet." Marjorie brought a beau to Prides, and Margarett flirted with him, even, Betty thought, took him to bed. But the friendship survived this, as it had Margarett's marriage and the offense of the last-minute telegram.

At the end of her life, Marjorie did not believe Margarett had ever loved her, and when she described Isabel Pell, the woman whose visits to Prides supplanted hers, she used the word "wicked." Margarett would never have admitted she treated Marjorie callously, would have described herself as "devoted"—"incredulous" at her friend's indignation. In 1926, leaving out the tension in their friendship, she did a watercolor called *The Quilt*—Marjorie asleep, beautiful and dreamily rendered in pale washes, both hands resting carefully on her chest, the quilt covering her a splash of vividly painted squares, an opening path.

Margarett's second New York exhibition, at Kraushaar in March 1927, included a group of large watercolors, *The Quilt* among them. "Though slight, their note is clear and fresh," the progressive critic Forbes Watson wrote in the *New York World.* "Her attack is not in the least literal," he continued, "and where a hint will do she does not, so to speak, insist upon writing a chapter." Margarett also showed three new plaster panels, to be the last she'd exhibit. Life at Prides pulled her from the studio and its solitude. What had been confined to her sketchbooks—the vitality of the household—she began to treat in large pastels.

Marjorie sits at a dressing table, hands in her lap, having her hair washed by Miss McNamara from Manchester. Margarett puts Margie behind her; in short underwear, spindly legs bare, she scrutinizes a book. Jenny looks up from a book on her lap; and a small black-and-white dog, slash of red for his collar, poses on the floor.

A woman, reclining on a green chaise longue, wears a rose peignoir, its ostrich collar languorously open. Margarett uses colors as dusky as those Lautrec painted Paris prostitutes, so the little girl is a surprise. In short dress and hair ribbon, she sits on the edge of the chaise, hand resting on the woman's. Marjorie, wearing Margarett's peignoir, hair dark around her face, could be Margarett, if Margie, who was the child, did not remember it was Marjorie's hand she held and her mother who quickly and quietly drew.

The announcement of Margarett's third Kraushaar show, in February 1928, was illustrated by the pastel of the unmade bed. For the first time, she did not show sculpture, just pastels and watercolors. In the *Brooklyn Eagle*, Helen Appleton Read remarked on her "new-found vivacity and interest in reality," and Henry McBride, in the *Sun*, noted her search for "free expression and simplicity. . . . Occasionally in the effort for the last named quality she misses a direct contact with life, but occasionally also, she gets it precisely."

Although Margarett was showing in New York, she had become a presence in the Boston art world. Kraushaar advertised her New York shows in the *Transcript*, and in December 1927, she was included in a group exhibition of American portraits at the Boston Art Club. "It is here that a Bostonian, Margarett Sargent, makes her first local appearance in a general exhibition," Harley Perkins wrote in the *Transcript*, "saying the essential things with the fewest of means."

By showing at the Art Club, Margarett allied herself with the group of insurgent painters, Perkins among them, who were turning the venerable organization into a venue for artists who looked toward what was new in New York and Paris. Though Margarett was more interested in work that distorted the recognizable than she was in abstraction, and though her temperament was more "avant-garde" than her taste, it was in Modernism that she found her aesthetic home. Its expressiveness reassured her; it seemed natural to be more interested in color than in fidelity, to experience distortion as revelation. Her rage at "those dreadful hunting prints," transformed to a hunger to see things in her own way, would soon change her art.

Easily and naturally, she sought the like-minded. "Modernists respect the past," she snapped to a reporter in 1928, "but why copy it?" Two years later, when Florence Cowles of the tabloid *Boston Post* came to interview her, Margarett was more diplomatic. Smiling, she said she understood why her work was considered modernist: "We must be called something. If you say a girl is pretty or ugly, I know what you mean, but literally of course, we are not 'modern' as many of the painters who belong to the school were painting 60 or 70 years ago. It is that the public is just becoming aware of us."

Boston associated Margarett with modernism not only because of her work but because of the paintings she and Shaw had begun to collect. She had always collected what she aspired to in her own work. When she was sculpting, she bought heads by Despiau and Lachaise, and when she was rendering women in pastel and watercolor, she purchased female likenesses by other women artists—Mary Cassatt, Berthe Morisot, Marie Laurencin. In the autumn of 1927 in New York, Margarett began to buy bold paintings by French Modernists— in September, *Mademoiselle X*, the head of a young woman by André Derain; in December, *The Storm*, a landscape by Maurice Vlaminck. On the last day of the year, she bought a painting the Reinhardt Gallery listed as *Head of the Artist's First Wife*, by Picasso.

It's possible the title was a nod to propriety; the subject of Margarett's Picasso was not Fernande Olivier, the woman considered his first wife (they never married), but a courtesan. In 1901 in Paris, twenty years old and under the influence of Lautrec—Blue Period and Cubism still years ahead—the artist painted a woman with a strong, hard face, a twist of red lips, a pompadour of orange hair, a huge, curling yellow hat with an enormous black plume. In Boston, where there were no Picassos on public view and few in private collections, Margarett's purchase got publicity—in the *Transcript*, a large reproduction announced acquisition "for the McKean collection of Boston" of "A Painting by Pablo Picasso, a Leader of the Modern Movement in Paris."

Margarett's Picasso was no longer avant-garde, but the artist's name, even on a work barely twentieth century, was a salvo in the battle between the Young Turks at the Boston Art Club and the old Tarbell-Benson establishment. In December 1925, the club had mounted an exhibition of thirty-nine Post-Impressionist paintings, the first significant display of modern European painting in Boston since the Armory Show. Crowning it were Seurat's *Sunday Afternoon on the Grand Jatte* and Matisse's *Woman Before an Aquarium*. In a long essay in the *Transcript*, Margarett's friend Harley Perkins cheered on the Art Club's campaign to ease acceptance in Boston of the work it had so vehemently rejected in 1913.

The paintings in the exhibition belonged to Frederic Clay Bartlett, a Chicago artist and collector who had just purchased a house on the sea at Beverly, not far from Prides. Like Margarett, he was a child of the upper class who had declared himself an artist. He wrote with sacred intensity of his youthful apprenticeship in Munich, described touching a bowl decorated by Dürer, its surface "made gloriously beautiful, most holy and divine by the great master." He'd traveled in Italy, studied with Whistler in Paris, and met Puvis de Chavannes, whose allegorical murals inspired him. Within a few years of his return to Chicago, his commissions decorated many of its buildings.

Margarett immediately sought him out. He was, like Luks, an older man with a great deal to teach her about art, and she was, like his wife who had just died, a strong and artistic woman. Frederic fell a little in love with her, and Margarett considered him a godfather. By the time they met, Bartlett had turned away from murals and was painting canvases in a vivid, School of Paris style; it was through him that Margarett first took a good look at the painters who became her major influence. Bartlett had always been a collector as well as an artist, but it was not until his marriage to Helen Birch, a younger poet and composer, who shared with her friend Harriet Monroe, editor of *Poetry*, a passion for modern art, that he began to buy Matisse and Seurat, Gauguin and Modigliani—avant-garde works, Helen wrote with excitement to a friend, "which someday not far in the future will be seen."

In 1925, Helen died of cancer—they had been married just six years—and Frederic offered their collection to the Art Institute of Chicago. After a fractious debate among its conservative trustees, the museum accepted the gift, and in the spring of 1926 the Birch-Bartlett collection opened, in an explosion of publicity. "Americans who wish to enjoy the acquaintance of European modernist artists must make the journey to the metropolis of the Middle West," a New York editorial advised, "for since the disposal of the John Quinn collection here, there has been no representative aggregation of their work in this neighborhood."

In fact, the Barnes Foundation, with its collection of nearly a thousand Impressionist and Post-Impressionist paintings, had opened in monumental limestone galleries near Philadelphia in March 1925, but admission was granted, irascibly, only to a chosen few. In New York in 1920, Marcel Duchamp and Katharine Drier had founded the Société Anonyme to introduce European abstraction—Kandinsky, Mondrian, Malevich—but the Museum of Modern Art, its inaugurating collections rich in the Post-Impressionists, would not open until 1929. Bostonians had to wait even longer. The Institute of Contemporary Art (founded as the Boston Museum of Modern Art) was not to be incorporated until 1936.

Despite the exhibition of the Birch-Bartlett collection, the climate in 1926 for Margarett and her fellow Boston modernists was, as Harley Perkins put it, "a tight lid." That February, in the Boston column he wrote for *The Arts*, he flew the idea of a Boston Independents show, open to any painter who wished to accept the invitation. He believed the Museum of Fine Arts, which had barely flirted with European modernism, would never embrace contemporary American art. "It is time for another Revolution," he wrote, "with minute men in ambush."

The revolution came in the form of Jane Houston Kilham, a tall Californian redhead trained as an artist in New York and Paris, who paid her six children a dime an hour to pose. She envisioned a Boston exhibition in the tradition of the Salon des Réfusés of 1863 and the First Impressionist Show of 1874, and rented a derelict stable on Beacon Hill. Margarett enthusiastically joined Kilham's Boston Society of Independent Artists, which proclaimed itself "reactionary toward no existing institution, but open to all." The New York independents had been organized by Robert Henri and John Sloan, great men; the Boston group was led by women—"one of the most striking points of the whole undertaking," Perkins remarked. Kilham was president, an anonymous Boston woman paid renovation expenses, and, from New York, Gertrude Vanderbilt Whitney and Juliana Force lent support by encouraging the participation of several New York artists.

Margarett and Shaw were among those who arrived at the Beacon Hill stable on the very cold afternoon of January 16, 1927, entering the exhibition space through a "tea room and eating place where the visitors may dally" and a central court "lit from above and hung with flowering plants." Hundreds of paintings, each fully illuminated by the specially designed lighting grid, jammed every foot of available wall. Harley Perkins praised the show's "robust vitality" and assured readers of the *Transcript* that they would find "a goodly number of very able achievements pricking through the rift of mediocre and nondescript offerings."

Among the "considerable percentage" of female exhibitors were Margarett Sargent, Jane Kilham, and the Boston Impressionist Lilla Cabot Perry, seventy-nine years old and a friend of Monet. No checklist of the first show survives, but when the *Transcript* reported works sold from the Independents' second annual, the following winter, all three Margarett Sargents were on the list.

§

THE SKETCHBOOK is eight by ten inches. On its mottled black-and-white cover is the date, 1927. On its first page, Margarett draws a young man, half of him. Her line is thick as a wire hanger not meant to bend. She gets what's gentle about his mouth, the tentative angle of his head, then contradicts with a swagger of lapel. On the reverse page is his other half: bottom of jacket, hand, crayon-jagged legs crossed at the ankle. If an entire face does not hold her, she excerpts. Of an anguished man, she draws just a balding brow and eyes that don't balance.

There are pages of men drawn with that hanger line. They wear ties. Their hair is slicked back. They are weak and weakly drawn, don't look up from their reading or out through their glasses. Then, abruptly, Margarett is no longer bored. She draws a man in a tuxedo, places him at an angle on the page. Poker-straight lines as random as pick-up-sticks cohere as his jacket, and above the tall starched collar and the black tie, a densely drawn swarthy face. He looks up—dark hair, bristling eyebrows, sunken eyes, turned-down mouth, gutted cheeks. This in charcoal, then across the surface, like bird tracks in sand, the odd delicate line exposes the pain beneath: a quick moment, like certain silences in conversation.

The drawing is of Roland Balay, a French dealer, member of the Knoedler family and director of its galleries. Margarett met him in London, walked with Shaw into an exhibition of old-master flower paintings, asked to see the person responsible. Roland came forward— a small, quietly witty man with a spark behind his eyes, no sign of the darkness Margarett later got in the drawing. They had dinner immediately, talked in French and English, talked about, among other things, Donatello and della Francesca. Roland was, by his own account years later, undone. "Surréaliste," he said of his new friend. "The essence— aristocracy, intellectuality, vulgarity."

Roland was married, but in the French way he continued his amorous adventures. When he got to New York, he did not hesitate to telephone Margarett. He was coming to Boston, he said, to deliver a Braque; perhaps she might like to see it. They had lunch at the Ritz, and afterward, when he rose to go up to his room to get the picture, Margarett stopped him. "I'll come with you," she said.

"No, no," Roland said, "I'll bring it down."

"I'd like to come with you—"

"But no, Margarett, I—"

She insisted. Telling the story, Roland shrugged and, disingenuously, blushed.

It was the beginning of a long affair. "In and out," Betty Parsons said, "as the wind blows." Afternoons at exhibitions and evenings in hotel rooms in Paris and New York, the tango at El Morocco, nights in Harlem at the Cotton Club. Roland understood Margarett in a way she wasn't used to. She had "*fantaisie,*" he said, purposely avoiding an English word. Soon he and his wife were visiting Prides, and Roland was hunting and fishing with Shaw. One night, hours after Roland and Mimi had gone to bed, Margarett appeared in the garden outside the guest room. Roland was not surprised, just eager she not wake Mimi. "Roland!" Margarett said in a stage whisper.

"Shhhhhhh." He gestured through the window, putting on his robe.

"I have something extraordinary to show you," she said, leading him to the pool. There, by the light of the moon and its reflection, calmly floated a Canada goose. Again Roland was not surprised, as he had come to expect from Margarett a confusion of life with dreams. The next day, he took her aside. "That was certainly one of the most interesting things I've ever seen." "Well," she said, "I tied it there for you to see."

If Margarett was to move on entirely from sculpture, she would need a medium to accommodate and amplify what had such force in the drawing of Roland. The face with gutted cheeks burned through pages of children, nursery twins, tentative young men, and a woman beautifully drawn with a supple, fluid line. "George Luks met me and told me I should be a painter," Margarett said. Her old friend had guided her through every transition she'd made as an artist, but the urgency had always been her own. The shift to oil was swift. In February 1928, she had shown pastels and drawings. That summer, she began to prepare for a January show at Kraushaar, in which she would exhibit twenty-four oil paintings.

"Your photograph irks me that I did not seize your face in paint," she wrote me once. Seize: Margarett's most characteristic paintings took possession with the unapologetic directness of that word. Her bravado was another gift from Luks. In 1927, he visited Prides, and Margarett commissioned a portrait of Jenny, who was then four, dressed as an infanta. Little Jenny stood as with frenzied dispatch Luks laid in brocade with a housepainter's brush, muttering, "Velázquez, he was the baby," and producing a delicate and vital likeness.

Margarett took from the older painter, sixty that year, what served her—spirit, nerve, speed, an emotional approach—but not color or brush technique. His palette evoked the Spanish or the Dutch: colors rich and dark, lighter hues emerging from darkness like light in a night fog, figures modeled with an abundance of paint. Margarett painted with bright, clear colors, diluting pigment so the color became almost transparent, or modeling a faint impasto across the canvas.

She began to use oils in Vermont the summer of 1927, the family's first in Dorset, the village where Marjorie Davenport lived. In the countryside, large working farms interrupted a landscape of mountains, meadow, marshland, and abandoned quarries. In town, the sidewalks were slabs of white Vermont marble, and in the clapboard farmhouse Margarett and Shaw bought for four hundred dollars and moved to a plateau on West Road, everything that could be was marble—bathtub, windowsills, thresholds, the terrace out back.

For a month, the McKeans lived, as the Sargents had at Wareham, a life that could be described as simple. Everyone ate at a big table at one end of the open living room, then sat around after supper on furniture Margarett picked up at farmyard auctions and draped with patchwork quilts. Margarett and Shaw shared a room that adjoined the only full bath; the girls and Senny the only other bedroom. The twins slept in a loft above the big room.

Margarett often left the house at six in the morning. She took ink, charcoal, and watercolor, made sketches, then, at home, enlarged and enhanced the images with oil paint on canvas. She painted Vermont people without sentimentality: country women, whose gaunt faces showed both their intelligence and the harshness of their lives; a tall thin man in a dark, derelict doorway; Annie, a neighbor girl who played with Margie and Jenny, wearing a white dress, bent over sewing, too large for her chair.

When Margarett returned at dusk, Shaw was often at the stove. He had learned camp cooking in his copper-mining days, and he and Senny split the job in Dorset. "I imagine you painting boys with apples, or women with arms covered with soap suds," Dan wrote Margarett. "Shaw has a white chef's cap on when he cooks. He heats up the sauce in a blue sauce-pan, stirring it with a wooden spoon. 'Taste this,' he says."

There had been artists in southern Vermont for decades, and painting was in the air. Margarett got the children to paint, and in the ease of the country even Shaw set up an easel. In the 1928 summer annual at the Equinox Hotel in Manchester, Margarett showed paintings, Jenny McKean a portrait in the children's division, and Shaw McKean a group of oils—colors faithful, edges definite, contours restrained: the bone china tureen on a table between two windows in the big room; little Shaw, blond, sitting neatly on a chair.

In a photograph, Margarett stands grinning on the marble-slab terrace behind the house. "She loved it there," Margie said.

By the autumn of 1928, back in Boston, Margarett was painting with assurance. If you looked for American resonance, you saw the women Alfred Maurer painted in hot Fauve colors; the stylized, chic restaurant habitués of Guy Péne du Bois, the 1920s figures of Walt Kuhn. Or you saw Paris: the abrupt, committed intensity of her own Picasso, the unnerving challenge in the gaze of that woman in the yellow hat. Margarett brought this directness to her most compelling subjects, women and men of social Boston who like herself chafed against its suppression of sensual will, its curb on the demonstration of feeling, its social requirements. How this conflict came through a face was what she painted.

At first, the portraits were ironic. Like Margarett, her subjects rebelled with charm and wit, a tossed-off light-touch arrogance, as in a 1928 portrait of a woman in a cloche hat, devil-may-care "Whoopee!" scrawled across the top of the canvas. As she became more experienced, the paintings challenged and deepened, leaving behind the pale lyricism with which she'd made watercolors of Marjorie Davenport, the buoyant entertainment of her Prides pastels. When she first used oils in Boston, Margarett hired a round-faced model named Edna, of whom she painted disengaged, placid portraits, but there was nothing, it seemed, in Edna's presence to knot the elements of composition into a tough, energetic whole. But in 1928, when she began to paint her cousin Bobo's widow, Maria, all that changed.

The wall behind the woman is pale pink. Next to her, loosely painted, a table; on it, a large Chinese lamp, white porcelain and white silk shade swirled light and dark blue. Visible behind the lamp is the edge of a gilt frame, and in the foreground, a vase of pink flowers cropped at the right edge of the canvas. It is a background for a lyric Cupid or a languishing Venus, but Margarett has introduced a modern Diana. Sitting tall, the dark-haired woman holds a dog, a fox terrier that sprawls across her lap. The dog looks at us; we see the woman in profile. Her alabaster skin shimmers with faint undertones of blue, pink, and yellow, and the effect is luminescence, paleness that shocks in contrast to the black of her hair, short and pulled behind her right ear. Her nose is slender, aquiline, her long neck elegant, chin delicate. Her shirt with its flipped-back man's collar is deep cornflower blue; its faint purple glow sets off a luscious violet jacket. All of this would recede in pleasing harmony if it weren't for the bright-red hat, close to the head—a crimson crown—not modest or restrained.

Maria deAcosta was born in New York, one of eight children of a Cuban father of Spanish ancestry and a Castilian mother whose noble birth, beauty, and inheritance eased the deAcostas to the center of New York society. Their daughters became unreluctantly famous: "Oh, she was one of the deAcostas," people would remark. The youngest, Mercedes, was an intimate friend, possibly a lover, of Greta Garbo, and in her 1960 autobiography published photographs of herself with Garbo, Cecil Beaton, Stravinsky, and Marie Laurencin. The oldest, Rita, was a famous beauty, whose portrait by Boldini is in the collection of the Louvre.

Maria was a dozen years older than Margarett, who met her when she was married to Charles Sprague Sargent's only son, Robeson. After Bobo's death, of flu in 1918, Maria lived in Harvard, Massachusetts, with her son and a woman named Miriam Shaw. "A Boston marriage," a niece explained: Maria flamboyant, effusive, and Spanish in her picador hat; Miriam a bluestocking and, though younger, "more like Maria's governess than anything else."

In another of Margarett's portraits, Maria wears a plum-colored beret. Her right hand rests on her knee, her left is half hidden in a pocket. Her sharp Spanish features are animated. One eyebrow is nearly obscured by the angle of her beret; the other is raised, bemused and disdainful. Her expression is mischievous, her mouth about to laugh. The taupe suit she wore for this portrait could be called "mannish," an effect accentuated by the tawny vest, the pale-blue ascot. "Oh, I'm sure she was a lesbian," exclaimed another niece, telling a story—Maria greeting her from bed, wearing a black lace slip, holding a glass of whiskey, the two of them alone in the house. At lunch once at a women's club in Boston, Maria malapropped: "I wouldn't be in town at all, but I needed a new pair of bisexual glasses." Margarett called the portrait *Tailleur Classique.*

"Oh," said Betty Parsons, looking at a slide. "That was Maria deAcosta. She had a *passion* for Margarett."

What sort of passion? If the red hat were a faded letter in a torn envelope, a page from a journal, it might answer that question. If *Tailleur Classique* were a short story, one might find clues to the mysteries of a half-hidden eyebrow, a hand almost concealed in a pocket. What passed between the two women when Margarett wasn't painting, when Maria wasn't posing with a dog or, as in a third portrait, sporting a bright-red smock and holding a cigarette, its ash hot and live?

Margarett and Maria may have had an affair or they may not have, but Margarett's lovers were not all men. More than one woman testified to having been approached, to having reciprocated with confidence. "Margarett had love affairs with women, there's no doubt about that," Betty said. But, also, "Margarett was a very subtle woman. She wouldn't tell you." When Margie was in her late twenties and curious about her mother's life, she sat Margarett down and recited a list of certain women who had come to stay at Prides for weeks at a time. "They were all lesbians. Surely you had affairs . . . !" Margarett faced her daughter down. "I've only known one lesbian in my life," she declared, and mentioned a woman with whom she had no particular friendship. She knew that as long as she was discreet, she could do as she pleased. If she was a lady in her behavior, her secret life, however well known it was, would not interfere with invitations to dinner.

Margarett had admired—had even had a crush on—Eleo Sears when she was a child and Eleo and Alice Thorndike were Amazons of the pony rink at the New Riding Club. Eleonora Sears had never married. She was the first national women's squash champion, four times the national women's tennis doubles champion, and the first woman to play polo, and was famous for the long walks she took from Providence to Boston accompanied by Harvard undergraduates, escorted by a chauffeured limousine stocked with refreshments. Eleo was both open and discreet. Protected by great wealth, her mystique enhanced by tall good looks, she lived a proper Bostonian life and, apparently, loved women. "Everyone knew it, but it was never spoken of," said Nancy Cochrane, one of Vivian Cochrane's daughters.

Miss Sears, as she was known to servants and children, was eagerly received by every North Shore and Boston hostess, and invitations to the famous dances she gave in the ballroom of her house in Prides Crossing or, in the winter, in Boston were prized. "She was such fun," said Margie. "I loved Miss Sears," said Paul Moore, who would marry Jenny. "Even a stuffy banker like my father loved her!" On a Thursday afternoon, Eleo might play bridge with a group of North Shore wives, on the weekend receive her particular friend, a young French actress who'd take the train up from New York. "Mother would take us to tea at Miss Sears'," Nancy Cochrane said, "and there she'd be, Mademoiselle. Eleo was madly in love with her, gave her a Duesenberg. Oh, they were so glamorous!"

The young actress had displaced another woman in Eleo's life. Isabel Pell, of New York, London, and, later, Paris, was tall, lean, and, Margie said, "handsome, *wonderfully* handsome." By the late 1920s, Isabel was visiting Prides three or four times a year for weeks at a time, and she and Margarett were seeing each other in New York. It was she whom Marjorie Davenport had characterized as "wicked." Among other lesbians, Isabel had a reputation as a sexual predator, and in her dominating character even those who admired her found a streak of duplicity.

Like Margarett, Isabel had broken an early engagement, and like Eleo, she lived an independent life unprotected by marriage or a married name. She was also an adventurer. Margarett pasted clippings of her exploits in her scrapbook, one of which recounts the rescue, sometime in the early thirties, of two "sporting" women off the coast of Denmark by a German freighter. Isabel had taken a seaplane voyage with Mrs. Henry T. Fleitman, an attractive brunette and "habituée of London's Mayfair equally with Long Island's Hamptons." Mr. Fleitman had not heard from his wife since she'd sailed for France months before, and "knew nothing of the crash."

Shaw seemed to be no more aware of the nature of Margarett's relationship with Isabel than of the erotic element in her association with Roland Balay. He and Isabel talked about golf. The children loved her so much they asked to call her "Cousin" rather than "Miss" Pell. They'd never seen a woman wear anything but a nightgown to bed until Cousin Pell appeared in pajamas cut from heavy silk crepe, "exactly like a man's." She drove a succession of maroon Duesenbergs named Olga, her perfume—Tabac Blanc—was musky and sexy, and she wore her honey-colored hair smooth and short. She was reputed to own forty pairs of riding boots, and if she abandoned jodhpurs or slacks for a skirt, she wore, Margie said, a "marvelously tailored" suit.

Nothing documents what Margarett and Isabel said to each other, the defiant wit they apparently shared, or what they actually did behind closed doors, but Margarett made one ink drawing after another of a woman with bobbed hair and prominent eyebrows who always wore pants. Her first painting of Isabel was of a mannish woman in leather jacket and necktie, cigarette hanging from her mouth, background fire-engine red. In a second portrait, she enthroned Isabel in an arched chair of pale gray and painted the wall behind her almost lavender. Her jacket is the color of flesh; her white shirt, which must be silk, is open at the collar, its shadows watery gray. She has large hands, and the look on her face is surprisingly tender. Pepe, her black Scottie, sits in her lap.

Soon after Isabel appeared, Marjorie Davenport challenged Margarett about the nature of her new friendship, but Margarett would tell her nothing. Marjorie, at last standing up to her, accused her of betrayal. "You've changed," Margarett retorted, "ever since you inherited that money from your uncle. . . ." It was dark, a late afternoon at Prides, and they shouted until Marjorie threw down her glass, shattering it on the tile floor. "She and Isabel deserved one another," she said bitterly at eighty-eight. "Finally Margarett got someone whose cruelty matched hers."

Thirty years later, not having seen her since the afternoon of the broken glass, Margarett arrived at Marjorie's house in Vermont, bringing flowers. Marjorie opened the door, and Margarett gave her the bouquet. They stood there at the door for a few minutes but said very little. It was the last time they saw each other.

When Margarett's first oils were exhibited, in 1929, two portraits of Maria deAcosta Sargent were among them. The walls at Kraushaar bristled with color, Margarett's strongest work since the sculpted heads of Luks and Chaffard, her freest since the model walked naked in her studio in 1919. A cigarette hung from the mouth of a woman in a striped sweater; a cook and a kitchen maid played cards at a table; two blond children mixed with a pattern of vivid red-and-blue pinwheels. Maria as *Tailleur Classique* bore little resemblance to the woman washed in watercolor who, dressed like a Greek supplicant, had raised a draped arm to obscure her face.

This, Margarett's fourth Kraushaar exhibition, allied her with other American Modernist and Post-Impressionist painters whose works were on display in New York that month—Marsden Hartley, Jane Peterson, and Edward Hopper. Henry McBride considered her in the context of her famous relative: "Miss Sargent seems more than careful not to let a suggestion of the relationship extend to her art. She burns her incense before the later gods." *Art News* noticed the shift in her work and found a way to patronize: "Miss Margarett Sargent has quite evidently grown a trifle weary of the sedate muse she used to follow and has mounted a more fiery Pegasus who has taken her for a somewhat breathless ride among the colorful phenomena of modern art."

But many reviews wholeheartedly affirmed Margarett's work in the new medium. "Her subjects," Forbes Watson wrote, "seem ready to step from their frames and become really alive." And *Vanity Fair*, whose editor, Frank Crowninshield, himself a collector of modern art, was a distant cousin and friend, reproduced three paintings: "Unfortunately the black and white reproductions fail to convey their beauty and importance."

Les Arts à Paris was published in Paris by the dealer Paul Guillaume to promote his own artists and collectors; in particular, his most famous collector, Dr. Albert Barnes. The magazine rarely discussed American painters, but in January 1929, it reproduced Margarett's *The Striped Sweater* (*Le Sweater Rayé*), and its columnist Jacques Villeneuve wrote enthusiastically of *"la femme peintre américaine dont l'exposition cet hiver aux Galeries Kraushaar à New York a été si remarquée par les connoisseurs."* He continued:

> Her expressive art reveals some praiseworthy affinities in inspiration and also in intention with the painters who work in France. There will be a time when the French public, enlightened or ill informed, will take account of the efforts of the young school of American painting, the passionate admiration that has borne witness for a quarter century to the painting which comes from France. . . .

The revolution in painting that exploded in Paris before the war had resumed in a shifting international community of artists in Montparnasse, some of whom, like Alexander Calder, Max Jacob, Jean Lurçat, Jean Pascin, and Isamu Noguchi, Margarett knew, collected, or came to know. She was also aware of the American expatriate writers Janet Flanner reported to be "richer than most in creative ambition but rather modest in purse" and had read their work in émigré journals like *transition* and *Broom*.

In the years after the war, navy surplus and shipping yards hot with a new capacity to build had swelled the count of great ocean liners from 117 in 1918 to 328 four years later. Daily columns in the Paris editions of the *New York Herald* and the *Chicago Tribune* reported arrivals and departures of notable and moneyed Americans. The impoverished crossed in steerage for fifty dollars; the prosperous strolled first-class decks and drank champagne at captains' tables. Each season, Paris couture emblazoned American magazines, beckoning women of fashion to its source, and American men like Shaw, who had fallen in love with France during the war, returned with their wives in pursuit of pleasure and the postwar business opportunities that waited all over Europe.

It was not unusual to read of the arrival of thirty-five hundred tourists in one day or of the railroad's scramble to schedule seven extra trains for transport from Cherbourg or Le Havre to Gare Saint-Lazare. It was less expensive to sail to Le Havre than to take the train to California, and France was cheap. In 1926, the exchange rate peaked at fifty francs to the dollar; later, it leveled off at twenty. A meal *haute cuisine* might be had for a dollar or two, a suite in a first-class hotel for six dollars a night. The *bar americain* was devised to quench the thirst of those in flight from prohibition: "10,000 Yankee Cocktails 'Go' in Nice Daily," exulted a *Herald* headline in 1924, the year Margarett and Shaw made the first of their trips abroad.

"In those days you met anybody anywhere," wrote Gertrude Stein. Margarett and Shaw were as likely to run into friends from New York or Boston at the Ritz in Paris as they were at the Ritz in New York or Boston. Dan and Louise Sargent stayed at the Hôtel de Cambon; the MacLeishes had an apartment on rue Las Cases; and Dickie Ames took two rooms at the Ritz, the second to store his paintings. In 1927, the *Herald* reported Marjorie Davenport at the American Women's Club, and on Easter Sunday, 1928, the marriage of Margarett's cousin Hollis Hunnewell to Mary Frances Oakes at the American Cathedral on avenue George. "Paris has now frankly become an American suburb," wrote the American Elizabeth Eyre in *Town and Country* in 1926. "One warm night, Paris suddenly turned American."

When Margarett first visited Paris in 1924, she found her friend Betty Parsons hungrily living the life of an artist, sharing a house on rue Boulard in Montparnasse with the painter Adge Baker, an Englishwoman, with whom she would live for six years. The exchange rate multiplied her alimony to a small fortune, and marriage had convinced her that her sexuality was inspired more by women than by men. She was twenty-four years old and burned, as she put it, with a "love for the unfamiliar."

On her arrival in Paris, she had enrolled in Antoine Bourdelle's sculpture class at the Grande Chaumière. There she met fellow Americans Caresse Crosby and Alexander Calder and shared their teacher's most enthusiastic encouragement with a tall, quiet sculptor named Alberto Giacometti. She canoed the Seine with Caresse's husband, Harry, and went dancing with Sandy Calder, "twice a week," she said, "for exercise." She was invited to the Saturday lunches Natalie Barney gave for young people at her salon on rue Jacob, where "All the men were homosexual, all the women were lesbian, and the conversation was brilliant. Brilliant."

She had tea with Gertrude Stein and Alice Toklas, and she met Janet Flanner, who would soon begin to write her "Letter from Paris" for Harold Ross's new magazine, *The New Yorker.* Flanner, eight years older, took her in hand, guided her to theater, concerts, and exhibitions. In the galleries of Paris and the studios of Montparnasse, Betty began to develop the eye that fifteen years later made her a revolutionary dealer in the history of American art. "After years of knowing only people who did what they were supposed to do, I suddenly knew people who did nothing whatsoever that was conventional," she said.

When she and Betty met in 1919, Margarett was an unmarried daughter defying family expectation by pursuing art in a great city. Now it was Betty who lived and worked with heady excitement, meeting everyone, allowing herself to be changed by a city at the center of the world. Betty took Margarett to hear *les diseuses,* "those *fantastic* woman singers," and to Le Boeuf sur le Toit, Cocteau's jazz club, hung with Picabia's paintings and Man Ray's photographs, where the Montparnasse model Kiki sang and artists gossiped and drank.

If Margarett had been ten years younger and still unmarried, she might have gone to Paris to seek her fortune as an artist. As it was, she checked into a Right Bank hotel with a businessman husband who played squash at the Travellers Club with his friends from Morgan's Bank. As Madame Q. A. Shaw McKean, she plied the glistening shops

along the curved phalanx of Place Vendôme. She bought handker-
chiefs, *"crêpe uni couleur,"* the latest accessory, "to be caught in the exact center and carried with all four points waving," had several
monogrammed "Maria" and "Vivian." She bought lingerie and gloves
at La Grande Maison de Blanc on the Place de l'Opéra, and at Goupy,
under the arcade on rue Castiglione, a dress of raw silk. For the children, left at home with Senny, she shopped at "Fairyland."

The earliest Paris document I have, a bill of sale for a Mary Cassatt
aquatint, *Mère et Enfant,* places Margarett and Shaw in Paris in February 1924. The following month, Cassatt, going blind, would offer for
sale "those of her works which she had guarded with jealous care." A
receipt for an unidentified Cassatt from the venerable dealer Hode-
bert, had Margarett and Shaw back in Paris on May 5, 1925, in time
for L'Exposition des Arts Décoratifs, the first international exhibition
of Art Deco. Though there are no documents for 1926 or 1927, "They
went every year," Margie said, "and stayed three or four months." And
Betty, sentences racing as Margarett must have—from taxi to shop,
luncheon, galleries—said, "Yes. Oh, yes. They did the life of Paris in
the spring." Expensive restaurants, horse races at Longchamps, Maurice Chevalier at Casino de Paris, Mistinguett at the Moulin Rouge,
and then on to Monte Carlo, London, or Berlin.

They visited the Princes at their foxhunting estate in the mountains at Pau. Margarett liked Freddie Prince, who was one of Shaw's
Myopia polo friends—"he was far more aesthetic in his business," she
wrote once to Betty, "than most painters are on canvas." In Paris, they
dined with Hope Thacher, Margarett's childhood playmate, and her
husband, "Bunny" Carter, head of the Paris office of Morgan's Bank.
At Harry and Caresse Crosby's parties on rue de Lille or at their converted mill outside Paris, they mixed with guests as likely to include
Bunny Carter as D. H. Lawrence, Kay Boyle, or Hart Crane.

The novelist Louis Bromfield became a great friend. Because of
two best-sellers and a Pulitzer Prize at thirty, he was celebrity enough
that when he accidentally tore up his steamer ticket on his way to the
pier, the *New York Times* reported it. Janet Flanner declared his "the

finest flower garden of any American in the Île de France territory, except Mrs. Edith Wharton, whose white garden was celebrated." He was such a gracious host, it was remarked that in another life he might have run a great hotel. At the Bromfields' converted monastery outside Paris, Margarett and Shaw met Gertrude Stein and Alice Toklas, and Edith Wharton. There is no record of Margarett's response to Gertrude and Alice, but as an old woman she yelped with scorn at the mention of Wharton, whose books she admired but whose approach to decorating she found extremely dreary.

More than once Margarett pulled Betty from class at the Grande Chaumière for the morning auction at the Hôtel Drouot. She bought one of Betty's sculptures—a red clay cat—and took her to meet Marie Laurencin. She went to Durand-Ruel for Cassatt and Morisot and, at Georges Aubry, bought *Women and Children* by Bazille, whose work was so scarce—he had died young in the Franco-Prussian War—that any acquisition was a coup. When she got to Paris in April 1928, an exposition of one hundred lithographs by Toulouse-Lautrec had just opened; she would eventually own two of his drawings and eleven lithographs—among them three of Yvette Guilbert, one of Jane Avril.

If Shaw was in Berlin or Amsterdam on business, Margarett went to auctions with Dr. Barnes, who was still buying Renoir and Modigliani, or to galleries with Frederic Bartlett, who, not yet remarried, unabashedly courted her. Out for the afternoon in Montparnasse, he sketched them having an apéritif at the Dôme. "You couldn't get an inning with Margarett. Bartlett was always there. He was mad for her. Mad for her," Betty said. "She was happiest when he was her boyfriend."

Check stubs dated 1928, checks made out to Betty Parsons, Harry Crosby . . . I am leafing through a messy stack of papers: pages torn from a 1930s sketchbook—"Île de France, 1931." A man with a funny fat face slouches in a deck chair; a figure in a green coat climbs a gangway; then a photograph, dusky with age, creased and bent. It takes a moment to recognize her. Her irises rest above the horizon of her lower eyelids; the stare fixes me. This was not the Margarett who glittered in a silver Poiret gown, fragrant with L'Heure Bleu, out for the evening with Shaw, who walked with Frederic Bartlett along rue La Boétie, or drank with Betty and Sandy Calder at le Boeuf sur le Toit. This was Margarett, by herself, at the age of thirty-six. On the back of the photograph, the inky stamp: "*Photographie de Berenice Abbott.*"

Abbott left a darkroom job with Man Ray in late 1926 and in January 1928 moved to a "big old daylit studio" near the Palais Luxembourg. It was to this studio, a top-floor room with a large, north-facing skylight, that Margarett went to have her portrait made by the talented, unusual young woman, an Ohio refugee in Paris. In 1926, Abbott's first exhibition of portraits, invitation card designed by Jean Cocteau, had opened at Au Sacre du Printemps, where André Kertesz had shown photographs, Kiki of Montparnasse paintings, and Calder sculpture. A month after she photographed Margarett, in April 1928, twelve of her portraits, exhibited with work by Kertesz, Man Ray, Nadar, and Atget, would make her international reputation.

Margarett climbed the five flights at rue Servandoni. "A stranger. Out of the blue," Abbott told me at ninety-three, chic in trousers, hair still elegantly short, scarf tied like an ascot at her neck. "I didn't know her well." The photographer, eight years younger than her subject, saw Margarett first on the threshold, illuminated in a spill of north light. She invited her to make herself at home while she set up. "I didn't have many props. The studio was simple. I used odd things." Margarett was immediately curious. They talked about what they had in common. Art? Paris? The old woman couldn't summon up their conversation, but she remembered Margarett's energy. "Paris was a magnet for a woman like that, looking for freedom."

Margarett had pulled back her hair rather severely and parted it on the side. She wore a suit with a pleated skirt, which reads gray in the black-and-white photograph, and under her jacket, to which was pinned an artificial flower, a thin sweater with narrow diagonal stripes. Abbott directed her to a mahogany chair with a curved back, the same chair visible in other seated portraits she made that spring: of André Maurois, Leo Stein, James Joyce.

"I relied on the instincts of the moment," Abbott said, a gesture in which the person "would reveal something about herself." Margarett crossed her legs, leaned forward, set her right elbow on her knee, chin on her fist, and looked straight at the lens. "A portrait was a collaboration?" I asked. "An exchange," the old woman answered. What Margarett gave was a gaze that followed one everywhere in a room. Nothing remained of the girl Arnold Genthe caught in a youthful smolder of romantic challenge, or of the young mother shot by a studio photographer at Prides, smiling, baby on her hip.

Margarett looks strong but uneasy; female but stripped of effeminizing clutter; handsome but not beautiful, not genderless exactly. You could imagine this woman lived and worked in Paris, that she was one of Abbott's famous female subjects: Sylvia Beach in a shiny black raincoat, face caught in an almost violent expression; Jane Heap, hair cut like a man's, tuxedo and black tie, full lips darkly rouged; Janet Flanner, cross-legged on the floor, top hat decorated with one black, one white mask. But Margarett was not a resident of Paris who sought likeminded friends in a café at the end of a day or labored in the solitary light of a Left Bank studio. In spite of the sophisticated angularity of the photograph, the unassailed, even enraged, determination in her expression, the look in her eyes is lonely and frankly sad.

Margarett stands at an easel. A woman sits facing her, and Margarett is painting, not the woman's anger, but the longing and sadness beneath it. Abruptly she picks up a wooden chair, slams it down on the floor. "Her face must disturb like a sudden, dangerous sound," I imagine her saying to no one in particular, then see her for a moment looking at herself in a mirror. The intensity in her eyes is not sadness and fear but what remains of work pursued that day, ideas argued through the night with artists who are her friends. Margarett paints and then she erupts into her loud, deep laugh and, with abandon, sitting in her chair, rocks back and forth in a rapture of having got it right.

"It was a time of hope," Berenice Abbott said, "that was the thing."

vii

*I like arms and
their movements, and
striped blouses*

(1930–1932)

Margarett in her Boston studio, 1930
(from a newspaper photograph)

PRIME THE TALL CANVAS, lay her in quick with charcoal. The mirrored walls of the bathroom reflect her, sitting on the *moderne* gray satin vanity stool, legs apart, black pumps, a short pink circus gown, low-cut, string strap falling from her shoulder. She wears a top hat. A shiver of magenta vibrates a yellow aureole of wall, dark teal scribbles a cloud of gray-blue floor. She is young and slender, beautiful, you would say, but for the—what?—disconsolate fury given off by dark eyes, scraped at by the stick end of a brush, asymmetrical. The left eye is encircled with a shadow of teal and finished with a glint of white; the right is its dimmed double. The shadow of the hat brim colors her forehead lavender. Her cheeks are flushed the fluorescent melon orange that also glimmers on her lower lip. The upper lip is red, bigger, messed at.

The North Shore *Breeze and Reminder,* which chronicled "society" north of Boston, had not caught up with soignée girls wearing top hats, foreheads turned lavender with intensity.

"The District Offers More of Beauty, Romance and History Than Any Other Spot in the Country," read a headline at the start of a late 1920s season. An article might authenticate Longfellow's "The Wreck of the Hesperus" as the true story of a shipwreck at Norman's Woe right up the road, or, reproducing a period engraving, recall the Salem witch trials. Photographs enshrined gardens of great estates, and captions described as "charming" oceanfront houses that rivaled the sea palaces at Newport in dimension. Each issue tracked the residents who moved from Boston to the Shore in summer; traveled in winter to

Boca Grande, Palm Beach, or Aiken, South Carolina; booked state-rooms on steamers for Europe.

Margarett, identified as "Mrs. Q. A. Shaw McKean (Margarett Williams Sargent)," was reported "busy with her art work all summer," in a column that followed the art colonies of Rockport and Eastern Point and activities of noted local painters like Cecilia Beaux and Charles Hopkinson. Margaret Fitzhugh Browne, breezing through as the portraitist who lured the retired golfer Bobby Jones to her studio, was the region's fierce opponent of "Modern Art." Its advocate was Mrs. Morris Pancoast, who exhibited "selected groups of paintings by the modern men" in "an unusual gallery in East Gloucester."

The *Breeze* never mentioned the stock market crash. Margie, then almost eight, overheard her father tell "some terrible story" of a man he knew throwing himself from a window after learning he'd lost all his money. Harry and Caresse Crosby's visits to Apple Trees, his parents' estate in Manchester, were always reported, but the *Breeze* was mute on his suicide in New York (surely the talk of Boston), six weeks after the crash. Crosby's death had nothing to do with money, but it marked the end of the 1920s "innocents abroad" and coincided with the turn in financial circumstance that brought the Gerald Murphys, the Archibald MacLeishes, and many other Americans home.

The crash affected Margarett and Shaw less than it did some of their friends. Bebo and Josephine Bradlee let servants go, sold a great house, moved to a smaller one, and Mrs. Bradlee opened a dress shop. The alimony Betty Parsons lived on abruptly ceased, and she was forced to leave Paris. Marjorie Davenport lost her uncle's legacy and left New York to live the year round in Vermont. For the very, very rich like Shaw's mother and Harry Crosby's parents, nothing much changed. Margarett and Shaw did not go to Europe in 1930 or 1931, but they went to Cuba in 1932 and returned to Europe in 1933. Margarett kept her studio on St. Botolph Street, but she and Shaw closed their Boston town house on Commonwealth Avenue in 1931, put it on the market, where it moldered unsold for years, and wintered at

Prides. What Margie remembered was Shaw sitting at the edge of Margarett's bed, whispering, "We're all right."

Asymmetrical eyes slant like the eyes of a jungle cat. Muscled arms bulge from a short-sleeved shirt. His green sweater vest is patterned yellow and red and black. No one knows who he is. Outsize hands loose on a knee. Where did she find him, this no-account sitting in the corner? Walls a saturated sky blue, broken by gray the color of storm clouds. She crops the top from his cap, the feet from his legs. The cuffs of his gray trousers billow. His chair is deeper yellow, more orange than butter, and it's coming apart—disrupted, perhaps, by his unsettled, piercing, contemptuous gaze. Its ladder back tilts—bands of gold sprung from proportion—so he seems pushed toward us, as if what caused the bright chair to fall apart were emptying him from its arms.

Painting the growl that came from the young man's eyes, Margarett pulled from herself what she could put nowhere else, turned that furor into something that could exist independently, seared what she felt and saw into the eye of the viewer. The girl with the lavender forehead and the boy in the yellow chair represent her at the height of her powers. From these paintings she has sheared the clutter of life as Mrs. Quincy Adams Shaw McKean. Margarett Sargent burns fiercely, with a burning that both divides her from those around her and enables her to live her double life. Her painting protects her, as magic does a sorceress, but it also endangers her. As her work homed in on the truth of her circumstances, Margarett became more vulnerable.

In the wake of the crash, Shaw closed down the investment banking firm he'd started after the failure of Richardson, Hill and "pretty much retired," John Spanbauer said, to devote himself to "sporting interests"—fishing and hunting trips to Canada, golf at Myopia, bridge in the evening. Prides Hill Kennels was a going concern. Shaw's fox terriers, with names like Bounce and Miss Barbarian, were advertised monthly in the kennel pages of *Vanity Fair*; in 1928, a dog called Style won the Best American Bred Bitch at the Eastern Dog Club Show in

Boston, where her competitors in other breeds were dogs shown by Shaw's North Shore friends. Margarett hated fox terriers. They were small and they yapped. They were Shaw's pride, and just one of their differences.

In October 1928, Paul Gauguin's great portrait of Meyer de Hahn was delivered to their rooms at the Ritz in New York. Margarett had bought it for $3,500—a huge sum—at Kraushaar. She knew what Shaw's reaction would be, even relished its inevitability, but his anger made no sense to her, at least not as much sense as the painting. She hung it like an icon at the entrance to the great hall at Prides, so that from anywhere in the room, you could see its audacious diagonal divide darkness from light; the pensive, magical, inward-looking face; its flagrant blaze of reds and yellows.

Increasingly, where Shaw was concerned, Margarett's lack of ease overcame her natural courtesy. The difference now was that their friends knew it. "They were physically drawn but mismatched," said Ted Weeks of the *Atlantic Monthly*, one of Shaw's golfing friends. "Shaw always stood to the side," said Garson Kanin, who met them in the 1930s. "She was so artistic, so creative," said Mabel Storey, with whom Margarett rode to the hunt. "Margarett needed something . . . else."

Guests were quiet when she got a laugh at his expense, when she taunted him at the table, Marie Laurencin's *Femme au Balcon*—black rail restraining her, hat abundant with pink roses—gazing down from above the fireplace.

"Fights about what?" I asked Margie.

"Nothing. The sugar."

The children joined in when Margarett suggested a game: Name the most appalling combination of food you can think of. "Oh, for God's sake, Margarett," Shaw would yelp. She invented an ongoing story she told the children, of Lizzie and James, a married couple who did nothing but argue. Shaw took Mountain Valley spring water along whenever he traveled. Margarett forged a letter from the company awarding him a certificate as its most esteemed customer and roared

with laughter as his delight turned to speechlessness when she exposed
the hoax. Once, during a party, she hid behind the curtains and kicked
at his ankle as he passed. Sometimes he was able to laugh. Often, suppressing rage or hurt, and with natural tenderness and a kind of hopeless faith, he continued to try to please her.

In 1931, Shaw finally launched an enterprise that pleased Margarett very much. His friend George Thomas, dog judge and breeder,
had two extraordinary dogs, which had been imported from England
by Zeppo, the youngest Marx brother. Afghan hounds were virtually
unknown in America and had been bred in Britain only since 1921,
when Begum, a pale dog with large brown eyes and perfect carriage,
was glimpsed by an English horsewoman galloping the plains of
Baluchistan. By acquiring Zeppo Marx's pair, Shaw became the first
American breeder of Afghan hounds. "Can kill leopards," he wrote in
the Prides Hill brochure, quoting a Britisher who used Afghans to
hunt white leopard in North India. The centerfold photo had Shaw,
two leads in each hand; a twin son to either side, a lead in each of their
hands; eight dogs attentively flocked to face the camera, pale fur ruffled
by the breeze.

The dogs entranced Margarett. After Sunday lunch, as guests stepped
from the darkness of the house into the bright afternoon, she saw to it
the kennelman opened the runs. "You couldn't believe it," a visitor said.
"There they'd be, thirty Afghans, leaping across that great green lawn."

Some of her friends considered Prides Margarett's greatest achievement. John Walker, a Harvard student in the late twenties, saw it as an
exquisite net in which she ensnared herself. "She would have been
much better," he said, "if she had broken the net and flown away." For
Margarett, Prides was not a prison but a context, and she worked to realize it as single-mindedly as she worked on a painting. When she
talked to Joe Leland about the shape of an addition, with her gardener,
George Day, about a plan for a topiary hedge, she spoke with creative
excitement. The house continued to evolve; in the summer of 1929,

another addition was completed. The big room, the living room since Margarett moved her work to the studio on the hill, had been extended thirty feet, an entryway added.

"Room" is the wrong word to describe what Margarett had composed to resemble the great hall of a Florentine villa—two stories high, giant skylights facing north. If you came through the iron gate that separated the entry from the living room and turned to look back, you saw, to the right, the portrait of Meyer de Hahn, and to the left *The White Blackbird*, George Luks's portrait of Margarett. The way paintings were hung, how sculpture and furniture were placed across the vast expanse, suggested landscape rather than decor.

Odd decorative ends of antique wrought iron, a multitude of Italian and Spanish chairs, a pair of Venetian corner cupboards, challenged Calder's wooden giraffe and Ossip Zadkine's brass bird for attention as sculpture. Lengths of tapestry or textile—tawny terra-cotta, dusky blue—lay across surfaces. A huge abstraction—flags and banners, all gray and black, Jean Lurçat's *Les Bateaux à Voiles*, traded from the artist for two Afghans—commanded the south wall. Over the fireplace hung a narrow horizontal Derain still life of a loaf of bread. Small Degas bronze horses gathered on an open desk, and near the fireplace, a polychrome marble head of a woman by Gaston Lachaise gazed from the top of a Shaker cabinet. During the day, shafts of light fell through skylights, breaking the shadow and brightening the creamy walls. At night, the light of candles and hanging lamps rose into the darkness so the high beamed ceiling was barely visible. The glow illuminated a profusion of cut flowers and was reflected when dark floorboard interrupted an expanse of pale Oriental carpet or a maze of American hooked rugs.

It was here, in the big room, that drinks were replenished until dinner was called, here that Margarett wandered, adjusting an imperfect flower arrangement or exchanging one painting for another so that she could see each anew. Looking out a sequence of leaded windows nearly the height of the room, she could see the arborvitae topiary, the espaliered apple trees, the pool, and beyond it the schoolroom, with its own kitchen, where the children had their lessons in the morning.

Senny's older brother, John Neary, had arrived when the twins were old enough for a teacher. He was a warm, funny, intellectually passionate, hard-drinking Boston Irishman. When he wrote Margarett a note accompanied by some of the children's writing, he commented that their poems had not sprung "full-fledged, like Minerva, from the brain of Jove." He did not think them too young—Margie was eight when he came, the boys five—to insist that they reflect before choosing a word, and he criticized the results "with a little imaginative baiting now and again." Nothing fine could be finished without reworking, he told them.

The children took to John as they had to Senny, and he was perfect for Margarett's requirements. She remembered her boredom at Miss Winsor's and was convinced the local private school, organized by one of her childhood friends, would be deadly. She didn't care that the children longed to go to school with their friends; she wanted them to be inspired. With the Nearys, she devised a curriculum that was intellectually serious and unusually advanced for children so young. John and Senny took care of literature, geography, and history, and twice a week, "Madame," Mrs. E. Power Biggs, the wife of the organist and renowned interpreter of Bach, came out from Cambridge to teach French and piano. John introduced Latin when the boys were five, and by the time she was nine, Jenny used it to write letters to Margarett.

When the girls were tiny, Senny sat at the foot of their beds at night, wrote down what they said about the day, and later typed it up. John would direct all four children to keep their own diaries. They also published a mimeographed newspaper, *The Prides Hill Gazette*, and occasional books—a collection of poems and stories when Margarett and Shaw went abroad in 1933, and, the next year, for their wedding anniversary, *The Onion River Anthology*—poems in the voice of everyone in the household, including the divorced Joe Leland: "It seems to me/ That all of life/ Is just the problem/ of a wife."

On rainy days, Senny and the girls climbed to the attic, pulled out trunks of Margarett's out-of-date clothes, dressed up, and put on plays in the schoolroom. The *Gazette* of April 1932 reviewed Jenny, aged nine, as Macbeth ("She had a good costume and her acting was marvelous") and Margie, eleven, as Macduff ("did it very well especially fighting Macbeth"). The art column covered exhibitions by Freddie Hall, an artist friend of Margarett's ("I liked Mr. Hall's etchings better than his paintings"), and Margarett Sargent ("She is a great artist. Her work shows ability and strength of character—one or two of her pictures I feel could be more finished—especially the young woman holding a child"). Once, when Margarett and Shaw were in Europe, the children put on their own exhibition and invited friends of their parents who they knew were interested in art. "4 under 8" was the name of the show, and Harry sold two nudes.

§

ONE AFTERNOON early in 1930, the last winter the family spent in the house on Commonwealth Avenue, a big man in a mustard-colored suit lugged five large, battered suitcases to the door of number 205. "Paris," read layers of labels and luggage tags. *"Calder,"* read the large painted signature. Margarett greeted her old friend at the door, summoned Walsh, the chauffeur, to help with his bags, and offered Sandy Calder a drink. The children had been told Mr. Calder would bring a circus, but what kind of circus could possibly fit into a suitcase? Margie and Jenny knew he was going to make portraits of them later in the week. They were accustomed to Margarett painting them, shouting "Hold that pose!" as they scampered away, but Mr. Calder was going to use wire, Margarett told them, instead of ink or paint.

Margarett had met Calder in New York, probably in 1922 or 1923, when he was studying with George Luks, painting city scenes with a bright palette inspired by John Sloan and emulating Luks's fast, blunt brush. He always called her Maggie. When she saw him again in Paris with Betty Parsons, it was 1927, and Josephine Baker was his subject. Margarett was entranced by the witty ease of his wire line. Any household quandary was an occasion for sculpture—the broken spigot he replaced with a wire dog that lifted a leg when the water was turned on; the fish Betty Parsons found, wire head and tail out either end of the toilet paper, after he left one evening.

Calder began the circus by accident. He'd always made toy animals to entertain his family; now he'd sell them to make money. "A lion with a wire body and tawny head of velvet and wool led to a cage on wheels," his sister wrote. His Paris friends loved how he moved the animals with his fingers, making animal noises. Soon he was manipulating a score of creatures and trapeze artists with a web of pulleys or by hand so deftly his pudgy fingers seemed to disappear. "He was lightfingered like a thief," said one enthusiast.

After a year, he had made enough figures to fill two suitcases and had printed bright linoleum-cut announcements. Circus performances at Calder's studio became the rage of Montparnasse. Isamu Noguchi cranked the gramophone, and Mary Butts brought Jean Cocteau. Sylvia Beach and Janet Flanner came, André Kertesz and Tristan Tzara, Mondrian and Miró, Adge Baker and Betty Parsons. Wherever Margarett saw the circus first—in Paris or at a New York performance in 1929—she was utterly charmed. Who could resist? The figures, seemingly thrown together with spit and paste, had the quirk of life, the poignance of a cripple hurling aside a crutch to break into dance.

The occasion for Calder's Boston visit was an exhibition of his wire sculpture at the Harvard Society for Contemporary Art in Cambridge. The story got out that he arrived at South Station with nothing but pliers in his pocket and a bolt of wire slung over a shoulder, but actually, he wrote later, "I took the circus along." His exhibition opened in Cambridge on Tuesday, January 27, and a circus performance at Harvard the following Friday was packed with students. The performance in Margarett's huge living room would be the only one in Boston, and she invited a crowd.

Margarett did not mind Sandy pushing the furniture into rows or constructing bleachers from boards and pails. He rolled back the rug, threw sawdust on the floor, and set out the peanuts. He unrolled a bit of green carpet and laid out a ring made of red and white rounds of painted wood. Crawling around the floor and talking to himself, he erected two steel poles about three feet high, a miniature French flag fluttering at the top of each. He suspended trapezes and a tightrope between them, looped a red-striped curtain to either side of the ring so his "performers" would have "privacy" offstage, and aimed a homemade spotlight at the center of the ring.

After dinner, Margarett summoned her guests, bespangled in evening clothes, to sit on the "bleachers," the children to sit on the floor. "Ladies and gentlemen," Sandy declaimed, and music cranked from a gramophone heralded a grand procession led by Monsieur Loyal, the spool-faced ringmaster. Applause! Loyal blew his whistle, and wooden horses with manes of string circled the ring, powered by an eggbeater, wire cowboys leaping to their backs. Enter clowns, Sandy's fingers effecting stumble and pratfall, then he barked for seals and roared for the lion, which leaped as the tamer lashed his whip.

Skinny tightrope walkers, feet weighted with fishing sinkers, traversed the high wire. Dalmatians sprinted between spokes of a buggy's spinning wheels, and a flock of doves—bits of white paper, weighted, spinning down a wire—fluttered to the creamy shoulders of the bejeweled passenger. Drum roll! Rigoulet, the strong man, strains at his dumbbell. Drum roll! The sword swallower is fed his sword. Are the children still awake? How thirsty are Margarett's patient guests, who have been eating peanuts for two, maybe three hours?

The trapeze act was the *pièce de résistance.* Sometimes the girl did not leave hold of her swing, and the act failed. Would she tonight? Would she spin through the air, hook her wire hands through her fellow's wire feet? A net reassured beneath. Sandy hesitated as if taking aim, then jerked the wire and released her into the air, wire arms outstretched. It was over in a moment, and there she was, hooked to her consort, swinging like a pendulum!

Calder and his circus had come to Boston through the efforts of three imaginative Harvard undergraduates. One fall afternoon in 1928, Lincoln Kirstein, John Walker, and Edward W. W. Warburg had marched into the university's new Fogg Art Museum and confronted Paul Sachs, its assistant director: "Why is there no modern art at Harvard?" Sachs—a bond trader turned connoisseur, who was heir to the Goldman, Sachs investment house—had collected his first Picasso drawing in 1920. He considered Modernism "the work of actuality," but his opponents on the Harvard faculty had balked at endorsing works that had not stood the test of time, and so the Fogg included nothing newer than the Impressionists. "Why don't *you* do it?" Sachs suggested to the three students. The result, six months later, was the Harvard Society for Contemporary Art.

Through Sachs, Margarett soon met the three "executives" of the new organization. For each, as for her, art was a redemptive passion. After an "excessively affluent" childhood in Pittsburgh, John Walker contracted polio at thirteen and was taken for treatment to New York, where he discovered art while spinning through the galleries of the Metropolitan Museum in his wheelchair. By the time he got to Harvard, he wanted to be a curator, and one day, drawn by reports of Picasso reproductions on his walls, his traveled classmate Lincoln Kirstein turned up, "dark, saturnine, shaved-headed," to discuss modern art.

Earlier in his Harvard career, Kirstein launched *Hound and Horn*, which shared writers, artists, and point of view with journals published by Americans in Paris. In England, with his sister, Mina, he'd gone to Bloomsbury parties and met Virginia Woolf and Roger Fry, and in Paris he'd seen Diaghilev's company dance on sets by Picasso and Derain. On his return, Boston seemed, as it often did to Margarett, "a combination of a prison and Friday afternoons at the symphony." He enrolled at the Museum School but soon ran up against "old Philip Hale who loathed Modern Art and any young twit like me who tried to draw from casts in the manner of Wyndham Lewis or Eric Gill."

Eddie Warburg had also traveled in Europe, but until the summer of 1929, when he bought Picasso's *Blue Boy* in Berlin, his taste for simplicity and directness had drawn him to the Renaissance rather than to modern art. The gouache portrait of a humble young man was a far cry from the brocaded, luxurious taste of his collector father, Felix

Warburg, whom he immediately recruited for the board of the Harvard Society for Contemporary Art. "Eddie was our clown," said John Walker. "He raised us a lot of lovely money."

Money was easy to come by in early 1929, and Paul Sachs helped connect his protégés with patrons and lenders—dealers and collectors of modern art in New York, Boston, and Chicago. For gallery space, the three leased two rooms above the Harvard Cooperative Society in Harvard Square. They painted the ceilings silver and the walls white, furnished one room with steel café chairs and tables, the other with a large rectangular table Lincoln and John constructed by balancing a highly polished metal top on marble legs from an old soda fountain.

When they asked to close their first year with a full retrospective of Margarett's work, she enthusiastically accepted. The Society's first exhibition, "Americans," included the abstract work of Marin, O'Keeffe, and Demuth, set off by the figurative and landscape painting of George Bellows, John Sloan, Arthur B. Davies, and others. The second show, an exhibition of European artists, brought "the work of thirty-three painters and sculptors, regardless of nationality, who have been working in Paris and who have made the influence of 'Modern' art what it is today."

Not only did Kirstein, Walker, and Warburg share Margarett's frame of reference as far as painting and sculpture were concerned; they also understood her impulse, demonstrated at Prides, to mix crafts like American quilts and hooked rugs with modern paintings. For the first time in an American art context, the Society showed contemporary design, folk art, and works in media not then considered art. Their first season also acknowledged the aesthetic attributes of certain technological advances; a photography exhibition included not only works by Americans and Europeans but aerial photographs, pictures from astronomical and surgical laboratories, and photos from the daily press. Their most sensational show, revived the second year by popular demand, was of Buckminster Fuller's Dymaxion House, a " 'machine-for-living-in' that could be constructed by mass productive methods, cost approximately $500 a ton."

As the Harvard Society for Contemporary Art was getting under way, some of its lenders and patrons, including Paul Sachs, Frederic Bartlett, and Margarett, became involved in a project in New York. When the Museum of Modern Art opened, on November 8, 1929, Bartlett and Sachs were on its board of directors, and Margarett's Gauguin hung on the walls of its temporary galleries, four rented rooms at 730 Fifth Avenue. Alfred Barr, recommended by Sachs as the new museum's director, had chosen for its inaugural exhibition the four painters he considered preeminent in "the genealogy of contemporary painting"—Cézanne, Gauguin, Seurat, and Van Gogh. When he characterized their work in the catalogue essay, he might have been articulating the aesthetic of Margarett's painting. "For soft contours they substitute rigid angularities; instead of hazy atmosphere they offer color surfaces, lacquer-hard."

It was at this new museum in New York that the eclectic experiments of the Harvard Society for Contemporary Art would eventually become exhibition policy, but by the time Margarett's exhibition closed the Society's first season, its reputation had already reached beyond Boston, and the debates that had roiled Back Bay art clubs for decades had become obsolete. The conservative Boston painter Ives Gammell could sneer in his diary that Lincoln Kirstein's discussion of Margarett's paintings at a dinner at Prides was "too broad a caricature for slapstick farce," but something new had taken root in Boston, and Margarett was close to its center.

Two women—boisterous, naughty, and big. They wear swimming costumes cut high on the leg. It's a close-up that crops heads at midbrow, legs at midthigh. One woman, her back to us, wears bright yellow; black stripes encircle buttock, hipbone. The other, facing us, wears aqua, four thin black stripes low on her hips. Two women— color against blue sky, flappers rowdy at the beach to jazz in the air. They have confidence and size. Yellow looks away, black cap, face in profile, eye a line, orange cheek, lips open. She has hips. She moves. Aqua has a brown bob, red mouth, full-face, no eyes, as she leaps to catch a yellow ball with big hands. Margarett has fixed them, hip-to-hip.

"First reaction: Immense thrill," read the dispatch from Cambridge to the *Chicago Evening Post.* "It's her colors. Her loving feeling for colors, her sensitiveness for grading colors, molding colors, contrasting colors." *Bathers* illustrated the review by a writer named H. von Erffa. "I like arms," Margarett told her. "I like arms and their movements, and striped blouses." At the galleries of the Harvard Society for Contemporary Art, twenty-eight of Margarett's paintings hung on bright white walls, their colors reflected in the silver ceiling. This was her first one-person show in the Boston area and included fifteen watercolors, two pastels, a wall of drawings, and the bronze heads of George Luks and Chaffard.

At the private view on Thursday, February 7, 1930, collector friends like Frederic Bartlett and John Spaulding circulated among Harvard and Radcliffe students and old friends like Emily and Henry Cabot Lodge and Vivian Cochrane. Maria deAcosta Sargent greeted the portrait of herself as *Tailleur Classique,* and Paul Sachs bought a drawing. Marian Haughton bought a watercolor of her grandchildren, rascals around a table. Freddie Hall gazed back at himself on canvas—about to laugh, intelligent eyes through round spectacles, cheeks flushed, a gardenia in his buttonhole. His wife, Evelyn, wore purple and carried an alarm clock in her purse, set to go off when she wished to depart. The children crowded near two paintings of Jimmy Durante—"If you can find enough oils, paint that schnozz of mine again," he'd written Margarett on a photograph he sent after the first time he sat for her.

"She is an out-and-out modernist in style as well as spirit, and her special field seems to be the interpretation of the post-war life that is our modern world," wrote the *Transcript* reviewer. Margarett was now considered a major Boston artist, and the writer met her on her own terms:

> Her style is slap-dash, but when she confines herself to a few bold colors, and a few bold slashes of the brush, she has an uncanny knack of saying everything with the most powerful economy. Her drawings reveal this gift in its greatest purity.

Here a line will betray a whole trend of emotion or indeed an
entire personality with the lift of an eyelid, the slouch of an
arm, the sag of a mouth. . . .

§

"SHE WAS A GOOD PAINTER at a time when that kind of expressionism
was not very much in vogue. I felt then and feel now that she's not
been appreciated enough," said John Walker at eighty-two, his careers
as assistant to Bernard Berenson and director of the National Gallery
in Washington years behind him. His dark hair had gone bright white,
and the effects of polio had returned in old age.

In 1930, he was a young man whose life had been saved by art,
and Margarett was an artist, a glamorous woman, fifteen years older
than he. "She had a big mouth, I remember that. And a deep voice."
He was physically drawn to her. She appreciated him, he said, flattered
him, but always seemed to withhold something. He was fascinated.
"She never seemed to do things like other human beings," he said.

Sometime during the spring of 1930, Margarett began to imagine
John Walker's face in paint—vivid dark eyes, wide brow, dark hair.
He met her at the studio on St. Botolph Street. It was not the first time
he'd been there; he'd come before, to choose paintings for her Harvard
exhibition. "She had an idea of what I looked like—which may not
have been what I actually looked like, but very few portraits are of the
sitter: they are rather an idea of the sitter."

Margarett painted him as a romantic young man, swooped at the
canvas with her brushes, painted a ground that was almost mauve.
"Her rapidity was what struck me," Walker said. She sculpted his suit
with soft browns, modeled the salmon-pink tie so it seemed to stand
up from his chest. He sat just once for that portrait, which she framed
in white and hung over the fireplace in her Art Deco bathroom.

Margarett was painting ferociously that spring and contributing to
Mrs. Pancoast's series of group shows, "Moderns at Pancoast." She
went to Palm Beach in April, and when she returned, John saw her
whenever he could. Often they went to galleries, to museums. The

way she thought about painting converted him to an instinctive way of looking that cracked open the formalism he'd learned at Harvard. "She was a great teacher," he said.

"What did you learn?" I asked him.

"I learned how to look at pictures."

"How?"

"You couldn't show it with words. She'd grab my arm and point. That was it."

"Did you have a crush on Margarett?"

"What?"

"When you met her—"

"Of course I did," the old man snapped, as if it should have been self-evident. "She was the love of my youthful life."

The culmination of their relationship came one evening in June 1930, just after his graduation from Harvard and before he left for Italy to work for Berenson. He was invited to Prides for the night. Shaw was away, but the children were in the house. He and Margarett had dinner alone, or perhaps there were guests who then left. She'd given him the tower room, with its silvery mirrored ceiling. "I feel quite sure I could find the room if I were in the house again," the old man said. "What I remember is a bed and a chair."

Margarett came to him, unexpectedly, in the night, wearing a filmy dressing gown and carrying a candle. He was a virgin.

"She seduced me. No, that's not right. I wanted to be seduced."

John Walker was not the only young man whom Margarett visited in her negligee. Nor were all the men she seduced as young as he was, nor is there any possibility of coming up with a complete list. The translator Louis Galantiere, wandering up and down the road in Dorset, calling her name; Artur Schnabel, a frequent guest at Marian Haughton's, in Boston to perform a concerto under Koussevitzky or an evening of violently swift, heartbreakingly delicate Beethoven sonatas. "We saw Mr. Schnabel," Jenny wrote Margarett in Europe in 1933, "and he

told us how wonderful he thinks you are." And of course there was
Roland Balay, in New York or in Paris, for years.

And, like a descant, the women.

Attention still came to Margarett naturally, and to respond, she
believed, transgressed nothing. She fixed you with her eyes, and if you
looked back at her, the room disappeared. Then she began to talk, to
smile at you, and you were riveted, fascinated, caught. She did not
miss the erotic subtext to a smile or gesture.

She must have been lonely, living as she did in the midst of a
crowd of people, intimate with none of them—not even with the children once they passed the age of coming unbidden to her arms, except
in the quiet moments when she drew or painted them, or when she got
them laughing in a game. Certainly not with Shaw, with whom, now,
tenderness was rare—with whom she now had something that could
be called an arrangement.

Shaw looked away when it came to Margarett's romances, or perhaps he genuinely didn't know about them—no one is sure. What
bothered him was her drinking, a vague problem at the beginning of
their marriage, which now alarmed him. She was late coming in to
dinner, or she fell asleep at the table. She was present in a conversation, then she was not. He wished she would not drink, and after a
while he began to ask her not to, to exact promises she'd take it easy,
have just one drink or none at all—for the sake of the children, for the
sake of health. He could handle her selfishness when it came to her art,
even when it came to the Harvard boys she kept inviting to the house,
whom he found boring and somehow threatening. But he could not
bear the humiliation, becoming more frequent, of her behavior after a
few drinks.

The roar of the twenties had reached Boston halfway through the
decade and emancipated an entire generation to the cocktail, to booze
procured through bootleggers. Dressed to the nines, the young of old
Boston drank at dinner parties, at speakeasies in New York or Chicago, and in Paris at Scheherazade, the Blue Room, Bricktop's. Mar-

garett drank with Betty Parsons, who matched her drink for drink but she said she never saw her drunk. She drank with Roland Balay and she drank with Isabel Pell. She drank with Maria Sargent and with Vivian Cochrane, who drank in New York as a young actress, in Boston as a young widow, and who later, as Mrs. Dudley Pickman of 303 Commonwealth Avenue, made sure her house had a bar on every floor and that her butler greeted all who knocked with the offer of a martini.

Margarett and Shaw drank through the clamor of their parties and in the gleaming quiet of the dining room at Prides. They had cocktails with Harry and Bessie McKean, with Ham and Ruthie Robb, who lived up the road. "They all drank," said Ruthie Robb's daughter, "and it turned on many of them." Alcohol turned on Shaw's brother Harry and Eddie Morgan. And it turned on Margarett. By the time the stock market crashed, she'd been drinking almost ten years, and it had started to show around her eyes. Her body began to betray her. A woman's liver, which succumbs to alcohol sooner than a man's, separated her drinking from Shaw's. The genes of the poet grandfather who sang sluiced with claret presented themselves, partnered by the depression that felled Hunnewell women at the prime of life. Increasingly, Senny greeted the children at breakfast with "Your mother has a headache. Please be quiet." Margie and Jenny had a word for it before they knew what *it* was: "Mama is languid today."

Apparently, Margarett had forgotten how extreme Eddie Morgan's drinking had seemed to her as a girl. She drank as much as she wanted. Or, if it pleased her, she didn't drink for weeks or months at a time. Her appetites were hers, and her capacity to satisfy them put her at a kind of liberty. She held to that liberty despite promising Shaw she'd never drink again, in spite of her love for her children. Her beauty and her talk still attracted anyone she wished for company, and she never drank when she painted. If she could not drink when she and Shaw were out together, she would drink by herself, hiding bottles in the bathroom, among the spangled shoes in all those mirrored closets. If she could not drink at Prides, she would drink elsewhere.

Margarett liked the release alcohol gave her, but she had no idea what it might take away. She was willing to sacrifice a few evenings to early drowsiness, a few daylights to the dark room of the headache, in order to have that particular vivid intensity. It did not threaten her in the slightest to stop or to promise to stop; she could stop, she kept proving, whenever she pleased. What she did not understand was that in abdicating to Shaw the responsibility for managing her drinking lay the threat of losing everything she had, that in months or years of lies and slips from his straight and narrow, she might lose her freedom, her upper hand, her magic.

" 'Beyond Good & Evil' is the picture of me," Margarett wrote to Frederic Bartlett. She had painted the self-portrait during the summer of 1930, had been photographed in her smock painting it, by Bachrach. She placed the image of herself almost diagonally across a ground of pale, smoky blue—slender, black hair pulled to her neck in a chignon, her skin translucently pale, eyes wide and light, light blue. Her hands, one on the other, press into her lap; her arms are tensely extended. Animals crowd the canvas, as if eager to push her from it—a leopard, a goat, a dove. The dress, string straps, is patterned magenta, poison green, and aqua. This is a self-portrait not as an artist but as a woman. The woman restrains herself, keeps her breath in. She is frightened, without defense.

In September 1930, Margarett mailed an exhibition checklist to Frederic, who had arranged an exhibition for her in November at the Arts Club of Chicago. Incorporated in 1916 by a group of collectors, the Arts Club soon became an innovative forum for modern art, years before New York, let alone Boston, had any such venue. By 1921, it had shown Marin, Demuth, and Lachaise, and, among the French, Seurat, Delaunay, and Cézanne. In 1924, it presented the first one-man show of Rodin's sculpture west of New York and the first American exhibition of Picasso's drawings, with a catalogue essay by Clive Bell. In the late 1920s, Marcel Duchamp installed a major Brancusi exhibition and Léger showed his film *Ballet Mécanique*. In its small theater, Igor Stravinsky and Serge Prokofiev performed their music, Edna St. Vincent Millay and Robert Frost read their poems, Marsden Hartley lectured on art, and Ford Madox Ford spoke on literature.

At nine o'clock in the morning on the day of the opening, Margarett met Alice Roullier, the club's secretary, and Isabel Jarvis, her assistant, at the Arts Club, then housed in the Wrigley Building on Michigan Avenue. Miss Jarvis was skeptical about the woman whom Mr. Bartlett had praised as "married, but a very good artist," but fifty years later, she remembered "an unusually beautiful woman, a very good painter, very informed about modern art." In the largest of the club's three galleries, they supervised the hanging of forty paintings, twenty-five watercolors, and fourteen drawings. Like the show at Harvard, this was both exhibition and retrospective. Two of the paintings were loans from Frederic Barlett, who, in his home, hung them on a wall with a Matisse and a Utrillo. "The three women have all the beauty of color of Marie Laurencin," a society columnist wrote, "and an underlying primitive power of their own."

Unlike Boston, where a gathering to celebrate modern art had the feel of a conspiracy, Chicago had boisterous pride in its innovation. The opening was celebrated with a tea, and fashionable Chicago crowded the gallery. Margarett arrived on Bartlett's arm, to be greeted by Mrs. John Alden Carpenter, the club's president, and by Mrs. Potter Palmer, daughter-in-law of the great collector who had commissioned Mary Cassatt's mural for the Woman's Building at the World's Columbian Exposition in Chicago in 1893.

In its weekly magazine of the art world, the *Chicago Post* headlined Margarett's exhibition. Bartlett, who personally handled the publicity, made sure photographs were provided, and *Blue Girl* took all of page one under a banner headline. The city's most prominent critic, C. J. Bulliet, was a conservative who usually panned the Arts Club's shows; he hated abstraction and would declare in 1936 that Modernism "began with Cézanne and ended with Picasso." In Margarett's work, however, he saw a kinship to his beloved Post-Impressionists; she was, he wrote, the leading Modernist in a city "where 'Modernism' has even a tougher row to hoe than it has here," and a rebel "regarded over in her hometown as a lost soul because of her art bolshevism." The strength of the exhibition was reflected in the clarity of Bulliet's review. As influences he cited "Matisse, principally, and Picasso and Chagall and Modigliani" but concluded that "despite the influences, there is a unity of effect running thru her work—something distinctively 'Margarett Sargent.' " He praised her gift for capturing character, in particular her ability, unusual in a woman, to paint men. "Given another three years like the last three and Margarett Sargent will have sublimated all her 'influences' and stand revealed in all the power of her own high talent."

When the exhibition closed, Margarett, long back in Boston, cabled Frederic to have her paintings packed. She had set up her easel backstage at the Metropolitan Theatre, she told him, and, with the company standing about, had painted Harpo Marx, first with a flaming corkscrew crown of orange hair, then with a parrot on his shoulder and his scribbled caption, "a portrait no artist would paint." Frederic directed the Arts Club to ship half the paintings to a New York warehouse to await Margarett's third exhibition of the year, which was to open on January 3. Harpo with his parrot illustrated the Kraushaar announcement. "Burlesque Picture a Hit," read the headline of a *New York World* report that the painting had "attracted many to the gallery."

Margarett showed fourteen paintings at Kraushaar, all of which, except for Harpo, she had shown in Chicago, and a group of drawings and watercolors, of which she sold six. The exhibition was her first in New York in two years, and the critics took note of her development. The *Post* reported a burst from prior reticence "into a full-fledged palette." Like Bulliet in Chicago, the New York reviewers were interested in what lay ahead. "If she is ever able to forget, or conceal, her somewhat noticeable admiration for Matisse she will prove an artist that has to be taken very much into account," Henry McBride wrote in the *Sun*. "A little more concentration and what used to be known as 'slogging' would do wonders for this gifted and imaginative painter," Margaret Breunig wrote in the *Times*.

There was no need to tell Margarett to keep working. She brought her sketchbook to the breakfast table and took watercolors out to dinner. Her most significant attention to her children was the command "Hold that pose," and when they came up the hill to visit her studio, she might ask them to sit for an hour and a half, "hardly entertaining if you're seven and prefer baseball," said young Shaw. Jenny escaped to the barn and her pony, so Margarett got her, dark-eyed, in the bathtub, a pink towel turbaning her black hair. Of the children, Margie was her favorite subject: prim and solitary in a chair; in the library with Senny reading to her; face resting in her arms; a solemn portrait, her blond hair, a slate-blue ground.

Often Margarett hired a model. Betty Fittamore arrived on the train from Boston, and Margarett painted her over and over again—chestnut hair, deep-set black eyes, and smooth, lean face. Betty was the Blue Girl, with a hawk-wing swoop of black hat, forbidding gaze, hands grasping the white chair. She was the Amazon, with a crimson headdress, eyeing the miniature man she held between thumb and forefinger. And a woman stripped naked to the waist, her luxuriant, flowered yellow hat vibrating against a deep black ground.

Margarett sketched at Elizabeth Arden, on the train to New York. She carried her supplies in a neat leather case. She did watercolors "at restaurants and night clubs," reported the *Breeze*, "aboard ship, from the tailboard of a truck, from a garden chair." She took canvas and paints to Florida, ventured inland from Palm Beach cabana and beach club and returned with a painting of a young black girl, fierce and meditative, sitting at a table. She visited Frederic Bartlett at his beach-front estate in Fort Lauderdale and painted his caretaker and friend, Fred Lockheart, an older black man, with a chicken under his arm. She did not, as *Town Topics* reported, spend all her time chatting at Sea Spray beach.

Her Boston School forebears had painted in the New Hampshire landscape or the quiet of a Back Bay living room. Margarett painted in the dining room at the Ritz. She took her paintbox to a party given on Beacon Street, billed as "an imaginary voyage to interesting places in the Mediterranean." While the travelers projected "moving pictures," Margarett took pencil and wash to the back of the invitation: a man, black-tuxedoed back to us, a woman to each side. He raises a hand to his face as if to express—what? It's not evident from the diffident profiles of his female companions.

Later, in the studio, Margarett made a painting from the sketch: the three figures on a hot-yellow ground; the gentleman's black back and arm take the breadth of the canvas. The lift of his hand to his face expresses ennui, which, if one removes the humor, the trick of the turned back, cuts deep. Margarett was inside social Boston, but as an artist she stood outside, looking at its back.

§

"I NEVER COULD UNDERSTAND," Gertrude Hunnewell often said, "how two such dear people as Uncle Frank and Aunt Jenny could have produced such *unusual* children." Gertrude had never questioned her own destiny, but Margarett and her sister and brothers all suffered from the requirements of the life they were raised to lead. Jane Cheever, well married and the mother of six children, was by 1930 an annual guest in a sanitarium, overcome like her grandmother by panic that alternated with debilitating depression. After a few years, Dan's marriage to Louise became the torment Jenny had predicted: "When Dan became an instructor at Harvard, Louise went to bed and never got up," Margie said. He cowered at demands she delivered from her chaise, getting his attention with the rap of her cane on the floor. He supervised the care of their children as best he could, wrote his poems, his biographies of saints, and prayed fervently at daily mass.

Harry, still unmarried, lived with Jenny and her hired companion, Eva Niblock, in Wellesley, Boston, and Wareham. He had left banking to become "an explorer," first in the fjords of Norway. In 1929, he financed a film about the lives of seal hunters, and in March 1931, went along to Newfoundland for the final shoot. On March 16, a front-page article in the *Transcript* reported that an explosion on the seal steamer *Viking* had killed twenty-five. One hundred men walked nine miles across the ice to safety, but there were no Americans among the known survivors. Though no body had been found, the *Transcript* ran Harry's obituary on March 17. When news came that he was alive, Margarett and Shaw sailed to Newfoundland.

Harry was alive, barely. He had spent two and a half days on an ice floe, his eyes burned temporarily blind, first by the explosion and then by the glare of sun on ice. He nursed a fire of ship debris, feeding cans of beans to two wounded crewmen until, three days later, a rescue ship crashed through the ice and carried him to shore with one surviving companion. In a hospital bed, he read he'd drowned.

When Margarett and Shaw brought her brother back to Boston, Margarett had a portfolio—sketches of seal men and caricatures of the Boston reporters who scavenged the *Viking* explosion, a watercolor of a cab stand in Quebec, a gouache of bellboys at the Chateau Frontenac. There was nothing, it seemed, she did not turn into art, and when that was true, the balance she managed between her life as an artist and her life as a woman was no feat at all. Florence Cowles celebrated Margarett on a full page of the *Boston Post*, under the headline "Applies Her Artistic Skill to Make Her Home Beautiful; Mrs. McKean's Hobbies Modern Paintings and Old Doors."

The article was nationally syndicated, and at least two versions were published, one illustrated with a portrait of the artist, brushes in hand; the other, by a collage—the children, a view of the big room, Margarett at the pool with her sculpture of Pilgrim. Cowles was promoting Margarett's first North Shore exhibition. Frederick Poole, an antique dealer, had suggested she hang her contemporary work throughout the twenty-six rooms of his shops, two seventeenth-century houses at Fresh Water Cove. By the summer, Poole, a friend and often Margarett's portrait subject, had died. It was he who had reproduced the Venetian corner cupboard, so that two cabinets might frame the end of the big room, he who repaired the sticks of American furniture she bought at auction in Vermont. His daughter insisted the show proceed.

It was Margarett's fourth exhibition in nineteen months—nearly two hundred paintings, watercolors, and drawings. "Into such a setting of antiquities come hundreds of people in fashionable cars each day to see her pictures," wrote the veteran *Globe* critic A. J. Philpott, who went on condescendingly to praise her work as "out of the ordinary . . . distinctive and outré and all that sort of thing." The *Transcript* listed spectators, leading off with Justice Oliver Wendell Holmes, just retired from the Supreme Court. "Margarett Sargent Exhibition Popular, Pictures Attract Hundreds at Gloucester," read the *Globe* headline.

Margarett had had five major exhibitions in New York, one in Chicago, and one in Cambridge. Now she had shown a large selection of her work to a popular audience in an unconventional venue just miles from her home. She had painted for only three years, but she was recognized as a painter, collected, exhibited, and reviewed by those who were bringing an aesthetic she shared into the mainstream of American art. At thirty-eight and at the height of her productivity, she was well positioned to take advantage of her opportunities, but she seemed to harbor some ambivalence. Tucked into the *Transcript* coverage was the unexplained news that she had been "indisposed" since her return from Vermont for the exhibition, unable to supervise hanging the pictures or to attend the opening.

viii

Isolation is delicious,
especially in a crowd

(1932–1936)

Margarett and her children at Prides, c. 1934
(from left, Shaw, Harry, Margie,
Margarett, Jenny)

In 1932, Emlen Etting, a young painter Margarett had met in Paris, visited with his camera. He set up a screen outdoors and posed her for a series of photographs. She wore pearls around her neck and on her wrist, a loose white silk shirt, a dark crepe pinafore fastened aside with a gardenia. Her hair, cut to a length above the shoulder and pulled back from her face, blurs as it recedes in the depth of field. Faint blemishes in her skin are visible in the high-contrast light, and her lips are painted dark with lipstick. The beginning of creases shadow her neck. She throws back her head and closes her eyes.

Later, she sits, legs pulled up under her, on the leaf-strewn grass, arms loosely folded on the brocade seat of a stool placed in front of her. Because of the whiteness of the screen behind her and the darkness of her hair, the extremely pale color of her eyes is strikingly evident. At forty, Margarett no longer has the slenderness of a girl, but she has come into her stature as a woman, and her age shows as fierceness and certainty.

When Margarett agreed to have her first one-person show in Boston, she chucked the gallery's usual exhibition notice, which looked like an invitation to a debutante tea, and designed her own—bright-black letters and Mondrian lines. Doll and Richards, a venerable gallery on Newbury Street, was where "everyone" sent a Barbizon landscape or a Boston School portrait to be cleaned or reframed. Exhibitions of paintings by Freddie Hall and Margarett's friend the watercolorist Marian Monks Chase occasionally interrupted displays of English silver, Persian antiques, or sculpture by Katherine Weems Lane, who, in 1932, showed a sleek bronze of Caresse Crosby's black whippet, Narcisse Noir.

Margarett showed thirty paintings and a group of watercolors and pastels. At the opening, Dan escorted Jenny Sargent, and Margarett's friend Vivian, newly married to Dudley Pickman, brought her daughters. Frederic Bartlett, John Spaulding, Robert Treat Paine, and Freddie Hall lent Margarett Sargents from their own collections. Josef Stransky of the Wildenstein Gallery in New York bought an oil called *The Blue Hat*, and Margarett's cousin Aimée Lamb, whose own paintings were strictly Boston School, purchased *The Next Table*, a gouache of a woman alone in a café, smoking—"I found it convincing," she said. The *Transcript* acknowledged Margarett as perhaps "the leading figure in our non-conservative art movement" because "the influence of her brush and pencil is traceable in the work of others," and called her "the most direct link between this city and Paris."

Until she and Shaw sailed for a holiday in Cuba on April 9, Margarett turned up frequently at the gallery, often with the children, whom she directed to count the red "sold" dots on the wall labels. In Cuba, she did watercolors, and when she came home, quickly completed a painting—a Cuban woman in a maroon dress, wearing a Spanish comb—which she placed in a group show organized at the Museum of Fine Arts by the New England Society of Contemporary Artists. Aside from the Boston painters, the exhibition included artists like Edward Hopper and Blanche Lazelle, and works by a group of African American painters lent by the Harmon Foundation of New York. Margarett's *The Watteau Hat*, of Betty Fittamore in deep browns, vivid blues and yellows, illustrated reviews in both *Art and Archeology* and the *Transcript*.

Margarett's exhibition in 1931 had been her last at Kraushaar. Antoinette Kraushaar recalled "no unpleasantness" to account for the end of the association, but in the years of the Depression, New York galleries closed down, and the number of exhibitions declined dramatically. Kraushaar did not close, but it mounted fewer shows, and Margarett began to focus more of her artistic attention on Boston. In return, Boston claimed her as an artist. A gentleman wandering through the 1933 Jordan Marsh annual, in which Margarett showed a painting called *The Opera,* was heard to remark to his male companion, "I'll tell you who that's by without going up to it—that Sargent girl!" A Brookline matron complained about the same painting in a letter to the *Herald*: "Here, indeed, was field for use of the favorite brand of soap . . . to remove daubs of this and that, in which case the lady might feel she was in the company of a gentleman not an ape."

Margarett's *The Opera* resonated with a painting by George Luks. In 1906, from a sketch made at the Café Francis, in New York, Luks painted a buxom brunette with dark eyes and high color, her white gown cut low, a bouquet of pink plumes waving from her hat, and, helping her out of an ostrich wrap, a mustached, solicitous gentleman. In the far background, mellowly lit, are a man with a guitar, and, farther on, other revelers. Because it was painted the year of Stanford White's murder, Luks may have intended a comment on the kind of high-life adultery that brought the womanizing architect to his death. Twenty-five years later, with a memory of Luks's *Café Francis,* Margarett painted a brunette, slender in a ball gown, with her own tuxed gentleman.

Luks's model offered her cleavage like a Mediterranean market woman might proffer a basket of fruit. Margarett's brunette gives us her back, bare to the waist, her face turned back toward us over her shoulder. Margarett painted her escort in the tuxedo as an unshaven, leering grotesque, and those who gather in the distance on the opera stage are not revelers but an angel in white dancing with a devil, her mortal partner vanquished at their feet. Luks's heroine seemed to relish her seductive power; Margarett's has a look of wide-eyed apprehension.

In painting *The Opera* as she did, Margarett reflected on her situation as she did not in conversation. A woman turns away, but seduces with an expanse of creamy back. She looks back at us, pleading, before disappearing like Persephone into the arms of a tuxedoed hell. Margarett has pulled back from the female face to reveal not only the woman but her female circumstances and, in doing so, finds herself more vulnerable than she ordinarily let on.

"Margarett was not an introspective person," said Dorothy DeSantillana, a book editor who met her in the late thirties. Others ascribed Margarett's discretion to manners: She was a "lady" and did not discuss certain things. Betty Parsons said Margarett talked about events in her private life only in exclamatory bursts. She was in love with someone, angry at Shaw, mad for a painter, had bought an extraordinary strain of Dutch tulip. Once, she was in love with "a Spaniard. Carlos was his name. Oh, how in love she was with him!" But Margarett did not talk through difficulty or emotion. She had seen her father take things in and move on. She had watched her brother Frank's depression bring suicide, her mother's mourning turn paralytic, her sister Jane's despair send her yearly to Silver Hill or Austen Riggs. But like them, Margarett considered the direct expression of feeling a weakness.

For those whose desires do not conflict with how they live, restraint has a kind of elegance. People admired Margarett's courtesy as if it were a rare and exquisite artifact. All her life, she had disguised her defiance with one aesthetic form or another, but increasingly now, her authentic self came through. When life at Prides meshed with her imaginative design, it was enchanting, and she moved through it with creativity and vitality. When things did not go as she planned and her efforts to correct or embellish failed, when she drank too much or could not drink enough, her body rescued her with headache or illness, and she retired to her bedroom and pulled the shades. Sometimes the headaches came even if she didn't drink. As the children grew older, Shaw more distant, the elixir of lovers less powerful, quiet hours in her room became less a comfort than the visitation of a pestilence, less a refuge than a fortress.

Only to the family, her household, and a few close friends was the woman in the dark room as truly Margarett as the joyous, powerful, infectiously attractive woman who greeted a guest or a journalist. When Louise Tarr arrived at Prides in October 1932, Margarett exuberantly received her in linen lounging pajamas—black trousers and a bright plaid jacket. Tarr, a friend and a reporter from the tabloid *Boston Sunday Post*, had conceived an article on the racy subject of "feminine charm." She would interview Margarett, the "well-known artist and leader of Boston society," as an authority. The piece took up a full page of the color feature section and was illustrated with tinted photographs of Sonja Henie, Sarah Bernhardt, and on a ship's deck with a bevy of her models, Coco Chanel.

The interview was a performance, and Tarr must have heightened the drama in her text. "Women try to charm attractive men by doing what the men want them to do—to the point of lunacy!" she reports Margarett declaring. "But charm is infinitely more dangerous than beauty," Margarett continued, gesturing toward her aviary, where drab females chirped at brilliantly plumaged mates. "Men are scared of the sorceress type, the flagrantly beautiful ones; they are warned against Helen of Troy in school. Charm is a plainclothesman who gets us before we know what he's doing." The housekeeper, Mary McLellan, served Dubonnet, Margarett opened the aviary, and a parakeet flew to her shoulder. The conversation continued, punctuated by the French-taxicab calls of zebra finches.

At the end of the interview, Margarett seemed to become personal. "There is no reason why women should not grow more charming as they grow older, but few of them do. The loneliness that overtakes a woman, the gradual fading away of admiration, and the knowledge that she is no longer held by someone to be the most important thing in the world—all this is hard to weather. The years from 30 to 50 are the dangerous years for women with charm. If she gets up to 50 without losing it—she can be a wallop at 80."

In 1933, Margarett and Shaw went to Europe for the first time since the stock market crash. They traveled with Arthur Hobson, one of Shaw's younger business associates, and his wife, Tiny, a small, gregarious redhead. The Depression drop in prices allowed an extended stay in Paris at the Ritz, a chauffeured Rolls-Royce, the hiring of ladies' maids and valets. The day after the new German Lloyd liner, the

Bremen, docked at Cherbourg on June 7, 1933, the *Paris Tribune* announced the arrival of Mr. and Mrs. Q. A. S. McKean for the summer. Their itinerary also included weeks in London and a visit to Berlin, where Shaw and Hobson had a business venture.

In Germany, the Weimar Republic had finally fallen, and Hitler, who had been named chancellor on January 30, was consolidating his power. In February, the Reichstag burned in Berlin and Communists were attacked in the streets and rounded up. In March, the Nazis and their Nationalist allies won the Reichstag majority, Hindenburg ordered the German flag replaced by the swastika, and the first concentration camp was opened, near Dachau. In early April, the Nazis enforced a ban on Jewish businesses, and in May, bonfires of books did away with Mann, Hegel, and Marx.

The new chancellor made sure to meet Americans interested in doing business in Germany. Facilitating many of these encounters was Ernst Franz Sedgwick Hanfstaengl, a robust man of six feet four with a booming voice, known as "Putzi" or "little doll," and an old college friend of Shaw's. Half Bostonian and half Bavarian, Putzi had been famous at Harvard for piano impromptus, his huge deft hands pounding out selections from Beethoven or Wagner. After the Munich Beer Hall putsch in 1923, the Hanfstaengls hid Hitler in their castle in Bavaria, and he and Putzi became intimate friends. Hitler was beginning to think about writing *Mein Kampf*, and Putzi was composing "The German Storm," which in time would become familiar as a Nazi march.

Sometime during June 1933, Putzi engineered a dinner with the chancellor for a group of potential investors and their wives, including the McKeans and the Hobsons. When he met rich Americans, Hitler was at his most seductive and devious, as he had been just a month before when he delivered his "Peace Speech" to the Reichstag, assuring the world that Germany supported Roosevelt's call for the abolition of all offensive weapons. The dinner Putzi organized was small enough for Margarett to have a good look at the newly ascended dictator. Janet Flanner, in a 1936 *New Yorker* profile, would describe how Hitler looked during conversation: "In anything approaching serious talk, his sapphire-blue eyes, which are his only good feature, brighten and glow heavily as if words fanned them."

Margarett had no interest in politics. If she voted, she voted Republican as her father had, and if she took a position, she came to it on instinct. When she spoke of the dinner with Hitler, she talked about the eyes Flanner described so impeccably. They drove her from the dinner table, she said, as soon as she could manage it: "I thought he was absolutely mad."

As always, Margarett had looked forward to Paris, but she found it a changed city. The movements in art that had excited the Continent in the twenties had been reined in by the Depression, which by 1933 had spread to France. In the 1920s, as F. Scott Fitzgerald put it, "even when you were broke, you didn't worry about money, because it was in such profusion around you." By 1933, many of the shops that catered to American tourists had closed down, and Charles Ritz was touring American cities to drum up business for his hotel. The Bromfields and the Carters were still in residence, but Betty Parsons had left France, as had Sandy Calder, and Caresse Crosby would shortly give her last party at Le Moulin before returning to the United States, to live in Virginia.

But there was Roland. Margarett and Shaw saw him with his wife, Mimi, and Margarett saw him alone at one of two or three restaurants they loved, where they could be, Roland said, "as we always had been." Of all the men in Margarett's life, Roland most enthusiastically entered her psyche, emboldening the part of her Shaw considered slightly mad, the part of her that, thwarted, could pull her down into darkness. Margarett confided in Roland, and he watched her carefully. He noticed when she got bored and removed herself from a conversation, and he saw what her marriage was like. Once, in New York, he and his wife had the McKeans to a dinner party. "Everyone was gay and joyous," he said. "Margarett was telling a riveting story." As the maid passed a vegetable dish, Margarett made "a grand gesture," and the peas in it spilled.

"Margarett!" Shaw shouted. "Look what you've done!"

"I'll pick them up," she said, retrieved one pea, put it back in the dish, and continued her story.

"Intellectual sensuality is the most rare and the most devastating," Margarett had said in the Louise Tarr interview. Perhaps she was referring to Roland. "An affair built up by a person exciting you verbally is much more intense than an affair which is all gin and chest." In Margarett, Roland sensed a companion for his own wildness, an echo of his dissolute youth at the edge of Cocteau's circle. "I was very deeply in love with her," he said, "and I think she reciprocated that love."

One day when they met, Roland announced that he had a surprise for her. As they drove toward the river, Margarett needled him. "Where are we going?" He kept silent, a feline grin spreading across his face. At the edge of the Seine, they left the car, and, Margarett saw birds of every description and breed chirping, singing, and whirling through the air in capacious cages. There were birds for decoration, birds that talked, fowl for eating, prize chickens for breeding. Roland remembered the goose in the moonlight and Margarett's delight when he once suggestively jiggled the handle of his umbrella—a swan carved from ivory—turning it into a discreet instrument of seduction as they sat at the Ritz in Boston for lunch with her children.

Margarett collected birds as if they were works of art—a finch of an obscure variety, a canary that was orange rather than yellow, a pair of gray-cheeked parakeets. Her aviary at Prides was a carnival of sentient color and living sound. She bought several birds and several cages that day. She planned to keep them with her for the rest of the summer, take them home on the *Bremen*. She had them delivered to the Ritz, and she and Roland celebrated in the bar.

Margarett was in the room when Shaw returned.

"My God, Margarett," he said.

"Aren't they beautiful?"

Shaw opened the windows, then the cages. Perhaps Margarett rushed to rescue her birds, or perhaps she stood there, helpless, as they flew out the window onto the Place Vendôme. Roland had never heard her so upset, so inchoate with rage, so close to tears, as when she telephoned and told him what "that damn Shaw" had done. Shaw detested how Margarett disrupted things, but Roland thrived on what he called her refusal of rational life—birds in the bedroom, phone calls that interrupted him at Knoedler's with improbable emergencies, her deep voice telling him about a new pair of *extraordinary* chartreuse pumps.

Shaw was having an affair with Beatrice Dabney, a Bostonian, younger than Margarett, divorcing or divorced, slender and dark-haired. She spoke with a lisp—particularly amusing when she addressed a pet goose she'd named Pompous Ass. She was also a friend of Margarett's and, like Margarett, had a talent for enchanting men. Beatrice had not hired a maid for her sojourn in Paris, which coincided, not by coincidence, with Margarett and Shaw's. For weeks, at Shaw's behest, when not ironing or mending for Mrs. McKean, Margarett's personal maid attended to Mrs. Dabney, who was staying at another hotel. Of this Margarett had no knowledge, but the arrangement eventually upset the maid, who, in tears, reported the story to "Madame McKean." "And do you know," Margarett said later to Dorothy DeSantillana, "he had *my* maid taking care of Beatrice Dabney!" No matter that she herself had affairs; the humiliation stung.

In September 1933, an interviewer arrived at Prides from *House Beautiful*. Margarett entered the room, "fit as always," wearing something black with quick interruptions of silver. "With her comes the steady, deep flow of gorgeous conversation, a steady cruising speed of about 110 miles an hour," wrote the reporter. "She never stakes all on a brilliant crack; her patter flows along on the income of a tremendous wit, she never spends from her capital account." The enthralled journalist had come without paper. Margarett supplied a handful of the pink laundry checks she occasionally used for sketching.

They settled themselves in the library, the reporter taking in what hung on the walls: George Luks's painting of the original house at Prides, a dark saltbox in a luminous field of snow; Mary Cassatt's aquatint *The Coiffure*, a nude sitting in front of a mirror, her pale back to us, bare arms raised to tie up her hair.

The reporter remarked on the food—a first course of baked cantaloupe, "warm and swimming," rack of lamb, fresh green beans, whipped potato. After supper, the children performed their poems, and Jenny brought out the biography she'd written of her mother: "Margarett Sargent was born in Boston. She took up sculpturing at an early age. Mr. Gutzon Borglum taught her, but she hated him and still does hate him." The interviewer left with glossies of three paintings, and a Berenice Abbott portrait in which Margarett, smiling at the camera, wears a dark smock and a black-and-white-striped polo shirt. The article in *House Beautiful* introduced an artist with "an artistic quality of immense candle power." But it misread the woman. "She laughs off everything," the reporter wrote. "Whatever it is, nothing is serious on the surface."

A month after the *House Beautiful* interview, Margarett went down to New York. She would go to the theater and to some exhibitions, and as always, she would see George Luks. At sixty-six, he continued to be celebrated as an artist—in 1931, he'd won the Clark Prize and Gold Medal from the Corcoran Gallery—but he'd broken with his dealer, who had forbidden him to come drunk to the gallery.

On an evening the previous December, it had been advertised that at eight o'clock, at the Artists' Cooperative on East Thirty-fourth Street, Luks would paint a demonstration portrait of Doris Humphrey, the dancer, and speak afterward on painting technique. Instead, he mounted the stage and escorted the model from her stand. "I'm George Luks, and I'm a rare bird," he began, and lectured the audience of five hundred on the appropriation of American taste by "French superior salesmanship." Americans were victimized by "cheap little lawyers who become diplomats," he fumed, "and financiers who let their wives buy pictures from dealers who perfume them with bombast and saddle them with trash."

The evening's organizer came forward to direct him to the easel and meekly offered a smock. Luks threw it on the floor. The audience began to shout. He shouted back: "I can paint and you know it. Now shut up and listen to me." People surged toward the stage, and Luks took hold of a large man who had called him a braggart. "You're talking to Chicago Whitey, the best amateur boxer and barroom fighter in America."

"Luks Lecture Drives Most of 500 from Hall," read a *Herald Tribune* headline the next morning; the reporter wrote that Luks had exercised "the gusto and delight of a child tearing apart his mother's favorite tapestry." His friends knew from the account that he must have been drinking. Even his most recent wife, Mercedes, had thrown up her hands. When Luks left after supper and told her he'd stay out just long enough to observe dawn come to Seventh Avenue, she knew he was going to a bar.

Early on the evening of October 28, Luks and Mercedes argued, and he stormed from their apartment on East Twenty-eighth Street. Margarett had not yet seen Luks—on arriving in New York she'd come down with bronchitis, which had quickly become pneumonia— and she was too ill to travel back to Boston, so her maid, Anna de Schott, had come to New York to take care of her.

By two A.M. on October 29, Luks was in a bar on Sixth Avenue, drunk and drawing on a napkin. In no time he was "Chicago Whitey," picking a fight. In early morning, he was found propped up in a doorway under the Sixth Avenue el. The sun cast light and shadow as it did in his best painting, but the figure dimly visible in the center of the field of vision was Luks himself, and he was not drunk or down on his luck; he was dead. Margarett's telephone number at the Hotel Weylin was in his pocket. He had died of injuries sustained in Chicago Whitey's last brawl.

There is no document of Margarett's response to the phone call, only Dan's testimony that it was she who identified Luks to the police, she who called Harrison Tweed, the lawyer to whom she had introduced him all those years ago. Had Margarett worried about the new intensity in Luks's drinking? Or had she, like his drinking buddies, denied it, believing what the newspapers said, that "Lusty" Luks "had been in good health"? She stayed in New York another month, grief deepening her cough. Luks's resilience had convinced her he'd always get back on his feet. His death was a promise broken, the loss of the most consistent witness to her life as an artist. When Frank killed himself and her father died, the unambiguous momentum of youth had pulled her forward, but she could imagine nowhere to go from this death. She stayed on as editorials and obituaries pronounced the "famous painter" dead of cardiac arrest, repeated stories of his Rabelaisian exploits, and fictionalized his demise: "He had died of a heart attack while studying the effect of the sunrise on the elevated structure for a picture he planned to paint."

Something happened to Margarett as letters from the children and Senny arrived day after day, full of get-well greetings, condolences, and family news: "Cara mater," Jenny wrote. "Esne melior?" Margarett wrote to Prides of having had a "good" night or a "bad" night, of news from the doctor, of a visit with Isabel Pell or Artur Schnabel. She did not write about her grief, how in the weeks after Luks's death, as the pneumonia held, sadness cut into her belief that she would always transcend the events that waylaid other, weaker beings.

It had been years since Margarett worked, Luks at her shoulder urging her on, as if with his coaching she was sure to score a knockout. But he inhabited her spirit. He was a source of courage should her ambition flag, should she be distracted by life or vanity. "To hell with your hats!" he'd shouted when she was a young woman, and she had learned to rely on the solace of blank paper, the feel of clay in her hands, the rapture of color on canvas. The times she had seen Luks work, wielding brushes like a flamethrower, had shown her paint as an expression of appetite, a means to renew with each emerging image her sense of a connected self.

At the opening of a Luks retrospective she curated in Boston in 1966, thirty-three years after his death, Margarett sat in a wheelchair, silent in pale-blue satin as friends viewed a room of his Boston paintings and drawings—among them, his portrait of Jenny and *The White Blackbird*. "The details of his death were typical of him," Margarett had written in an exhibition handout. "He was found in early morning,

dead, having been assaulted beneath the elevated on one of the sidewalks he loved so well." She did not respond to any greeting that day
with more than a monosyllable. Luks's death had marked the end of
her youth, of the New York years in which she worked with such passion. It had brought back the death of her father, of his love without
conditions, his moral and spiritual protection. Margarett's family hon-
ored her grief, but they did not understand the depth or significance of
her loss. She suffered it by herself.

A doctor made the suggestion that she recuperate from her pneumonia in Atlantic City, take the sea air even though it was November.
Just before Thanksgiving, she returned to New York, where Shaw met
her to take her back to Prides. After the New Year, they sailed for Europe. The children, as usual, stayed behind. By the end of January,
Margarett was in the Sicily sun.

That something had shifted was evident when Margarett and Shaw returned from Europe. Margarett now drank with impunity, even before
she appeared in the morning. She drank from bottles hidden in the
bathroom, in the closet, or under the bed. If she invited friends for
lunch, four or five women in the middle of the week, Margie or Jenny
was sent out to greet them. Margarett could keep guests waiting as
long as forty-five minutes, and so Margie, dying to be grown up,
would make conversation and summon Mary McLellan to pass hors
d'oeuvres and offer drinks. She knew that something was often wrong
with her mother, something connected with her long mornings in the
dark bedroom, but she and Jenny still didn't know what they were describing when they said to each other, "Mama is languid again."

"She'd look perfectly lovely, and she'd be absolutely blasted,"
Margie said years later, describing her mother entering the living room
to greet guests. Margarett would seem different from how she usually
was—scary, imprecise in her movements, slow in her speech. The guests
would be terribly kind, behaving as if she were all right or suffering
an unidentified malady. Eventually someone might suggest she excuse
herself to lie down. Once, as she slowly retreated along the corridor

toward her bedroom, Tiny Hobson recommended that Margie, then twelve, call a doctor. Margie was too embarrassed to ask Mrs. Hobson to make the call, and it was Senny's day off. Later that afternoon, when the doctor emerged from the bedroom, he assured Margie her mother would soon be fine: "Just let her sleep."

No one in the household talked openly about Margarett's drinking. They talked about her headaches. They complained about her temper, joked about her perfectionism. And they continued to seek her approval and pleasure. The children wrote get-well notes, which were sent in on the breakfast tray, the lunch tray, the supper tray. In their mother's place, they had Senny, who, never speaking ill of Margarett, distracted and protected them the days the shades were lowered. When Senny was not around and Shaw was at his office, Margie stood in: "Senny's days off were 'doozies.' "

As Margarett's behavior came more to obstruct her life with Shaw, her drinking became more clandestine and her existence more alienated from the life of her family. For Margie, there was still no greater pleasure than to be close to her mother, but she now distinguished between two Margaretts—the one she adored and the one who frightened her. Jenny fled the sarcastic dining table, the shouts that echoed up the hallway from Margarett's bedroom, and was wary even when her mother did not drink. The arguments that erupted between her parents with increasing frequency terrorized and embarrassed her; never again would she feel close to Margarett. She escaped to the stable and her horse, Me Too, and never, she told me, invited friends home. Margarett noticed her coolness and when Jenny started to win blue ribbons, boasted about her own childhood riding exploits; without Jenny's consent, she began to enter them in mother-and-daughter events at Myopia horse shows.

No one wanted the twins, still very young, to encounter their mother's unfocused eye or slurring tongue, and so, as her habit became predictable, they were kept out of her path and away from her bedroom. One day, after a lunch in Boston, Margarett burst into the house at four in the afternoon. Shaw and Harry, playing in the living

room, watched as she opened the door, as she fell to the floor in her ex-
quisite black suit, iridescent hat feathers wobbling in the failing light.
They raced to the library. "Papa," they said, "Papa, Mama is drunk."
They stood there as Shaw sat down and dialed his mother's number.
"Mama," he said, as if tolling a knell, "the boys know."

Not even work calmed Margarett's despair. It shows in a portrait
of Margie: ground of dry white daubed onto dimmer gray, blond head
of hair an abundant sculptured shape, face a pale oval settled like a
mask, golden hair springing from behind, expression benumbed and
too world-weary for a thirteen-year-old.

In another painting, the subject, a woman, wears yellow. Black hair
frames her face. Margarett paints her arms folded, a cigarette burning in
her left hand, a garish smear of red lipstick on a mouth set mid-anguish.

And in a third painting, a woman's dark hair is pulled back into a
knot at the base of her neck. Her eyes are downcast, seem, to the
viewer, closed. Her arms are folded, each hand grasping its opposite elbow, so that her simple black tunic dress appears to be a straitjacket.

❧

HARRY SNELLING WAS TALL and he was younger than Margarett. Ruby
Newman's orchestra was playing at a dance Eleo Sears was giving in
the same Boston ballroom where Margarett had made her debut
twenty-two years before. She and Harry Snelling danced right off the
floor. He had red-blond hair, and he made her laugh. She made him
laugh. Perhaps his wife hadn't come to the dance; perhaps Shaw hadn't
come either. Harry didn't live on the North Shore, but from time to
time he came up from Weston to play golf at Myopia. That was how
Eleo knew him.

At eighty-two, Margarett, reclining on a hospital bed in an apartment high above Boston, told me the story. Her hair was dyed tawny
brown and carefully waved. Her bones held the shape of her face. Her
eyes were still wide and blue, and her mouth was lipsticked carmine
red. A practical nurse brought old red wine, a silver tray of smoked
salmon, crumbled hard-boiled egg, capers and lemon. Margarett held

forth like a dowager queen, evening darkness encroaching on a room lit by lamps that illuminated the paintings, hers among them, ganged on creamy walls.

Her affair with Harry Snelling marked, as far as Boston was concerned, the same sort of change in direction as the clothes she wore after Florence or the breaking of her engagement to Eddie Morgan. By the time Margarett told me the story, her articulation had been impaired by a stroke, so I cannot be sure how accurately I heard her: We danced right off the floor, then we went to a hotel, purposely not the Ritz. Her voice was deep, somewhere between laughter and scorn.

They fell in love. They planned a trip abroad. They plotted divorce, the abandoning of young children. They were intoxicated, enthralled with one another, by what had happened on the dance floor, what followed in the privacy of the hotel room, where they spent, apparently, a few days. "And Shaw came to the hotel! Imagine!" Margarett laughed in the gloom of the winter lamplight. The hotel lobby was brightly lit, and Shaw, his face set, walked toward her, across a parquet floor. "Him or me," he said. She laughed. "Can you imagine that?"

When she met Harry at the ball, Margarett was wearing black velvet and her section of Empress Eugénie's pearls. Grandpa Hollis had purchased the full strand as a financial favor to Napoleon III and, after Isabella's death, split them between his daughters, who in turn divided them between their own. Harry wore a tuxedo, was big and blond like the man Margarett had painted sitting next to Betty Fittamore as a redhead bored to death, dancers whirling in the background.

"He was attractive to women," Dan said. He did not mean it as a compliment.

"He was a great amateur golfer," said Shaw's friend Ted Weeks.

"He was a dreadful man," said Margarett's son Harry, repeating what he heard as soon as he was old enough to play the links at Myopia. "A real rotter. He was considered to be very amusing and terrific fun, but he was a great woman chaser, a heavy drinker and gambler and all that stuff. A rough guy—certainly a complete nonconformist in Boston."

Harry Snelling had been married since 1928, and he and his wife had two small children. When Margarett met him, he was thirty-five and she was forty-two.

"Did he drink?"

"Well," said Margarett's friend Mabel Storey, putting a hand to her face, "he had a ruddy complexion. They all drank."

He had a car. He and Margarett left the ball and went straight to the hotel.

"So he was a big sexy guy."

"Yes."

Mabel repeated a story, apocryphal perhaps, that Margarett tagged the children before she ran off, each with the name of a friend to whom she wished that child sent.

"Shaw's friends all rallied during the Snelling thing," said Ted Weeks.

"They went abroad," someone said.

"They planned to go abroad," someone else said.

"Mrs. Haughton went to the hotel to put a stop to it."

"Margarett came out to Wellesley," Dan said, "and we went for a drive in Mama's car." Though he did not overtly approve of his sister's nonconformity, a part of him applauded it—he himself was a Catholic convert among Unitarians and Episcopalians, a poet among investment bankers. Because Margarett believed he understood her, he got the calls when she retreated to the dark room—if not from her, from Shaw, sometimes even from Mrs. Haughton. He'd listen patiently and make suggestions, grateful his religious practice shielded him from her kind of suffering.

"I'm going to leave Shaw," Margarett announced once they were settled in their mother's car. "Everything will change," she said. "I'm going to marry this man and begin again." The window between front and back kept the conversation from the chauffeur, and Dan was silent. "Are you with me?"

"No," he answered. "I'm not."

"At the time, I knew something was wrong," Margie said, "but I didn't know what. Mama had Harry Snelling to the house years later. He was terrifically dull."

"I don't know how long it went on," said Ruthie Wolcott, daughter of Ham and Ruthie Robb, "but I know it must have been pretty violent, you know. Because it was hot—pretty hot." What was unusual was not that the affair occurred but that it was public enough to be a scandal, public enough that friends and friends of friends walked past a particular Boston hotel to gaze up, with amusement or distress, at a certain row of windows.

Margarett took Harry to New York.

"I'll ruin you in business," Shaw told Snelling.

Ted Weeks climbed the stairs to the second-floor dining room at the Ritz, and there he saw Harry Snelling, sitting with his wife, her eyes red-rimmed.

Harry had trained himself for business by working first in a foundry, later in machine shops in the Midwest. He'd gone to school to learn the textile trade, had then helped to finance Franklin Rayon, which later became the Textron Corporation. Unlike Shaw, he had to work, and he worked hard. In a photograph taken his senior year at Harvard, hair parted up the middle, he has a wide, placid face, a delicate mouth, and large, light eyes. By the time he posed at forty-six for his twenty-fifth-reunion photograph, his hair had thinned, his eyes had narrowed, and his cheeks had dropped, but when Margarett fell in love with him, he was still in possession of the tension between delicacy and masculine heft that made him "attractive to women."

"Margarett was terribly in love with him, and he ditched her," Mabel Storey said.

"He did?"

"Oh, yes."

One evening, Ham Robb received a phone call. He had been in Harry's class at Harvard, and Harry had confided the affair. Now Harry told Ham he had broken it off and that Margarett was extremely upset. He simply couldn't go through with it, he said. He wasn't going to leave his marriage. He wasn't going to risk the talk.

"Him or me," Margarett reported at eighty-two, red mouth swerving in a smile of triumph. "Can you imagine?"

When Ham and Ruthie reached Prides, Margarett was distraught, had opened a window to fling herself from. Ham pulled her back. For hours she wept and raged. Out of her feeling for Harry Snelling had come a resolve to leave Shaw, a belief that she could be free of the guilt of her failed marriage, her inadequate motherhood. Her brother Harry drove her out to Wareham. They walked to the end of the pier. The tide was out. The rocks glistened, but there was no water. "All I want to do is dive in." Harry pulled her back. The rest of the family heard about it from Jenny Sargent: "If only we hadn't sent her to Europe!"

When Shaw learned Harry Snelling had thrown Margarett over, he returned to Prides. He had been staying with his mother, had probably taken the children with him. In morning-after daylight, Margarett greeted him. They went to see Mrs. Haughton, who spoke sternly. The marriage must be saved, she said, for the good of the children. As soon as they could manage to sail, she would send them to Europe. The events of the spring would, in the course of things, recede, and they could return to Boston, if not in happiness, at least in an appearance of tranquillity.

Margarett didn't tell me, on that winter afternoon, what she felt when she and Shaw left her mother-in-law's house. Apparently she took her pain in stride and packed her trunks for Europe without protest.

§

ON MAY 29, 1935, the family, including Senny, sailed on the *Bremen*. The twins, at almost eleven, were clowns, especially Shaw, who was beginning a career as the family subversive. Jenny, at twelve, had outgrown her nickname, Dizzy, given because she seemed to dance rather than walk or run. Margie, at thirteen, was ready for the diary Margarett had given her—"To my Margie, from her publisher & mother"—and she kept a running commentary of the trip: "Read. Write. Listen to rebukes and commands." It was Shaw's job to manage logistics, and he was mercilessly teased for any blunder. Margarett threw herself into the trip. She wanted to give her children what Europe had given her at eighteen, and she routed guidebooks for excursion ideas, with which she regaled them as the twins rolled their eyes.

Hardy, a chauffeur, met them at Southampton in a Rolls-Royce. He had been advertised as trilingual but spoke English with a thick Cockney burr, German when French was required, and, as it turned out, French for German. They settled first at Bournemouth, where Margie and Jenny had begged to go because it had a professional skating rink. They stayed for a month, and when the girls weren't skating, Margarett began her sightseeing campaign, with Hardy in the driver's seat. Jenny took snapshots of Margie and young Shaw at Stonehenge, of the ruins at Beaulieu Abbey, of swans at Abbotsbury. She caught her father, eyes downcast, in boredom or melancholy, sitting on the grass; her mother in a garden chair, sketching. Margarett looked straight into the camera, pencil in hand, sketchbook on her lap. "Isolation is delicious, especially in a crowd," she wrote in a sketchbook. She drew all the time that summer, filling book after book with watercolors.

They arrived at Brown's Hotel in London with forty trunks, and it rained for four days. A maid had joined the party. "Olga can be heard for miles shrieking about what 'Madame' has forgotten to pack," Margie wrote. "Jenny got sick, Senny was homesick." Everyone, including Margarett, played Monopoly, the latest game. "Shaw going slowly bankrupt. Harry gloating. Jenny making casual remarks, causing fistfights. Senny shushing from the bathroom next door." The girls skated at Streatham. Lady Astor, whom Shaw, because she had been married to his uncle Robert Shaw, still called "Aunt Nancy," escorted the twins through the members' entrance into the House of Commons. "Terrific amount of hailing taxis, buying paints & painting boxes, presents for people," Margie wrote.

Margarett took the girls to every possible museum. Without seeming to teach, she seduced them into looking, and they loved it. In the National Gallery, she showed them the Florentine painters, pointing out a particular color, the embrace of angels in a Botticelli nativity, an incidental vase of lilies in a painting of a Madonna and child. Almost without words, she communicated that a painting wasn't just something pretty, that it hadn't just gotten there but had been made by a person whose name it was important to remember. Looking with them at paintings, she infused her daughters with the language most precious to her. "Victorious happiness with Margie and Jenny," she wrote on July 22. "Everything is easy now—everything is evolvable—everything is worthwhile."

For August, Lady Astor provided her house in Plymouth, the town she'd represented as the first woman in Parliament since 1919. The acerbic wit that had always delighted Shaw only hinted at the combative parliamentary style that bore out her campaign slogan: "If you can't get a fighting man, take a fighting woman." In 1936, when Chamberlain accepted Hitler's invasion of the Rhineland without protest, Astor would position herself firmly with the appeasers, but in August 1935, Plymouth was a pretty town on the sea and Aunt Nancy was, to her guests, not the object of controversy, but a generous, though absentee, hostess. William, the butler, took care of things, serving breakfast on the porch before the children's morning lessons with Senny. After lunch, the family would set off to sightsee. "The landscape has a noble haunted tinge," Margarett wrote in her sketchbook. "Hurry to motor to one town," Margie reported. "Hurry to motor to next town."

After Plymouth, they moved on to France, to Guéthary, a small seashore town on the Spanish border, only a short drive from the casinos of Biarritz. Margarett and Shaw had decided they would not return to Prides in September. They'd spend the autumn in Paris, perhaps even stay into the winter to see Shaw's niece Sis McKean compete at the Olympics in February. At the end of September, they moved into a flat in a silver-gray pension that stood on avenue Marceau just where the avenue begins to slope; from one set of windows, you could see the Arc de Triomphe. The children settled back into their lessons with Senny, and two days a week, Mademoiselle Yvonne James, who spoke no English, arrived to supplement the French they'd learned at Prides.

Soon after they got to Paris, Margarett decided Margie should be painted by Marie Laurencin, and telephoned. "I don't do portraits," said the artist, then fifty, still in her prime and never kindly disposed to commissions. "You haven't seen my daughter," Margarett retorted. Laurencin did not say no. Margarett took the girls to shop at Elizabeth Arden, to see the fall collection at Rochas, and one day, coming down the staircase after an exhibition at the Grand Palais, she introduced them to Mrs. Edith Wharton, dressed all in black. Often the family went to the Bromfields' for Sunday lunch, and once, before the grown-ups sat down, Margie and Jenny were introduced to Gertrude Stein and Alice Toklas.

Shaw's niece Butsy McKean was living in Paris that winter, and Margarett invited her to avenue Marceau, to the theater, the circus, sightseeing, and museums. Butsy was sixteen and aware that the trip had been precipitated by a crisis. She admired Margarett, so she paid attention. Margarett seemed to her more removed than usual, quieter, but at the same time more attentive to her family. Butsy didn't remember Margarett drinking or even ill that fall, but Margie recorded a darkened room more than once. "Came back to find Mama stretched out on bed with bad headache."

One evening, they all went to the circus. Margarett wore a white evening suit with long white gloves, her pearls, the emerald ring that had belonged to Pauline Agassiz Shaw glinting from her hand. The family, including Senny, sat in a box, watched the pony act, the dog act, an acrobatic elephant. The boys held their breath as a hypnotist began his exhortations. Such concentration, such silence, and then, with no warning, the sound of Margarett falling in a stone faint from her chair. "Of course what we were told was that she had been hypnotized by mistake," Harry said. Years later, Margarett was diagnosed as having a vascular disorder that caused her, periodically, to faint, but at the time, what went unsaid was everyone's assumption she was drunk. She was carried from the tent.

In late January, with Hardy at the wheel of the Rolls-Royce, the McKeans left Paris for the Winter Olympics, the first phase in Hitler's full-dress campaign to present his new Germany to the world. They drove east toward Bavaria, where, in September at Nuremberg, Hitler had announced laws denying Jews citizenship and forbidding marriage between Jews and "Aryans." At the border, swastika flags fluttered from passport control and police sauntered to the car to demand identification. Shaw pulled out the family passports and by mistake a hidden fifty thousand marks. The police asked questions in loud German, and Hardy broke forth with French excuses. "For God's sake," Shaw shouted with horror, "don't speak French!" After a moment, with a frown, the guard waved them on.

Half a million converged for the games at Garmisch-Partenkirchen, a small winter resort nestled in the Bavarian Alps near the Austrian border. Two million would attend the Olympics that summer in Berlin and see Jesse Owens, an American of African descent, win four gold medals, an unprecedented triumph for one athlete. Garmisch was a smaller affair, a prelude to the summer and, for the McKeans, a Boston reunion. Butsy's older sister, Sis, had been in Garmisch for weeks, practicing with the American team for the first women's Olympic ski competition. Her mother, Bessie, came from Boston, and Butsy came over from Paris.

The McKean children had their own ski teacher and when they weren't at the games were on the slopes learning to telemark, boots fastened to their skis with rawhide. Shaw and Harry saw a man with a black face and tails ski down the mountain; he was a chimney sweep, their teacher told them. Margie dispensed quickly with ski lessons to skate on the Eibsee, the huge lake that stretched out from the hotel, whose staff kept its surface free of snow.

Garmisch had been refurbished for the games, but it was short of accommodations. Nazi officials had taken all the hotel rooms, and foreign journalists were relegated to pensions. The McKeans' rooms, procured weeks in advance, and their extraordinary seats at the stadium and on the final curve of the bobsled run, across from Hitler's box, were arranged by Shaw's German business friends, in particular Putzi Hanfstaengl, who, since they'd seen him in 1933, had become notorious in America.

In the spring of 1934, Putzi had made his first visit to the United

States since Harvard. When a "storm of protest" followed his invitation to serve as a twenty-fifth-reunion marshal at the Harvard commencement, he declined the honor but agreed to attend the reunion if his duties to the Reich permitted. Jewish alumni were openly enraged, but vocal Gentiles supported the university's position that every Harvard graduate must be accorded freedom of speech, no matter what his beliefs—the *Harvard Crimson* even suggested Putzi be awarded an honorary degree. Most of Putzi's friends on the North Shore would not have gone that far, but a number of them, including Shaw and Margarett, did not allow themselves to understand what the Nazis intended until the brink of war. An attitude toward Jews as "other," a casual, unexamined anti-Semitism, was a fact of life in most of Brahmin Boston, in spite of Jewish friends, assimilated like Shaw's business partner Clement Burnhome, or unassimilated like Fanny Brice.

In the days before the Harvard commencement, Putzi came to dinner at Prides and played the grand piano in the living room, entertaining his old friends as he had when they were young at Harvard, never suspecting that at home Hitler was moving to execute Ernst Roehm and hundreds of others for suspected treason. As the details of the Night of the Long Knives made their way across the Atlantic, Putzi stood on the lawn of his Harvard roommate, Shaw's cousin Louis Agassiz Shaw, and declared to journalists his fealty to Hitler's "providential mission" and his belief that the chancellor had "proven himself never greater, never more human than in the last forty-eight hours."

Official Harvard remained silent about Hanfstaengl's politics and, on the morning of commencement, called in state troopers to restrain demonstrators at the gates of Harvard Yard. Aware of his celebrity, Putzi greeted classmates with the Nazi salute and responded, deadpan, to questions about Germany's "Jewish Problem." "It will be restored to normal soon," he said cheerfully. "By extermination?" a Boston rabbi shouted, before Hanfstaengl was hustled to safety by the police. When the press asked political questions, he dodged, saying "his visit was not official" but "for the sole purpose of attending his class reunion and renewing old friendships."

The Reich took precautions at Garmisch. Under pressure from the International Olympic Committee, the customary anti-Semitic signs were torn from trees and fence posts in town, and later, under further pressure, from highway markers along entrance roads to the city. But one could not escape the Nazi presence. Near the stadium, gangs of Hitler Youth and Nazi Labor Battalions marched and sang, shovels held to brownshirt shoulders in lieu of the guns forbidden at Versailles in 1919, torches throwing eerie light across the snow.

Forty years later, Harry recalled the unmistakable feel of war in the atmosphere, but there is no record of his mother's feeling at Garmisch-Partenkirchen, and only one photograph places Margarett there. She is standing on a snowy slope with a group of friends, her arm around a photographer's shill costumed as a white bear. Her head is thrown back, and she is laughing. She left behind no opinion of Putzi Hanfstaengl or of the Olympics, nor do sketchbooks survive. Nothing but the children's testimony: Margarett and Shaw had lots of friends whom they saw at night.

On March 7, 1936, three brigades of German troops crossed bridges on the Rhine and entered the demilitarized zone of the Rhineland in defiance of the treaty at Versailles. The action was opposed by neither the French nor the British. Immediately, Shaw booked passage home.

Back at Prides, Margarett painted a woman and two blond children around a table in a garden of red tulips. On the table sits a white rabbit, ears erect. The woman is blond and angular; the children could be Harry and Shaw, and one of them looks toward us. The garden is enclosed by a tall green hedge. Outside, a ring of soldiers in uniform point rifles over the hedge, into the circle, toward the woman and the children.

§

FROM THE POINT OF VIEW of the family, the trip had been a success. Whatever sadness Butsy McKean intuited in Paris, whatever the occasional crisis, marriage and family returned, on the face of it, repaired.

"She was wonderful there," Butsy reported to her parents and to Marian Haughton. The family resumed the round of North Shore life—"McKean Twins Have Eye on the Big Leagues," announced the caption beneath a newspaper photo of the not altogether happy-looking eleven-year-olds; another caption, identifying a photograph of two well-dressed women, announced the presence at a dog show of "Mrs. Quincy Adams Shaw McKean and her friend Miss Isabel Pell."

There is nothing in a photo of Margarett taken at a church fair later that weekend—slender in a black sheath to midcalf, smiling glamorously, black Parisian hat at an unexpected angle—to suggest she was anything but delighted with herself on their return from Europe. She began to ride with Shaw to the hunt at Myopia. She returned to the garden, to entertaining, resumed her trips to New York and her friendships. She redecorated the still unsold house on Commonwealth Avenue—black and white, stark chrome furniture—and the family moved back into it for the winter. But six months later, when she posed indoors with five of the Afghans at her feet, her face had no animation, she had gained weight, and a circular white collar lay on her dark tailored shoulders like the ruff of a clown suit.

By June, Jenny Sargent, now eighty-five, was bedridden with cancer; by August, in and out of coma. "I hope," she told Margarett, "that you will never be afflicted in this way." On August 31, Margarett had her forty-fourth birthday, and on Tuesday, September 2, she was called to Wellesley. Jenny died in her sleep on Wednesday, and Margarett remained at her bedside, keeping watch as her mother lay "so serene in all her lovely patience." On Friday, she wrote thanking Mabel Storey for sending a gardenia plant. "I dread tomorrow when she is moved from her bedroom. I have been here ever since Tuesday in my old time little bedroom almost adjoining hers, and they have been days to love. I wish I did not feel so lonely about tomorrow."

Margie and Jenny arrived Friday morning and were brought in to see the old woman with tissue-paper skin who lay dead on the bed where she had slept all her married life. "How incredibly beautiful she looks," Margarett wrote, "and the voice that in any pain still asks me if everything is all right speaks no more. It's the only difference. It seems everything I ever gave her is on her or near her. She said they brighten the room." Shaw and the boys drove down from Prides for the funeral on Saturday, arriving at the Unitarian Church in the family Rolls-Royce, the twins, dressed alike, sitting next to the chauffeur, "like footmen," Sargent Cheever remembered.

As his grandmother was lowered into the ground at Mount Auburn Cemetery, Harry, not knowing what else to do, wept until he noticed his father's disapproving glare. Jenny was buried beside her husband, not far from her daughters Ruth and Alice, whose small, identical gravestones were etched, each with a single lily.

Ever since her marriage, Margarett's relationship with her mother had been evolving. When she named her second daughter Jenny, she seemed to forgive the years of conflict, and since then, in her flamboyant way, she had been a dutiful daughter. Still, in light of their stormy history, Margarett's surviving reference to her mother's death seems surprisingly tender. She would not have confided her own recent losses, but perhaps, now, she could have deeper compassion for what Jenny had suffered.

"So much gratitude to you for saying what I believe," she wrote Mabel Storey. "In love there can be no separation."

ix

I turned to horticulture

(1937–1945)

Margarett in the garden
at Prides, c. 1944

THE WOMAN'S LEGS ARE BARE, her shoulders are exposed. She has dark hair, wears a slip of patterned silk pulled up to reveal her thighs. She sits on a low rush-seated chair painted robin's-egg blue. Large bust, narrow waist, broad hips, slender ankles, small graceful feet. She and another woman are having a conversation. The other woman wears a kimono. She has a modest little face and red hair, and she stands, body facing the mirror, face turned toward Margarett as if to speak to her, but she doesn't seem to be speaking. Margarett herself—for the woman with dark hair dressed only in a slip is Margarett—sits, hands on her hips, face turned toward her model.

On the left side of the painting is a standing mirror with a white wood frame. In the mirror is reflected the part of the room where an artist would stand to paint the scene, but we do not see her, see instead a Sheraton sofa, the pale-brown floor, corner of a rug, tawny walls. Logically, Margarett, posing in her chair, should be reflected in the mirror, but she is not. She should see herself in the mirror, but she does not. The woman casts no reflection, and there is no evidence of the artist. Knowing we cannot be sure, let's say this is Margarett's last painting—herself with no face, casting no reflection in a mirror she clearly faces.

Fifty-five years later, two women lay slides on a light table, arrange them according to catalogue numbers. One of us is the granddaughter who rescued the paintings from a warehouse room; the other, a young art historian. We list individual works, note characteristics—use of paint, of color, approach to drawing or outlining, the swag of an eyelid, treatment of hands. The eye of the artist comes into us as slides flash and images startle the dark. On the basis of the few paintings Margarett dated, of illustrated reviews, ages of children, and exhibition catalogues, we date the slides. We confirm that Margarett Sargent began to sculpt in 1914, that her work evolved to paint on plaster in 1925, and that she began to paint with oil in approximately 1927. Using our dates, we arrange the slides in chronological order, and again images flash, one by one, onto the wall. We observe her increasing mastery, a swift, intense development. In our excitement, we have almost forgotten, until the wall burns white after the final slide, the bare fact that Margarett stopped painting.

When the family returned from Paris in 1936 after the year abroad, Margarett's most recent exhibition was four years behind her. If she had not intended to stop painting when they left, by their return the distance to the studio had become unbridgeable. She exhibited *The Ritz Waiter* both in a biennial at the Worcester Museum in 1935 and in the Ninth Annual of the Boston Society for Independent Artists in 1936, but there is no painting that can be dated, with certainty, later than 1936.

No event punctuated the end of Margarett's painting. Instead, there ceased to be solo exhibitions for which to prepare work; later, when invitations to exhibit in group shows arrived, she turned them down or left them unopened. Eventually there were unfinished paintings, a studio used less frequently, then not at all, palettes and tubes of color hardening. By the early forties, there were people whom Margarett met who had no idea she had been an exhibiting artist, people to whom the sketchbook she continued to pull from her bag and fill with drawings was evidence only that she was a gifted amateur.

A nurse opens the door. Wearing a fuchsia satin jacket and makeup as porcelain as Empress Josephine's, Margarett sits in a hospital bed. It is 1975, and she's eighty-two. Scrapbooks crammed with yellowed reviews overflow onto sheets the color of daffodils, a salmon satin blanket cover. She looks up. "Why, I'd forgotten these!" she exclaims, shocked, genuine, and then, inconsolably, "Why did I ever stop?"

It will be years before I catalogue her paintings in a warehouse room. I stand there, mute, my eye drawn first to her face, then to newsprint Blue Girl and Harpo Marx, her artist face by Bachrach and Abbott unfolding from scrapbook pages.

This is the visit I keep going back to, the first and only time Margarett and I talk about her life as a painter. I haven't walked my way through it for years, not since I set off from Margie's, armed with that portfolio of Margarett's drawings and photographs, in search of answers to the questions I was never able to ask: What must I do not to "go mad" as you did? What must I do to live fully both as an artist and as a woman? Tell me about your life.

As I write now, I shelve that memory of Margarett on the hospital bed, freeze it in time like a moment from one of her paintings, walk again into the apartment on Tremont Street and look at her there, the salmon blanket cover, the mass of yellowed reviews.

"Why, I'd forgotten these!" she exclaims, waiting for my response. "Why did I ever stop?"

"Why *did* you stop?"

"It got too intense," she answers slowly, articulation blurred by the stroke.

Margarett, I want to ask, what do you mean? Too hot? Color blooming across canvas after canvas that gets hot, hotter, then too hot for any brush, and explodes, burns out, leaving just a tiny pile of ash? But my chest tightens, and, instead, I am as silent as I was the last time. I see her pull herself together before she says the next sentence.

"For twenty years I worked," she says, "and then I turned to horticulture."

She speaks as if the transition had been orderly, as if she'd made a conscious decision to stop. The expression on her face tells me she did not. Her answer says both everything and nothing, and it stops the conversation.

At the time, I believed that if I could have said something more, I would have got more information, but now I understand that Margarett made it difficult for me, that her locution, "I turned to," was itself a turning away. She turned from my question, as she had from painting all those years ago, leaving me mystified, silenced, and, I realize now, angry.

But what did I want? What did I imagine a deeper conversation might give me?

With the young art historian, I show slides of Margarett's work to a museum director, herself a young woman. Again we wheel through the bright images, again come to the cruel ending. I make aesthetic conversation, but beneath its veneer is my shame that Margarett stopped painting and, beneath that, grief and fear for my own creative life. What I wanted that day was for Margarett to rise from her bed, for paints magically to appear, for me to watch her at the easel as she painted herself back into the room with the mirror, for her to answer my questions by sitting me down and seizing my face, as she once said she wished to, in paint.

"I think she hated herself for not continuing," Margie said. "Once, in the sixties, I suggested that she have an exhibition," Al Hochberg said. He was her lawyer the last twenty years of her life. "What did she say to that?" "She didn't want to."

In fact, there had always been gardening; the difference now was that it had no rival. In the absence of canvas, Margarett's appetite to seize the entire world in paint—every face that interested her, every configuration or movement that caught her eye—went unsatisfied. To do so now seemed too revealing: the erotic appreciation with which she painted women, the weakness in his image the few times she painted her husband. That she continued to draw—to outline, to catch on the run, on the train, in a restaurant, the striking face or posture—was no substitute for hours in the studio, the full-bodied satisfaction of color on canvas. Bury it instead, in the earth when you plant a bulb, and it will come up acceptable, looking for all the world like anyone else's tulip.

She bought hundreds of bulbs—one year, seven hundred *Narcissus poeticus*—supervised their planting, planted some herself. She was up at six, worked until dusk, perhaps stopping to have people for lunch, perhaps not. The arborvitae at the end of the pool had grown full and high enough to cut back, and she directed the clipping—topiary not to rival her grandfather's Italian Garden but certainly to pay it homage. When the grounds at Prides would take no more work, she did gardens for friends like Emily and Henry Cabot Lodge, or picked up a shrub for someone as a favor and arrived with Fusco, her gardener, to put it in. Eventually she designed gardens professionally, for friends like Nat Saltonstall, a Boston architect and art patron, younger brother of the Salts, and Lily Saarinen, a writer once married to the architect. By the early 1940s, she had clients like Helena Rubinstein, whose penthouse garden she designed in New York.

In 1938, Shaw bought a nursery north of Prides, and he and Margarett began to collaborate, his Magnolia Nurseries providing stock for her landscape design. For a while, she had a flower shop in Boston on Newbury Street. A sheaf of garden plans turned up among some gouaches in a suitcase in an auctioneer's attic, along with a note: "This came near being a very good plan—it just isn't—naturally the color proportions are not right—as I do not plan ahead properly but sketch in free—therefore follow the locations—but not proportions." She'd drawn the pool, then blocked in color with cut-out patches of gouache, labeling them with names and numbers of bulbs: "Murillo Pale Blue Hyacinth 150. Murillo Pale Pink Hyacinth 125." In the spring, pink hyacinths alternating with blue bordered the pool, and behind them, banners of white narcissus quivered in the breeze.

When the force with which Margarett approached painting lost its object, those around her felt the consequences. She talked all night, spilling virtuosic, hilarious stories. She planned a party to bring this person together with that one, to celebrate a new friendship. She planned a garden. She got angry. She went to New York. "Margarett needed a project," Dorothy DeSantillana said. She discovered an artist. She bought six boxes of watercolors and used only one of them. She

ordered a new suit. She drank. One morning, Shaw accosted Mary
McLellan on her way to Margarett's room with a breakfast tray; he
lifted the teapot lid, smelled whiskey, sent Mary back to the kitchen. Or
she didn't drink at all, which confused him: for weeks, even months,
there would be no incident.

Once, he took her to New York for dinner and a play she was dying to see. When he left her upstairs in their hotel room, she looked
lovely, was herself, even gave him a kiss. "You go downstairs, I'll be
there in a second." But when she turned up in the dining room ten
minutes later, "She was absolutely blasted." This became a talismanic
story. Shaw couldn't comprehend how in just ten minutes she could
have drunk enough to get "blasted," did not understand that in its
progressed form addiction to alcohol needs barely a glass to ignite a
full-dress binge. He thought that perhaps on her evenings out with
Roland in Harlem, Margarett acquired drugs, that "dope" was responsible when her condition changed so quickly. He and Margie searched
her bedroom, the closets, the bathroom, but what they found were
bottles—bottles in the backs of closets, in garment bags, slipped into
riding boots.

When they were fifteen and fourteen, Margie and Jenny invited
their father out to the Ritz for lunch. Margie was, in her own opinion,
finally grown up, short blond curls held back by a headband, eager to
begin wearing lipstick. Jenny, the tomboy, still felt awkward wearing a
dress, and so she wore jodhpurs most of the time. Tall and slender,
with pale skin and jet-black hair, she was less outgoing than her older
sister. His daughters were paying for the lunch. Shaw was amused and
delighted.

As they'd become more wary of Margarett, the girls had turned to
Shaw, whom they could count on. They saw him as a victim in the
hostilities: Their mother lashed out, he cowered, dodged, exploded, or
did not fight back, proceeded as if nothing had happened. Margarett
seduced them with her affection, but tell her something in confidence,
and she'd broadcast it with a sarcastic twist to get a laugh at the dinner
table, no matter who was there. And they were terrified Senny would

leave. Late at night in their rooms on the top floor of the old part of the house, they conspired to talk to their father. They wanted him to know that it would be all right if he divorced her. In fact, their purpose in inviting him to lunch was to *ask* him to divorce her.

Shaw refused. He understood how they felt, he was touched they had taken him to lunch, but the divorce laws were such, he said, that their mother was likely to win custody, and he could not allow that to happen. But you're so unhappy, Papa! They imagined a family without Mama, her headaches, her chaos, and her cruelty. They imagined a mother as calm and loving as Senny, as authoritative and responsive as Grandma Haughton, a mother who would put their interests before hers. They believed Margarett's suffering was entirely of her own making. "If the house burned down," young Shaw said, "and there was a choice between a child and a Renoir, the Renoir would win, hands down."

But even Margie admitted that when Margarett was well, "she could be *great fun*." The young people, friends of the children, who came to Prides characterized Margarett as "great fun," "very warm," "interested." She would engage you in a real conversation if she found you sitting alone at a party, or she would draw out of you what you wanted to do with your life and encourage you, particularly if your ambition involved leaving Boston or becoming some sort of artist.

Ben Bradlee, one of the children of Margarett's second cousins Bebo and Josephine Bradlee, came to Prides often. After "being ditched by Margie," he "fell hard for Jenny" and turned up to court her and to absorb at Prides the first glimmer of life beyond cold roast Boston, a glimmer that later led him to become a journalist. "Margarett would be talking about painting or about music, or there would be interesting people there," he said. "The house had an enchanted quality, but with slightly ominous overtones. Some days Margarett would be in a good mood—there was more joy on those days."

Ben's older brother, Freddie, an aspiring actor and writer, worked up a mean imitation of his Prides hostess. He loved setting the pitch of his voice to capture Margarett's. One day it was chilly, and she turned to him. "Dahling"—as he mimicked, he let his voice settle—"will you go up to the octagonal room and if that window's open, close it, and if it's closed, put your foot through it?"

Their younger sister, Connie, a friend of Jenny's, came for lunch or supper or to spend the night. Once, at lunch, Margarett complained about the gloom of her bedroom. The standing lamp simply did not give enough light to read by.

"Well, Mrs. McKean, have you seen those new lamps for night reading that clamp right to the headboard?"

"Seen them? I've been married to one for fifteen years!"

"Like that," Connie Bradlee said, "one after another, so fast you got almost unpleasantly sick laughing."

One day, an enormous box arrived at Prides addressed to Margarett, with instructions to open it immediately. Hardly visible were small holes at intervals on each side. Margarett set upon the package, tearing at its wrappings, only to find beneath it another carton, then still another. Inside the third carton was a huge cage in which sat a large green macaw, a gift from Shaw, in appeasement, perhaps, for the finches set loose in Paris.

Margarett immediately named her new bird Jack. Very soon he was shrieking Margarett's name with a broad Boston *a*, and when the phone rang, he'd summon Mary McLellan. One evening, Margarett had a young Harvard friend to supper by himself, and Jack sidled along the table, moving at a microscopic pace. Just as he was about to strike with his beak, the young man, watchful, moved his hand, and Jack tumbled to the floor.

One morning, he laid an egg. "Oh," Shaw said, "you're Jacqueline!"

"Go to hell!" Jack replied.

On one of Shaw's birthdays, Margarett had the floor of the big room strewn with hay, fodder suspended from the Venetian lanterns, tables set out for dinner. For music she hired an Italian accordion band, and at the climax of the party, a donkey led a procession of animals through the front door (built to accommodate monumental sculpture) and into the living room. To entertain at another party, Margarett hired wrestlers. In a ring, constructed for the evening, a very large man, his head shaved bald, threw around his Greek opponent. Another evening, waiters carrying trays of champagne executed pratfalls without spilling, and when one guest requested an ice cube, the waiter returned struggling under the weight of a chunk of ice "practically the size of a boulder."

If Margarett could not manage to disturb the surface of a canvas, she could certainly disrupt social expectations. In time, the sheer profusion of her pranks exhausted her family. "It would be Papa's birthday, and everyone would be complimenting Mama on the brilliance of the party!" Margie said. Margarett would invite thirty to dinner: "Come to my owl party!" And a multitude of stuffed owls, peering through the candlelight, would mutely rebuke stuffed shirts. Or telephone her friend the actress Hope Williams in New York: "I'm planning the most extraordinary evening." That Saturday night, the guests cooked and served, and the Prides staff sat for dinner at the table; afterward everyone drank and danced into the night.

One Christmas Eve, Shaw's brother, Harry, and his wife, Bessie, gave a family party. Their five teenage children, the Shaw McKeans, Bessie's aged mother, and assorted cousins were guests at a dinner large enough to be catered by Creed, a figure so familiar he and his staff added to the *bonhomie* of any North Shore party. Once in a while, if it was a big dinner, as this was, the hostess hired an "extra," as Bessie had this evening.

Margarett, whom Creed always called Maggie, was expected later, and though Shaw reassured Bessie when she asked, he could never be sure these days if his wife would turn up. When the additional waitress appeared, Bessie's daughter Butsy was sorry Aunt Margarett wasn't there to sketch her. She had wild, curly red hair, and she smiled strangely to obscure a missing tooth. Over the regulation black uniform, she wore a garishly ruffled apron, and on her feet were brown-and-white saddle shoes. It seemed to Butsy, as the woman lunged toward her, that she had a slight limp.

"Would you care for an hor d'oeuvre, miss?" she asked, in a "ghastly Irish accent," passing the plate so high Butsy couldn't see what was on it, and then so high it came within an inch of her grandmother's nose. Mrs. Lee, in her eighties and an Italian aristocrat, pushed the plate away so that she could see the canapés. "We'll all just rise above it," she said to Butsy under her breath.

A cousin arrived late. "Better get at it," the redhead told her at the door, yanking off her coat. "The drinks are flowing like glue." Later, in the parlor, the maid returned to Mrs. Lee with another tray. "What's going on, mum, have ye had too much to drink?" Grandma Lee lost her temper. "If you don't behave, I'm going to tell Mrs. McKean to throw you out!"

Butsy's sister Sis was furious her mother wouldn't tell the woman to leave. Butsy kept her own feelings—more amusement than disapproval—to herself, and suddenly, as she walked across the room to join her father near the fireplace, realized who the maid was. As the redhead let loose another raucous "Excuse me," Butsy's father also caught on, and the two of them began to laugh. "Stop laughing," fumed Sis, still thinking the woman was a maid.

When the guests entered the dining room a few minutes later, they found Margarett, red wig off, blacking smudged from her tooth, feet up on the damask-draped table, cocktail in her hand, laughing with Creed, who'd been as taken in as anyone but hadn't dared complain to his client about her hired extra. Only Bessie had been in on the secret.

"Nobody could get over it," Butsy said. "It was so clever and so good." It occurred to no one that their habitual lack of attention to hired help had greatly helped Margarett to carry off her disguise.

"What's a den of iniquity?" Margie asked her father once, on returning from a visit to Wellesley.

"Why do you ask?"

"Because Uncle David Cheever says we live in one."

§

By 1934, the generation of curators Margarett had known as students at Harvard were bringing European Modernism into the mainstream of American cultural life. Their new prominence was announced that February, when A. Everett "Chick" Austin, a Harvard product and the new director of the Wadsworth Atheneum, mounted the world premiere of Gertrude Stein and Virgil Thomson's *Four Saints in Three Acts*. Margarett made a pilgrimage to Hartford for the opera, cast entirely with black gospel singers, designed by the painter Florine Stettheimer (the scenery was a bouillabaisse of cellophane and colored light, the costumes pale-blue robes and white gloves), and directed by John Houseman, a young German-born director newly arrived in American by way of London.

When Margarett went to New York, she encountered Harvard graduates on the staff of the Museum of Modern Art and in the directorships of two major galleries. In a small brownstone on Madison Avenue, Julien Levy showed the group of young European painters who called themselves the neo-Romantics (among them, Pavel Tchelitchew and Leonid and Eugene Berman) and, in 1936, mounted the first significant American exhibition of the Surrealists, including, most sensationally, Salvador Dalí's *The Persistence of Memory*—limp pocket watches in a desolate landscape. At Durlacher Brothers, on Fifty-seventh Street, Kirk Askew exercised a flawless eye for old-master drawings, an instinct for the then unfashionable Italian Baroque, and a tough but effective gift for nurturing new American artists. Later, when he inherited them from Levy, Askew showed the neo-Romantics; in 1948, when a young Yale graduate, George Dix, became his partner and brought them along, he took on the British painters Francis Bacon and Ben Nicholson.

Kirk Askew and his wife, Constance, were friends of Margarett's, and by the mid-thirties their salon was one of her New York destinations. At their brownstone on East Sixty-first Street, Kirk, slight of stature, with bright, prematurely white hair, and Constance, blond and statuesque—her "relaxed visage," Virgil Thomson wrote, "as calm as that of Garbo"—received their influential friends: curators from the

Museum of Modern Art, artists, composers, writers, theater people, and collectors. Tea and drinks were served Sunday afternoons from five o'clock on "during the R months," John Houseman wrote, "like oysters," in a large sitting room whose windows overlooked a garden. On the fringes simmered an unrepressed erotic life one habitué characterized as "extremely bisexual—nobody worried much about the gender of the other person in bed." But excess in flirtation, drink, or shoptalk was not to interfere with the purpose of the gatherings, which Kirk, "smiling and efficient," kept to an elegant blend of repartee and an exchange of ideas that might lead to collaboration.

At the Askews', Margarett reencountered Lincoln Kirstein, Archibald MacLeish, and Paris friends like the artist Jean Lurçat and the dealer Valentine Dudensing, from whom she had bought her De Chiricos. Aaron Copland, the three Stettheimer sisters, and George Balanchine turned up from time to time, and when they visited from England, Elizabeth Bowen and the Sitwells always stayed with the Askews. In the forties, Pavel Tchelitchew joined the Sunday parties, bringing his companion, the poet Charles Henri Ford, who edited the avant-garde magazine *View*. As the decade wore on, the crowd got younger—Leonard Bernstein, the librettist John LaTouche, the composer and writer Paul Bowles, and his wife, the writer Jane Bowles.

In Kirk Askew, Margarett found a sharp-tongued companion and a compassionate friend. At his parties, she was marveled at by aspiring artists and writers—mostly young men—drawn by her combination of what the writer Leo Lerman called "granite solid background," intelligence, wit, and an ability to talk about art. "When she spoke, she delivered a thought as if it were a poetic phrase, almost like an actress, with low voice," said Gloria Etting, one of the dancing Braggiotti sisters, who as a child had known Margarett in Boston. To this younger generation, just a few years older than her children, Margarett represented rebellion, all the more admirable because it came from within, all the more important to them because it was sexual as well as aesthetic. "She knew things," Bowden Broadwater said. "She had," said the playwright William Alfred, "fauve majesty."

Margarett's new admirers were the kind of people who had always attracted her—engaged in art or theater, in the intensity of aesthetic argument or creative collaboration, people for whom gossip was a medium of intelligence rather than social control. To them her talk was unusual but not alien, her taste welcome but not intimidating, her appetites familiar.

In New York, she danced on the table. In Boston, she passed out. Life there, increasingly, was tolerable only if she drank. She went to New York once, often twice, a month. Or she went foxhunting in Virginia. She went to Vermont, with and without the children. Sometimes she was happy there. "Mrs. McKean was extraordinary the whole time," Connie Bradlee wrote her brother Freddie from Dorset in 1937. "She is really blissfully happy up there as she can do exactly what she wants without anyone criticizing her."

But often now, even in Vermont, Margarett wept for hours at a time, had what Margie described as "terrible crying jags." Once in a while, when she came out of a spate of sadness, she would, in a burst of high spirits, make a false start at painting—buy sketchbooks and paints and hire a model, even rent a studio in Boston. Or she'd rip up a garden and lay out a new one, over Shaw's protests at her extravagance. But her discontent had become harder to disguise, and she exploded unpredictably now, even at friends, with whom she usually concealed her pain.

Hope Williams, the actress, had become a friend. She had a dry sense of humor and a walk so distinctive that her first Broadway entrance, in Philip Barry's *Paris Bound*, got laughs and applause before she spoke a word. Margarett met her through Betty Parsons and pursued her, "like a schoolgirl," Hope said. They had a slight affair. Hope would come up to Prides on the Sunday train after the matinee, Margarett would meet her in New York, or they would go to Dorset for the weekend.

One spring day in Vermont, after lunch and in the middle of a conversation, "Margarett walked away from me," Hope said. "I could see by her walk that she had become another person, and when she

turned back, she turned on me." Hope did not recognize the unfamiliar and frightening look in her friend's eyes, or her loud, cruel voice.
She packed her bag for New York and left immediately. "After that I
never loved her again," she said. Or saw her.

In Dorset for a weekend with Betty Parsons, Margarett woke from
a dream. "A little golden flower in a snowbank," she said. "I dreamed I
was a golden flower in a snowbank."

Most of Margarett's friends treated her torment as if it were the
weather. Even those few in whom she felt free to confide, like Betty,
felt powerless to help her; but in 1937, she began find some solace
with the help of her old friend, Maria deAcosta. Maria, now married
to Teddy Chanler, credited the Catholic Church with much of their
happiness. Related by marriage to Vivian Pickman, Teddy was a composer, who had skipped Harvard to study in Paris with Nadia Bou-
langer, "an experiment," Virgil Thomson archly observed, "in upper
class male education." He was considered one of the more talented of
the generation that included Thomson, Aaron Copland, and Walter
Piston, but music had failed to restrain him from a life his family considered dissolute: "Drink, drugs, sex of all kinds, as I understand it,"
said his friend Bill Alfred. Maria met Teddy in Paris, abandoned her
Boston marriage to Miriam Shaw, and, to his family's everlasting gratitude, married him. Both had been born Catholic, and by the late 1930s,
each had returned to the Church.

Maria and Teddy were not unusual; for many conflicted bohemians,
the Church was a safer haven for spiritual longing than art or sex. To
many in trouble with drink, it offered the kind of spiritual surrender
Alcoholics Anonymous, then in its infancy, would later provide. The
Chanlers, knowing Margarett's suffering, took it upon themselves to
encourage her, Maria with what Bill Alfred called a "loopy" sort of faith,
and Teddy with "a gift of mirth" that amounted to grace. "Nobody
could resist him," Alfred said—it was Teddy who would successfully
encourage Alice Toklas's deeper embrace of Catholicism in the 1950s.

That summer of 1937, Father Thomas Feeney, a Jesuit, gave a

preaching mission at Saint Margaret's Church in Beverly Farms. The first week was for women, and Margarett refused to go, but eventually Teddy persuaded her to meet Father Tom, as he was called, and Margarett invited him to Prides for lunch. "A lot of fancy people were flirting with the Church in those days," Paul Moore said, and charismatic priests like Feeney and his brother Leonard were in part responsible. Margarett recognized in Tom Feeney, a professor of French and English at Boston College, a literate sophistication akin to her brother Dan's, and they talked all afternoon. When Teddy told Father Tom after the lunch at Prides that he sensed Margarett was close to conversion, Feeney replied, "Wouldn't it be nice if she came in soon, while she is still young and beautiful?"

Margarett listened to the priest's passionate talk and to Teddy and Maria. She began to imagine there was a way to ease what she suffered in the darkened room, to bring her close again to her children, to make peace with Shaw. She imagined a return to the clarity she'd had when she was painting and showing, imagined giving herself over to a connectedness resembling what she'd felt in the studio, or early mornings in the garden. If she could be relieved of the terrible sense she had of her own imperfection and simply call herself a sinner, if she could lose herself to a force of beauty and forgiveness outside her knowledge, why not relinquish some of her prized independence?

That weekend, Margarett went to Lake Placid, where Margie and Jenny were spending the month with Senny, taking lessons and skating in the all-weather rink built for the 1932 Olympics. She was planning to convert to the Catholic Church, Margarett announced to her daughters. To the girls it was as if she had announced a trip or the purchase of a new coat. "By then I didn't gave a damn what she did," Margie said. Neither believed anymore that their mother could or would change for the better, particularly under the influence of a church they perceived as a peculiarity in the lives of Uncle Dan's odd family.

On Sunday evening, back at Prides, Margarett was no longer sure of her decision, but Teddy and Maria persuaded her to come hear

Father Tom's first sermon the second week of the mission, which was devoted to men. "We sat upstairs," Teddy wrote Dan, "so as not to distract the male congregation." They returned Monday night, and Tuesday Father Tom began to address his preaching to Margarett. At lunch at Prides, he'd admired the way Jack spread his wings when Margarett asked him to, and so, when he preached of angels, he said, "Isn't it hard on these wonderful beings to be near us and over us every minute of the day and night and never to receive a word of recognition from us—never to be asked to 'spread their wings'!" And then he invented a parable: A princess lives in a "beautiful tower surrounded by gardens." A beggar comes to her gate with an invitation "from the Queen of Heaven to attend a banquet where you will be fed the Bread of Angels." Pray for her, he exhorted the congregation of men.

The final night of the mission, at a ceremony for the renewal of baptismal vows, Margarett again sat upstairs. She watched the congregation below, and as each man lifted a lighted candle up into the darkness, and Father Tom "spoke like a sort of child-soldier to us," she turned to Maria, in tears. "I cannot stay as I am any longer."

Teddy and Maria took her to the rectory after the service to talk to Father Tom. "Have you been crying?" he asked.

She refused his offer to be baptized the next morning. "The devil's tail," Teddy wrote Dan, "was still sticking out from under the lid." He sharply informed Margarett that Jesuits were not in the habit of making such offers, and at the church the next morning after seven-thirty mass, Father Tom greeted Teddy and Maria, smiling, a note from Margarett clasped in his hand: "I desire to become a Catholic."

She was baptized that morning at ten.

The Church reached her through its aesthetics—the light of candles in a darkened church, the liturgy sung in Latin, the antique Spanish crucifix she hung beside her bed. Its promise of absolution moved her to believe that her most private, unshared agonies might be lifted. Once she joined the Church, Margarett never disavowed her faith, but she kept her belief private. Asked once why she converted, she replied,

"There was nothing else to do that year to shock Boston." Only the few religious people—her brother Dan, for one—with whom she became intimate understood the depth at which the Church reached her. Dan went to mass every morning, but Margarett would not take communion from a priest she didn't like. David Challinor, born what he called a "WASP Catholic," was one of Jenny's boyfriends and a frequent Prides houseguest the summer of 1942. He remembered Margarett, then five years a Catholic, calling him to her room to discuss the nonconformist faith of François Mauriac.

Margarett's new religion did not forestall the inevitable. Two months after her conversion, she and Shaw and Mary McLellan became the only residents at Prides. For years the children had clamored to go away to school, to lead, as Jenny put it, "normal lives." Now they were old enough, and Margarett was no longer in a position to keep them at home. Margie, at sixteen, was dying to go, as her mother had, to Florence, but the threat of war prevented travel abroad, and in the autumn of 1937, she went instead to the French School for Girls in New York. Jenny, who wanted to go to a school that would prepare her for college, went to Madeira in Virginia. The twins, because of the deficits of their Neary education—"We were stars of French, but we'd never heard of science"—were sent to the Fay School in Massachusetts to prepare for Saint Paul's in New Hampshire.

After a year, Margie finished school, and for her seventeenth birthday, the autumn of 1938, Margarett and Shaw gave her a coming-out party. Margie was pleasantly surprised. "That whole year, I never saw Mama drunk. She was absolutely marvelous." And marvelous again the winter of 1940, when, longing to see Machu Picchu and Cuzco, she took Margie to Peru. They sailed on a cruise ship. "God knows Mama was attractive," Margie said, "and so we had quantities, swarms, of unattached males lurking around."

In less than a year, Margie was engaged. Walter "Wally" Reed was from New York and had gone to Harvard. He was tall, with romantic, dark-haired good looks. "Very smart, very funny, and a drunk," his daughter said. What Margie said later was that she married at nineteen to get out of the house.

On a spring day in 1941, Margarett sat in the Ritz dining room. Whomever she'd lunched with had long gone, and the dining room was empty except for waiters tidying up, who were trying, tactfully, to persuade her to leave. She refused, first falling asleep and then laughing at the headwaiter. She was heavier than she'd been—not overweight but certainly full-bodied—and she could feel it. She drank the last of her wine as the room darkened. She asked for another drink, and a waiter filled her glass with water. She cursed him and began to laugh. "Mrs. McKean," the headwaiter kept pleading, politely.

At Prides, the telephone rang. It was the Ritz calling, Mary McLellan reported to Shaw. Apparently, Mrs. McKean would not leave the dining room. She was shouting at the waiters.

"Mrs. McKean, we must close the dining room." Margarett just sat there. "Mrs. McKean." Shaw walked toward her across the long floor, young Shaw, then sixteen, behind him. The waiters pulled the table from the banquette, and together Shaw and young Shaw lifted Margarett's dead weight to standing, escorted her from the dining room, down the stairs, into a waiting car.

Barely six months later, on November 19, 1941, Margie married Wally Reed in a small ceremony at a church in Beverly and Margarett organized a lunch at Prides. She arranged the flowers and orchestrated the seating, saw the newlyweds off to New York and an apartment on East Tenth Street, made sure they had furniture, linens, and silver. This was another occasion on which, as Margie put it, Margarett pulled herself together. She adored Wally, whom Margie had met through a group of his Saint Paul's classmates, and who, while he was at Harvard, had come to Prides often for Sunday lunch or for the weekend. The relatives and friends who wrote effusive notes of congratulation would soon observe that Margie had chosen a husband who shared not only her mother's wit and verbal skill but her weakness. Wally drank too much and disappeared for days, returning nonchalant and without explanation.

In the autumn of 1940, Jenny had entered Vassar. She appeared to her classmates very much a product of Madeira, but beneath a veneer of what one of them called "saying all the right things," she carried a powerful sense of the peculiarity of her background—"shame," she would call it later when she described her childhood to me. But she concealed it, in writing class transforming her mother's character in pieces of writing, once wittily imagining Margarett and Margie on the boat to Peru:

MARGARETT: Mr. Cross gave me a letter to a man who has a private zoo filled with honey bears ... but the boat doesn't stop there.

MARGIE: Who's Mr. Cross?

MARGARETT: Margie, don't look as though you had unearthed a scandal, Papa knows him very well.

During the summer of 1941, Margarett was hostess at Prides as young men courted her younger daughter, and Jenny eased into what Paul Moore, who would become my father, called "a golden summer." The specter of war hovered as Roosevelt declared a national emergency and Hitler invaded Russia, but the blandishments of July and August on the North Shore kept the ominous news just outside awareness. Young Ruthie Robb, Bob Potter, Paul Moore, and Jenny cleaved together in no particular romantic configuration and called themselves "the younger set." They spent days at Singing Beach or playing tennis, had dinner at one or another of their parents' houses, and at night danced to Ruby Newman's orchestra at the Magnolia casino, drinking martinis, more than once spending the night in a hungover heap on someone's living room floor.

As the Germans subdued Ukraine in August, as Leningrad stood against the Nazis and winter halted Hilter outside Moscow, young men began to make decisions about war. When the Japanese bombed

Pearl Harbor, on December 7, even Shaw decided to enlist. He'd missed combat in the first war, now he'd have his chance, as a major, he imagined. When he was rejected because of high blood pressure, he helped organize a Boston center for GIs. Marian donated her house at 13 Commonwealth Avenue and moved across the street to the Ritz, and Margarett organized cabaret evenings for soldiers on leave. Jenny's friends Bob Potter and Paul Moore were called up, and in the summer of 1942, Wally Reed was drafted. He left for India in October, just after Margie gave birth to Margarett's first grandchild, Jenny.

In July 1943, a month after their graduation from Saint Paul's the twins were drafted. Harry wanted to join the air force, but his father advised against it. Asked in his entrance interview why he wanted to join the infantry, he replied, "Because I like to shoot." By November, he was stationed in England, living in a hut on the Salisbury Plain, hiding the luxurious packages Margaret sent from S. S. Pierce, claiming Lady Astor as a relative, and taking weekend leaves at Cliveden, the Astor country house in Buckinghamshire. Unlike Harry, who at first felt uncomfortable with his fellow enlisted men, Shaw took to the company of soldiers and reveled in leaving Prides behind; a hernia diagnosed the day before embarkation kept him in America throughout the war, in spite of his father's efforts to have him assigned to combat. In 1944, Harry would fight in the Battle of the Bulge, following, as his division advanced, the road on which Hardy had driven the family to Garmisch-Partenkirchen eight years before.

With the household now essentially dissolved, Margaret spent even more time in New York. She'd stop at Durlacher's, with its old-world ambience, then mount the elevator in the next building west on Fifty-seventh Street to visit Betty Parsons who by then was working at Mortimer Brandt's gallery. Betty had settled in California after Paris, and in 1935 returned to New York. In 1940, she opened a gallery at the Wakefield Bookshop on East Fifty-fifth Street where, combining audacious taste and a gift for persuasion, she built a controversial stable of artists that included Saul Steinberg, Theodoros Stamos, Hedda Sterne, and Joseph Cornell.

In 1946, Betty took over Brandt's entire suite of galleries, stripped away architectural detail, and painted the walls flat white. "A gallery isn't a place to rest," she said of her new space, and created a sensation showing the bold, vibrant assertions of the revolution in American art being made by the painters who would come to be called the Abstract Expressionists—among them, Barnett Newman, Jackson Pollock, and Mark Rothko.

At Christmas, 1946, Elsa Maxwell's effusive account of a group show there was syndicated on society pages nationwide, and soon after, Rosalind Constable published an article in *Time.* For the first time since the Eight, American art was chic. Maxwell dropped the names of artists like Newman, "Rathko," and Sterne, and finished off the column with an exhortation: "Some dissenters scream, 'Hang the abstractionists!' I echo, 'Certainly, but why not on your walls.' "

Margarett was amazed and impressed by Betty's enormous success, but she was also intimidated. The new art that was making her friend's name seemed to have no roots in the European Modernism that had inspired her. Betty had always admired Margarett's eye, had in fact shown her collection at the Wakefield in 1942, but her own taste had always been the more obviously experimental. Though it is possible that if Margarett had not stopped painting, the visceral relationship to paint central to the Abstract Expressionist aesthetic would have entered her work, she never turned to those artists as a collector. Instead, she bought from Betty the artists who carried forward, more clearly, a European aesthetic—not Newman or Rothko, but Steinberg and Stamos.

The turn in Betty's fortunes came at a difficult time for Margarett, who now felt less able to call on the friend who had always been her confidante. When she appeared in Betty's gallery, she carried on with her usual bravado, but alone in her hotel room, she often panicked. She was afraid to go out on the street, afraid to go back to Prides, afraid to go by herself to Grand Central. She'd call and ask Margie to pick her up in a taxi and take her to the train, but Margie, terrified in any case of her mother's desperation, was alone in an apartment on

East Tenth Street with an infant. More than once Margie telephoned Betty, who left her gallery to take the friend she once called "the most talented woman I've ever met," weeping, to the train.

§

MARGARETT'S ISOLATION was in part a consequence of her drinking, but her loneliness was real. She no longer had the companionship of the studio, Prides was bleak without the children and their activities, and the war had closed off part of her world. Roland Balay was in Paris and would not return to America until peace was declared. Isabel Pell was also in France, living with a marquise near Grasse in the south, where she would remain until the war's end. By 1942 or so, shorn of these old allies and friends, Margarett began "to see a great deal of" Florence Shaw, the widow of Shaw's cousin and Putzi Hanfstaengl's old friend, Louis Agassiz Shaw.

Florence, "Auntie Floto," to the children, was a brassy, flirtatious sportswoman with a beautiful figure and a buoyant spirit, who reminded the boys of the "younger set" of Lauren Bacall. Louis, who had died in 1941, had done early research on decompression sickness (the "bends") and, with Cecil Drinker, had invented the Drinker Respirator, which came to be called the "iron lung." He and Florence had been frequent dinner guests at Prides, had had, by all accounts, a felicitous, even blissful marriage. After Louis died, Florence divided her time between houses on the North Shore and in Boca Grande, Florida, where Vivian and Dudley Pickman also had a house, and where Maria and Teddy Chanler wintered in a small cottage.

During the 1940s, Margarett and Shaw visited Florence in Boca Grande nearly every winter, and Margarett often stayed on. When a young Hunnewell cousin visited there, she assumed Florence's house belonged to Margarett. Florence liked to drink and laugh as Margarett did, and eventually the two became lovers. It was this relationship that made people outside the family aware that Margarett McKean was given to more than one kind of romance.

"Did you know your grandmother had love affairs with women?" a friend of my mother's asked me when I was thirty.

"I had that feeling. . . ."

"There was a woman named Florence Shaw."

"Was it a long relationship?"

"More than ten years."

Margarett's discretion was total as usual, and so her liaison with Florence was another love affair about which everyone knew and nobody spoke.

"Did you know about my grandmother and Florence Shaw?" I asked Nancy Palmer, one of Vivian Pickman's daughters.

"Oh, yes, everybody knew."

"Well, if nobody spoke of it, how did you know?"

"Mother told me."

Since she lived nearby, Florence did not come to Prides as a houseguest, like Isabel or Marjorie. As she had when her husband was alive, she came to dinner or to lunch, in turn inviting Margarett to her house in Beverly Farms. Or, guests at the same party, they would leave at the end of the evening, one at a time, often going on to Florence's or, if Shaw was not there, to Prides. As always, if Shaw noticed the affair, he made it his business to look away. No one has a story of an erotic moment witnessed, and there are no letters. Only Margarett's sketchbooks attest to what was, from time to time, a life together.

"Margaret S. McKean, Boca Grande, Florida, March, 1942." The cover is calf stamped to look like lizard: inked, rotund scribbles for Florence's black Pekingeses; a woman through the window of a green-blue car, yellow broad-brimmed hat, naked ear, eyelash, fingers obscuring her mouth; pencil drawing of a woman with a cigarette, just her face, the line as effortless as exhaling; in gouache, the captain of a pleasure boat: "No Smoking." In pencil, a long-legged woman in a well-cut jacket, a man in a uniform: "So you're living in a rented house.'"

At a restaurant in Tampa, as Margarett makes her portrait in ink, a little girl asks: "Do you just draw anywhere—anything you want?"

Or anyone she wanted. Margarett had never been a monogamist.

A small sheet of paper, ripped from a sketch pad: Hair that stands straight up. Mouth from two brush strokes, pale orange; black eyes daubed with a loose brush, circles beneath them the same color as her lips. Her hair is wild black grass, diluted to purple across her brow. She looks right at you. Diminutive body, pink puffed sleeves, dress a criss-cross of black stripes. The likeness is unmistakable. It is a portrait of Jane Bowles, at the time twenty-eight years old, and Margarett had done her from memory.

The summer of 1944, Wally Reed, now separated from Margie, frequently visited Jane and Paul Bowles in their rented house in Ama-gansett, and that autumn in New York, he introduced Margarett to the Bowleses. Jane, who thrived on flirtatious pursuit and was given to obsessive romance, was undeterred by the fact that Margarett, at fifty-two, was nearly twice her age. She had a penchant for older women: "She was no longer beautiful," she wrote in her novel *Two Serious Ladies*, "but in her face I found fragments of beauty which were much more exciting to me than any beauty that I have known at its height."

Two Serious Ladies, peopled with odd characters in baldly original configurations, had been published a year before by Alfred Knopf. Margarett certainly talked about the book with her friends at the Askews'. Like them, she marveled at Bowles's disjunctive, deadpan style and recognized her bisexual characters, her opposition to senti-mentality, and the ache she evoked in fleeting moments of human connection. *Two Serious Ladies* had a cult success, and overnight Jane became, in Ned Rorem's phrase, "a major minor writer."

When Jane was fourteen, her widowed mother had sent her to pri-vate school in Massachusetts, where she became painfully conscious of her difference as a Jew. At fifteen, she fell from a horse, broke her right leg, developed tuberculosis of the knee, and spent two years in a sani-tarium in Switzerland, most of it in traction. There, in an agony of pain and loneliness, she found her vocation as a writer and developed "a fear of dogs, of sharks, or mountains, of elevators, of being burned alive," phobias that, along with her stiff right leg, gave her a perverse sense of uniqueness. "Crippie, the kike dyke," she called herself with the bravado of self-hatred.

Jane was small, gamine or boyish, depending on your point of view, and "brilliant," Betty Parsons said, "just brilliant." By the time Margarett met her, her marriage to Paul Bowles resembled a sister's dependence on a beloved older brother, and she lived for part of the year on a farm in Vermont (not far from Dorset) with a woman companion—in an astonishing coincidence, Helvetia Orr (now Perkins), with whom Margarett had occasionally skated afternoons forty years earlier at Miss Porter's School. Helvetia had given her life over to caring for Jane, keeping her from the chaotic New York life that, Helvetia believed, made her drink too much, depressed her, and led her to slit her wrists the first summer they were together.

Margarett had no interest in taking care of Jane; she recognized her talent, and if at first she resisted her young admirer's insistent pursuit, she soon capitulated. Jane courted her in New York and followed her to Massachusetts. It was rare that Margarett had this sort of rapport with a woman. Jane delighted in Margarett's mode of expression, which she called "controlled non sequitur," a phrase she might have used to describe her own prose style. By the same token, Margarett, in the single slinky line with which she drew women, might have been describing Jane's fictional characters.

When in New York, Margarett stayed at the Gladstone Hotel, on Fifty-second Street, where the socialite Alice Astor and Gerald Murphy's sister Esther kept apartments, and where the international arts patron Mabel Dodge and Tony Luhan, her Indian husband, took a suite when they visited from Taos. On the left as you came in was a tiny crowded bar, legendary as a meeting place for women who loved women but by no means confined to them. There, in the smoky crowd, you might encounter Marlene Dietrich in a backless gown or the novelist Sybil Bedford. A friend of Margarett's, a young actor, rang her once from the desk at the Gladstone and was directed up to her suite. Margarett greeted him at the door, stockings down around her ankles, Jane trailing out of the bedroom behind her, both of them laughing and high.

Unlike most of her earlier liaisons with women, Margarett's relationship with Jane was discussed openly—at the Askews', at the Gladstone, even in certain Boston circles. Kirk Askew remarked that Jane's crippled leg and the difference in their sizes—Margarett was robust and five feet ten, Jane petite and five feet three—must have made certain aspects of the relationships "inconvenient." Maud Morgan, a Boston artist, told a story of Margarett and Jane in her Andover kitchen, pursuing each other, laughing and brandishing skillets. Betty Parsons worried about their drinking and later blamed Jane for "ruining Margarett, ruining her." But Oliver Smith disagreed. "They had conversation and engagement with one another," he said, "not just booze."

Jane talked and talked to Oliver about Margarett, first with enormous excitement about her wit, her articulateness, her voluptuous body, later with disappointment that after a while Margarett no longer shared the degree of her sexual passion. At first, he and the others with whom Jane lived, in a revolving commune on Tenth Street, thought Margarett was a character Jane had invented, but eventually "Margarett McKean" turned up in chic suits, elegant hats, and beautiful shoes for dinners Jane marshaled from a narrow galley kitchen.

Margarett took to Jane's friends immediately. She was enthralled by the double piano Bobby Fizdale played with Arthur Gold and by Oliver's connection to the theater—he was about to design and produce *On the Town*, which would launch his extraordinary career and introduce Leonard Bernstein's music to Broadway. At Tenth Street, Margarett also met John La Touche, a young lyricist and librettist, who became a new combatant in repartee. Margarett's new friends soon came to feel protective of her. They could not understand why she returned to Prides when it was so clear she belonged in New York, why she remained married to a husband they heard her only revile and ridicule. Jane was at work on a play; "My husband never loved me," one of its characters moaned, tipsy and out of control.

Once, Bobby Fizdale and Oliver Smith had lunch with Margarett and Jane and another woman, to whom Margarett took a dislike. Bobby knew it was just a matter of time before Margarett made her opinion known. "What type are you?" she finally asked the woman, who looked back at her blankly. "Hmmm, it's coming to me," Margarett said. "I know what type you are. You're the type my husband likes; you're the restaurant type."

§

WHEN PAUL MOORE APPROACHED his father for permission to marry Jenny McKean, the senior Paul Moore expressed concern. It was not that he disliked Margarett McKean—in fact, she made him laugh— but he feared her daughter might inherit the instability evidenced in Margarett's drinking and her rumored sexual career, and in her brother's suicide. He wanted his son to consider his choice carefully, but Paul was madly in love and already a rebel. He planned to marry Jenny and, when the war ended, enter theological school to prepare for the Episcopal priesthood—which pleased his mother, infuriated his father, and delighted Margarett, who always made a point of engaging him in theological discussion.

The easy friendship of the "golden summer" had intensified when Paul returned to New York to recuperate from a war wound. He'd been shot straight through the chest by a Japanese soldier while commanding a platoon at Guadalcanal and had returned to New York with three medals for bravery. In a newspaper photograph taken at El Morocco, zebra upholstery behind them, he is identified as a Marine hero, Jenny as a "socialite." But Paul's experience in combat had traumatized him, and he was uncomfortable thinking of himself as courageous. To Jenny he could express his confusion about killing, could even cry, as she did when she talked about her mother's drinking or showed him Margarett's studio at Prides. Paul, with his successful father and his kind and effusive mother, represented to Jenny a hope for authentic family happiness, "a normal life."

The Moores lived in an apartment on Fifth Avenue overlooking the Central Park Zoo and on a farm, called Hollow Hill, in New Jersey. They summered at Rockmarge, the huge white Beaux Arts house Paul's grandmother maintained on the ocean at Prides Crossing, next door to the Fricks. Paul's mother, Fanny, and Margarett were friends in North Shore dog show, gardening, and dinner party circles, but his grandmother, Mrs. William H. Moore, and Marian Haughton, intimate enough to have played golf every week for forty years, had always stopped short of calling each other by their first names.

Margarett and Shaw gave an engagement dinner at the Somerset Club in Boston on November 10, 1944, but the wedding was planned for New York. Three years before, Margarett had pulled herself together to plan Margie's wedding, but Jenny did not want to take any chances. Fanny Moore, whom she would one day call "the only mother I ever knew," made the arrangements. The ceremony at the Church of the Resurrection was preceded by an Episcopal nuptial mass. Jenny wore Jenny Sargent's 1881 bridal gown, Paul his full-dress Marine blues. That night, soldiers forgot their dead comrades, and their foxtrot partners forgot they would soon be alone again. Early the next morning, the newlyweds left for Virginia and the tiny plantation cottage where they would live while Paul taught at the Officers Training School in Quantico.

At the wedding, Margarett had looked nervous when the photographer caught her, long dark fingernails to her face hiding a lipsticked smile. Afterward, she wrote Jenny a series of letters, as if to make up for her deficiency as mother of the bride: Her brother Harry had sent a check rather than a gift; she'd send an alarm clock if they needed one; their wedding, Paul's good looks, Jenny's radiance, were the talk of the North Shore. "Last night I was tempted into calling you," she wrote, "to wish you 'Bon Voyage' on the move to the box planting & wizardry of Virginia landscape—but you & Paul were protected—you were out, and so I took mercy and cancelled the call."

When Margarett fell into abject depression days later, Shaw was prepared. He suggested she check into Four Winds, a sanitarium near Katonah, New York.

Jane Bowles was appalled when she heard, as was Oliver Smith. They had not lived with Margarett through years of utter powerlessness, as Shaw had, and so they saw her situation in simple terms. The problem was her split life, the division between her artistic self, represented by New York, and her Bostonian self, represented by Shaw. Oliver remembered a visit to Prides. "Shaw was in the house. They didn't speak. I heard shouting, but they didn't speak to one another."

On December 29, Margarett wrote Shaw from Four Winds. He was bird shooting in Aiken, South Carolina, had spent Christmas with Jenny and Paul at their honeymoon cottage. "The watercolor of Prendergast is still being framed—I swapped a Luks drawing to get it," she wrote, and, without a transition, continued her letter as if what followed simply filled out a list of household loose ends. "I can't understand how most people can take these shock treatments. My headaches recently have been fierce, unlike any I have ever had. Dr. Lambert says, all right, cancel treatments, but that seems so senseless that I said keep on. . . ."

X

Nothing equalled the day I left

(1945–1978)

Margarett in Brittany, c. 1954
(from a snapshot by Joseph Gelli)

EAST OF KATONAH, New York, along a country road, a lawn slopes up to an enormous Tudor edifice situated on a three-hundred-acre estate. "The whole place is very reminiscent of Wellesley," Margarett wrote Shaw, "with polite ladylike furniture & safe taste—Cousin Gertrude might be in a corner—most harmoniously and consistently." Thirty years later, under different management, Four Winds Hospital would become a model facility for the treatment of alcoholism, drug abuse, and mental illness, particularly among young people, but in the 1940s, it was a model of a different kind—a sanitarium for the wealthy, particularly women, whose depression, mania, alcoholic excess, or untoward sexual enthusiasm rendered their presence unacceptable.

The grand house was furnished with antiques Dr. Charles Lambert and his son, "Dr. Jack," picked up at auction. The women who served breakfast at eight, lunch at twelve-thirty, and supper at six were uniformed in apple green during the summer and in black with white trim after Halloween. A Norwegian chef produced aspics, rarebits, and, on Sundays, roast beef and Yorkshire pudding; a Swiss baker did the desserts. Certain "guests" were permanent residents. An Eagle Pencil heiress built her own house on the grounds, and a Delano aunt of President Roosevelt's resided there for years, visited on Sundays by her husband, with whom she dined, a cameo at her throat, a fork in one hand, his hand in the other.

Electroshock was administered out of sight, on the third floor of the main building, and was not referred to by name in the brochure

that characterized Four Winds as "a home-like neuropsychiatric sanitarium" with "laboratory, studios, gymnasium, swimming pool, bowl-
ing green, trails, trout streams . . ." Patients in the midst of treatment
or too depressed to meet company took meals in their rooms, where
social life was limited to visits from Dr. Charles Lambert and, after he
died, Dr. Jack.

Electroshock treatment, or ECT, was instituted in the United
States in 1938, and its heyday was the 1940s, before the discovery and
availability of lithium, psychotropic drugs, tricyclic compounds, and
MAO inhibitors. No one then knew that those treated with ECT were
more apt to return to the hospital than those who had not been, or
that shock itself altered the course of manic-depressive illness, later
called bipolar affective disorder. Later research would confirm that
electroshock caused hemorrhages in the blood vessels of the brain, but
in 1944, the important fact was that the seizure it brought on dissolved certain constellations of depression. No matter that relief was
usually not permanent and that the biological consequences were irre-
versible; very few patients suffered the most extreme side effects—
permanent epilepsy, extreme memory loss, or death.

At Four Winds in 1944, Margarett's alcoholism was considered a
symptom of her manic-depressive illness. No one then theorized that
alcoholism in a patient like her was a separately occurring illness; fur-
thermore, treatment of alcoholism was in transition. Alcoholics
Anonymous had been founded in Ohio in 1935, but the first national
announcement of the group's successes, an article by Jack Anderson
in the *Saturday Evening Post*, did not appear until 1941, and only in
1972 did the American Medical Association proclaim alcoholism a
disease. In 1944, it was possible that even a physician might consider
Margarett's drinking weakness, moral failing, or self-indulgence.

Decades later, the experiences of manic-depressive alcoholics in Alcoholics Anonymous would open new avenues of treatment for patients
like Margarett, but when she entered Four Winds, it was assumed that if
her manic-depressive illness was relieved, she would no longer medicate
herself with alcohol. Treatment that combined sobriety, medication with

lithium (not introduced until 1968), and group support would not become commonplace until more than a decade after her death.

Margarett also contended with an attitude that confused a woman's rebellion with mental illness. It was this mind-set, made institutional with asylums that changed only superficially with the times, which Charlotte Perkins Gilman protested in her classic *The Yellow Wallpaper* and that, nearly a hundred years later, the feminist therapist Phyllis Chesler challenged in her book *Women and Madness*. Chesler called for a reexamination of "the relationship between the female condition and what we call madness—that divinely menacing behavior from whose eloquence and exhausting demands society protects itself through 'reason' and force."

More recently, the psychologist Kay Redfield Jamison has questioned society's lack of subtlety when dealing with the artist and "madness." In a book called *Touched with Fire*, she compares an artist's ecstatic, engaged creative state to the euphoria a bipolar patient enjoys before being overtaken by mania. She points out that great writers have had the illness—William Blake, Mary Wollstonecraft, Virginia Woolf, F. Scott Fitzgerald, and Sylvia Plath among them—and suggests that culture has benefited. Her work raises a question that Margarett, when her mood was flattened by treatment, must often have asked herself: Is there no way to have the ecstasy of creativity without suffering its darkness?

For all their good intentions, the physicians at Four Winds in 1945 were practitioners of what Chesler called "reason and force." Margarett was confined to her room, entertained only by Dr. Lambert's visits and his tales of former guests, "such as the man who tried to take 50 drinks a night but couldn't quite make it." She had her first shock treatment immediately. She was taken to the third floor and secured to a treatment table with straps to prevent her breaking bones or injuring an attendant during the involuntary thrashing that always followed the surge of electrical current. Next, the doctor fit a metal plate to either side of her head. "He buckled them into place with a strap that dented my forehead, and gave me a wire to bite," Sylvia

Plath wrote of electroshock. "I shut my eyes. There was a brief silence like an indrawn breath. Then something bent down and shook me like the end of the world. Whee-ee-ee-ee-ee, it shrilled, through an air crackling with blue light, and with each flash a great jolt drubbed me till I thought my bones would break and the sap fly out of me like a split plant."

"They were no doubt efficient, but extremely disagreeable," was how Margarett described her treatments in a letter to Shaw. Patients led out of the third-floor laboratory at Four Winds seemed woozy to those who observed them, and Margarett suffered severe headaches after treatment, but no one denied that the results could be miraculous. Margarett's depression did begin to lift, and so, when she complained of headaches and Dr. Lambert again offered to stop the treatments, she waved him off. She wrote proudly to Shaw that "many patients could not take them at all," but that when she completed eight treatments, she'd asked for more.

When the course of treatment was over, Margarett found Four Winds "conducive to application." She ordered seeds from Burpee's and planned the vegetable garden for Prides—"radishes (good varieties), parsley, lettuce and tomatoes (yellow)." She considered writing a book and discovered that Van Wyck Brooks, author of *The Flowering of New England*, had, at Four Winds, "pulled off his masterstroke. . . . He was a chain smoker, coupled with breakdowns, I believe." She resumed the cutouts she had been doing before she came to Four Winds, now combining them with watercolor. "I am crazy over a paint box of strange dry oriental colors that make drawings look almost like aquatints—or Lautrec colored lithographs—(nothing like self-complacency)."

Friends sent books and she read them—books on art, books on herbs from E. Ames Parker—and she ventured out to occupational therapy. She liked the young woman in charge—"a merry kid about Margie's age—daughter of a Yale professor—crazy over art but obliged to teach every type of activity from weaving to playing jacks which must drive her mad." Soon Margarett and she were talking about art magazines, and Margarett was "rather unobtrusively" drawing the other guests:

"one had the most wonderful coloring—I loved her; she looked like a very valuable Carriere *the best period.*" Eventually she was seriously at work: "My pen drawings have been successful—my pencil ones stupid. There is not enough danger to them in execution. I hate being able to correct with eraser etc."

There is nothing in Margarett's letters to Shaw to suggest she suffered much that winter at Four Winds, and no other letters survive. She had wanted Margie to have a new fur coat and was delighted to hear that Marian had given her a broadtail. She regretted she had not been able to invent "some wonderful letters" for Harry, still in combat. And she was grateful to those who thought of her: "your mother has been extraordinarily wonderful about writing—and when I think I am one needle in her haystack of correspondence—" She still wrote as if her illness were a cosmetic condition to be corrected, a head of hair to be permanently waved—but of course she was reporting to Shaw, to whom she had to prove she was capable of behaving, or recovering. "Please write frivolous news of Aiken," she urged him. "Please write voluminously & indiscreetly—"

On April 12, to celebrate the death of President Roosevelt, Shaw cracked open a very good bottle of champagne. Margarett had left Four Winds and was visiting Florence Shaw in Boca Grande. She sent Betty Parsons a postcard—a tarpon on a line, leaping, the background a garish sunset: "Not because it's a Winslow Homer, but entirely for the slogan—'Hooked but gamely fighting.'" Her battle was not over, but she considered her time at Four Winds a success and gave the impression that her loss of short-term memory—any recollection of, for instance, Paul and Jenny's wedding—a small price to pay for relief. Her New York friends were not so sure. Oliver Smith, when he saw Margarett after Four Winds, thought she looked as if she'd been hit over the head.

The end of the war, in August, brought Harry and Shaw home. Either they were not told what had happened to their mother or it did not register. Each complained that neither parent treated him as the adult he had become. Young Shaw was at Prides for two days before he moved into the house Marian had leased at 15 Louisburg Square. Living there, he could go out as he pleased or sit for hours talking to the grandmother he considered far more canny than either of his parents. Harry, unlike Shaw, had seen battle and the worst of war. The banner—"Welcome to Beverly"—that greeted him made him sick to his stomach, and he was appalled to hear his parents' friends complain about the rationing of gas and sugar, when he had seen people starve. No one wanted to hear his stories of combat or of the spectacle of death he encountered when his company liberated Mauthausen concentration camp. In Vienna, he'd given money and ration cards to Marian's musical friends. He had met people who'd escaped the Warsaw ghetto and had seen hundreds of young women from Czechoslovakia walking west in flight from the Russians. When he began to send money, all his money, to CARE and the Red Cross, Marian stopped him. In the spring of 1946, both he and Shaw entered Harvard.

Writing to Betty Parsons after Four Winds, Margarett referred to 1945 as a year to be ashamed of. She apologized for lunches and confused letters. She criticized herself for "indulgence," for allowing Helvetia Perkins, Jane Bowles, and Betty to help her onto a train to Florida—"all your nursing and first aid in Penn Station . . ." She thanked Jane for "being so patient with me." When she learned Helvetia was jealous, she wrote Betty over and over for advice. "I think if I had not been in such an alcoholic mirage, I would not have made such involved mistakes about the Vermont pair. It never occurred to me any one could consider me as a *plausible* or *passable* foe." That Jane and Margarett drank together particularly provoked Helvetia, "the jury of Mr. & Mrs. Alcohol," who still tried to keep Jane sober, in Vermont, and away from New York and other women.

Four Winds had not helped Margarett to adjust to a life without work or a household without children. By the end of the year, her friends in New York were concerned. Wally Reed hated the idea of her spending the winter "alone" at Prides and suggested she return to the hospital. Others suggested she move to New York. Oliver Smith invited her to lunch "en famille" at Tenth Street on New Year's Day,

1946. "You belong here, with us," wrote Briggs Buchanan, another Tenth Street communard. But by April, she was back in Four Winds.

Margarett sat alone in her room. "I must have been ossified to have made this decision." The first week, Dr. Lambert came to see her only once. "The only way I survive is I have countless books." She read Elizabeth Bowen's short stories, asked Betty to send *The Death of the Heart*: "Do you believe it is too out of print to obtain?" She read E. M. Forster—"He is my new friend, have you read him?" She wrote Jane and Helvetia for French books and a French dictionary. She wanted to study, to read Italian poetry, to memorize. "Please lay any practical task before me," she wrote Betty. "I am in a grim, grim fix—I must make it positive." In long letters, Jane encouraged her to draw and write. "It would be easier to walk a tight rope," Margarett replied, but Jane's caring stunned her: "I had truly no idea she was upset beyond her mercy & her imagination for my pain."

In "the terror—of losing everything," she wrote Betty nearly every day:

> If I were *well, I would go crazy*—I still have not cried but my horror of the place—has become so extreme—because I doubt it—& think all they want is the weekly money—I admit I sought them—but in pain anything can look easier—& I was not responsible for my decision—all of which I admit is my fault— But if Shaw & I were in any way compatible he would comprehend what I mean & I could explain—sign a pledge— go into a convent or the Bowery or Sing Sing—the only thing I *don't crave* is alcohol—& for the first time I can soberly think of destruction, including self—I have said nothing of this to Shaw—

It was Wally Reed who had prevailed one night at Prides when Margaret couldn't sleep. She'd allowed him to see behind her drunken state and into her distress, and when he insisted she go back to Four Winds, he stated his position so strongly she believed he was right.

I never analyzed (like a maniac) what it would mean—& allowing no telephone or telegraph drives me mad—I would be
willing to have anyone in the room as I spoke—but I will burn
up with this bed life—

When she complained about the isolation and the lack of treatment, Dr. Lambert told her his strategy was to deprive her of alcohol
and allow nature to take its course. Her only regular visitor was the
woman dressed in apple green who brought her breakfast: "Well—the
day is about to clear." Or her supper: "I declare it's clouding over."
Margarett wanted "counsellorship & conversation," but psychotherapy was not offered, and she resented the money spent for what she
considered "just isolation—& a whistling neighbor—a mowing machine—& tea house food. . . ."

I cannot understand about last year—I can only say it must
have been the shock treatments which made me oblivious &
this year—they refuse probably to give them—at least they
smacked of danger— It really is a race with idiocy now—not
depression—the sharpest arrow in my side was when Dr. Lambert brought in 2 narcissi—I recognized them "Thalia"—he
had bought the bulbs from me—the most poignant of white
flowers—an old crocked tub remarked, "Is that an orchid?" The
answer is no, it's rarer—& far more innocent—& topping it
all it's no parasite—orchids are. Betty Dear, there are always
two to a stem—Thalia—and I am cut off from it all—with my
own hand—

Betty suggested confiding her dissatisfaction to Shaw, but Margarett was certain he'd say "they did so well before." In her isolation,
she began to doubt her friendships. When she didn't hear from Jane
for a week, she became convinced Helvetia's jealousy had destroyed
her place in the Tenth Street group, that she would lose all of them—
in particular Oliver, who represented to her "the standards of intellect
& office in the world." Kirk Askew, who was storing a Delacroix pastel

Shaw had inherited, was going to England. Margarett realized his gallery wasn't fireproof but was ashamed to write him "from this address." She was amazed at his response, "a touchingly thoughtful letter—even sending me books." On top of her fear for herself, she worried about Harry, whose reaction to the war had rendered him so vulnerable she considered his life in danger. "No Beverly life is safe," she wrote Betty.

The only document of Jenny's graduation from Barnard, aside from her election certificate to Phi Beta Kappa, is a color snapshot. She stands, twenty-three years old, in black cap and gown, a baby on her hip. I am the baby, Jenny's oldest child and Margarett's second grandchild. There is no sign of Margarett in the photograph, but she and Shaw were at the ceremony. She had managed to "knock down the bars" of Four Winds, not only for the graduation but to have lunch with Betty: "I must see you."

I had been born eight months before, in October. In the baby book kept the first years of my life, Jenny noted that her daughter's first visitors were "Grandma and Grandpa McKean." I was one day old. Margarett and Shaw also came to my christening, in December 1945. Obviously, I remember none of this. What Jenny, my mother, told me when I was a child was that I rarely saw Grandma Kean, as we came to call her, not because she didn't love me but because she was ill. She explained carefully what this meant, even touched her head to communicate what mental illness was. She also told me about "shock treatments," which she compared to the shock you feel touching an electrical plug when a wire is loose or your hands are wet. She explained that shock treatments made Grandma feel better, but that they also caused her to forget things.

When I try to summon an early memory of Margarett, or of my mother, Jenny, in her early twenties, telling me about her mother's illness, I hear a voice coolly explaining and I'm pulled into shadows, noise in the night, and darkness. I think I must have overheard tele-

parties at Prides. My mother seemed less sad about her mother than exasperated. Only now, approaching Margarett's age at the time of her treatments and reading her letters to Betty Parsons, do I begin to understand what she suffered. I remember her sad face. I remember that she wore dark suits and talked slowly in a deep voice.

At the graduation, Margarett was uncomfortable. There was scant warmth in her encounter with Jenny, who kept her usual self-protective distance. By contrast, Margie, in the wake of divorce from Wally, had recently surprised her with letter after letter, "holding nothing back . . . She even writes she loves me." To Margarett, Jenny's "secure existence" seemed a rebuke from which she, in her vulnerable state, had no protection. She didn't want to go back to the Moores' farm in New Jersey after the ceremony. She had planned to spend the night at the Gladstone, but she was relieved when Wally offered to drive her back to Katonah. "I wish I could 'do over' our lunch," she wrote Betty. Probably what shamed her about lunch was that she wept, unacceptable in her view, and that Betty, austere in her emotional manner, had not allowed her compassion to show. After seeing Margarett at the graduation, Shaw, "rather startled when I described how literally nothing had been done," directed Dr. Lambert to begin another course of electroshock.

An aging envelope Margarett addressed to Betty is garish with flower stickers, as if by merely drawing she could no longer communicate the required gaiety. In the envelope is a sheaf of drawings. If they had been drawn by a cartoonist, the effect would be comic, but they were not. Margarett calls one of them "Bus Stop." At first, it looks like the reflection of a cloud in rippling water, but on scrutiny you see six figures clustered on a sidewalk. A buxom woman wears a tall hat. Two men talk. Another woman—large, behatted—stands with a child who comes only to her waist. Margarett's line oscillates, as if the shock to her head had animated her hand. "How do you like my wiggle technique?" she wrote Betty.

The effect of the course of shock treatments was not as dramatic as it had been the year before and did not reassure Margarett about the integrity of Four Winds; she continued to complain that the two hundred fifty dollars per week was exorbitant, but she came out of her depression and by mid-June had taken herself in hand:

> I like to sweep things very clean but understand what I am sweeping. . . . It was a very difficult decision coming here and I do not think a particularly astute one but a gullible one on my part—I believed because of last year but I was wrong—however I think the discipline of facing myself in this brutal light is excellent and necessary.

At the end of June, against Dr. Lambert's advice, she made plans to leave Four Winds, but she panicked at the thought of going home. "I would prefer not to be around Prides on the 4th," she wrote Betty. "Maybe I can 'call' on you." Betty was moving to Gloucester for the summer, near Rockport, where some of her own artists—Stamos and Barnett Newman—had also rented studios. To her next letter, as if aware her loneliness might overwhelm even her oldest friend, Margarett added a postscript: "Please be as stern as you want with me. I can take it. I would rather be scolded than receive silence."

Margarett made no pencil compromises in the little notebook with brown covers. Her line is single and clean. She dated the first drawing July 5, 1946. Consider the sketchbook a diary. At Singing Beach in Manchester, thirty minutes up the coast from Prides, on an afternoon during the July Fourth weekend she had dreaded, Margaret sits drawing. As usual, her sketchbook, pen, and pencils are in her bag, among an overstuffing of paints, scarves, seed packets, wallet, and notebooks. Let's say she sits with friends for lunch at the beach club, at an umbrella-shaded table overlooking the ocean, and that she takes notice of a particular little boy, newly allowed to walk by himself.

As the child stops to look at something, Margarett draws his expression as suspicion, his bangs neatly across his forehead. Then she renders his socks, his legs, and the outline of his shoes with an ink line as conscious of his gawkiness as he is. She draws the fingers of his right hand to look like spider legs, nearly obscures them with a pouch of stomach. At his left hip, she cuts off his forearm at the wrist. Read the look on the child's face as an expression of Margarett's own doubt, his physical awkwardness as the portrait of a new discomfort in her own bodily self.

For all her assertions of a cure, the visits to Four Winds had been an assault. An electrical current had repeatedly disrupted her body, competing with her own energy for control of her nerve and her brain. She had become passive, a patient, had entered a realm where the qualities that made her uniquely herself, which gave her the capacity to draw, which had driven her to sculpt and to paint, had been assaulted by "polite ladylike furniture & safe taste."

It is true she had been desperate, had needed a cure, someone or something to do for her what she could not do for herself. She had taken a risk, had looked to doctors for caring, and what were the results? "She looked as if she had been hit over the head," Oliver Smith repeated.

No one can figure out exactly how he did it, since the doors to Dudley and Vivian Pickman's dining room were terribly heavy and, it seems, could not be easily or quietly opened, but that is the story. Margarett was in Boca Grande with Florence late the winter of 1947, and Vivian invited Shaw to dinner on the North Shore. At cocktails, he was introduced to Kay Winthrop, whom he'd met at a party once with Margarett. She was a competitive tennis player, recently the national women's doubles champion. She was thirty-four years old (twenty years younger than Margarett), vibrantly attractive, very wealthy, and, as a descendant of John Winthrop, a member of one of the oldest Boston families.

Shaw quietly left the cocktail hour, opened the dining room doors, and switched the place cards. At dinner, he discovered that Kay loved dogs, horses, and foxhunting. She had a quality of kind attentiveness and honey-colored hair. She loved to laugh, and was both delighted and flustered at his attention. After dinner, he asked her for a ride home. His car had broken down, he told her, though it hadn't. "He said he hadn't been happily married for years," Kay told me. "And then one thing led to another."

When Margarett returned from Boca Grande, there was already talk among the staff at Prides, some of whom had seen Miss Winthrop's car in the driveway at odd hours. Shaw let Margarett know that he wanted to divorce her. She was incredulous. After the Snelling affair, since her conversion, she had never considered leaving him, and she had not believed he would ever leave her. She went immediately to Marian, who in the past had always insisted they keep the marriage together. She loved Shaw, Margarett told her mother-in-law. How could he leave her? She had been ill; her religion forbade divorce. Marian was upset with the precipitousness of Shaw's decision, but, she told Margarett, he had made up his mind. The children had grown up; she would not intervene.

The children were jubilant about the separation. "It was what I had always wanted him to do," Shaw said. "It wounded her pride more than anything else," said Margie.

Shaw hoped for an early-summer wedding, but one morning the upstairs maid presented Margarett with a gold earring she'd found while tidying his room. Margarett decided to contest the divorce. The maid would testify about the earring, and Shaw couldn't use the Snelling affair because he condoned it by taking her back. Rather than risk litigation, he planned a Nevada divorce and postponed his marriage. He would leave Margarett practically everything—Prides and the house at Dorset; furniture, paintings, and china they jointly owned; anything Margarett believed belonged to her. Margarett's lawyers advised her to agree to his terms, and eventually she did. For weeks afterward the two sniped and fought, passed each other in the house in frosty silence.

Because Wally Reed had become a close friend, Margarett was not enthusiastic when, just two years after her divorce from him, Margie announced that she planned to marry Barclay Warburton III, a handsome, swashbuckling Vanderbilt relation and a Newport sportsman, who loved sailing. Buzzie Warburton, Margarett wrote Betty, "irrespective of his innocuous charm & courtesy . . . is merely all I have avoided." He was younger than Margie and still at Harvard when the wedding took place, on March 29. Margarett and Shaw put up a united and cordial front for the ceremony and the celebratory luncheon at Prides. The newlyweds had barely left when young Harry's grief about the war brought on a serious depression—"a severe and ghastly shock to me," Margarett wrote Betty. She was reminded of her brother Frank's visit to New York before he killed himself.

In the wake of all this, Roland Balay arrived in Boston. Margarett had not seen him for six or seven years, not since before the war. They met in Boston, walked in the Public Garden, dined at "odd restaurants," visited "French churches." They went to Mrs. Gardner's museum at Fenway Court, to galleries and to the Museum of Fine Arts. As always, Margarett talked openly to him.

"I found a great change in her," Roland said, "when I came back after the war."

"As if something had broken?"

"Something—yes, something had happened."

"We had three days of strong happiness," Margarett wrote Betty. On April 5, she took the train with Roland to New York, returning the next morning to Prides. The following week, she left for Boca Grande, trusting Harry's care to his father.

On June 15, Shaw packed a suitcase and moved out of Prides. Young Shaw accompanied him to Reno to wait out the divorce and shocked his father by romancing an older blonde who was divorcing Milton Berle. When he left Prides, Shaw determinedly began a new life. He never spoke against Margarett to Kay, but he had no desire to hear news of her, and once, questioned about her at a party, he abruptly turned on his heel and left. He and Kay married on October 24 and spent the winter in California. When they returned to the

North Shore, they purchased Bayard Tuckerman's estate in Hamilton, where Margarett had been celebrated as a debutante. For two years, Shaw wrote courteous letters to Margarett's lawyer, asking, futilely, for the few things from Prides to which he believed he was entitled. On August 7, 1948, John McKean was born, the first of five children he would have with Kay.

In May 1948, Margarett had sent out an invitation: "You are invited to a private viewing of the recent landscape designs of Margarett Sargent McKean." Sometime later, she hired Mark Pagano, who'd once worked for Kirk Askew, to direct a gallery—which she christened the Belvedere—on the roof of Driscoll's, the elegant Boston dress shop where she bought her clothes. She planned exhibitions of drawings, paintings, and sculpture (not her own), and renovated the space at her expense. There was a publicized opening, and an article in the *Sunday Herald*: "Mrs. McKean, Fabulous Resident of Beverly, Returns to Art Again," which gushed her associations with Borglum and Luks and showed Margarett, heavier now at nearly sixty, holding forth in the garden at Prides.

She was her old self, creative and productive. She received guests at Prides: Robert Lowell and Elizabeth Hardwick, the writer Alan Pryce-Jones, George Dix, the Askews. In New York she saw Betty and scouted artists for the gallery. She hired a young Marine veteran, Charlie Driscoll, to be her chauffeur, but he soon became a friend as well—planting trees, hanging paintings, and keeping her company at supper. Eventually, she overcame her aversion to Buzzie Warburton and invited him to lunch. Sketchbook in hand, she visited her grandchildren—Margie had had a second child.

Margarett hadn't taken a drink since Four Winds, but in time, to have a glass of wine did not seem to be courting danger. She began to drink now and then. She began to argue, to criticize, to fight with Mary McLellan, or with Driscoll, once opening the car door to jump as they sped down the Merritt Parkway. She shouted angrily. The Belvedere Gallery lost tens of thousands of dollars, and her lawyers closed it down. She accused a friend's maid of stealing her jewelry. She struck a Washington taxicab driver with her purse. By her birthday, she was back in the darkened room, weeping as if the world had ended.

As I sifted through letters, medical bills, and legal correspondence, it became clear that the worst depression of Margarett's life had come after Shaw left. His departure finished off the idea of Prides as a household. Though there had certainly been times when she'd wanted to be rid of him, his presence had provided a structure. When, at Shaw's insistence, John Spanbauer stopped paying Margarett's bills and keeping her accounts—in effect, managing the household—that structure, in place for twenty-seven years, utterly collapsed. Margarett did not admit she was frightened, and she grieved with the self-destructive intensity of a Euripidean heroine.

In Shaw's absence, Mary McLellan telephoned Margie, and Margie turned to Buzzie, who went immediately to Prides. What greeted him as he walked the corridor to Margarett's bedroom was his new mother-in-law screaming, shouting, shrieking, throwing things. At the suggestion of a friend, Buzzie called Dr. Max Rinkel, a Viennese psychiatrist who practiced in Boston. Dr. Rinkel came up to Prides and suggested Margarett be hospitalized. He would call his friend Dr. George Schlomer, of Baldpate Hospital, in Georgetown, just forty-five minutes north. After some resistance, Buzzie gave in. "I said, get the wagon and the man and the straitjacket and do it."

The ambulance, with Margarett sedated, in a straitjacket, and lying on a stretcher, sped north from Prides and swerved up a small hill, through entrance gates, to the "Inn" at Baldpate, a towering clapboard Victorian, garish with turrets, porches, and windows, and painted barn red. When Robert Lowell arrived manic and violent six months after Margarett, he was put in a cell padded with leather to keep him from injuring himself. Baldpate Hospital advertised the same amenities as Four Winds and, in addition to shock treatment, offered "Prolonged Sleep Treatment, Psychoanalysis, Fever Therapy, and Definitive Psychotherapy." Car service was available for day trips, and the telephone was not off limits. Families were informed they would be charged for any property damage a patient incurred. After a few days in the infirmary, Margarett settled into an outlying "bungalow" with a sitting room.

"Half dozen treatments like Katonah—have made me love life again," she wrote Betty on March 11, 1948. ". . . I am at Baldpate—& now triumphant & wanting to paint & draw all the time—This is *my first letter*—except to my young—I would not have dreamt of such a performance a fortnight ago—but I am grateful to you—& do not worry . . . it *was* unadulterated agony—however . . ."

After the initial crisis passed, Margarett took frequent outings, but by November 1948, it was clear her stay in the hospital was not temporary. The bills at Prides were piling up, and the staff went unsupervised. On behalf of the children and after consulting Dan, Buzzie wrote Dr. Schlomer, asking for a letter on the subject of Margarett's competence. The doctor quickly replied that he did not consider her able to take care of her financial affairs.

In the spring of 1949, Margie visited Baldpate and found Margarett drunk. She complained, visited again, and found her mother slurring words, as if drugged. The nurses searched Margarett's room and discovered barbiturates—she'd had a Beverly pharmacist telephone a doctor, who'd written a prescription. Dr. Schlomer wrote both the doctor and the pharmacist, asking that the prescription not be refilled. On May 5, 1949, a citation was published and filed in court appointing the Old Colony Trust conservator of Margarett's assets: "To all persons interested in the estate of Margarett Sargent McKean of Beverly in said County, a person of mental weakness. . . ."

The staff at Prides, now four or five people, was reduced to two, Charlie Driscoll for the grounds and Mary McLellan for the house. Plans were made to heat only a few rooms. Without Shaw's contribution, after the extravagance of the Belvedere and with the postwar rise in prices, Margarett could not afford both Prides as she had known it and Baldpate. Before she was hospitalized, her response to financial pressure had been to send a painting off to New York to be sold—through Roland, through Kirk. One turned up in the cloakroom of the Gladstone Hotel: Margarett had sworn the attendant to secrecy. Once in a while a long-unpaid bill arrived in the mail, and the Old Colony officer in charge of her affairs wrote to Buzzie, "There's little we can do other than to pay it." Eventually the bank suggested Margarett's charge accounts be shut down.

Two weeks after the conservatorship was announced, Buzzie wrote Dr. Schlomer that the children, in consultation with Judge Cabot of the Essex County Court, had decided it was in Margarett's best interest that they formally commit her. The decisions as to when she might leave the hospital for the day or be discharged would now be Baldpate's, her "madness" under the legal authority of someone other than herself. On June 8, Dr. Schlomer dictated a legally binding letter: "In accordance with the rules and regulations of the department of Mental Health of the Commonwealth of Massachusetts, we are writing to notify you that Mrs. Margarett Sargent McKean was committed to Baldpate, Inc. by the Justice of the Central District Court of Northern Essex, on June 7, 1949."

Her friends came to expect to find her at Baldpate. It was the place she went to dry out, to overcome a depression, to receive a course of ECT. By the end of her long acquaintance with it, she considered the place nothing better than a prison. Like other such facilities in the forties, Baldpate attended to a patient's symptoms rather than to the life that had produced her illness. Electroshock and hospitalization kept Margarett from alcohol and pills only temporarily. She'd leave, live at Prides, and, when it became necessary, return to endure an existence that barely broke the surface when she was out in the world.

"You could tell when it was coming," her friend George Dix said, "because she would dance on the tables in the bar of the Gladstone Hotel."

After nearly a year and a half in Baldpate, Margarett returned to Prides in the fall of 1949 as if washed up on a shore, as dazed as the survivor

of a shipwreck. She was fifty-seven years old. She began to draw, and
to write, in a large bound book:

> It is a delight to throw away empty bottles, even if they have
> only contained oil. It is startling to make plans without per-
> mission & not to have it breaking a law, merely mending a
> habit. I am nursing along a very different type of good fortune
> than encountered by most people. I am looking at Society
> with the other end of the telescope. I am aware of a fresh cli-
> mate. I am alone, on my own, in unmedicated air.

On page after page, in charcoal, she drew rows of women's legs,
crossed, their feet in high-cut pumps. Then she switched to ink and
drew a sequence of women with a fine, sure line. At a desk. In a chair.
Elbow on a table. There is an ease to this drawing—an arm across a
lap, the open collar of a simple dress, a female body comfortably filling
the dress, a compassionate face.

> The greater the complication, the clearer the drawing it neces-
> sitates. Simplification & elimination of line—is equal—no
> *exceeds* the opening of a window in stifling air. It includes for-
> getfulness of agony & absorption akin to delight. There is no
> explanation of the line that obeys smoothly & suavely & the
> line that balks the finger. The result is totally disconnected
> from discipline & reason,—that is its hypnosis for me—its
> lure. There is no cheating with a line in ink.

Margarett saw Dr. Rinkel for thirty-minute sessions twice a week in
Boston. He courted, complimented, and dispensed the alcoholism
remedy paraldehyde, an ether derivative, which, when Margarett took
it instead of a drink, put her right to sleep. He and his wife were frequent guests at Prides, and Margarett's family and friends did not like
him. They insisted he cheated her, but Margarett defended him, took
his side against her brother Dan, against her children. "Dr. Rinkel
was wonderful yesterday," she once told Dorothy DeSantillana. "He
told me I should always wear gray stockings because my legs look

beautiful in them." When he invited her to a dinner party, he sent her the bill. When a society writer lunching with him at the Ritz asked if Margarett McKean would be home by Thanksgiving, he was heard to reply that it made no difference to him, just as long as he got his stipend. "She liked admiration," Dorothy DeSantillana said. "She'd been a beautiful girl and she was used to it."

Dr. Rinkel wrote the children in 1949 that he assumed Margarett would recover from her current illness, that she now seemed "nice and quiet and calm." Closer to the truth was what another psychiatrist wrote them in 1964: "I think it unlikely Mrs. McKean can return to a relatively normal state again." The children were now in their twenties and thirties, and their mother still scared them. Because there were months when she carried on with full command of her intelligence and perception, months in which she did not drink, she also confused them. They did not want to deprive her of what she enjoyed, even though the conservators advised that the sale of Prides would make her life financially much more secure.

The clarity Margarett felt after leaving Baldpate was short-lived. In the early spring, by herself, she took a trip up the Mississippi on the paddle steamer *Delta Queen.* She sketched in restaurants in New Orleans, visited every museum, sent postcards to Betty from Cincinnati—"Blow up 57th Street & I'll be waiting for you in Louisiana"— but by the winter of 1951, she seemed lost again. In letters, she made self-effacing distinctions between Betty and herself: Betty was the famous dealer, Margarett privileged to be her oldest friend. The isolation of the hospital, disorientation brought about by repeated shock treatments, the grip of alcohol, gain of weight and the displacement of beauty with a tenuously maintained handsomeness, had made her a supplicant.

During the autumn and winter, Margarett gave occasional dinners at Prides. She saw Florence, the DeSantillanas, the artist Gardner Cox and his wife, and her brother Harry. She telephoned her brother Dan every day just as he and Louise sat down to lunch. Charlie Driscoll drove her to New York. She saw Betty and the Askews, John La Touche and his new lover, a tall blond taxi driver named Harry Martin. With Touche, Margarett settled back into laughs and repartee. Harry Martin, twenty-two, just out of college, and an aspiring artist, was dazzled: "She entertained so marvelously—her knowledge of painting was so exciting. . . ."

One snowy winter day, Margarett, Touche, Harry, and a couple of other people piled into Alice Astor Bouverie's Rolls-Royce and set off for a weekend at Alice's house in Rhinebeck. By the time they reached Harlem, all drinking in the car, the light snowfall had become a blizzard, and the chauffeur would drive no farther. They turned back to Manhattan and continued their carousing in the lobby of the Gladstone. Touche began a wild monologue in which he told the story of every Christian martyr, miming the fate of each. Everyone was laughing. Margarett could not keep from laughing, laughing until tears rolled down her cheeks. "Stop! Stop!" she protested as if the next blasphemous vignette would send her to hell—she was, after all, a Catholic! Finally, drunk and laughing, she got up for another drink and fell to the floor. In a flash, Touche put his foot on her large fallen torso and raised his right arm heavenward as if holding a sword aloft. "Saint George and the Dragon," he said.

"You have to remember, we all drank so much. Frankly, I don't know how any of us got away with it," Harry Martin said. Among her usual friends, Margarett's drinking was merely the extreme of what everyone did, but Jane Bowles, who was trying to control her own heavy drinking, could no longer bear to be in her presence. Margarett's wit, which Jane continued to find "keener than anyone's in New York," now seemed to her a smoke screen for "an endless plot which she herself ignores." Unlike Margarett's young male friends, who were content to laugh at her jokes or respond to her generosity, who in some sense accepted her condition, Jane turned away.

Before long Jane withdrew from Margarett altogether. "Do you think there is something wrong with me that I am able to turn so on someone I once liked as much as I did Margarett?" she wrote to her friend Libby Holman, the singer. "In those days of course she was selfish as hell and a fat tyrant but now is just humble and could be slavish if she had the energy or sobriety to run errands and she is fatter than ever." Margarett telephoned repeatedly that winter in New York, and repeatedly Jane refused to see her.

> She called me up today and whispered to me that she was telephoning from the Algonquin as if she was revealing the formula for the hydrogen bomb. The poor woman is just hunted and haunted all of the time. She is of course drinking like a fish, gallons of cider in public and alone in the bathroom, gin out of her purse, I'm convinced. Naturally she is disturbing because of her disembodied talent. . . . The terrible thing is that while all along I thought she liked my feeling for her but never me, I now feel that perhaps I was wrong because she seems dead set on me, though she behaves in a most distinguished manner and never makes me feel either guilty or uncomfortable.

Jane was not the only friend from whom Margarett's drinking separated her. By the end of the 1940s, she had fallen out with Vivian Pickman and with Florence Shaw. She spent time in Gloucester at John Hammond's antique-filled castle, where poets and painters of a younger generation gathered, and she invited more of her New York friends to Prides. Her children associated her new friends with her drinking, and Harry, who still lived at home, resented it when she entertained them. When Harry Martin and Touche came to dinner one night during the summer of 1951, the evening led to Margarett and Touche's usual raucous performance. At about one A.M., Harry appeared on the balcony above the living room and shouted to his mother, "Get those awful people out of here!"

Margarett saw a lot of Harry and Touche that summer, both at Prides and at John Hammond's, where they were staying. She also continued her friendship with Nat Saltonstall, an architect and collector, the closeted homosexual younger brother of the "Salts," and often visited him at a settlement of bungalows he'd built on Cape Cod. One night, with Harry, Touche, and Whitey Lutz, a sculptor friend of Betty's, Margarett drove down to Wellfleet to visit a friend who'd rented one of Nat's cottages.

They arrived drunk and carried on so loudly that Nat appeared at the door to complain. He was startled to see Margarett among the offenders, even more startled that she was preparing to bed down on the floor with people like Touche and Harry. He recovered himself and introduced the young man with him as "my protégé." "Hmph," said Margarett, when she told the story, "and there was Nat at the door with a young man who had nothing to recommend him but two cowlicks and central heating!"

Whitey Lutz was living at Prides that summer, quietly working in the old greenhouse, sculpting angels. He and Margarett talked about sculpture, and she commented on his work.

"I'd give anything to see Margarett start painting again," he wrote Betty.

Sometime in the fall, Margarett rented a studio on Bearskin Neck in Rockport, "but she never went there much," Margie said. By the spring of 1952, she was planning a trip to France and Italy.

On May 31, 1952, two weeks before Margarett left for Europe, young Shaw married Linda Borden in Rumson, New Jersey. The children were nervous: though Margarett had invited Kay to lunch once at Prides, she had not seen Shaw since the divorce. She arrived at the rehearsal dinner wearing a black dress and a satin cape that was orange on one side, magenta on the other. She stopped all the guests in their tracks with her old beauty and, Jenny said, swung her cape like a matador.

"Shaw," Margaret said, coming quietly up to him, "aren't the trees in New Jersey beautiful?"

"Yes, Margarett, they are."

At the reception, he took her for a turn around the dance floor, and she returned to the table, Charlie Driscoll reported, with tears in her eyes.

§

WHEN MARGARETT arrived in Paris in June, she checked into the Saint-James et d'Albany on rue de Rivoli, a small, elegant hotel surrounding a courtyard. The city was slowly coming to after the war, but its vitality had been as compromised by the intervening decades as Margarett's. The giddy jubilance of the 1920s was not the mood with which to greet devastation that was both spiritual and material, a devastation of ethics as well as economics. That spring, six heads of state had signed the agreements that would lead to the establishment of the North Atlantic Treaty Organization, but when Margarett arrived, Paris was still occupied by American GIs.

On the Left Bank, at the Café de Flore, Sartre and de Beauvoir debated existentialism; on the Right Bank, a new generation of couturiers, led by Dior and Balenciaga, flourished, and as old social barriers began to collapse, young women who modeled on the runway were for the first time invited to certain society dinners. A revolution in theater had exploded in the work of Jean-Louis Barrault and Madeleine Renaud, and in March 1953, Samuel Beckett's *Waiting for Godot*—"a curious and interesting two-act play," Janet Flanner wrote—opened at Théâtre Babylone, a tiny space hidden in a court behind an apartment house on the Left Bank. From Vallauris in the south came news first of Picasso's experiments with ceramics and later that Françoise Gilot was about to pack up and leave him.

Margarett had come abroad to reclaim the parts of herself from which she had been torn, as she said, by her own hand. In France, she sought herself as she had been in the Paris of the late 1920s and early 1930s; in Italy, the exuberance she'd brought to Florence as a young girl. She was to remain in Europe for three years, through France's first disenchantment with de Gaulle, the bracing regime of Mendès-France, the national strikes of the summer of 1953, and the deaths, in 1954, of Colette, Derain, and Matisse, emblems of the passing age. When Margarett took a sentimental journey to Betty's former house on rue Boulard, she was starkly reminded that her friend was in New York, her attention turned to American art, and that the days "with my acrobatic finches on Place Vendôme when Frederic Bartlett was godfather to us both" were long past.

On her arrival at Le Havre, Margarett was welcomed by Joseph Gelli, in uniform and driving a black limousine. He was a short, dark-haired Florentine, a famous driver among certain American travelers. He looked like the actor Rossano Brazzi and was terribly kind. Enthusiastically, he drove Margarett anywhere she wished, through the car-poor streets of Paris, out into the countryside, down through France and northern Italy to Florence. Europe was much cheaper than America in the 1950s, and the exchange rate relieved nervousness at home about Margarett's extravagance. The conservators issued a monthly stipend that allowed her to live well in hotels but restrained openhanded visits to galleries and shops. "I have no checking account," she complained to Betty.

In Paris, she saw Roland, and in Florence that summer she saw Harold Acton and Bernard Berenson, whom she revered from her days as a girl in Florence and had met briefly in 1929. Young Shaw had a job with a law firm in Paris, and after a wedding trip in Spain and Portugal, he and Linda arrived to set up housekeeping. They were greeted by a telegram from Joseph in Florence. Day after day, he told Shaw, he found Madame weeping for "her past happy time." And she drank, he said, even if he told her it would do no good, even when he refused to buy her alcohol. She drank, Margarett told him, because she was alone and there was nothing to do. She drank, Joseph said, even the cologne.

Shaw cabled Margie, and Dr. Rinkel contacted a doctor in Paris, who administered "sedative therapy"—a pattern of medication that made it possible for Margarett to sleep through the night. What Rinkel had given her had her sleeping all day and wide awake all night. Two weeks after Dr. Pichaut first saw her, she emerged from her depression and resumed her travels.

She fell in love with Brittany, and she and Joseph returned four times in eight months. "I am in *your* country," she wrote Betty, who had painted there every summer she lived in Paris. "And don't you admire the Bretons—I believe they are almost my favorite people, & their oysters certainly are my favorite oysters!!" She took photographs of women in Breton dress with wide faces, tall narrow lace caps clipped to their hair. She abandoned herself to the austere Romanesque architecture, the anguish of belief in the faces of stone saints that balanced, in wild feats of sculptural genius, on ancient crosses that aged against a bleak and purifying sky.

Her other headquarters was Florence, and that winter she and Berenson became friends. Margarett was such a frequent guest at I Tatti that his companion, Nicky Mariani, apparently became jealous. "Why?" Dan asked in a letter. "Well," Margarett replied, "the kisses he gave me were pretty terrific." She was almost embarrassingly grateful for Berenson's kindness. "Surfeited as you must be with admiration— and its attendant adorations," she wrote him on January 14, "I cannot with any possible comfort bottle mine. What an incredible magic you deal out when you see fit." The great man was eighty-nine, just five years from his death, and so fragile it was said his wristwatch was heated to prevent a chill when it was put on his arm.

Before Margarett left for Naples in mid-January, her friends Robert Fizdale and Arthur Gold, the pianists, performed in Florence. She went backstage and the next morning telephoned to tell them Mr. Berenson wished to see them that afternoon for tea. At I Tatti, they waited for "the presence," who materialized, on Nicky's arm, at the far end of a long hallway. He came into the room and, Bobby remembered, "plunked himself down right next to Margarett on the sofa." Bobby saw him cuddle up as if to get warmth from her large body.

Margarett reported her travels to Berenson by letter. From France, she wrote of the Apocalypse tapestries at Angers—the "beautiful *un*-emphasized bodies" reminded her of William Blake; and of seeing at Rouen "with a semi-braille system" in "the one *un*lighted gallery" the drawings of Géricault. In his replies, Berenson directed, recommended, and referred. At the Von Maries murals in Naples, his name sent the librarian, "a Jane Austen character," scuttling off to find the director, who rushed to Margarett's side, coattails flying. In Otranto, Margarett was enraptured by a mosaic of Noah and his animals, and at the museum in Taranto, "which opens at the extraordinary hour of 8:30 a.m.," the "flawless unimpaired fragile figures" held her "a voluntary prisoner" day after day.

From Sicily, she wrote she had finally found the "right" hotel in Siracusa, "overlooking Arithusa's Spring." Like Goethe, she fell out of love with Neptune's temple at Paestum when she saw the pink ruins of Agrigento:

> ... though I saw them at many different hours—& lights—
> nothing equalled the day I left when the sea looked like a mad-
> dened opal—still & wild simultaneously—everything excites
> me so superbly here—even the clouds which choose to lie on
> the land rather than remaining in the sky. ...

She photographed four columns rising Olympian to the sky and stood beside the Temple of Concord as Joseph took her picture—"rightfully insignificant," the ruin towering behind her, battered by the sirocco but intact and sacred.

> What you prophesied of orange—lemon & almond was all
> beautifully true. Now more is happening—& the wild stretches
> of earth are "dappled—dimpled" with small sweet things—
> valerian—noscaria & small sultry poppies—all stridently in
> bloom.

Much was made back in Massachusetts of the great distance Margarett traveled to see a particular door. "Imagine that," said Dorothy DeSantillana, astonished. "She drove a hundred miles to see a door, and it wasn't the famous door of a church or something, it was just a door in some village!" As it had when she was a girl in Florence, "just looking" came to Margarett's rescue. Seeing had become a matter of life and death. She sought out beauty not merely to please her eye but to bring the spiritual equilibrium she had once found in the studio. She was sure Betty understood:

> You have been so true to your beliefs—and that is wonderfully and incredibly rare. I could not bear for you to suffer as I do at times when I am not frenzied with visual joys, I can feel shipwrecked. The change of my routine of life came too late I can see now, and this prison of trustees drives me crazy. . . . Europe has meant more independence, therefore. I have written you nakedly. Please do the same to me.

Joseph photographed Margarett in Florence at dusk, dressed in black, tall and romantic, opening a high wrought-iron gate, a garden behind her. "My hair obstinately is not gray for some odd reason, but the color is displeasing increasingly—and my thoughts are often gray." He photographed her among the suppliants on an Assumption Day pilgrimage in Brittany. Chic among the Bretons, walking the eight kilometers up a country road, she wore sunglasses and lowered her eyes. A white length of chiffon swathed her dark hair, and her long black coat fell to narrow ankles. Put a magnifying glass on the tiny snapshot and you see a face loosened on its bones, a dark lipsticked mouth.

Margarett's stay in Europe stretched to six months, a year, then two years. She planned her itinerary a little at a time. In October 1954, she wrote Berenson she'd turn up in Florence in early December, which was no guarantee she would. When Dan arrived in Paris that spring to meet her, Margarett was not at the Saint-James et d'Albany, and Bunny and Hope Carter had not seen her. She was not at her Florence pensione, nor on the lists of tourists each hotel registered with the police. Distressed cables crossed the Atlantic. When Dan heard from her, Margarett reported she *had* been in Florence, staying not at the Albergo Berchielli but with Joseph Gelli and his family.

"The Easter dinner was horrifying!" she said.

"Oh, why?"

"I admired their two Belgian hares. Such beautiful animals, I said.

And Joseph told me their names, and then for our meal we had the most glorious stew, and when I asked after the hares, Signora Gelli pointed at the stew pot."

Margarett did not report the mornings she wept for the past when she was happy in Paris. She did not write letters about Joseph's kindness to her when, having persuaded him to let her have just one glass of wine, she could not keep her head from falling into the soup. Instead, her children got letters from those who came across her in Paris. Bunny Carter, visiting Boston, telephoned Oliver Wolcott he'd heard Margarett was in "very good shape." More frequent were complaints: "Why don't you do something about your mother!?"

On August 31, 1954, Margarett's sixty-second birthday, a hurricane hit Prides. She lost one hundred fifteen trees, forty of them matched lindens that bordered a walk. "I am rightly considered fortunate," she wrote Betty, "but mine are not like others' trees—Thank God I was not there. A spring return may be workable." But she did not return until late the summer of 1955. One day she went silent in Paris, and Joseph Gelli made a decision. He escorted her across the Atlantic and home to Prides. Within two weeks, she was back in Baldpate.

§

In April 1958, Margarett hired a New York lawyer. She had been out of Baldpate for more than a year and believed that with the help of a bank, she could manage her own affairs. Margie, Jenny, and Shaw were skeptical, but with Harry's support, their mother prevailed and, in July 1958, was declared competent. The conservatorship was replaced by two trusts: Margarett again had control of her own income.

To the distress of her children, she soon began to sell things. She sold three parcels of land at Prides. She wrapped the Gauguin in brown paper and took it on the train to New York, where Roland sold it for her to David Rockefeller for ninety thousand dollars. "It wasn't that we minded her selling things, it was that she rarely got a fair price," young Shaw said. She sold one of her own paintings, *The Watteau Hat*, to buy liquor. Furs disappeared, and jewelry—her engagement ring and Pauline Agassiz Shaw's emerald, which Shaw had intended young Shaw have for Linda.

There were rumors she propositioned models at Driscoll's, that when she arrived in the store, the girls hid in the back. Once, Buzzie got a call from the police. Margarett had refused to leave a restaurant; she'd been arrested and jailed. Buzzie called a lawyer friend to keep it out of the paper. In September 1958, just after her sixty-sixth birthday, she was again admitted to Baldpate. By the time she was released three years later, in October 1961, Margie and Buzzie had divorced.

That January, Margarett moved to New York for the winter, into an apartment in the Gladstone. But the change Oliver Smith and Jane Bowles had suggested so long ago came too late. In February, she began to drink, and by the twenty-first was admitted to Regent Hospital, whose supervising physician reported her difficult to evaluate "because she was so angry." She refused to answer questions, he said, and when he asked what change she should receive from five dollars after purchasing one item for twenty-five cents and another for fifty, she replied that she was an artist and had never been very good at figures. "Mrs. McKean possesses superior intellectual endowment and abundant creative artistic talent," he wrote, "but it would appear she has always been emotionally labile, eccentric, opinionated, egocentric and not a little sadistic." He concluded that Margarett suffered from four illnesses: manic-depressive illness; alcoholism; cerebral arteriosclerosis and associated "senile changes"; and basic psychopathic personality.

In the fall of 1962, having spent a good summer at Prides, Margarett planned another trip to Europe. "I feel reasonably certain," her new Boston psychiatrist reported, "that if she will not use alcohol, the outlook for the immediate future is not too bad." What he did not understand was that his patient could not stop using alcohol. Joseph met her at the Florence airport in a new limousine, and they began to travel as they had ten years before. After a few days, Margarett had a severe fainting spell. "Her skin was like ice," Joseph told the doctor who arrived to help him massage her back to health. Gloria Etting, a younger friend from New York, joined them for an excursion to Nice. "I was with this extraordinary person I adored, going to my favorite place." When Margarett retreated into silence and alcohol, Gloria fled, and Margarett and Joseph traveled on to Naples. Then Margarett failed again, and the doctor diagnosed a minor stroke. She soon recovered enough to take a cruise in the harbor, and Joseph snapped her on the deck, smiling—"When the sun came out in Naples," Dan captioned the photo he glued into his scrapbook.

The third week in January, Margarett and Joseph reached Madrid, where Margie's daughter Jenny was studying. When Jenny arrived at the hotel to see her grandmother, she found her lying in bed with her clothes on, not drinking but unable to move, insisting that Joseph never leave the room. Jenny called Harry, who now lived and worked in London, and he flew to Madrid. His mother was unable to understand what he said when he spoke to her. She was panicked about her health but adamant she would not go to a hospital. Eventually she agreed to go to London to stay with him. She and Joseph would drive up through France, stop in Paris to see Dr. Pichaut, who'd helped so much in the past.

When Harry got home to London, he wrote to my mother, Jenny, whom he had attacked in his campaign to have their mother declared competent: "She is very ill not just physically. I now see no hope." Days before she was expected in London, Margarett cabled Harry from Paris that her "present state of acute anxiety and depression" would prevent her coming. He flew to Paris. She had no money for food, she told him. He suggested she go home to Prides, but she said she was afraid. Margie would trick her into Baldpate, and she'd lie in the dark for days without a doctor's visit. The house would be empty—the lawyers said she had to sell her pictures. There was no one to meet her, because Driscoll was sure to be out at lunch.

Margie met the plane, and on April 7, 1963, Margarett was admitted to Westwood Lodge, a sanitarium in Dedham, Massachusetts.

While Margarett was in Europe, Jenny and Shaw had consulted a Boston lawyer, Alvin Hochberg. He was their contemporary, a kind and intelligent man. He suggested that Margie become her mother's legal guardian. In an account of a meeting among her children, lawyers, and a doctor about her future, the only record of Margarett's voice is the testimony of her psychiatrist. He had recently suggested she might sell her house and paintings, and she had "reacted violently," showing "more spirit than he had observed before." Her response was, in his view, "really quite uncommon"; he expected that she would also protest becoming, in effect, her daughter's ward.

In fact, after some persuasion, Margarett agreed. On June 17, the register of probate for the County of Essex certified that Margie had been appointed "guardian of the person of Margarett Sargent McKean—mentally ill person," and, with the Boston Safe Deposit Trust, guardian of her assets. The guardianship confirmed what had been true for some time, that in the collision of talent and illness, of an uncommon woman with a particular historical circumstance, Margarett had lost her power. She never recovered from the anger. "The change in my life came too late, I fear," she'd written to Betty almost ten years before. It was certainly too late for a return to the freedom of the past. When Al Hochberg offered, thirty years after she'd stopped painting, to organize an exhibition of her work, she brushed him off. How could he understand that it wasn't the pictures that had sustained her, but the act of painting? When she had strength she raged, and when she didn't, she fell silent. Only the pleasures of drawing, of looking, of company, restored her to herself, to the radiant carpet of talk.

"Mrs. McKean is living at Westwood," Al Hochberg wrote Joseph Gelli in Italy, canceling the visit to Prides Margarett had planned for him the spring of 1964. She was again having shock treatments, and her friends knew they wouldn't find her at home. "Am being mesmerized by your painted stone," Margarett telegraphed Betty on February 23. Betty was painting stones she picked up on the beach. "The colors are bright and the design successful," Margarett continued. "I miss your gallery announcements. You can send them here." But when Roland called her at Westwood, she refused to come to the telephone. To him she was as she had always been; for her, talking to him would have been too bald a reminder that she was not.

Ironically, it was Al Hochberg, the architect of the guardianship, who restored Margarett to a form of freedom. After a first hostile encounter at Westwood, they met at Margie's for lunch. "I saw it happen," Margie said. "Mama fell in love." And Al was utterly fascinated—not just by Margarett's charm but by her intelligence and her history. "She taught me all I know about art," he said much later, gesturing at the paintings on his walls. There was nothing he did not want to hear about, and for years he sat, bemused and rapt, as she told him about George Luks, about Prendergast, about her days in Paris and New York; as she taught him how to look at pictures, what was good, what was important.

On February 12, 1966, an attendant brought Margarett her supper at Westwood. She was feeling depressed but was otherwise perfectly well. She was seventy-four years old. She walked over to the supper table, sat down, and began to eat. Suddenly she lost feeling in her right leg. She returned to bed and tried to lift her leg from the floor onto the bed. She could not. In the morning, an ambulance arrived to take her to the emergency room at Massachusetts General Hospital, where, on examination, she was found to have difficulty talking and a weakness of the right side. She had had a stroke. In her confusion, she named Buzzie, now divorced from Margie for seven years, and Dan as her two nearest relatives.

On February 14, Dr. Raymond Adams, a neurologist, visited Margarett in her hospital room. Though she was in pain and the action of her tongue had slowed, he found her completely aware she was in a hospital, able to name and spell, to comprehend written and spoken language, and to make the appropriate sound when he mentioned a particular animal. On the telephone with Dan that afternoon, she exuberantly imitated herself barking, cawing, and oinking. Later, when Dr. Adams asked her to, she scrawled, slowly and with great difficulty, on a yellow pad: "Margarett" and "Hospital."

But she could no longer draw.

After a month, Margarett was well enough to begin physical therapy. She hated it. She shouted and wept when she was forced to walk, first with a cane and finally on her own. She moved to the Phillips House, where she'd had her children, and, as she recovered, hung her room with paintings from Prides. When I visited her, she was leafing through some of her George Luks drawings, planning an exhibition of her collection of his work for a gallery in Boston. I promised to be there.

On June 15, the exhibition opened at Joan Peterson's gallery in a Back Bay brownstone. The small room was hung with more than thirty paintings and drawings—Jenny as an infanta, *The White Blackbird, Women in the Doorway of St. Botolph Street,* governesses pushing their strollers on Commonwealth Avenue, the old part of Prides in the snow, called *Cottage in Winter.* Margarett dressed in pale-blue satin and arrived in a wheelchair. It was a muggy summer day, and the gallery was jammed with friends and family, visitors from New York, Boston artists and museum people.

By the time I arrived, the room had become terribly close. When I said hello, Margarett did not speak. It was as if she couldn't hear me, and her face did not move. She sat that way, silent, all afternoon. As I stepped out of the heat onto the street, I fainted on the sidewalk. Margarett knew she would not recover from the stroke and that she would not draw again. It was as if the heat in that room were that realization, vivid and closing in. "Simplification & elimination of line—is equal— no *exceeds* the opening of a window," she'd written twenty years before.

Now, for relief, her doctors considered shock treatment, but in the end, Dr. Adams prescribed drugs—Dexedrine and antidepressants when she was low and, when she was manic, something to calm her down. At various times, he gave her lithium. "None of them seemed to work," he said, meaning that Margarett continued to have her usual cycles of hypomania and depression. She stayed at the Phillips House for nearly two years. In November 1967, she moved to the apartment on Tremont Street and, once or twice a week, went out to Prides for the day.

The apartment was high above the Boston Common, with a panoramic view of the city where she'd been a famous beauty, whose post office had once, in her youth, delivered a letter to Hereford Street addressed, simply, "Margarett Sargent, Boston." She had visitors there, and as her cousin Aimée Lamb remarked at ninety-nine, "she had parties." In her bedroom, she hung her own painting of three children in a green field and, where she could see them, *The White Blackbird* and the watercolors of single women Prendergast had given her when she was young. The living room walls were crowded with Schiele and Luks, Lurçat and Prendergast, and furniture from Prides civilized the boxy high-rise rooms.

When she had parties, Margarett directed her nurses to set up card tables to seat two dozen—museum curators, art dealers, family, old friends. "Always such interesting people!" said Al Hochberg's young associate, Sylvia Cox, who came often with her husband. During the early seventies, guests came for cocktails and then walked in summer twilight to the Shubert Theatre or the Wibur, returning to the apartment after the play for supper, often with the cast. Once, Margarett commandeered her sister Jane's grandson to push her wheelchair. "For God's sake, Russell," she shouted as he wended her along Tremont Street through sidewalk construction. "Hurry up!" Margarett saw the Boston tour of *Godspell* so many times the cast knew to look up toward her box during performances.

Dan visited every week, often before going for supper to the Tavern Club. If he brought along their nephew Sargent Cheever, a surgeon at Mass. General, Margarett was apt to say, "Oh, Sarge, why did you bring my brother along, he's so dull!" sending Dan off into gales of laughter. Louise Sargent was long dead, and with her, the only obstacle to Dan's passionate affection for his sister. Intimacy restored, they talked at least once a day on the telephone, about their parents, their sisters and brothers, about the death of Ruth, about Wellesley, about everything, filling in each other's details like a finely tuned duet.

Margie and Al Hochberg supervised, and several times a week, Margie's third husband, Stephen Vernon, stopped in after work: "We talked about trees; she taught me how to prune." Jenny came to Tremont Street twice a year, Shaw called every Sunday, Harry visited from time to time, and every few weeks, Margie brought her needlework and sat until Stephen arrived later in the afternoon. "Do you know, Margie," Margarett said after one of her strokes, "that you've done needlepoint every time I've been dying?"

Margarett's grandchildren—Margie's six, Jenny's nine, Shaw's three—brought boyfriends or girlfriends. Sometimes Margarett would be silent and answer our greetings only in monosyllables. More often she fought to be clear through the blur of her stroke-damaged articulation. "I have something to tell you," she said to Margie's daughter Minnie one day in 1968, at the height of protest against the Vietnam War.

"What, Grandma?"

"Something I don't want anyone else in the family to know."

"Okay," Minnie said, bracing herself for the revelation.

"I've become a Democrat."

§

Margarett still had sieges of depression, but by 1970, Dr. Adams was able, for the most part, to keep her on an even keel with medication. He made house calls to Tremont Street and recruited an associate who was an expert on Italian art. He himself never tired of her conversation. "I got her away from the psychiatrists," he said. Margarett was attended by a covey of nurses, whose population shifted. It took a particular kind of woman to withstand her orders, her shouts of pain, the willful perfectionism that had never changed. On day visits to Prides, she continued to plant trees and once, behind Margie's back, planned a garden on the site of her studio, which had burned in the early sixties. "Sargent's Secret," she called the projected garden—a vast checkerboard, thousands of dollars' worth of imported tulips. Her conflicts with the trustees now had the feel of comedy. When they heard about the garden, they canceled the bulb order.

On August 27, 1971, Shaw died of a stroke, and Harry called Margarett. "Thank you for telling me," was all she said. She was silent for several days, and then, Jenny observed, seemed almost happy to have survived him. When Harry cleared out Prides, he found photographs of Shaw "under every blotter in the house." That fall, Dickie Demenocal, a Catholic convert whom Margarett had known since the 1930s, telephoned. He had been a lay brother in a monastery for years and had returned to Boston to paint. He came often to visit, sometimes bringing his paints. "We'd talk about flowers," he said. "She'd tell me about a particular tulip, and she'd start weeping. She was so profoundly moved. I'd say, describe it to me, and tears would start pouring from her eyes."

Now that Al had brought her financial affairs under control, Margarett no longer clung to her paintings. He encouraged her to look on her collection as bounty she could take pleasure in giving away, and she did so, amusing herself by alternately seducing and fending off the curators, museum directors, and dealers who circled like courteous vultures. She gave paintings—including her own—to grandchildren and to friends she cared about. She cut drawings from her sketchbooks, had them framed, and handed them out like party favors to visitors at Tremont Street. She determined which paintings in her collection should go to which museums—the Cassatt pastel, for instance, she lent to the Museum of Fine Arts but left to the museum in Philadelphia because Cassatt had lived there.

Once in a while, she sold paintings to raise cash. One designated afternoon, a dealer came to Tremont Street to see her de Chiricos. The doorbell rang, and Al, who had arrived beforehand, brought the man into her bedroom. Margarett, perfectly made up and coiffed, suddenly became convincingly drowsy, and when the dealer was introduced, asked him to repeat his name. Al pulled out the first painting.

"Well, Mrs. McKean, how much do you want? It isn't a very good painting, you know. . . ."

"Twenty-five thousand dollars," she said, closing her eyes, seeming to fall asleep.

"That painting isn't worth twenty-five thousand dollars," he said, and ran a medley of what was wrong with it.

Suddenly, as if jerked awake, Margarett said, without opening her eyes, "Twenty-seven thousand, five hundred dollars." When the dealer protested, she opened her eyes and said, calmly, "You had your chance to buy it for twenty-five thousand." She got her twenty-seven thousand five hundred dollars for the painting of the horses and her asking price for the others.

Ordinarily, when Sylvia Cox arrived with papers for her to sign, Margarett charmed her with stories from the past—how Shaw McKean had been so furious to see *The White Blackbird* in a New York gallery window ("My wife, dressed like that!") that he'd bought the painting; how she'd commissioned Sandy Calder to make her a wire head of Harpo Marx. She was fascinated that Sylvia had a career and that she'd kept her own name when she married. "Call me Sargent," she said one day, not telling Sylvia about the days of Frank Bangs and MacLeish's sonnet "Sargent on a city street . . ."

But one day when Sylvia arrived, Margarett turned on her. "I don't know who you think you are, trying to be a lawyer," she said evenly. "You're nothing but an incompetent nobody." Sylvia, dark-haired, brown-eyed, and small, waited until Margarett signed the papers, and left in silence, bursting into tears when the door closed behind her. Though Margarett never attacked her again, Sylvia withdrew, did not, for instance, reveal that it was her birthday when she arrived one day a few weeks later with another sheaf of papers. As she turned to leave, Margarett summoned the nurse, who presented Sylvia with an enormous basket of red anemones.

"As I walked down Tremont Street, the flowers were so abundant they almost hid my face," she remembered. "I saw that people were looking at me as they never had before, and I understood what it must be to be a beautiful woman."

During the late spring of 1973, Margarett gave an enormous party at Prides, a sit-down dinner for what seemed like hundreds of her friends, relations, acquaintances, people who had worked for her. Creed, the caterer, set up tables throughout the house—in the bedroom, the loggia, the dressing rooms—as Margarett, dressed in pink satin trousers, supervised from a wheelchair in the big room, her hair finally gone gray but carefully curled, her face beautifully made up, her eyes pale and wide. The cast of *Godspell* would be out to perform after their matinee, and a friend's grandson's rock band was to provide dance music. The white weeping tree wisteria were in bloom; it was a perfect May evening.

As cars pulled up and Driscoll directed them to parking, Margarett's brother Frank's son, then Governor Sargent of Massachusetts, stood on the front lawn, talking to the composer Randall Thompson and to Dan. Mabel Storey came, and Jane Cheever's grandchildren; I flew up from New York, and one of my brothers drove out from Cambridge. Inside, guests crowded at tables set with linen and crystal, laughing and talking just like the old days. "Margie," someone joked as a multitude of waiters served veal and poured champagne, "you better enjoy this—it's the last of your inheritance."

Earlier that spring, Jenny had been diagnosed with terminal cancer. Margarett showered her with paintings and drawings—the George Luks painting of her at four as the Spanish infanta, the Mary Cassatt aquatint of a dark-haired mother lifting her blond child in a very green garden. Toward midsummer, Jenny took a turn for the worse, and Margarett fell into a depression. When Sylvia or Al or Stephen came to the apartment, she spoke of her worry about Jenny or ordered another painting sent. She knew that Margie had gone to Washington in mid-September and hadn't returned.

On October 3, Stephen called to tell her that Jenny had died early that morning. At first, Margarett didn't want to go to the funeral, but he encouraged her. He worked for an airline and was able to arrange, at the last minute, first-class seats on the shuttle. When he pushed the wheelchair down the long white marble aisle of Washington Cathedral, Margarett bent and swathed in black lace, the service had already begun. "She upstaged Jenny," my father, Paul, said, "even at her own funeral."

In 1977, it became clear to Margie and Al that keeping a full-time nursing staff at Tremont Street would soon become impossible. Margarett had suffered a few more small strokes and now required even more care. That summer, she was moved, against her will, to Oakwood, a mansion turned nursing home, overlooking the ocean in Magnolia. She would never return to Prides. Without her knowledge, the house was emptied of furniture and pictures, and an auction was held on the front lawn. That fall, without her knowledge, Prides was sold to a developer.

§

HER BLUE EYES, still like lakes. Skinny, skin fallen back to her bones, hair no longer dyed, no makeup. Vulnerable as a child, she lies on her side in a hospital bed. "Hello, Grandma," I say, hating that I speak as if to a child to a woman who has lived eighty-six years. "Oh, hello, dahling," her voice very low. "Hello. Hello." She's been repeating things since she came to Oakwood.

"How are you?" "Not very well. Not very well." It is August. In the bare but spacious room, the only photographs are five of Jenny, and one of me. Beside Margarett's bed is a copy of the anthology I've edited, my first book, new plays by women, including one of mine. I'd sent a first copy to her months ago. A week later had come her call: "I read your book, read your book, read your book. I've read it twice. Twice." The nurse, worried I haven't understood, explains before hanging up: "When she finishes reading it, she begins all over again."

On Thursday, January 19, Father Duquette, a friend of Dickie Demenocal's, brought Margarett communion at Oakwood. On Friday, January 20, Stephen visited, and early Saturday morning, January 21, 1978, Margarett died alone in her room.

When I got the call in New York, it was dark and snowy. I was sitting at the breakfast table with friends and one of my sisters. It was my uncle Shaw. "Your grandmother died last night," he said. "The funeral is on Wednesday." I told everyone, then I took out the telephone book, looked up the number of the Betty Parsons Gallery, and called to tell a woman I'd never met that her friend had died.

Sixteen years later, on an early-summer afternoon, I sat surrounded by paper—scribbled-on and crumpled typescript, photocopies of Margarett's drawings, books open to certain pages—the storm of finishing her biography, this book. When I wrote her death, that one sentence, I dropped my head to the table and cried.

I wrote the end on a Friday. Saturday night I dreamed we were in Paris together, at the Saint-James et d'Albany.

The room is hung with crimson and gold. Healthy and in possession of her beauty, Margarett reclines on a bed, in an elegant black sheath. I sit by her side, notebook on my knee, interviewing her. In the way of dreams, I am both viewer and participant. As I watch, I can see we are both laughing. I want to sleep forever if I can keep dreaming this, me asking, Margarett exclaiming, telling me all her answers.

Acknowledgments

THERE ARE a few people, in particular, without whom, literally, this book could not have been written. With great generosity, Margarett Vernon opened her memory and her house, provided leads and archives, and persevered in a decade-long conversation about her mother, which could not have been as riveting for her as it was for me; it is with gratitude and love that I have dedicated the book to her. In addition, I thank Shaw McKean, his wife, Linda, and Henry P. McKean II for the hours they spent talking to me; and for the memoir she wrote before her death, I am grateful to my mother, the late Jenny McKean Moore.

Ingrid Schaffner included Margarett Sargent in "The Feminine Gaze," an exhibition she co-curated at the Whitney Museum (Stamford, Connecticut) in 1984, and subsequently brought her intelligence, wit, perseverance, and curiosity to the project as a research collaborator. Diane Gelon, armed with camera, lights, and expertise as an art historian, accompanied me to the Metropolitan Warehouse in Cambridge for a week of photographing and cataloguing; without her slides, I would not have the visual record that formed my understanding of Margarett as an artist. Patterson Sims introduced me to the New York art world, shared his knowledge of American painting gleaned from years as the curator of the permanent collection of the Whitney Museum, and directed me to sources I would otherwise not have found.

Alvin Hochberg, Margarett Sargent's lawyer in the last twenty years of her life, generously made available files that clarified the years she spent in mental hospitals. The late Daniel Sargent, a great raconteur with an extraordinary gift of recall, painted, in hours of interviews, his favorite sister's childhood and youth, and their unusual relationship. In the last years of her life, Betty Parsons, in many interviews, situated Margarett in the New York art world of the 1910s and 1920s, and, with an artist's insight, cast light on the convolutions of her friend's character. After Betty's death, her friend Gwyn Metz made available the revelatory letters Margarett Sargent wrote from Four Winds and Baldpate.

For *The Writer on Her Work* (Volume I), Janet Sternburg commissioned "My Grandmother Who Painted"; it was in writing that essay that I decided to write Margarett Sargent's life.

Margarett's friends, family, and associates, the friends and families of those who knew her, and those who guided me to them were extraordinarily generous with their time and memories. I would like to thank Dr. Raymond Adams, William Alfred, K. K. Auchincloss, Lyn Austin, Mr. and Mrs. Roland Balay, Mrs. Frederic Bartlett, Susan Blatchford, Benjamin Bradlee, Frederick Bradlee, William Brice, John Malcolm Brinnin, Sargent Cheever, Susan Sargent Cooper, Jonathan Coppelman, Sylvia Cox, Richard Demenocal, Millicent Dillon, George Dix, Gertrude Hunnewell Donald, Charles Driscoll, Laura Delano Eastman, Kenward Elmslie, Katharine Evarts, Evelyn Evers, Hamilton Fish III, Robert Fizdale, Michael Gladstone, Stephen Green, C.Z. Guest, Lee Hall, John Hohnsbeen, Jane Hunnewell, Mrs. and Mrs. Walter Hunnewell, Phyllis Jenkins, Buffie Johnson, Garson Kanin, Walter Kilham, Lincoln Kirstein, Alida Lessard, Mrs. John Lodge, Lily Lodge, Jane Lyman, Russell Lyman, John McGovern, John McKean, Katharine McKean, Agnes Mongan, Edwin Denison Morgan, Jr., Daisy Oakley, Gina Ogden, Morton Palmer, Eve Pell, Robert Pell-Dechame, Stephanie Pell-Dechame, David Pickman, Perry Rathbone, Rosemary Rawcliffe, William Roerick, Mr. and Mrs. Daniel Ignatius Sargent, Francis W. Sargent, Joan Sargent, Charlotte Sheedy, Dr. Pamela Sicher, Jenny Slote, John Spanbauer, Constance Tilton, Katharine W. Tweed, Stephen Vernon, John Walker, Theresa Walsh, Minnie Warburton, Sylvia Whitman, Eugene Williams, Ruth Robb Wolcott. I am also grateful for conversations with Billie Sorenson, Dr. Terry Twichell, and Polly Abel of Four Winds Hospital.

A great many of the people most central to my understanding of Margarett Sargent have died since I spoke with them. I remain grateful to Berenice Abbott, Elizabeth McKean Bourneuf, Emily (Lodge) Clark, Fanny Perkins Cox, Marjorie Davenport, Dorothy DeSantillana, Hamilton Fish, Sr., Antoinette Kraushaar, Aimée and Rosamond Lamb, Leo Lerman, Archibald MacLeish, Harry Martin, Father Hilary Martin, Elizabeth McKean, Nancy Cochrane Palmer, E. Ames Parker, Joseph Pulitzer, Oliver Smith, Marian Valliant, Barclay Warburton, Edward Weeks, Kay Saltonstall Weld, Annie Laurie Wetzel, John White, and Hope Williams.

Certain people gave crucial direction to my research or thinking, sometimes without knowing it. I thank all of them, in particular Miranda Barry, Bowden Broadwater, Dr. Leonard Glass, Philip Grausman, Jasper Johns, Moira Kelly, William Koshland, Gail Levin, Arthur Lewis, Eleanor Munro, Toby Quitslund, John Richardson, Dr. Susan Robertson, Mira Schor, Dr. Sue Shapiro, Michael Steiner, George W. S. Trow, and Gillian Walker. I also thank my friends and colleagues who read the manuscript during its composition, providing encouragement to clarify and deepen my writing and thinking: Louise Bernikow, Helen Brann, Joyce Chopra, Michelle Cliff, Kennedy Fraser, Suzannah Lessard, Nancy Mowll Matthews, Dr. Phyllis Meshover, Arthur Miller, and Victoria Wilson.

A number of scholars and biographers have been invaluable teachers, some through their work and others with advice and direction. In particular, I would like to thank Carol Walker Aten, Deirdre Bair, Shari Benstock, Lawrence Bergreen, Flora Biddle, Liana Borghi, Milton Brown, Shareen Brysac, William Coles, Janis C. Conner, Blanche Wiesen Cook, Wanda Corn, Stanley L. Cuba, Courtney Graham Donnell, Louise DeSalvo, Trevor J. Fairbrother, Joseph E. Garland, Françoise Gilot, Cleve Gray, Kathryn Greenthal, Barbara Grossman, Nancy Grossman, Gillian Hanna (who also provided translations of Italian poems), Ann d'Harnoncourt, Anne Higonnet, Erica Hirschler, Kay Redfield Jamison, Temma Kaplan, Bernice Kramer Leader, Eunice Lipton, Celia McGee, Joan Marter, Diane Middlebrook, Nancy Milford, Alexandra Murphy, Linda Nochlin, Judith H. O'Toole, Arlene Raven, Joseph Rishel, Charlotte Streifer Rubenstein, Jean Strouse, Judith Thurman, Louise Tragard, Carol Troyen, Nicholas Fox Weber, and Judith Zilczer. I have also been privileged to participate in five years of discussion about biography and women as a member of the Women Writing Women's Lives Seminar, first at the New York Institute for the Humanities, and later at the Graduate School and University Center of the City University of New York.

No book about an artist is complete without its visual component. I am grateful to Gloria Etting for permission to use the photograph of Margarett Sargent by her late husband, Emlen Etting, for the jacket; to Rebecca Busselle, Joan Barker, Sarah Jenkins, and Monica Stevenson for making exquisite copies of old photographs, often at a moment's notice; to Monica Stevenson, Robert Houser, and Gregory Heins for photographing works of art for use in the book; and to Rustin Levenson Art Conservation Associates for the care with which they have restored Margarett Sargent's works, and help beyond the call of duty. I am also grateful to Vincent Virga for his invaluable help with the black-and-white picture section. Most of all I thank the people at Viking Penguin who made the visual elements of the book possible.

For important research assistance, I thank Ann Butler, Martha Finamore, and the late Margaret Stevens; and for their transcriptions of interview tapes, Ellie Mikalchus, Laura Stroehlein, and especially Judith Herrick.

For their memories of Margarett and patience during the years I devoted myself more to my family of the past than to my family of the present, I thank my brothers and sisters, Paul, Adelia, Rosemary, George, Marian, Daniel, Susanna, and Patience Moore; my brothers-in-law and sisters-in-law; my nieces and nephews; my Moore and McKean cousins; and my aunt Pauline Nickerson. And for their love and support, I thank my father, Paul Moore, and his wife, Brenda.

During the years of composition, friends have sustained me practically and spiritually, and their insights have enriched what I've written. I especially thank Margie Adam, Ann Arensberg, Dorothy Austin, Judy Baca, Rebecca Busselle, Martha Clarke, Tom Cole, Jane and Tom Doyle, Karen Durbin, Gabriela de Ferrari, Lucy Flint-Gohlke, Carolyn Forché, Phyllis Foster, Gerald Freund, Nancy Fried, Francine du Plessix Gray, Venable Herndon, Christopher Hewat, Richard Howard, Howard and Susan Kaminsky, Joan Larkin, James McCourt, Kathryn Meetz, Inge Morath, Eileen Myles, Ginger Nelson, Peter Passell, Joan K. Peters, Maletta Pfeiffer,

Jane Rothschild, Victoria Rue, Christina Schlesinger, Paul Schmidt, Faith Stewart-Gordon, Susan Taylor, Vincent Virga, Kathryn Walker, Arnold Weinstein, Marguerite and Tom Whitney, Peregrine Whittlesey, and Sondra Zeidenstein.

Finally, I would like to thank Amanda Vaill, the editor who originally commissioned this book for Viking, Wendy Weil, the agent who first represented it, and Nan Graham, the book's second editor, for their enthusiasm at the beginning and along the way. I also thank my agent Andrew Wylie, whose tough criticism and vigorous encouragement came at crucial times, his associates Sarah Chalfant and Jeffrey Posternak, for their continuing contributions to my work, and Viking's publisher, Barbara Grossman, for her warmth and support. Last, but in no way least, I thank Courtney Hodell, my editor, whose passion for *The White Blackbird* and its subject has been the great gift of its publication.

This book has taken years to write, and it's altogether possible I've inadvertently failed to acknowledge someone who provided time and important assistance. If I have, I apologize; I did—and do—value your contribution.

H.M.

Kent, Connecticut
May 1995

Afterword

ALL THE WHILE I was writing *The White Blackbird*, which took twelve years, I was also coming to terms with Margarett Sargent's work. The first time I saw her paintings was in a dark closet at Prides. I began to deal with them a dozen years later, in 1980. My grandmother's executors had been unable to interest anyone in buying her paintings and drawings, and after various family members chose what they wanted, Margarett's work would be up for grabs or destruction. I had a contract for this book, and I knew I wanted to look closely at the paintings, so, in exchange for time to catalogue and photograph them, I agreed to pay rent to keep them stored in a fortress-like facility across the street from MIT in Cambridge and, after I'd finished, to distribute them to family members. Diane Gelon, an art historian who at the time was director of operations for the making and first tour of Judy Chicago's *The Dinner Party*, volunteered to help and teach me. For a week we worked, with lights, cameras, and newly printed catalogue cards, in the dungeon-like room.

At the time a working poet, I knew nothing of the history I would learn that would help me to put Margarett Sargent's work in the context of American art of the twentieth century, of the history of art in Boston, and of the newly emerging canon of women artists. I was looking at the paintings and drawings solely in terms of what I knew of my grandmother, the view of Margarett that opens this book—a woman who stopped painting in her early forties, was subsequently diagnosed with manic-depressive illness, and spent much of the rest of her life in and out of mental hospitals undergoing shock therapy.

Diane, on the other hand, steeped in the history of women artists, saw images that expressed a woman's power and her ambivalence about it. In Margarett's subject matter, she saw resonances with Mary Cassatt, Berthe Morisot, and Romaine Brooks, and in her formal approaches, influences of the School of Paris and German Expressionism. She thought it was interesting that Margarett had collected works by women artists, that she had spent time in Paris in the 1920s, and that she had numbered artists among her friends. I had much to learn.

That week photographing began a process. We had the photographs developed but not mounted as slides. Diane taught me how to clip an image from the strand of film stock, frame it with silver tape, and mount it to make a slide. I had a stamp made and labeled each slide with the artist's name. After photographing the works, we wrapped them in glassine, I rented a van, and with Diane, drove around the East Coast delivering paintings. I was left with what remained— more than two hundred canvases and drawings. Since many of the paintings were in terrible shape, I looked for an art conservator and, through museum acquaintances, found Rustin Levenson. Her conservation studio embraced the project enthusiastically and, because of its size, was able to discount the costly job of restoration; these works had been in damp places for years and, if not downright filthy, were often missing chunks of paint. I spent a decade driving from my house in Connecticut, where I stored the works, to the studio on West 27th Street—years marveling at the miracle of cleaning and restoration.

Through this work, I became intimate with the paintings (they crowded my walls), independent of my grandmother and of the Margarett Sargent I was trying to bring to life on the page. Learning what I had to understand in order to write was arduous—doing interviews, reading books on art history and criticism, just plain thinking. But also, for years, I was almost blocked. Eventually, I had plenty of information, but the fierceness that had drawn me to Margarett was absent both from my writing and from my working process, something I was afraid to admit. One day I showed an early chapter to some new friends, the playwright Arthur Miller and his wife, the photographer Inge Morath. He said, Throw away the research and write it like a novel. She said, Write it like Margarett draws, referring to my grandmother's elegant, exploratory line. And my agent, on reading 150 pages, said, These are a little dull. I've read your poems! Now write the book! I was, needless to say, disconcerted by these responses, but I was also thrilled. I had permission to do something as imaginative in writing the book as Margarett had attempted in her art. But how to move forward was still a mystery.

One day, despairing of writing yet another prosaic transition, I decided to look again at Margarett's work. From the carton of sketchbooks under my desk, I took one, opened it, then leafed through it. First I just looked, but then I laid it open next to my computer, turned my music up loud, and began to type, almost randomly. Soon I was writing from the drawings, constructing narratives, finding my way into the images like a poet rather than a biographer. After a few days of "writing" sketchbooks, I turned to the slides Diane and I had made of the paintings. I tacked an old window shade up on the wall, borrowed from friends a projector I placed next to my desk, loaded a carousel, and turned it on. Now I was "writing" the paintings— surface, color, dimension—often they seemed to speak back to me, even provide information I lacked. I later learned that writing from a work of art was a tradition that began with the Greeks. "*Ekphrasis*," it's called—one writes from the work of art, not merely describing it, but allowing the language it stimulates to take on a life of its own. In my case, writing from the visual record Margarett Sargent left was how I came to know something of her inner life, something of the stakes in her life as an artist. When Margarett came to stop painting and these images disappeared from the narrative, I felt their loss, and so, I thought, would the reader.

More than five years into writing the book, I sent slides to Susan Taylor, then the director of the art museum at Wellesley College. She was intrigued, and by the time the book was scheduled for publication, Wellesley College had a beautiful new facility—the Davis Museum and Cultural Center—and the opening of Margarett Sargent's first solo exhibition in more than half a century was scheduled to coincide with *The White Blackbird*'s publication in March 1996. While preparing to go to Wellesley to help hang the show, I spoke with Helen Miranda Wilson, a painter friend who'd been with me throughout the long process of writing the book. "Be sure to take half an hour alone with the paintings," she said. "You'll want to feel their presence."

It was raining the night Lucy Flint-Gohlke, my co-curator, met me at the train. I was carrying Margarett's bronze head of her teacher, the painter George Luks, which we'd decided at the last minute to include in the show. As I climbed the stairs of the old station at Route 128, it seemed impossibly heavy, like a burden in a fairy tale or a myth; I thought I would never reach my destination.

I did what Helen said. I remember the door closing behind me, the clear white light, vivid color, and the strong spirit of this grandmother I had finally come to know. The paintings, not yet hung, leaned against the walls of a large gallery; the expressions on the faces of their subjects seemed to vibrate. I stood at the entrance for a while, my head throbbing, tears coming. It had been fifteen years since Diane and I photographed in that dungeon room, almost twenty years since Margarett's death. I walked from one painting to another. From *The Blue Girl*, the first painting she had given me that had frightened me so much as a young woman, to her 1928 self-portrait, *Beyond Good and Evil*, which would later represent her in an exhibition of Boston women artists at the Museum of Fine Arts. I looked at *The Bathers*, cleaned and restored, buoyant as the women on the beach who'd entered Margarett's imagination sixty-five years before, at *Tailleur Classique*, the painting of Maria de Acosta that had helped me in my "slide writing" to introduce Margarett's sexual love for women. And at the drawings and pastels and watercolors of my mother and aunt and uncles as children, of Jane Bowles and others of

Margarett's friends. "You'll realize," Helen had said, "how much work you've done."

It's exhausting now to begin to remember all the work—it was my life for so many years—but the half hour I spent alone in the gallery stays with me, as does the opening of the exhibition a week later. This time I drove to Boston unburdened by sculpture or paintings or plans for interviewing or research. When I walked into the museum I saw many copies of my newly minted book stacked on a table in the lobby, books for sale that I would sign after a short reading and talk. Would anyone come? I could hardly speak as I passed through the empty gallery and back into the museum offices. I was ready when Lucy came to retrieve me, and when I entered the gallery where the reading would take place, the gallery next door to the one where Margarett's paintings hung, I was stunned to see that every chair was filled, that people stood against the walls and sat on the floor, that still others draped themselves over the rail of the balcony that encircled the space.

I would read about the painting I'd imagined Margarett's last: ". . . The woman casts no reflection, and there is no evidence of the artist. Knowing we cannot be sure, let's say this is Margarett's last painting—herself with no face, casting no reflection in a mirror she clearly faces. Fifty-five years later, two women lay slides on a light table, arrange them according to catalogue numbers. One of us is the granddaughter who rescued the paintings from a warehouse room. . . ." I ended the reading by directing those gathered to head into the gallery next door to look at those very paintings. The applause, I thought, was not for my reading but for the return of this artist, her survival in the paintings it had cost her so much to make.

Honor Moore

Peterborough, New Hampshire
2009

A Note on Sources

THE SOURCES, aside from interviews, that most intimately revealed my story are the scrapbooks, sketchbooks, diaries, photographs, paintings, and drawings left by Margarett Sargent McKean and now either in my possession or spread among her children and grandchildren. Family material relevant to Margarett's life was also generously provided by Sargent Cheever, Susan Sargent Cooper, Gertrude Hunnewell Donald, Alvin Hochberg, Jane Hunnewell, Mr. and Mrs. Walter Hunnewell, the late Betty Parsons, and the late Daniel Sargent.

But whatever the wealth of personal material, it cannot take shape without the resources of institutions. At the Sargent Murray Gilman House in Gloucester, Massachusetts, which was once the residence of Judith Sargent Murray, I found a profusion of Sargent family material to supplement the encyclopedic *Epes Sargent of Gloucester and His Descendants,* arranged by Emma Worcester Sargent, with biographical notes by Charles Sprague Sargent (Houghton Mifflin, 1923). At the Essex Institute in Salem, Massachusetts, I leafed through logs kept on ships owned by Daniel and Winthrop Sargent, and later through issues of the *North Shore Breeze and Reminder.* My major source for the Hunnewell family was *The Life, Letters and Diaries of Horatio Hollis Hunnewell, with a Short History of the Hunnewell and Welles Families and an Account of the Wellesley and Natick Estates,* edited by Hollis H. Hunnewell, privately printed, 1906.

By the Winsor School in Boston, I was given copies of Margarett Sargent's report cards; and with the assistance of Gloria Gavert, I consulted the rich archives of Miss Porter's School in Farmington, Connecticut. In the Harvard University Archives, I discovered a treasury of autobiography, personal statements written by Harvard graduates on the occasion of each important class reunion, called "Anniversary Reports." At the Arthur and Elizabeth Schlesinger Library on the History of Women in America, Radcliffe College, I consulted the papers of the Boston Junior League (including those of the Sewing Circle). In the Yale Collection of American Literature at the Beinecke Rare Book and Manuscript Library, Yale University, I consulted Francis Hyde Bangs's annotated *Letters and Verses of Archibald MacLeish, 1914–1942, together with poems sent to Francis Hyde Bangs from 1914–1942*, in the Archibald MacLeish Collection, an invaluable document originally brought to my attention by R. H. Winnick.

For information about the history of Ogunquit as an art colony, I consulted, with the guidance of Louise Tragard, the archives of the York Historical Society, York, Maine, and later read the excellent *A Century of Color: 1886–1986*, by Tragard, Patricia E. Hart, and W. L. Copithorne (Ogunquit: Barn Gallery Associates, 1987). At the Library of Congress in Washington, D.C., in the Prints and Photographs Division, I consulted the Arnold Genthe Collection; and in the Manuscript Division, the Gutzon Borglum Collection. For much of my information about George Luks, I am grateful to Arthur Lewis, who has amassed a great deal of material toward a biography of the painter. In New York, Larry Campbell answered questions about the history of the Art Students League. And in Chicago, Patricia Scheidt, then its director, gave me a tour of the Arts Club of Chicago, whose archives I consulted at the Newberry Library. For information about the Harvard Society for Contemporary Art, with the help of Phoebe Peebles and Abigail Smith, archivists, I consulted the Harvard University Art Museum Archives.

The Archives of American Art, Smithsonian Institution, and Robert Brown of its New England Regional Center, were invaluable resources for information and material about Margarett Sargent and her artist contemporaries. Carol Pesner, director of the Kraushaar Gallery in New York, kindly perused its archives for me. In addition, I consulted the libraries of the Art Institute of Chicago; the Boston Museum of Fine Arts; the Metropolitan Museum of Art; the Museum of Modern Art; the National Museum of American Art, Smithsonian Institution; the Wadsworth Atheneum, Hartford; and the Whitney Museum, New York

City. And at the Harvard University Center for Italian Renaissance Studies at Villa I Tatti, in the Berenson Archive, I found the letters written to Bernard Berenson by Margarett Sargent McKean.

For periodicals, the New York Public Library (Astor, Tilden and Lenox Foundations) and the Library of Congress were extraordinary sources. I also consulted the Elmer Bobst Library of New York University, the Lamont and Widener libraries of Harvard University, and the Fine Arts Department of the Boston Public Library. In Litchfield County, Connecticut, the John Gray Park Library of Kent School, Kent, and the Edsel Ford Library of the Hotchkiss School, Lakeville, graciously made their resources available.

To all these institutions, which seem particularly precious now, I extend my heartfelt gratitude.

Notes

Key to Initials

BB	Bernard Berenson
EB	Elizabeth McKean Bourneuf (Butsy)
FB	Frederick Bradlee
MD	Marjorie Davenport
DDeS	Dorothy DeSantillana
GHD	Gertrude Hunnewell Donald
HHH	Horatio Hollis Hunnewell, *The Life, Letters and Diaries of Horatio Hollis Hunnewell*
AH	Alvin Hochberg
EL	Emily (Mrs. Henry Cabot) Lodge, later Mrs. Forrest Clark
HMcK	Henry Pratt McKean, II (Harry)
QASMcK	Quincy Adams Shaw McKean, Sr.
SMcK	Quincy Adams Shaw McKean, Jr.
JMcKM	Jenny McKean Moore
EDM	Edwin Denison Morgan
EDM, Jr.	Edwin Denison Morgan, Jr.
BPP	Betty Pierson Parsons
DS	Daniel Sargent
FWS	Francis Williams (Frank) Sargent (Papa)
FWS, Jr.	Francis Williams (Frank) Sargent, Jr.
JS	Jane Hunnewell (Jenny) Sargent (Mama)
MS	Margarett Sargent (McKean)
MTS	Mabel Thayer Storey
MV	Margarett McKean Vernon (Margie)
JW	John Walker
RRW	Ruth Robb Wolcott
BW	Barclay Warburton, III (Buzzie)
MW	Margarett Warburton McInnis (Minnie)

Chapter i

5. *great-great-grandmother:* Margarett's husband, my grandfather QASMcK, was the grandson of Pauline Agassiz Shaw, stepdaughter of Elizabeth Cary Agassiz (1822–1907), who founded the Harvard Annex, which became Radcliffe College in 1879.

6. *De Chirico: Horses in Moonlight,* purchased in New York from F. Valentine Dudensing, February 1, 1930.

8. *"pitch pine forest":* Quoted in "A Garden for the Public: H. H. Hunnewell's Rhododendron Show," *Horticulture,* July 1978, p. 53. In 1873, at his own expense, HHH temporarily transplanted most of his rhododendrons and many of his tropical plants to the Boston Common, which he then enclosed in a giant tent. His intention was to encourage cultivation of shrubs then unknown to the American public. Forty thousand Bostonians attended the show. With his friends Margarett's cousins Charles Sprague Sargent of the Arnold Arboretum and Henry Winthrop Sargent of Woodenethe, and Frederick Law Olmsted, designer of Central Park in New York, Hunnewell believed that the cultivation of the landscape contributed to the social good.

9. *"No Vanderbilt":* HHH, vol. I, p. 118.

10. *"fully 200 years old":* HHH, vol. III, p. 190.

11. *old as Methuselah:* To her sister, Jane Welles Hunnewell, November 28, 1838; HHH, vol. I, p. 43.

11. *"It was in Europe":* Henry Sargent Hunnewell, *Recollections* (Boston: Privately printed, 1930), n.p.

12. *"the beloved wife":* HHH, vol. II, p. 148.

12. *Beacon Street lot:* HHH's mansion, at 130 Beacon Street, now houses Emerson College.

12. *"The Hunnewells aren't":* This and all subsequent quotes from Margarett in this chapter, unless otherwise noted, are from interviews with DS held at South Natick, Mass., between 1980 and his death in 1988; all quotes from DS are also from these interviews.

13. *the Sargent genealogy:* Emma Worcester Sargent, with biographical notes by Charles Sprague Sargent, *Epes Sargent of Gloucester and His Descendants* (Boston and New York: Houghton Mifflin, 1923). Unless otherwise noted, all Sargent genealogical material comes from this volume.

13. *the "triangle trade":* Though I was told by the librarian at the Essex Institute in Salem, where I looked through registries of cargo shipped on Daniel Sargent's ships, that he was not known as a slaver, no records were kept of slave cargo because the slave trade (distinct from slavery itself) was illegal after 1808. If he was not a slaver, certainly his participation in the triangle trade implicated him in the enterprise, which made so many New England fortunes.

13. *"the finest head"*: Emma Worcester Sargent, *Epes Sargent of Gloucester*, p. 161.

14. *put three sons:* The eldest, John Turner Sargent, emerged an abolition-ist preacher, who, with his wife, Mary, founded the Radical Club of Chestnut Street, where Unitarians met with Spiritualists, Calvinists, and Quakers, and women like Lucretia Mott and Julia Ward Howe spoke on equal terms about abolition, suffrage, and temperance with men like William Ellery Channing, Henry James, Sr., John Greenleaf Whittier, and Thomas Wentworth Higgin-son. Christiana (Kitty) Sargent's youngest son, Howard, became a physician.

14. *"I am a gentleman"*: DS, *Our Sargent Family* (Boston: Privately printed, 1992), p. I-6.

15. *"Thou art lost"*: Henry Jackson Sargent, *Feathers from a Moulting Muse* (Boston: Crosby Nichols, 1854), p. 123.

15. *youngest clipper captain:* His letters are collected in *The Captain of the Phantom: The Story of Henry Jackson Sargent, Jr., 1834–1862 as Revealed in Family Letters* (Mystic, Conn.: Marine Historical Association, 1967).

15. *"General Custer's daughter"*: My best efforts could not prove the exis-tence of such a daughter or of any Custer children. This story and all quotes from Sargent family members come from DS interviews unless otherwise noted.

16. *"great news . . . the gentleman"*: HHH, vol. II, p. 118.

18. *"When Baby was sick"*: *Boston Evening Transcript*, August 31, 1892, p. 1.

18. *"Jenny Sargent"*: HHH, vol. I, p. 173.

22. *"Only that I missed"*: GHD, author interview, Brookline, Mass., Sep-tember 1978. All subsequent GHD quotes from this interview, unless other-wise noted.

23. *"Sundays of course"*: pastel, n.d. Unless otherwise noted, all MS works noted are in the collection of the author.

23. *"Between the dark"*: Henry Wadsworth Longfellow, "The Children's Hour," The Library of America, *American Poetry: The Nineteenth Century*, vol. I: Freneau to Whitman, p. 409.

24. *"warm in his seaman's coat"*: Henry Wadsworth Longfellow, "The Wreck of the Hesperus," ibid., pp. 373–75.

27. *"The assassination"*: HHH, vol. II, p. 273.

27. *"January 1. 9 degrees"*: Diary kept by MS, 1902. Diary entries quoted come from this volume, until otherwise noted. All MS diaries and scrapbooks referred to are, unless otherwise noted, in the collection of the author.

28. *Boston Herald report:* Quoted in DS, *Our Sargent Family*, chap. 2, pp. 18–19.

31. *"They say Buster"*: MS diary, 1906. Entries quoted are from this diary, until otherwise noted.

32. *E. and O. Ames:* Elise and Olivia were daughters of Oliver Ames, heir to a farm implements company which had evolved into a manufacturer of railroad hardware and a lucrative railroad holding company. The Ameses were more ostentatiously rich than the Hunnewells, but not as rich as the Searses, who were "swells," Dan said, meaning not that their house was bigger or their carriages were more opulent, but that they observed certain amenities, such as having butlers rather than maids to wait at table.

33. *Lily and Phyllis Sears:* Once, at Wareham, as Frank Sargent plunged off the pier, Lily Sears said, "I should think you'd be ashamed that your father goes swimming in a topless suit." "Well," Margarett replied, "I should think you'd be ashamed that your ancestors dug clams on Cape Cod," referring to the Searses' fishing origins but not repeating the story that the Searses were rumored to have first made money by selling horses to George Washington at exorbitant prices.

33. *"power of concentration":* This remark, as well as Margarett's grades, are recorded on her report cards, still in the archives of the Winsor School, Boston.

35. *"It was quite":* Jenny Sargent to Alice Russell, July 11, 1907. All family papers referred to are in the collection of the author, unless otherwise noted.

Chapter ii

39. *"during the day":* Annual Circular of Miss Porter's School, Farmington, Connecticut, 1910–1911. Courtesy Miss Porter's School.

39. *Noah Porter:* Sarah's brother Noah was a philosopher and president of Yale; an ancestor was a founder of the town of Farmington.

40. *"hardly less . . . she required":* William M. Sloane, "Sarah Porter: Her Unique Educational Work," *Century Magazine* LX, no. 41 (penciled date "1900") p. 346. Courtesy Miss Porter's School.

40. *"the fixed organization":* Ibid.

40. *"sailed imposingly":* Clover Todd (Mrs. Allen Dulles) in a reminiscence, typescript, p. 3. Courtesy Miss Porter's School.

40. *"Homesick if I stopped":* From a diary kept by MS at Miss Porter's School, 1908–1909. All quotes, all notes from others, all drawings referred to in this chapter, are from (or preserved with) this diary, unless otherwise noted.

41. *psychology text:* This detail from Fanny Perkins Cox, author interviews cited below.

42. *"I have absolutely":* MD, author interview, Dorset, Vt., January 9, 1979. All MD quotes from this interview, unless otherwise noted.

42. *Fanny Perkins:* Her brother Maxwell would become the famous editor. One of her sons, Archibald Cox, was the solicitor general of the United States fired by President Nixon in 1974 during the famous "Friday night massacre" of the Watergate scandals. All FPC quotes are from an author interview conducted in Windsor, Vt., January 8, 1979, and a telephone interview conducted November 1983.

43. *"the dump":* Slang for the place set aside to wait for a partner's approach at a dance; also the place where wallflowers inevitably ended up.

46. *"close-fitting but inconspicuous":* Quoted without attribution in Charlotte Streifer Rubenstein, *American Women Artists* (New York and Boston: Avon Books and G. K. Hall, 1982), p. 92.

46. *"Ingres-like":* "On Our Street," *House Beautiful,* December 1933, p. 248A.

46. *Theodate Pope:* The design of Hill-Stead is often wrongly attributed to McKim, Mead and White, who provided practical assistance to the young architect. Pope (1867–1946) also designed Westover, Avon Old Farms, and Hop Brook Elementary schools, all in Connecticut.

47. *Cassatt pastel: In the Loge,* pastel and metallic paint on canvas, unsigned, now in the Philadelphia Museum of Art, gift of Margarett Sargent McKean.

47. *Rosamond Smith Bouve:* A member of the Boston Guild of Artists, the Connecticut Academy of Fine Arts, the National Association of Women Painters and Sculptors of New York, winner of a Bronze Medal at the Panama Pacific Exposition in San Francisco in 1915.

48. *"most sought after leading man":* At Miss Porter's, plays were put on by the Players Club and the French and German departments. Briefly rehearsed pantomimes like *The Peterkin Papers* were performed on weekends, and, for graduation, the Players Club, the Mandolin Club (seven girls poised with stringed instruments), and the Glee Club produced a comedy by Shakespeare.

49. *"my attractive blond":* MS to QASMcK, n.d.

49. *"the new member":* A caption from the scrapbook MS kept in Florence. All quotes attributed to her in Florence are from this scrapbook, unless otherwise noted.

49. *three finishing schools:* In a 1980 interview in Florence, Evelyn Evers told me that Miss Penrose's, on the Piazza Donatello, was for English girls, and Eversholm, a school run by her mother, an English widow, was international.

50. *"the most banal things":* DS, author interview.

50. *"not accessible to ladies":* Karl Baedeker, *Italy: Handbook for Travellers, First Part: Northern Italy,* 12th Remodelled Edition (Leipsig [*sic*], London, New York, 1903), p. 528.

51. *"just looking":* Lawrence Dame, "Mrs. McKean, Fabulous Resident of Beverly, Turns to Art Again," MS scrapbook clipping, *Boston Sunday Herald,* c.1948. Margarett kept intermittent scrapbooks, but she was not systematic. Often the clippings she preserved were not dated. Whenever possible, I've located the clipping in its original periodical. If unable to, I've simply labeled it as above and speculated a date.

51. *"sporting Italian":* E. Ames Parker, telephone interview, January 1979. All EAP quotes from this interview, unless otherwise noted.

51. *"If I were fire":* Cecco Angiolieri in D. G. Rossetti, trans., *The Early Italian Poets from Ciullo D'Alcama to Dante Alighieri: 1100–1200–1300: In the Original Metres Together with Dante's Vita Nuova* (London: George Routledge & Sons; New York: E. P. Dutton, n.d.), p. 337.

52. *great group portrait:* John Singer Sargent, *The Daughters of Edward D. Boit,* 1883, Museum of Fine Arts, Boston.

52. *Edward Darley Boit:* By 1910, Boit had a reputation as a watercolorist. In 1912, he and Sargent exhibited their watercolors jointly at Knoedler's in New York, and the Boston Museum of Fine Arts bought out the exhibition. The story is that Sargent would allow the purchase of all his watercolors only if the museum bought all of Boit's as well.

52. *Guincelli:* In Rossetti, *The Early Italian Poets,* p. 19.

52. *Ambrogio de Predis:* The portrait was either of Beatrice d'Este, patron of Castiglione and subject of da Vinci, or of Bianca Sforza.

52. *"ugly duckling":* Kay Saltonstall Weld, author interview, September 1978.

53. *"gigantic robustness":* Bernard Berenson, *Italian Painters of the Renaissance* (London: Phaidon Press, 1956), p. 40.

53. *"the greatest master":* Ibid., p. 131.

53. *In 1898, Berenson:* See Ernest Samuels, *The Making of a Connoisseur* (Cambridge: Harvard University Press, 1979), p. 297.

53. *"Berenson gives it":* Two years later, Berenson, in a new edition of his "gospels," again attributed the painting to Leonardo, but with the assistance of Credi.

53. *"rouse the tactile sense":* Berenson, *Italian Painters,* p. 40.

55. *"There's Margarett Sargent!"* Marian Valliant, author interview, Washington, Conn., December 1984. All MV quotes from this interview.

56. *early in 1912:* MS diary, 1912. MS quotes in the balance of the chapter are from this diary, unless otherwise noted.

57. *"philanthropic employment bureau":* Elizabeth Gray, "Talk to Debutante Sewing Circle," handwritten notes c.1912, Papers of the Boston Junior League. Schlesinger Library, Radcliffe College, Carton #1 79–M9.

57. *New York in 1901:* The history of the Junior League is told in Janet Gordon and Diana Reische, *The Volunteer Powerhouse: The Junior League* (New York: Rutledge Press, 1982).

57. *"promiscuous giving":* Gray, "Talk."

57. *"most preeminently popular":* *Town Topics,* c.1912. MS scrapbook clipping.

57. *"the rising generation":* *Boston Sunday Herald,* January 14, 1912, p. 18.

58. *"frequently pounded the table":* *Boston Herald,* January 12, 1912, p. 1.

58. *"Miss Sargent":* *Boston Traveler,* January 12, 1912, p. 11.

59. *"Young ladies should":* Florence Howe Hall, *Social Customs* (Boston, 1911; original edition, 1887), p. 182.

59. *"peach colored satin":* Boston Herald, January 13, 1912, p. 5. All descriptions of gowns quoted are from this article.

59. *"one of the veterans":* Ibid., January 14, 1912, p. 19.

59. *"a tall, slender":* Ibid.

60. *"She was good-looking":* Hamilton Fish, Sr., author interview, New York, February 16, 1981. All HF quotes from this interview.

60. *"a red wagon":* FB, author interviews, New York, April 1979, April 1986. All FB quotes from these interviews. Bebo (Frederick Josiah Bradlee) was the father of FB and of Benjamin Bradlee, executive editor of the *Washington Post,* 1968–1991, and of the late Constance Bradlee Devens.

60. *"Junius Morgan":* J. P. Morgan's grandson.

60. *Hall Roosevelt:* Eleanor Roosevelt's younger brother.

61. *only distantly related:* Three Welsh Puritan brothers had come to America in 1630: Edwin Denison Morgan descended from the eldest, James; John Pierpont Morgan from Miles, the youngest.

61. *"But the Morgans had no swank":* Eddie's father, Edwin Denison Morgan, called "Altie" (Harvard 1877), was heir to the fortune his grandfather, Civil War governor of New York and Lincoln confidant, had made in the boom the followed the opening of the Eric Canal. He was a serious yachtsman—his *Columbia* won the America's Cup—and, as an amateur engineer, made innovations in hull design that increased the speed of his boats. The dark side of his brilliance and his famous charm was a merciless vulnerability to alcohol, which he inherited from his father, who died young of drink, and passed on to Eddie, the elder of his two sons.

61. *He majored in Egyptology:* During the winter of 1910, Eddie's freshman year, an archaeological expedition sponsored jointly by Harvard and the Boston Museum of Fine Arts unearthed, at Giza, the slate sculptures of Mycerinus and his queen, now in the museum.

63. *"It was my first kiss":* JMcKM, unpublished memoir.

64. *"If only you could have seen":* EDM to MS, n.d.

65. *"Don't you think":* DS interviews.

65. *Frog Fountain:* "I want you to have another made in marble for Jim Breese's Long Island garden," was how Janet Scudder reported Stanford White's 1906 commission in her autobiography. Janet Scudder, *Modeling My Life* (New York: Harcourt Brace, 1925), pp. 196–97.

67. *"famously beautiful":* EDM, Jr., (EDM's son), author interview, New York, April 28, 1986.

67. *"Everybody's Doin' It":* The story of the impact of ragtime is admirably told in Lawrence Bergreen, *As Thousands Cheered: The Life of Irving Berlin* (New York: Viking, 1990), chaps. 4, 5.

67. *"so very attractive":* Katherine Morgan Evarts (EDM's sister), author interview, April 29, 1986, Kent, Conn.

68. *One hundred horses:* At Wheatly, he kept a hundred ponies and, with Thomas J. Hitchcock, Elliot Roosevelt, and Winthrop Rutherford (who would later marry FDR's mistress, Lucy Mercer), formed the first American team to compete in the International Polo League.

68. *"I'm going to Italy to sculpt":* MW, author interview. All MW quotes from interviews held between October 1979 and June 1989 on the telephone and in Newport, R.I.

68. *"no small talk":* Theo (Mrs. Charles) Codman told EDM, Jr., that Margarett had told her she couldn't marry a man with no small talk.

68. *"Eddie took to drink":* The Sargent family stories are from DS; the Morgan ones from Katharine Morgan Evarts.

69. *"Oh clay":* Diary of Adelia Moore, after visiting her grandmother, c.1973. Courtesy AM.

69. *"She didn't explain":* JMcKM, unpublished memoir.

Chapter iii

73. *"It will be remembered":* Town Topics, c.1913. MS scrapbook clipping.

73. *"experience underground":* QASMcK, Harvard College, Class of 1913, Secretary's Third Report, June 1920, p. 206.

74. *Jean-François Millet:* Quincy Shaw met Millet through the Boston painter William Morris Hunt. When his widow, Pauline, died, in 1917, her children gave most of the collection, which includes the famous painting *The Sower*, to the Museum of Fine Arts.

74. *"a party of Boston men":* Louise Hall Tharp, *Adventurous Alliance: The Story of the Agassiz Family of Boston* (Boston: Little Brown, 1959), p. 199. Horatio Hollis Hunnewell accepted stock in the new mines as payment of a debt owed him by Quincy Shaw, and Major Henry Lee Higginson, married to Ida, Pauline Agassiz's sister, invested, putting his trust in "Quin and Alex . . . with their ability, honesty, industry, nerve and power."—Russell B. Adams, Jr., *The Boston Money Tree* (New York, 1977), p. 164. No one could have predicted that by the 1870s, the Calumet-Hecla Mining Company would produce half the copper in the United States and that by 1898, an investor who purchased 100 shares at $30 each in 1868 would own 250 shares worth $530 each, his original investment having also earned dividends of $131,250. During his lifetime, Alexander Agassiz made gifts of more than $1 million to the Harvard Museum of Comparative Zoology, and in 1908, Quincy Shaw died New England's largest individual taxpayer.

75. *"The Grand Canyon":* QASMcK to MS, March 10, 1914.

75. *"I'm trying to become an outdoor girl":* MS postcard to her brother Harry, c.1914.

75. *"It was my accident":* EDM to MS, September 8, 1914.

75. *"At the time I got your letter"*: Ibid.

76. *"I know you love me"*: QASMcK to MS, March 10, 1914.

76. *"I'd like a shot"*: Story from DS.

77. *"the emancipated females"*: William Wetmore Story to James Russell Lowell, 1852, quoted in Henry James, *William Wetmore Story and His Friends* (Boston: Houghton Mifflin, 1903; New York: Grove Press, 1957), p. 257.

77. *"that strange sisterhood"*: Ibid.

77. *"Hatty takes a high hand"*: Ibid.

78. *"eternal feud"*: Harriet Hosmer, quoted in Rubinstein, *American Women Artists*, p. 79; from Cornelia Crow Carr, *Harriet Hosmer: Letters and Memories* (New York: Moffat Yard, 1912), p. 35.

78. *"I honor all those"*: Harriet Hosmer, quoted in Rubinstein, p. 79; from Phebe Hanaford, *Daughters of America* (no publisher cited) pp. 321–22.

78. *"white rabbits"*: Janet Scudder, *Modeling My Life*, p. 58.

78. *"I won't add"*: Ibid., p. 155.

78. *"If we men"*: Quoted in Janis C. Conner, "American Women Sculptors Break the Mold," *Art and Antiques*, May–June 1980, p. 81, from William Walton, "Some Contemporary Young Women Sculptors," *Scribner's Magazine* 47 (May 1910).

79. *"the study of melancholy"*: "$100,000 if Edith Deacon Weds," *Boston American*, July 1912, Boston Museum of Fine Arts School Scrapbooks, vol. V., p. 80.

79. *"occupied . . . passionate application"*: MS to her son SMcK, 1966.

80. *"their crowded little flat"*: " 'L' Ticket Seller Is Wonderful Sculptress," *Boston Journal*, July 6, 1914; MFA School Scrapbooks, vol. VII, p. 106. Courtesy Kathryn Greenthal.

80. *"the figure of a crouching"*: Jessie E. Henderson, "A Girl Sculptor Who Models in a Subway Ticket Booth,"*American Magazine*, June 1914; MFA School Scrapbooks, vol. VI, p. 109. Courtesy Kathryn Greenthal.

80. *"one of the ambitions"*: "Relief Portrait of Jane Addams," unidentified clipping, ibid., vol. VIII, p. 19. Courtesy Kathryn Greenthal.

80. *bohemian glamour*: William Koshland tells a story of Bashka Paeff visiting his family's house in Boston; it is his description that informs mine.

81. *"It was strange"*: All Sargent Cheever quotes from author interview, Wellesley, Mass., November 16, 1981.

81. *"My freedom"*: DS, "Freedom," *Our Gleaming Days* (Boston: Richard G. Badger, 1915), p. 29.

81. *"But tonight"*: "Rain—October 1914," ibid., p. 57.

82. *"a keepsake"*: "Miss Margarett Sargent Moulds Bust of Brother," c.1915. MS scrapbook clipping.

82. *"a frail swift passenger steamer"*: DS, *Our Sargent Family*, chap. 2, p. 15.

82. *"struck a rock"*: Ibid., p. 14.

82. *"The Sussex had been cut"*: "Fifty Lives Lost in U-Boat Attack on the Sussex," *New York Times*, March 26, 1916, p. 3.

82. *"had not received any word"*: "New Yorkers on Sussex," Ibid.

83. *"It was broad daylight"*: DS, *Our Sargent Family*, chap. 2., p. 15.

83. *"quaint little"*: "Dinner and Dance Precede Weddings of Miss Breese and Miss Claflin," *New York Herald*, October 10, 1915. MS scrapbook clipping.

84. *"Miss Margaret Sargent"*: *Town Topics*, October 21, 1915, p. 5.

84. *"Finding a Venus"*: Arnold Genthe, *As I Remember* (New York: Arno Press, 1979), p. 163.

84. *"Rossetti Mouth"*: ibid. p. 169.

84. *"unconscionable old goat"*: Interview with Dorothea Lange, n.d., original transcript in the Bancroft Library, UC Berkeley. Courtesy Toby Quitslund.

85. *"Thanks for your letter"*: JS to MS, n.d.

85. *"merely a metropolis"*: Herbert D. Croly, "New York as the American Metropolis," *Architectural Record* XIII (March 1903), pp. 193–206; quoted in Trevor Fairbrother (with contributions by Theodore Stebbins, Jr., William L. Vance, Erica E. Hirshler), *The Bostonians: Painters of an Elegant Age, 1879–1930*, exhibition catalogue (Boston: Museum of Fine Arts, 1986), p. 64.

85. *"army of professionial artists"*: William Howe Downes, "Boston as an Art Centre," *New England Magazine* XXX (March–April 1904), pp. 155–66. Quoted in ibid.

86. *In the Orchard:* Oil on canvas; Daniel J. Terra Collection, Chicago.

86. *"Exhibition of Post-Impressionists"*: Headlines, *Boston Herald*, April 28, 1913, p. 1.

86. *"a lady, quite bare"*: Philip Leslie Hale, quoted in Nancy Hale, *The Life in the Studio* (New York: Avon, 1980), p. 138.

86. *"the near-Vermeer"*: *American Art News*, December 12, 1916, p. 3.

87. *The Breakfast Room:* Oil on canvas; collection The Pennsylvania Academy.

87. *Mrs. C:* The disjunction between the actual lives of Boston School models and how they were depicted is studied in Bernice Kramer Leader, *The Boston Lady as a Work of Art: Paintings by the Boston School at the Turn of the Century* (Ph.D. diss., Columbia University, 1980).

87. *"a boor"*: Ibid., p. 26.

87. *Gertrude Fiske:* Portrait of Margarett Sargent, oil on canvas, private collection.

87. *"the march of Art Amazons"*: "John Doe," *American Art News*, January 23, 1915, p. 3.

88. *"painting & drawing"*: In Charles Woodbury scrapbook, shown to me by India Woodbury, daughter-in-law of the artist, Ogunquit, Maine, August 1984.

88. *"a highclass resort":* Brochure, "An Attractive Resort on the Coast of Maine" (1920); collection York Historical Society, York, Maine.

88. *"fanatically adoring disciples":* R. H. Ives Gammell *The Boston Painters, 1900–1930* (Orleans, Mass.: Parnassus Imprints, 1986), p. 138.

88. *"virginal wayfarers":* Author interviews with Louise Tragard, Ogunquit, July 1984, July 1985.

88. *John Singer Sargent's 1921 portrait:* Collection, National Portrait Gallery, Washington, D.C.

89. *Robert Laurent:* Laurent was a boy when Field met him in Brittany and undertook his education. Laurent was one of those responsible for introducing to American sculpture the technique of direct carving, which challenged the then accepted practice of modeling and casting. Together, Field and Laurent exhibited in New York, and in Ogunquit, one taught painting and the other sculpture. They lived with Laurent's family in a big house on an island at the end of Perkins Cove.

90. *"Good-lookin'":* Phyllis Ramsdell Eaton, author interview, Ogunquit, Maine, July 1985. All PRE quotes from this interview.

90. *"for the open discussion":* Pamphlets, "Thurnscoe Forum, Ogunquit, Maine: Meetings Held Thursday Evenings for the Open Discussion of Art, Music, Literature and Kindred Subjects: Season of 1918." Original, collection George Karfiol. Courtesy Louise Tragard.

90. *"the generator":* Interior (Chicago), review of *Mr. Bonaparte of Corsica,* by John Kendrick Bangs, quoted in advertisement on back of Bangs, *A House-Boat on the Styx* (New York: Harper & Brothers, 1895).

90. *"rich and expensive":* Pamphlet, "Two Weeks in Ogunquit-by-the-Sea," York Historical Society, York, Maine.

91. *"Pine Hill Girls":* See Tragard et al., *A Century of Color* (Ogunquit: Barn Gallery Associates, 1987), p. 17.

91. *"divergence of opinion":* Charles Woodbury, Lectures of July 8, 1916–August 12, 1916; on microfilm, Woodbury Collection, Archives of American Art, roll 1255, frame 482. Courtesy Louise Tragard.

91. *"a dreadful picture":* To Daniel Sargent, among others.

91. *"throw away all tradition":* Woodbury Collection, roll 1255, frame 490, Courtesy Louise Tragard.

91. *"I will say then":* Ibid., frame 482.

92. *"You will always":* Ibid., frame 508.

92. *"I am trying":* Ibid., frame 657.

92. *four works by Charles Woodbury:* Inventory of the collection of Margarett Sargent McKean, 1966; Collection of author. Works themselves were probably destroyed by fire.

93. *"Lily, red wool":* Archibald MacLeish, *Tower of Ivory* (New Haven: Yale University Press, 1917), p. 57.

93. *"kicked her legs"*: MS's Farmington diary, final entry, n.d.

93. *"fascinated"*: Francis Hyde Bangs, Archibald MacLeish, *Letters and Verses of Archibald MacLeish, 1914–1924, together with poems sent to Francis Hyde Bangs from 1914 to 1924, together with ms. and typewritten notes of explanation by Mr. F. H. Bangs.* Unpaged. Archibald MacLeish Collection, The Yale Collection of American Literature, Beinecke Rare Book and Manuscript Library, Yale University. Hereafter referred to as Bangs material.

93. *"O my brazen prophet"*: Bangs material.

94. *"I can't see"*: Grace Allen Peabody to MS. All GAP quotes from this letter, unless otherwise noted.

95. *"what he deemed"*: Bangs material.

95. *"One doesn't tell"*: Ibid.

95. *"She is all"*: Ibid.

95. *"Lo, the lady"*: Archibald MacLeish, *Letters of Archibald MacLeish 1907–1982,* ed. R. H. Winnick (Boston: Houghton Mifflin, 1983), p. 36. The poem in a slightly different version appears as "The 'Chantress" in MacLeish's first collection, *Tower of Ivory,* p. 50.

96. *"never would have known"*: Bangs material.

96. *"Did he fear"*: Ibid.

96. *"a considerable stimulus"*: Ibid.

96. *"like silver . . . has dreamed"*: *Tower of Ivory,* pp. 15–16.

96. *"she sat, self-mimicking"*: "A Portrait," ibid., p. 36. Years before, when MacLeish sent it to Bangs, he titled it "The Showman: A Portrait of Margarett Sargent." Bangs material.

96. *"Sargent, that Archibald should"*: Bangs material.

97. *"To wind her tresses"*: Ibid.

97. *"the great Nun"*: Ibid.

97. *"She does indeed"*: Ibid.

97. *"Like moon-dark"*: "Soul-Sight," *Tower of Ivory,* p. 60.

Chapter iv

101. *"War has begun"*: *Boston Evening Transcript,* April 6, 1917, p. 1.

101. *"most beautiful girl"*: Sargent Cheever, author interview, Wellesley, November 16, 1981.

102. *"I've never lost faith"*: Francis Williams Sargent to Jane Sargent Cheever, c.1917. Courtesy Russell Lyman.

102. *"I hate to think"*: FWS, Sr., to MS, July 1, 1918.

102. *"The Cheever Boys"*: Bronze, in the collection of Sargent Cheever.

103. *"It's all there"*: Lloyd D. Lewis, "Sculpture Exhibit Is Remarkable," *Chicago Herald,* November 3, 1916. Art Institute of Chicago scrapbook.

104. *"personal note":* Quoted in Milton Brown, *The Story of the Armory Show* (New York: Joseph H. Hirshhorn Foundation, 1963), p. 78.

104. *"we wish Mr. Borglum":* Ibid., p. 83.

105. *The Craftsman:* Gutzon Borglum, "Individuality, Sincerity and Reverence in American Art," *The Craftsman* XV, no. 1 (October 1908), pp. 3–5.

105. *"no such institution":* " 'What I Would Do with $10,000,000' by Gutzon Borglum, Sculptor," clipping from *The World Magazine*, March 29, 1914. Borglum Collection, Manuscript Division, Library of Congress, Washington, D.C.

105. *"the search for country homes":* "A Greater Stamford," newspaper clipping, source unknown. Borglum Collection, Library of Congress.

105. *"My name is":* MD, author interview.

105. *"Oh no":* Edward F. Bigelow, "Beauty in the Life of a Portrayer of Beauty," *The Guide to Nature: Education and Recreation*, IV, no. 5 (September 1911). All remarks of Borglum quoted about Borgland/Nature are from this article. Borglum Collection, Library of Congress.

105. *"most sacred recess":* Untitled typescript, p. 1. Borglum Collection, Library of Congress.

106. *"Through the neck":* Drawing in MS papers.

106. *"You can see it":* William Coles, author interview, Boston, October 9, 1986.

107. *"Those three years":* Dame, "Mrs. McKean . . ." clipping.

108. *"new art realism":* New York American, February 4, 1908. MS scrapbook clipping.

108. *"pink and white painters":* Quoted in Bernard B. Perlman, *The Immortal Eight* (Westport, Conn.: North Light, 1979), p. 175.

108. *"the dangerous habit":* Margarett Sargent McKean, "George Luks," printed sheet for Luks retrospective, June 1966, Joan Peterson Gallery, Boston.

109. *"any odd kitchen implement":* Ibid.

109. *"to protect me":* Ibid.

109. *"robbed by the Huns":* MS scrapbook clipping.

110. *"independent—free life":* QASMcK to MS, August 14, 1916.

112. *"unusually light-blue":* Bangs material.

112. *"My memories":* A. MacLeish, letter to author, October 28, 1981.

112. *"the Sargent gift":* FB, author interview.

113. *"just as the canoe":* These letters turned up in MS's effects.

113. *"She had such magnetism":* BPP, author interviews, May 1979–August 1980, New York City and Southold, N.Y. All BPP quotes from these interviews, unless otherwise noted.

113. *"mentally I feel":* MS to Gutzon Borglum, n.d., Borglum Collection, Library of Congress.

113. *"pay for a car"*: Dame, "Mrs. McKean . . ."

114. *Margarett may have seen Brice:* Fanny Brice material from Barbara Grossman's excellent *Funny Woman: The Life and Times of Fanny Brice* (Bloomington and Indianapolis: Indiana University Press, 1991); Norman Katkov, *The Fabulous Fanny: The Story of Fanny Brice* (New York: Alfred A. Knopf, 1953), and a telephone interview with Brice's son, William Brice, February 27, 1988.

114. *near-underworld cronies:* Author interview with Francine Julian Clark, daughter of Frank Biscardi, Sr.

117. *"I am glad"*: FWS to MS, July 21, 1918.

117. *"Get* Town and Country": George Luks note to MS, n.d.

117. *"Miss Sargent"*: Frederick James Gregg, "Miss Sargent Models George B. Luks; Ingres at Best in Leblanc Portrait," *New York Herald,* June 29, 1919. MS scrapbook clipping.

118. *"The eye was made"*: Benjamin deCasseres, "The Fantastic George Luks," *New York Herald Tribune,* September 10, 1933, p. 11.

118. *"I had the good fortune"*: McKean, "George Luks."

118. *"Don't tell me"*: Alexander Z. Kruse, "Luks Still Lives in His Work, Wit and Wisdom," *Greenwich Villager,* February 1934, p. 12.

118. *"Gutzon Borglum critiquing"*: Such a drawing, included in an inventory of Margarett Sargent McKean's collection made in 1966, is now apparently lost.

119. *"I should have been shocked"*: Author interview with MW.

119. *"To hell with"*: Quoted in Dame, "Mrs. McKean . . ."

119. *"Spontaneity and freedom"*: McKean, "George Luks."

119. *"Art!—my slats"*: Quoted by MS, from Van Wyck Brooks, *John Sloan: A Painter's Life* (New York: Dutton, 1955) pp. 44–45.

119. *"the paint before it"*: John Sloan, in preface to catalogue for George Luks memorial exhibition at Newark Museum, October 30, 1933–January 6, 1934, p. 12.

120. *"If a man"*: Quoted in Perlman, *The Immortal Eight,* p. 151. Gwendolyn Owens, formerly of the Prendergast Project, and Nancy Mowll Matthews, Prendergast Curator, both at the Williams College Museum of Art, provided information about Prendergast and women artists, and the provenance of Prendergast works in Margarett Sargent's collection. According to Matthews, the artist rarely sold single female figure studies but often gave them away to visitors. See also Nancy Mowll Matthews, *Maurice Prendergast* (Williamstown and Munich: Williams College Museum of Art and Presel, 1990).

120. *"having bought more pictures"*: McKean, "George Luks."

121. *"We've come together"*: Quoted in Perlman, *The Immortal Eight,* p. 154.

122. *"Vulgarity smites"*: Quoted in *George Luks: An American Artist,* es-

says by Stanley L. Cuba, Nina Kasanof, and Judith O'Toole (Wilkes-Barre, Pa.: Sordoni Art Gallery, 1987), p. 28.

124. *"passes a visit"*: DS to MS, April 14, 1918.

124. *"a memorable dent"*: DS to FWS, Jr. May 1918. Courtesy Susan Sargent Cooper.

124. *"a whale of a job"*: QASMcK to MS, August 15, 1918.

124. *"You needn't worry"*: Henry Jackson (Harry) Sargent to FWS, Sr., October 28, 1918. Courtesy Susan Sargent Cooper.

125. *"sensational advance"*: Edwin L. James, "Pershing's Drive Goes On," *New York Times*, November 4, 1918, p. 1.

125. *"told to apply"*: *New York Times*, headline, November 6, 1918, p. 1.

125. *"After this armistice"*: Harry Sargent to MS, December 1, 1918.

125. *"several thousand . . . down east"*: DS to MS, November 13, 1918.

125. *"so nearly"*: MS to BP, April 23, 1947.

126. *"I always understood"*: Russell Lyman, author interview, Needham, Mass., November 1986. All RL quotes from this interview.

126. *"We must cut him down"*: DS, author interview.

126. *"She worshiped him"*: MV, author interviews, Hamilton, Mass., September 1978–June 1992. All MV quotations from these interviews.

Chapter v

129. *"Oh, Marjorie . . . married"*: This story from MD.

129. *"Why, you serpent!"*: This story from EDM, Jr., told him repeatedly by his father.

129. *"Can I do"*: MS to Jenny Sargent, n.d.

130. *"Modernists"*: This information from *American Art News*, January–May 1919.

130. *"You will notice"*: George Luks on drawing by MS.

131. *"I know it will seem"*: Letter to author from Governor Francis Sargent, FWS Jr.'s son, June 3, 1988.

131. *"When did you"*: MS scrapbook clipping.

132. *"Instead of passing"*: "John Barleycorn Died Peacefully at the Toll of 12," *New York Times*, January, 17, 1920, p. 1.

132. *"Please come pick me up"*: DS, author interview.

132. *"Francis Williams Sargent"*: *Boston Evening Transcript*, January 19, 1920. Clipping from Harvard College Archives.

133. *"To have the children"*: JS to Louise Coolidge, n.d. Courtesy Susan Sargent Cooper.

133. *"naturalistic view"*: DS, Harvard College, Class of 1913, 25th Anniversary Report, 1938, p. 736.

134. *"I cannot wait"*: JS to Louise Coolidge, n.d. Courtesy Susan Sargent Cooper.

134. *"Sails Steerage"*: Undated, unattributed clipping. Courtesy Susan Sargent Cooper.

134. *"a girl"*: Katharine Winthrop McKean (the second Mrs. QASMcK), author interview, Hamilton, Mass., August 1986.

135. *"simply a mass"*: QASMcK to MS, August 15, 1918.

135. *"I guess I will"*: Author interviews with DS, Katharine Winthrop McKean, MV.

135. *"known internationally"*: "Name Master Mind in Great Bond Plot," *New York Times*, February 1, 1920, p. 1.

135. *"500 Banks Watch"*: *New York Times*, February 22, 1920, p. 1.

136. *"Boston Symphony"*: Marian's aunt Ida Agassiz Higginson was married to its founding benefactor, the financier Henry Lee Higginson.

136. *"woman suffrage"*: In 1882, Mrs. Charles Dudley Homans, Mrs. Randolph Coolidge, and Mrs. R. C. Winthrop founded the Boston Committee of Remonstrants and with it the American antisuffrage movement. When Margarett's suffragist aunt Isabella, Jenny Sargent's sister, encountered Dan at Tremont Temple and asked his opinion of the evening's lecturer, Sylvia Pankhurst, he answered, to his aunt's chagrin, "I think she's pretty good looking!" Margaret, at nineteen, was amused at the combination when a 1912 dinner conversation took up "Guinea pigs and votes for women" and, when her sister had a son, rejoiced, "I am not patriotic for my race."

137. *"who were at the time"*: QASMcK, Harvard College, Class of 1913, 25th Anniversary Report, 1938, p. 567.

137. *"Goodness!"*: Katharine Peabody Loring's remark is quoted in Joseph E. Garland, *Boston's Gold Coast: The North Shore 1890–1929* (Boston: Little, Brown, 1981), p. 124.

139. *"the biggest kind of a surprise"*: *Town Topics*, August 5, 1920, p. 6.

139. *"Leaving for Kings Chapel"*: MD, author interview.

140. *"You think"*: Identical stories of Margarett's account of the wedding trip were told me by MW, Stephen Vernon (November 1989), and BW (March 1982).

140. *"What's the definition"*: BW, author interview, Newport, R.I., March 20–21, 1982.

141. *Agassiz Hotel:* An apartment house built in 1872 by Shaw's great-uncle Henry Lee Higginson, one of three such buildings in the Back Bay, which accommodated the "newly wed and the nearly dead" (a phrase quoted without attribution in Douglass Shand Tucci, *Built in Boston: City and Suburb* [Boston: New York Graphic Society, 1978], p. 101). The address was 191 Commonwealth Avenue.

141. *"They were spellbinding"*: HMcK, author interviews, Manchester,

Mass., August and November 1980. All HMcK quotes from these interviews, unless otherwise noted.

142. *"Drop dead"*: Mrs. Winston (C.Z.) Guest, author interview, Old Westbury, N.Y., November 1989. All CZG quotes from this interview.

143. *"She thinks like a man"*: Quoted in an interview with Phyllis Leland, daughter-in-law of Joseph Leland, Beverly, Mass., October 1986.

143. *"She had the fattest lines"*: *Variety*, June 24, 1921, p. 17. Quoted in Grossman, *Funny Woman*, p. 123.

145. *"How could that awful woman"*: Quoted by Walter Vanderburgh in an unpublished typescript about George Luks. Courtesy Arthur Lewis.

145. *"I have lived"*: Quoted by Harley Perkins in *Boston Evening Transcript*, August 11, 1923, p. 6.

146. *"Sorry I'm late"*: This story from DS.

146. *"The work wreaks"*: *Boston Evening Transcript*, n.d., MS scrapbook clipping. *The Wrestlers* was exhibited at the Boston Art Club in January 1923.

146. *"in her artistic efforts"*: *Boston Evening Transcript*, August 11, 1923, p. 6.

148. *"engaged in what might"*: QASMcK, Harvard College, Class of 1913, 25th Anniversary Report, p. 567.

148. *"a Boston arrogance"*: JMcKM, unpublished memoir, 1973.

149. *"a born loser"*: SMcK, author interview, Rumson, N.J., April 1987. All SMcK quotes from this interview.

149. *"At times she drank"*: John Spanbauer, author interview, Brighton, Mass., June 1991. All JS quotes from this interview.

149. *"feeling deathly"*: MS diary, January 5, 1912.

151. *"May God bless"*: George Luks to MS, n.d.

151. *"I don't remember"*: Quoted by JMcKM in conversation, c.1972.

152. *"claimed the Greeks"*: Harley Perkins, *Boston Evening Transcript*, n.d. MS scrapbook clipping.

152. *"To a remarkable degree"*: Ibid.

152. *"Art World Amazed"*: *The Art News*, January 2, 1926, p. 1.

153. *"artistic anarchists"*: Kenyon Cox, "The 'Modern' Spirit in Art: Some Reflections Inspired by the Recent International Exhibition," *Harper's Weekly*, March 15, 1913, p. 57.

154. *"the fascinating Mrs. Q. A. Shaw McKean"*: *Town Topics*, 1926, n.d. MS scrapbook clipping.

154. *"She had a lot"*: Antoinette Kraushaar, author interview, New York, June 1979. All AK quotes from this interview.

154. *"an innovation"*: Henry McBride, *New York Sun*, March 6, 1926, n.p. MS scrapbook clipping.

154. *"amazing talent"*: *The Art News*, March 6, 1926, p. 7. MS scrapbook clipping.

154. *"the glamor":* *New York Herald Tribune,* March 7, 1926, n.p. MS scrapbook clipping.

154. *Helen Appleton Read:* "Boston Woman Shows Notable Work at Kraushaar Galleries," *Brooklyn Eagle,* March 7, 1926, n.p. MS scrapbook clipping.

155. *"that rare apparition":* "Kraushaar's New Find," *New York American,* March 14, 1926. n.p. MS scrapbook clipping.

Chapter vi

160. *"they could run very fast":* Jenny McKean Moore, unpublished memoir, 1973.

161. *"took to affairs":* EL, author interview, Beverly, Mass., November 1980. All EL quotes from this interview.

161. *"made me careless":* quoted by MV.

161. *"I've been seeing":* MD, author interview.

162. *"Though slight":* Forbes Watson, *New York World,* April 3, 1927. MS scrapbook clipping.

162. *three new plaster panels:* These were more engaging than those of 1926: *Nude* seemed almost a pastiche of the idea of a rhythmic study, a reclining nude with a fan of nude figures in the background, prescient of Busby Berkeley; the faces of the five subjects of *Heads,* a horizontal overmantel, "expressed character rather than mere mood," according to Helen Appleton Read, who also speculated in her review that Margarett was probably "the sole exponent of the decorative possibilities of colored bas relief in this country" and noted in the new work "a more profound sense of form which adds to the richness and variety of surface." *Brooklyn Eagle,* April 3, 1927. MS scrapbook clipping.

163. *"new-found vivacity":* Helen Appleton Read, *Brooklyn Eagle,* February 12, 1928. MS scrapbook clipping.

163. *"free expression and simplicity":* Henry McBride, *New York Sun,* February 11, 1928, p. 10.

163. *"It is here that a Bostonian":* Harley Perkins, *Boston Evening Transcript,* December 10, 1927, p. 10.

163. *insurgent painters:* A painter himself, Harley Perkins was a member of the Whitney Studio Club in New York and of a group of artists called the Boston Five, who showed together and fought to open venues in Boston for progressive art. Margarett's connection to the Five was through Perkins and Marian Monks Chase, a watercolorist who showed at Montross in New York.

163. *"Modernists respect":* Katharine K. Crosby, "Paintings by Margaret [*sic*] Sargent, Boston Artist, to Be Shown in New York Soon—Canvases Pos-

sess Modern Spirit, Design and the Influence of Sculptural Knowledge," *Boston Evening Transcript*, December 29, 1928, n.p. MS scrapbook clipping.

163. *"We must be called something":* Florence Cowles, "Mrs. Quincy A. Shaw McKean's Beverly Home Growth from 280-Year-Old House of the King's Tax Collector," *Boston Sunday Post*, August 10, 1930, n.p. MS scrapbook clipping.

164. *Head of the Artist's First Wife:* The painting, now known as *Woman Wearing a Necklace of Gems*, Paris, 1901, is in the Ayala and Sam Zacks Collection, Toronto, Zervos, VI, 85. I have never seen the Derain and have been unable to locate the Vlaminck, of which I have seen a black and white photograph.

164. *"for the McKean collection":* MS scrapbook clipping with illustration is unattributed. Another clip, from *The Art Digest* (Mid-February 1928, p. 10), reported that the *Transcript* had noted the Picasso purchase by "Mrs. Q. A. Shaw McKean, a new name among collectors. She has a flair for Modernism, and the *Transcript* says she recently purchased a fine Derain head and Vlaminck landscape."

164. *"In a long essay":* Harley Perkins, *Boston Evening Transcript*, December 9, 1925, p. 12.

164. *acceptance in Boston:* The renaissance would be short-lived; by 1930, the Boston Art Club was back in the grip of conservatives.

165. *"made gloriously beautiful":* Frederic Clay Bartlett, *Sortova Kindofa Journey of My Own* (Privately printed, 1965), p. 10.

165. *"which someday":* Quoted in Courtney Graham Donnell, "Frederic Clay and Helen Birch Bartlett: The Collectors," *Museum Studies* 12, no. 2, 1986, The Art Institute of Chicago, p. 92.

165. *"Americans who wish":* Ibid., p. 94.

166. *Bostonians had to wait:* Isabella Gardner had been given a rather restrained Matisse, which hung at Fenway Court, but John Walker, later director of the National Gallery, told me in an interview (Fishers Island, N.Y., 1990) that when he came to Harvard as a freshman in 1926, "There was nowhere in Boston to see a Picasso!" Robert Treat Paine II and John T. Spaulding bought Post-Impressionists, but their collections did not come to the Museum of Fine Arts until after 1935.

166. *"a tight lid . . . in ambush":* Harley Perkins, "Boston Notes," *The Arts* IX (April 1926), p. 211.

166. *"reactionary toward no":* Catalogue of First Annual Exhibition of the Boston Society of Independent Artists, Inc., Jan. 15–Feb. 16, 1927." Quoted in Jane Bock, "The Boston Society of Independent Artists," manuscript, April 20, 1978 (which also provided a good chronology), p. 2. Courtesy Walter Kilham.

166. *"one of the most striking":* Harley Perkins, *Boston Evening Transcript*, January 15, 1927, p. 10.

166. *"tea room and eating place"*: Ibid.

167. *"robust vitality . . . percentage"*: Ibid.

168. *"Surrealiste"*: Roland Balay, author interviews, New York, February, April, May 1981. All RB quotes from these interviews, unless otherwise noted.

169. *"George Luks met me"*: MS to Adelia Moore, May 2, 1971, recorded in her unpublished journal. Courtesy AM.

169. *"Your photograph"*: MS to the author, July 24, 1971.

169. *"Velázquez, he was"*: McKean, "George Luks."

172. *her 1960 autobiography:* Mercedes deAcosta, *Here Lies the Heart* (New York: Arno Press, 1975). See also Barry Paris, *Garbo* (New York: Alfred A. Knopf, 1995) pp. 257–259.

172. *"A Boston marriage"*: Daisy Oakley, author interview, Bedford, Mass., November 1990.

172. *"Oh, I'm sure"*: Alida Lessard, author interview, September 1994.

173. *"bisexual glasses"*: Quoted by Williams Alfred, author interview, Cambridge, Mass., March 1988. All WA quotes from this interview.

174. *"Everyone knew it"*: Nancy Cochrane Palmer, author interview, Hamilton, Mass., June 1990. All NCP quotes from this interview.

174. *"I loved Miss Sears"*: Author conversation with Right Reverend Paul Moore, 1980.

174. *"sporting . . . the crash"*: *Sunday News,* August 27, 1933, p. 10. MS scrapbook clipping.

176. *"Miss Sargent seems"*: Henry McBride, *New York Sun,* January 17, 1929, n.p. MS scrapbook clipping.

176. *"a more fiery Pegasus"*: *American Art News,* January 12, 1929, p. 7.

176. *"Her subjects"*: Forbes Watson, *New York World,* January 13, 1929, n.p. MS scrapbook clipping.

176. *"Unfortunately"*: "New Oils by Margaret [*sic*] Sargent," *Vanity Fair,* February 1929, p. 111.

177. *Les Arts à Paris:* Jacques Villeneuve, January 1929, p. 2 (translation by the author). In 1928 in Paris, Margarett took Betty Parsons to lunch at Paul Guillaume's, and he made cubist drawings of both women. Also at the table that day were his famously beautiful young wife, Dr. Albert Barnes, and Frederic Bartlett, who frequently escorted Margarett in Paris. Before the war, the poet Guillaume Apollinaire had introduced Paul Guillaume to the painters of Montparnasse. Guillaume became Modigliani's first dealer and the first dealer in Paris to organize a commercial exhibition of African art. Early in his acquisitions career, Dr. Barnes chose him as his representative, and by the end of the twenties, Guillaume was the most important advocate of Montparnasse on the Right Bank.

177. *"richer than most"*: Janet Flanner (Genêt), *Paris Was Yesterday,* ed. Irving Drutman (New York, Viking, 1972), p. 4.

178. *"10,000 Yankee"*: *New York Herald*, Paris edition, February 12, 1924, p. 1.

178. *"In those days"*: Gertrude Stein, *The Autobiography of Alice B. Toklas* (New York: Alfred A. Knopf, 1933; Vintage edition, n.d.), p. 197.

178. *"One warm night"*: Elizabeth Eyre, "Letters of Elizabeth," *Town and Country*, May 15, 1926, p. 58.

180. *"crêpe uni couleur"*: Sales receipt, "Mrs. Shaw McKean," Ed. Charvet & Fils, 8 Place Vendôme, Paris, 5 April 1928.

180. *"to be caught in the exact center"*: Rosemary Carr Benét, "Our Paris Letter," *Town and Country*, April 1, 1928, p. 72.

180. *"those of her works"*: *New York Herald*, Paris edition, March 4, 1924, p. 5.

180. *"he was far more"*: MS to BP, December 2, 1954.

180. *tore up:* "Tore Up Ship Ticket," *New York Times*, March 26, 1935, p. 16.

181. *"the finest flower garden"*: Flanner, *Paris Was Yesterday*, p. xvi.

182. *"big old daylit studio"*: Berenice Abbott, author interview, Monson, Maine, June 1990. All BA quotes from this interview, unless otherwise noted.

Chapter vii

187. *"The District Offers"*: North Shore *Breeze and Reminder*, June 19, 1928, p. 1.

188. *"busy with her art work"*: Ibid., September 16, 1926, p. 32.

188. *"selected groups of paintings"*: Ibid., May 4, 1928, p. 26.

190. *"They were physically drawn"*: Edward Weeks, author interview, Boston, November 1980. All EW quotes from this interview.

190. *"Shaw always stood"*: Garson Kanin, author conversation, New York, April 1989.

190. *"She was so artistic"*: MTS, author interview, Hamilton, Mass., June 23, 1979. All MTS quotes from this interview.

191. *"Can kill leopards"*: Promotional brochure, Prides Hill Kennels, Afghan Hounds, n.d. My source for the history of Afghan breeding was Constance O. Miller and Edward M. Gilbert, Jr., *The Complete Afghan Hound* (New York: Howell Book House, 1971).

191. *"You couldn't believe it"*: William Roerick, author interview, Tyringham, Mass., July 1979.

191. *"She would have been"*: JW, author interviews, Fishers Islands, N.Y., August 1989; Sussex, U.K., November 1989. All JW quotes from these interviews, unless otherwise noted.

193. *"full-fledged"*: John Neary to MS, n.d.

195. *"A lion with a wire body"*: Margaret Calder Hayes, *Three Alexander Calders* (New York: Universe Books, 1987), p. 209.

195. *"He was lightfingered"*: Billy Kluver and Julie Martin, *Kiki's Paris: Artists and Lovers, 1900–1930* (New York: Abrams, 1989), p. 239n.

195. *"I took the circus"*: Quoted in Jean Lipman with Nancy Foote, eds., *Calder's Circus* (New York: E. P. Dutton in association with the Whitney Museum of American Art, 1972), p. 14.

196. *"Ladies and gentlemen"*: The sources of my description of the circus are the circus itself, on exhibition at the Whitney Museum, New York; the accompanying videotape; Thomas Wolfe, *You Can't Go Home Again* (New York: Scribner, 1934), pp. 273–83; Carole Klein, *Aline: The First Biography of Aline Bernstein, Famed Stage Designer and Mistress of Thomas Wolfe* (New York: Harper & Row, 1979), pp. 248–53.

197. *"Why is there no modern art"*: JW, author interview.

197. *"the work of actuality"*: Quoted in Caroline A. Jones, *Modern Art at Harvard* (New York: Abbeville Press, 1985), p. 44.

197. *"Why don't you"*: Quoted by Agnes Mongan, author interview, Cambridge, Mass., March 1988.

197. *"excessively affluent"*: John Walker, *Self-Portrait with Donors* (Boston: Atlantic/Little, Brown, 1974), p. 4.

197. *"dark, saturnine"*: Ibid., p. 22.

197. *"a combination . . . Eric Gill"*: Lincoln Kirstein, letter quoted in *The Bostonians: Painters of an Elegant Age, 1870–1930* (Boston: Boston Museum of Fine Arts, 1986), p. 92n.

198. *"the work of thirty-three"*: Harvard University Art Museums Archives, Harvard Society for Contemporary Art files, First Annual Report, February 1929–February 1930.

198. *"not then considered art"*: Including Japanese and English pottery and weaving by people "wholly uninfluenced by the methods of modern commercial production" (ibid.); American cartoons, including examples from daily newspapers, and photography as "an individual medium of artistic expression." Harvard University Art Museum Archives, HSCA files, Second Annual Report, February 1930–February 1931. For a full account of the history of the Harvard Society for Contemporary Art and its influence on the founding of the Museum of Modern Art, see Nicholas Fox Weber, *Patron Saints: Five Rebels Who Opened America to a New Art* (New York: Alfred A. Knopf, 1992).

198. *" 'machine-for-living-in' "*: Harvard Society, First Annual Report.

199. *"the genealogy"*: Alfred Barr, *The Museum of Modern Art, First Loan Exhibition, New York, November, 1929; Cézanne, Gauguin, Seurat, Van Gogh* (New York: Museum of Modern Art, 1929), p. 11. Barr was a Harvard graduate, an alumnus of Sachs's museum course, and in the mid-twenties taught art history at Wellesley, where he mounted exhibitions of modern art and hosted multidisciplinary panels of modernist writers and composers.

199. *"For soft contours"*: Ibid., p. 13.

199. *"too broad a caricature"*: Ives Gammell, unpublished diary, January 7, 1930. Courtesy Williams Coles.

200. *"First reaction"*: H. Von Erffa, *Chicago Evening Post Magazine of the Art World*, February 25, 1930, p. 12. MS scrapbook clipping.

200. *"She is an out-and-out"*: "G.K.," *Boston Evening Transcript*, February 12, 1930. MS scrapbook clipping.

204. *"They all drank"*: RRW, author interview, Manchester, Mass., May 1991. All RRW quotes from this interview.

205. *" 'Beyond Good & Evil' "*: MS to Frederic Bartlett, The Arts Club of Chicago Archives, The Newberry Library, Chicago.

206. *"married, but"*: Isabel Jarvis, telephone interview, November 1980.

206. *"They have all the beauty"*: "Cousin Eve," *Chicago Tribune*, November 30, 1930, sec. 8, p. 1.

206. *"began with Cézanne"*: in C.J. Bulliet, *The Significant Moderns* (New York: Covici Friede, 1936), p. v.

207. *"where 'Modernism' "*: C. J. Bulliet, *Chicago Evening Post Magazine of the Art World*, December 2, 1930, p. 1.

207. *"Burlesque Picture"*: *New York World*, January 11, 1931, n.p. MS scrapbook clipping.

207. *"full-fledged palette"*: *New York Post*, January 10, 1931, n.p. MS scrapbook clipping.

207. *"If she is ever able"*: Henry McBride, *New York Sun*, January 13, 1931, n.p. MS scrapbook clipping.

208. *"A little more concentration"*: Margaret Breunig, *New York Times*, January 10, 1931, p. 60.

208. *"at restaurants"*: "Margarett Sargent's One-Man Show," *The Breeze*, n.d. MS scrapbook clipping.

210. *"Applies Her Artistic"*: Florence Cowles article (newspaper unnamed in MS scrapbook clipping) was syndicated, often with cuts, in newspapers as far away as Colorado Springs. With slight changes, it ran under headline "Mrs. Quincy A. Shaw McKean's Beverly Home Growth from 280-Year-Old House of the King's Tax Collector," in *Boston Sunday Post*, August 10, 1930, which MS also preserved in her scrapbook.

211. *"Into such a setting"*: A.J. Philpott, "Margarett Sargent Exhibition Popular," *Boston Globe*, n.d. MS scrapbook clipping.

211. *"indisposed"*: *Boston Transcript*, n.d. MS scrapbook clipping.

Chapter viii

216. *"the leading figure"*: Alfred Franz Cochrane, "Margarett Sargent's Paintings," *Boston Evening Transcript*, March 26, 1932, p. 10.

216. *"New England Society of Contemporary Artists"*: Formed by rebel members of the Boston Art Club (including Frederic Bartlett) in 1928, it showed for a while in Magnolia on the North Shore and lay moribund for two years until revived by this exhibition.

216. *The Watteau Hat:* Black-and-white reproductions of Margarett's portrait of Betty Fittamore illustrated reviews of the New England's Society's exhibition in both *Art and Archeology* XXXIII, no. 4 (July–August 1932), p. 177, and *Boston Evening Transcript,* June 25, 1932. MS scrapbook clipping.

217. *"that Sargent girl!"*: Alfred Franz Cochrane, *Boston Evening Transcript.* MS scrapbook clipping.

217. *"a gentleman not an ape"*: Mrs. Forest Shea, letter to the editor, *Boston Herald,* April 1, 1933. MS scrapbook clipping.

217. *a buxom brunette:* George Luks, oil on canvas, c.1906, Butler Institute of American Art.

218. *"Margarett was not an introspective person"*: DDeS, author interview, Beverly Farms, Mass., June 1979. All DDeS quotes from this interview.

219. *"feminine charm"*: Louise Tarr, "Why Feminine Charm Snares More Hearts Than Mere Beauty—and Is More Dangerous: Mrs. Sargent McKean, Noted Boston Society Leader, Famed as an Artist, Reveals Woman's Most Closely Guarded Secret—the Gift That Made Garbo, That Other Women Fear and That Turns Men into Slaves and Holds Them Without Dread of Rivalry," *Boston Sunday Post,* 2nd Color Feature Section, October 9, 1932, p. 3.

220. *Paris Tribune:* Also "News of Americans in Europe," *New York Herald,* Paris edition, June 8, 1933, p. 4.

221. *"his sapphire-blue eyes"*: Janet Flanner, *Janet Flanner's World, Uncollected Writings, 1932–1975,* ed. Irving Drutman (New York: Harcourt Brace Jovanovich, 1979), p. 9.

221. *"I thought he was absolutely mad"*: Quoted by AH, author interview, Boston, June 1987.

221. *"even when you were broke"*: Quoted without attribution in Tony Allan, *The Glamor Years: Paris 1919–1940* (New York: Gallery Books, 1977), p. 163.

222. *"Intellectual sensuality"*: Tarr, op. cit.

223. *"fit as always"*: *House Beautiful,* December 1933, pp. 248A–249A.

224. *"a rare bird"*: "Luks Lecture Drives Most of 500 from Hall," *New York Herald Tribune,* December 22, 1932. MS scrapbook clipping. Excerpted as "Luks Speaks Up," *The Art Digest,* January 1, 1933, p. 12.

225. *"Lusty" Luks:* "George B. Luks Found Dead in 6th Av. at Dawn," *New York Herald Tribune,* October 30, 1933, n.p. MS scrapbook clipping.

226. *"studying the effect of the sunrise"*: Ibid.

226. *"Cara mater"*: JMcK letter to MS, October 25, 1933.

226. *"The details of his death"*: McKean, "George Luks."

229. *"the boys know"*: Story from HMcK.

230. *"And Shaw came to the hotel!"*: MS conversation with author, c.1973.

231. *"They went abroad"*: The gossip about Margarett's affair with Harry Snelling, gathered from many interviews—MTS, Ted Weeks, DS, FB, RRW, MV—are a cacophony of contradictions and rumor one-upmanship. I've tried to reproduce the effect.

232. *"I'll ruin you in business"*: Quoted by Ted Weeks.

232. *"attractive to women"*: DS.

233. *"Read. Write"*: Diary kept by Margie on 1934–1935 trip to Europe. Courtesy MV.

234. *"Isolation is delicious"*: MS sketchbook, c.1934–1940.

235. *"Victorious happiness"*: MS sketchbook, July 22, 1934.

236. *"I don't do portraits"*: Quoted by Hilary Martin, author interview, Newport, R.I., February 1980. Laurencin was indeed turning down portraits at the time.

236. *Butsy McKean:* Many Paris details and all quotes attributed to Butsy are from EB, author interview, Beverly Farms, Mass., October 1986.

237. *"don't speak French!"*: This story and many details of the stay in Germany are from HPMcK, author interviews.

238. *"storm of protest"*: "Hitler Lieutenant Refuses Bid as Harvard Commencement Aide," *New York Times*, April 5, 1934, p. 1.

238. *the* Harvard Crimson: "Urges Harvard Honor Hanfstaengl by Degree," *New York Times*, June 13, 1934, p. 13.

238. *"providential . . . forty-eight hours"*: "World Now Safe, Hanfstaengl Says," *New York Times*, July 2, 1934, p. 2.

238. *"restored to normal soon . . . friendships"*: "Hanfstaengl Gives Multi-Topic Talk," *New York Times*, June 18, 1934, p. 8.

240. *"McKean Twins"*: April 26, 1936, source unknown. MS scrapbook clipping.

240. *"Mrs. Quincy Adams Shaw McKean"*: Newspaper photo, July 24, 1936, source unknown. MS scrapbook clipping.

240. *"never be afflicted in this way"*: Quoted in MS letter to MTS, postmarked September 4, 1936.

240. *"I dread tomorrow"*: Ibid.

Chapter ix

245. *a young art historian:* Ingrid Schaffner.

251. *"being ditched by Margie"*: Benjamin Bradlee, author interview, Washington, D.C., December 2, 1988. All BB quotes from this interview.

252. *"Well, Mrs. McKean"*: Constance Bradlee Devens, author interview, Marlborough, Mass., November 1991.

253. *"One Christmas Eve":* Story from EB, among others.

255. *"Chick" Austin:* As soon as he was named director in 1927, Austin bumped the Atheneum's Connecticut Impressionists to the basement, opened a loan exhibition of old-master drawings from Paul Sachs's collection and then an exhibition of works by Braque, Cézanne, Gauguin, Laurencin, Matisse, Toulouse-Lautrec, and Van Gogh, all borrowed from galleries in New York and Paris. Armed with a recent two-million-dollar bequest to the museum, he bought not only Tintoretto, Fra Angelico, Daumier, and Goya but Hopper and Demuth. He soon raised money for a new building, to include galleries, and a theater for productions of the Friends and Enemies of Modern Music, a showcase for young composers like Thomson, Walter Piston, and George Antheil.

255. *"relaxed visage":* Virgil Thomson, *Virgil Thomson* (New York: Da Capo, 1967), p. 215.

256. *"the R months":* John Houseman, *Run-through* (New York: Simon & Schuster, 1972), p. 98.

256. *"extremely bisexual":* Bowden Broadwater, author interview, November 1992.

256. *"smiling and efficient":* Houseman, *Run-through,* p. 99.

256. *lead to collaboration:* It was at the Askews' one Sunday that Chick Austin met Virgil Thomson; there also that Kirk directed John Houseman to have the conversation with Thomson that resulted in Houseman's directing *Four Saints in Three Acts.*

257. *"Mrs. McKean was extraordinary":* Constance Bradlee letter to Frederick Bradlee, July 17, 1937. Courtesy FB.

257. *"like a schoolgirl":* Hope Williams, author interview, New York, April 1984. All HW quotes from this interview.

258. *"an experiment": Virgil Thomson,* p. 75.

258. *Father Thomas Feeney:* "Father Tom" was one of three brilliant Jesuit brothers. John had a parish in New Hampshire, and Leonard, the editor of the Jesuit weekly *America,* would come to national prominence in the 1940s at the center of what came to be called the Boston heresy case, which resulted in his being censured by the Pope. Leonard was a published poet and a humorist, whose *Fish on Friday* had been a best-seller in 1934; later, Teddy Chanler would collaborate with him on a sequence of songs for children. Dan and Louise Sargent became followers of Leonard Feeney, as did Teddy and Maria Chanler. Margarett was never drawn to his kind of demagoguery and conservatism. For an extremely biased account of the Feeney controversy, see the book by his associate, Catherine Goddard Clarke, *The Loyolas and the Cabots* (Boston: Ravengate Press, 1950).

259. *"A lot of fancy people":* Paul Moore, author interview, New York, October 1991.

259. *"Wouldn't it be nice":* Account of Margarett's conversion from Teddy Chanler letter to DS, August 16, 1937.

262. *"Very smart":* Jenny Reed Slote, telephone interview, May 1993.

263. *"saying all the right things":* Lyn Austin, author interview, New York, March 9, 1993.

263. *"Mr. Cross":* Jenny McKean, loose-leaf binder of Vassar writings, c.1939–1940; collection of the author.

265. *"A gallery isn't":* Lee Hall, *Betty Parsons, Artist, Dealer, Collector* (New York: Harry N. Abrams, 1991), p. 77.

268. *"She was no longer":* Jane Bowles, *My Sister's Hand in Mine: The Collected Works of Jane Bowles* (New York: Ecco Press, 1978), p. 49.

268. *"a major minor writer":* Quoted in "Notes from the Director," program insert, *In the Summer House,* Vivian Beaumont Theater, Lincoln Center, New York, Summer 1993.

268. *"a fear of dogs":* Millicent Dillon, *A Little Original Sin: The Life and Works of Jane Bowles* (New York: Holt, Rinehart & Winston, 1981), p. 26.

270. *"They had conversation":* Oliver Smith, author interview, New York, February 18, 1987. All OS quotes from this interview.

270. *"My husband never loved me":* The play was *In the Summer House,* in Bowles, *My Sister's Hand,* p. 263.

271. *"What type are you?":* Robert Fizdale, conversation with author, June 1992.

272. *"the only mother":* JMcK conversation with author, c.1966.

273. *"the watercolor . . . keep on":* MS to SMcK, December 29, 1944.

Chapter x

277. *"The whole place":* MS to SMcK, December 29, 1945.

278. *"a home-like":* Four Winds promotional brochure, c.1944. Courtesy Billie Sorenson, director of public relations, Four Winds Hospital.

278. *more apt to return:* In "Convulsive Therapy and the Course of Bipolar Illness, 1940–1949," *Convulsive Therapy* IV, 2 (New York: Raven Press, 1988), pp. 126–32, George Winokur and Arnold Kadrmas reported they had come to this conclusion after scrutinizing the records of ninety-three Massachusetts patients given shock between 1940 and 1949. No clear reason for their findings emerged, but the authors did not rule out that shock itself altered the biological course of the condition.

278. *Later research:* This assertion has always been controversial; when, at the 1976 annual meeting of the American Psychiatric Association, Dr. John Friedberg gave a paper insisting "that, despite the importance of a negative finding, there has not been a single detailed report of a normal human brain after shock," he was vigorously rebutted, and his methods of data collection were criticized. John Friedberg, M.D., "Shock Treatment, Brain Damage, and Memory Loss: A Neurological Perspective," *American Journal of Psychiatry* 134:9 (September 1977), pp. 1010–18.

278. *No one then theorized:* In "Bipolar Affective Disorder and Alcoholism," *American Journal of Psychiatry* 131:10 (October 1974), pp. 1130–33, James R. Morrison, M.D., theorized that alcoholism was a disease distinct from bipolar affective disorder and suggested that for effective recovery, both diseases had to be treated.

279. *"divinely menacing behavior":* Phyllis Chesler, *Women and Madness* (New York: Doubleday, 1972), p. xx.

279. *Kay Redmond Jamison: Touched with Fire: Manic Depressive Illness and the Artistic Temperament* (New York: The Free Press, 1993).

279. *"He buckled them":* Sylvia Plath, *The Bell Jar* (New York: Bantam, 1972), pp. 117–18.

282. *Writing to Betty Parsons:* MS wrote to BP consistently between April 1945 and March 1959, and with particular frequency during her second Four Winds stay (May–June 1946). MS's descriptions of hospital life, of Jenny's graduation, and of her family relationships during that period are drawn from these letters, as are her remarks to BP, unless otherwise noted. The letters were given to me after her death by BP's friend Gwyn Metz and her biographer Lee Hall.

283. *In long letters:* Letters from JB to MS have been lost, but MS refers to them in hers to BP.

290. *"odd restaurants . . . strong happiness":* MS to BP, April 23, 1947.

291. *"Mrs. McKean":* Dame, *Boston Sunday Herald,* c.1948.

292. *"get the wagon":* BW, author interview, Newport, R.I., March 20–21, 1982. All BW quotes from this interview, unless otherwise noted.

292. *When Robert Lowell arrived:* See Ian Hamilton, *Robert Lowell, A Biography* (New York: Random House, 1982), pp. 158–60.

293. *"Half dozen treatments":* MS to BP from Baldpate, March 11, 1948.

293. *"To all persons":* Copy of citation mailed to BW, May 9, 1949.

294. *"little we can do":* A. C. Malm to BW, March 1, 1949.

294. *"In accordance with":* Dr. George Schlomer to Mrs. Barclay Warburton III (Margie), June 8, 1949.

294. *"You could tell":* George Dix, author interview, New York, January 1994.

295. *"It is a delight . . . in ink":* MS sketchbook, Boca Grande, 1949.

296. *"nice and quiet":* Dr. Max Rinkel to BW, November 15, 1949.

296. *"I think it unlikely":* Dr. Robert Fleming to Alvin Hochberg, January 15, 1964.

296. *"Blow up 57th Street":* MS to BP from Vicksburg, Miss., April 28, 1950.

297. *"her knowledge of painting":* Harry Martin, author interviews, Gloucester, Mass., July 1982, April 1984. All HM quotes from these interviews.

297. *"keener . . . uncomfortable":* Jane Bowles, *Out in the World: Selected Letters of Jane Bowles, 1935–1970,* ed. Millicent Dillon (Santa Barbara: Black Sparrow Press, 1985), pp. 168–69.

299. *"central heating":* Quoted by Harry Martin in author interview.

299. *"I'd give anything":* Herbert "Whitey" Lutz to BP, August 3, 1950.

300. *"curious and interesting":* Janet Flanner, *Paris Journal, 1944–1965* (New York and London: Harcourt Brace Jovanovich, Harvest edition, 1977), p. 197.

301. *"with my acrobatic finches":* MS to BP, December 2, 1954.

301. *"no checking account":* MS to BP, June 10, 1954.

301. *"her past happy time":* Joseph Gelli to MV, October 12, 1957.

302. *"And don't you admire":* MS to BP, June 10, 1954.

302. *"incredible magic":* MS to BB from Florence, January 14, 1954. Margarett's letters are in the library at I Tatti and are quoted courtesy of Villa I Tatti, Harvard University Center for Italian Renaissance Studies, The Berenson Archive. BB's side of the correspondence, referred to in her letters, has vanished.

302. *"the one un lighted gallery":* MS to BB, November 10, 1954.

303. *"a Jane Austen character":* MS to BB, January 9, 1954.

303. *"a voluntary prisoner":* MS to BB, April 8, 1954.

303. *"overlooking . . . in bloom":* MS to BB, March 27, 1954.

304. *"true to your beliefs":* MS to BP, June 10, 1954.

304. *"obstinately is not gray":* Ibid.

305. *"very good shape":* Quoted in Oliver Wolcott to Mrs. Barclay Warburton III (MV), June 18, 1953.

305. *"Why don't you do":* MV, author interview.

305. *"rightly considered fortunate":* MS to BP, October 26, 1954.

306. *"a little sadistic":* Dr. Harold W. Lovell, M.D., to Margarett's lawyer, Walter Powers, April 4, 1962.

306. *"I feel reasonably certain":* Dr. Robert Fleming to SMcK, Jr., December 17, 1962.

306. *"like ice":* HMcK to SMcK, MV, JMcKM, DS, and Walter Powers, January 29, 1963.

307. *"this extraordinary person":* Gloria Braggiotti Etting, author interview, Philadelphia, April 1987.

307. *"She is very ill":* HPMcK to JMcKM, January 30, 1963.

307. *"present state":* Quoted by HPMcK in a letter to SMcK, February 18, 1963.

308. *"reacted violently . . . uncommon":* Memorandum of family conference, May 10, 1963, at office of Dr. Robert Fleming, Boston.

308. *"mentally ill person":* Commonwealth of Massachusetts, Probate Court, Docket #276047.

308. *"The change in my life":* MS to BP, June 10, 1954.

308. *"at Westwood":* AH to Joseph Gelli, May 27, 1964.

308. *"Am being mesmerized":* MS to BP, telegram, February 23, 1965.

309. *"all I know about art":* AH, author interview, Boston, June 1987.

310. *"Simplification":* MS sketchbook, Boca Grande, 1949.

310. *"None of them":* Dr. Raymond Adams, author interview, Boston, October 1987.

311. *"she had parties":* Aimée Lamb, author interview, Boston, October 1986.

311. *"such interesting people!":* Sylvia Cox, author interview, Boston, April 1984. All SC quotes from this interview.

311. *"For God's sake, Russell":* Russell Lyman, author interview, Needham, Mass., November 1986.

311. *"We talked about trees":* Stephen Vernon, author interview, Hamilton, Mass., April 1984. All SV quotes from this interview.

312. *"I've become a Democrat":* MW, author interviews.

313. *"We'd talk about flowers":* Richard Demenocal, author interview, Cambridge, December 1980.

313. *"Well, Mrs. McKean":* This story from AH.

314. *"Sargent on a city street":* Bangs material.

Index

Illustration Credits

Chapter-opening photographs:

Black-and-white insert:

Color insert:

THE WHITE BLACKBIRD

Honor Moore

READING GROUP GUIDE

THE WHITE BLACKBIRD

Honor Moore

HONOR MOORE ON WRITING *THE WHITE BLACKBIRD* AND BEYOND

I was in my late twenties when I started to write seriously. In those early days I wrote only poems, and I hoped to follow in my artist grandmother's footsteps. She was still alive then, and once in a while I would send her a poem and she would write, in turquoise on pink paper or vice versa, some extravagant compliment. I always knew that she had stopped painting, but I hadn't seen any of her paintings, only one drawing. It was not until I was in graduate school and she sent me *Blue Girl* that I understood she'd been an artist of real power.

There is nothing like the ecstasy of completing a work of art, and nothing like the emptiness that follows it. As I became more experienced as a writer, I began to feel the powerful force of that emptiness. Would I ever write another poem? Or would I stop writing poems like my grandmother stopped painting and end up in mental hospitals, having shock treatments, like she did?

It was out of that fear, in the heady feminism of the late 1970s, that I began to dream of writing this book. I began a poem about Margarett that sat unfinished for months on my desk, and then, sometime in 1979, I was asked to write for an anthology called *The Writer on Her Work*. That essay, "My Grandmother Who Painted," was the germ of *The White Blackbird*. I had read "A Room of Her Own," and I was interested in pursuing Virginia Woolf's question further. What about a woman who had many rooms of her own? And an income much larger than 500 pounds a year? What if the woman in question was married and a mother and also an artist whose most active period as an artist had been the years when her children were small?

Margarett Sargent came into her prime in the 1920s, "a time of hope," as the photographer Berenice Abbott put it, for women of talent. But my grandmother was also born into Brahmin Boston at the end of the nineteenth century, a repressive and suffocating society in spite of the accomplished women it produced in the generations before Margarett's—women like the poet Amy Lowell and collector Isabella Stewart Gardner. I wanted to know about Margarett's generation, about the context of her achievement, and that task required biography, a book that would retrieve not only my grandmother's life but the world in which she lived.

Unconventionally for a biography, *The White Blackbird* opens with a sequence of memories. My mother declares to me as a young girl, "You will have a bosom like your grandmother." And I tell of my grandmother's first serious gift to me, the painting *Blue Girl*, and introduce the mystery of her life—that she stopped painting.

When I'd finished writing *The White Blackbird*, I gave the manuscript to the proprietor of a bookstore, a woman ten years older than myself, a mother and wife. "I finished your book," she said, "but there's something I don't understand. What happened? Why did Margarett stop painting?" I hardly knew what to say, and I don't remember what I did say, but I do remember wondering if my reader wanted the security of a diagnosis. I'd purposely let the story stand on its own—I'm not a psychotherapist, after all, but a writer. I was reassured by the response of another woman—twenty years older than me, a poet's wife, a mother, and later a clothing designer and entrepreneur. "I knew why she stopped painting even before I opened the book!" Margarett Sargent, who cultivated her contradictions, would have been delighted by the divergence of these responses.

When I began *The White Blackbird* in the 1980s, I never imagined that my next nonfiction book would be *The Bishop's Daughter*, a memoir of my relationship with my father. In contrast to Margarett's rebellious spirit, he then seemed, while courageous, bland and conventional. When his secret life was revealed to me in the 1990s, I learned how mistaken I had been. Now, in my thinking, his life takes its place naturally next to the life of his mother-in-law, born nearly thirty years earlier than him.

Like Margarett Sargent, Paul Moore was born into a society that was more conventional than he was, like her he sought spiritual freedom in a relationship with the unseen, and like her he was a sexual rebel born into a generation that would come into its own after a great war. While I barely appear in *The White Blackbird*, in *The Bishop's Daughter* I am a character, a daughter discovering her own complexity while coming to terms with her complicated father. It is a book about two people, written through the prism of memory, while *The White Blackbird* is a biography with elements of memoir.

As I launched into *The Bishop's Daughter* I felt myself, after two books of poems, returning to the familiar terrain of a life and the narrative freedom I'd finally been able to achieve in *The White Blackbird*. It turned out that having "written" Margarett's paintings served me well as I approached the spectacle of vestments, candlelight, and preaching, but even more important was the revelation—due to my search for the truth of Margarett Sargent's creative spirit and my discovery of its importance—that, in approaching him as a character, I could consider my father's calling as a priest analogous to the creative vocation of an artist.

In responding to *Darling* and *Red Shoes*, the two poetry collections I published after *The White Blackbird*, readers remarked on my use of color, something of which I was barely conscious. Now, just beginning new work, I look forward with curiosity to the elements of *The Bishop's Daughter* that will make themselves known as I write into the future.

DISCUSSION QUESTIONS

1. Instead of Margarett's birth, Honor Moore begins *The White Blackbird* with a scene of herself as a child, listening to her mother Jenny, Margarett's second daughter, discuss Honor's "crazy grandmother." Moore then devotes several pages to Margarett's ancestors. Why do you think Moore chose to open the book this way? What do these pages tell you about Margarett and the way Moore chose to write her book?

2. As a young woman, Margarett's life was punctuated by three major events: her trip to Italy (1910), her decision to break off her engagement to Eddie Morgan (1912), and her brother Frank's suicide (1919). What was significant about each of these experiences, and how are they related to Margarett's decision to become an artist?

3. In 1919 Margarett received her first critical praise in the form of a review in *Town and Country* magazine. The reviewer called Margarett's piece, her sculpture of George Luks in the annual show at the Pennsylvania Academy, "a refutation of the theory that nobody ought to pay attention to the work of a woman sculptor." When Honor Moore first published *The White Blackbird* in 1996, many reviewers—enthusiastically—praised its depiction of the life of a "woman artist." What role did gender play in Margarett's life as an artist? Would you consider Margarett a feminist? How does gender continue to influence our understanding of artists and their work?

4. Margarett "took to affairs as easily as to brushing her teeth," says her friend Emily Lodge. Does Moore depict Margarett's affairs as an essential part of Margarett's being or the consequences of a lackluster marriage?

5. Describe Margarett's friendships with Marjorie Davenport and Betty Parsons. What do these relationships signify about Margarett's capacity for intimacy?

6. Both New York and Europe seem to have offered Margarett an

artistic and personal escape. What did Margarett find so attractive about these places? How were they different from Boston?

7. Moore writes that Margarett's temperament was "more avant-garde than her taste." What does Moore mean? What is Modernism, and how did it influence Margarett's style as a painter?

8. Margarett and Shaw's home, Prides, has such a significant presence in the book that it comes to function as practically a character itself. What was Margarett's relationship to Prides—both as an artist and as a wife and mother?

9. "Seize: Margarett's most characteristic paintings took possession with an unapologetic directness of that word," Moore writes. Go to www.margarettsargent.com and view some of Margarett's paintings. Would you agree with Moore's assessment? How else would you describe Margarett's work?

10. In addition to her husband and four children, Margarett carried on affairs with men and women—some lasting a period of several years, such as with Roland Balay. Yet despite her gregarious nature, Moore writes that Margarett "must have been lonely, living as she did in the midst of a crowd of people, intimate with none of them." How is this possible?

11. In Moore's depiction of their marriage, Shaw often comes across as a passive figure—a man at a loss for dealing with his wife's mental anguish and addictions. Occasionally a more provocative side to Shaw emerges, such as when he sets free Margarett's birds in their Parisian hotel room in 1933. Why does Shaw stick by Margarett for so long, and how does Margarett cope when he finally leaves her?

12. How does Margarett's childhood compare with the lives of her own children when they were young? To what do you attribute the difference—changing times or Shaw and Margarett's abilities as parents? How do Margarett's children come to view her when they are adults?

13. Why does Margarett stop painting? Does the evidence point to Margarett's mental illness?

14. In the painting world, George Luks comes to serve as a mentor—a father figure—to Margarett. How does her relationship with him compare to her relationship with her actual father, Frank Sargent? Sargent dies in 1920, when Margarett is twenty-seven, and Luks in 1931. How does Margarett cope with their deaths?

15. Why do you think Moore chose to call her book *The White Blackbird*, the name of George Luks's 1919 painting of Margarett? What does this title evoke of Margarett's character?

16. "What must I do to live fully both as an artist and as a woman?" Moore asks in the opening pages of part six. Instead of presenting a straightforward biography, Moore chose to write *The White Blackbird* as a more personal project, subtitling it "A Life of the Painter Margarett Sargent by Her Granddaughter." In what ways does Moore herself become a character in the biography? How would the book be different if someone else had written it?

*Available only on the Norton Web site: www.wwnorton.com/guides